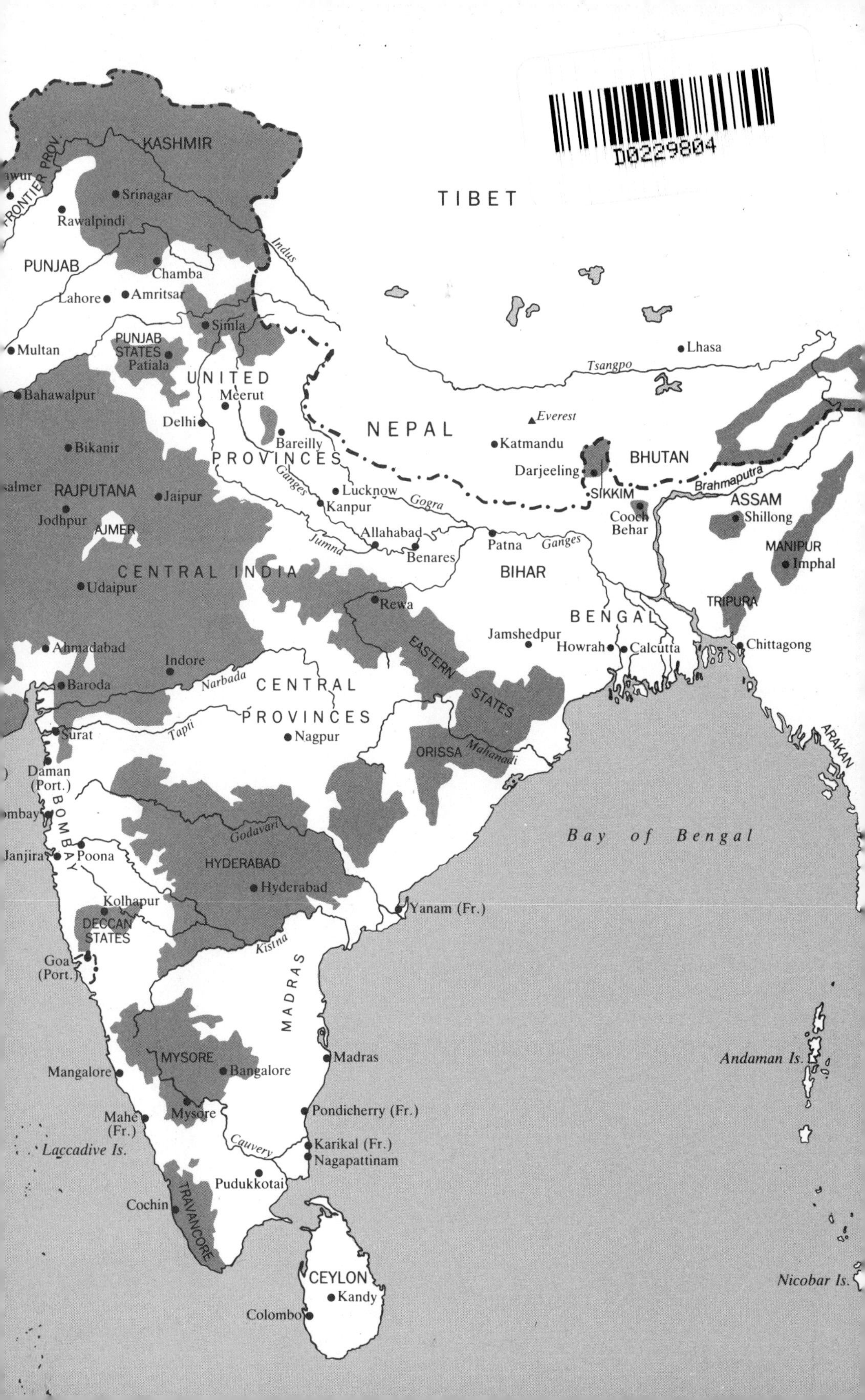

KASHMIR
Srinagar
Rawalpindi
TIBET
Indus
PUNJAB
Chamba
Lahore
Amritsar
Simla
Multan
PUNJAB STATES
Patiala
Lhasa
Tsangpo
UNITED PROVINCES
Meerut
Bahawalpur
Delhi
Bareilly
NEPAL
Everest
Katmandu
Bikanir
BHUTAN
Darjeeling
SIKKIM
Brahmaputra
Ganges
Lucknow
RAJPUTANA
Jaipur
Kanpur
Gogra
ASSAM
Jodhpur
Cooch Behar
Shillong
AJMER
Allahabad
Patna
Ganges
Jumna
Benares
MANIPUR
Imphal
CENTRAL INDIA
BIHAR
Udaipur
Rewa
TRIPURA
BENGAL
Jamshedpur
EASTERN STATES
Howrah
Calcutta
Chittagong
Ahmadabad
Indore
Narbada
CENTRAL PROVINCES
Baroda
STATES
Tapti
Surat
Nagpur
ORISSA
Mahanadi
ARAKAN
Daman (Port.)
BOMBAY
Godavari
Bay of Bengal
Janjira
Poona
HYDERABAD
Hyderabad
Kolhapur
Yanam (Fr.)
DECCAN STATES
Kistna
Goa (Port.)
MADRAS
Madras
Andaman Is.
MYSORE
Mangalore
Bangalore
Mysore
Mahe (Fr.)
Pondicherry (Fr.)
Laccadive Is.
Cauvery
Karikal (Fr.)
Nagapattinam
Pudukkotai
Cochin
TRAVANCORE
CEYLON
Nicobar Is.
Kandy
Colombo

VICEROY'S AGENT

by the same author

GEORGE II
CHARLEY GORDON
THE DESERT'S DUSTY FACE
MY MOTHER TOLD ME
PORTRAIT OF A PATRIOT
THE ROYAL MALADY
THE WESTERN RISING
THE GREAT DAN
A HISTORY OF HORSEMANSHIP
THE POACHER AND THE SQUIRE
THE FRONTIER SCOUTS

VICEROY'S AGENT

Charles Chenevix Trench

JONATHAN CAPE
THIRTY-TWO BEDFORD SQUARE LONDON

First published 1987

Jonathan Cape Ltd, 32 Bedford Square, London WC1B 3EL

British Library Cataloguing in Publication Data

Trench, Charles Chenevix.
Viceroy's agent.
1. India——History——20th century
2. India——Politics and government——
1919–1947
I. Title
954.03'5'0922 DS448

ISBN 0 224 02478 7

Phototypeset by Falcon Graphic Art Ltd
Wallington, Surrey
Printed in Great Britain by
Butler & Tanner Ltd, Frome and London

Contents

Illustrations

PLATES

MAPS *page*

The author and publishers are grateful to the following for permission to reproduce illustrations: BBC Hulton Picture Library (8); D.H. Biscoe (9); Miss Thora Bruce (4); Mrs J. Bradshaw (23, 24); J.R. Cotton (2); C.P. Hancock (19, 20); R.V.E. Hodson (31); India Office Library (British Library) (7, 25, 26, 27); Mrs Nancy Kirkbride (11); A.P. Low (3, 5); Mrs W.I. Moberley (18); Sir Fraser Noble (28, 29); A.W. Redpath (10, 12, 13, 17); Lady Reynolds (15); Lady Thompson (16). Other photographs are taken from the author's archives.

Preface

The Foreign and Political Department of the Government of India, which was re-named the Indian Political Service, had four main areas of responsibility:

> for relations between the Crown (not the Government of India) and the semi-independent Indian princes;
>
> for relations between the British and Indian Governments and some countries adjacent to India, viz. the Arab Emirates of the Persian Gulf, South and East Persia, Afghanistan, Sinkiang (Chinese Turkestan), Tibet and Nepal;
>
> for the administration of the North-West Frontier Province, Baluchistan and Aden Colony, and for relations with the semi-independent rulers of the Aden Protectorate;
>
> for relations with the Pathan tribes living in Tribal Territory, which was on the Indian side of the international border with Afghanistan but which was neither taxed nor administered (though efforts were made to stop the tribesmen being a nuisance to the British and to the Afghans).

In the first and fourth spheres of responsibility, officers were known as Political Agents and, more senior, Residents and Agents to the Governor-General; in the second, as Consuls, Consuls-General and Ministers; and in the third as Deputy Commissioners, Commissioners and Governors. They were very much the Viceroy's service, the selection of every officer having been personally approved by him.

This is not a history of the service, which has been admirably compiled by Sir Terence Creagh-Coen, but a book about some of the officers who served in it between 1919 and 1947.

1987 C.C.T.

for Mary
who remembers every stick and stone

Acknowledgments

The writing of this book was made possible by the unpublished memoirs of many former officers of the Indian Political Service and their wives, deposited in the British Library (India Office Library and Records). These, and the correspondence arising from them, are my principal sources, and to all who contributed I am most grateful. I will not catalogue their names, for they are all mentioned in the text. I used also my own family records, and the recollections of my wife of the years she spent as a girl in Gilgit and Udaipur, where her father was stationed. I am indebted to Mrs Olwen Barnes for access to her husband's letters and diaries, written in Waziristan in the 1930s.

Of published sources, the standard work on the service is Sir Terence Creagh-Coen's *The Indian Political Service.* I am very grateful to Jack Bazalgette and Edward Lydall for permission to quote from their autobiographies, *The Captains and the Kings Depart* and *Enough of Action*; to Lady Fry for giving me a free hand with her husband's *As Luck Would Have It*; to John Murray (Publications) Ltd for quotations from Sir Kenneth Fitze's *Twilight of the Maharajahs*; to Chatto and Windus Ltd in respect of B.J. Gould's *The Jewel in the Lotus* and E.B. Wakefield's *Past Imperative*; to Mrs K.P.S. Menon and the Oxford University Press for the use I made of K.P.S. Menon's *Many Worlds*; to Century Hutchinson Ltd for permission to quote from Charles Allen's *Lives of the Indian Princes*; and to the Indo-British Historical Society for quotations from Sir Conrad Corfield's *The Princely India I Knew.* My correspondence with Lakshman Singh of Dungarpur (formerly His Highness the Maharawal of Dungarpur) has been of the greatest interest and value.

The illustrations are mainly photographs taken by Political officers or their families. Like most snapshots taken with Kodaks in the 1920s and 1930s, they are of varying technical merit, and have been chosen mainly to illustrate the extraordinary variety of work in the service. The printing and enlargement of photographs fifty and sixty years old is not easy, and has in many cases been most skilfully accomplished by the Michael Lea Studio in Yateley.

Sir Cyril Hancock and Sir John Cotton took a great deal of trouble in answering my innumerable questions and guiding my research. Dr

Richard Bingle, Mr Victor Martin and the staff of the India Office Library and Records sorted out old files and photographs, provided me with copies of officers' memoirs and compiled the list of all officers mentioned in the text, with brief particulars of their service. To them I am extremely grateful.

Last, but not least, I must acknowledge the generosity of The Indian Political Service (Retired) Association for their financial support in the research and writing of this book.

1

The States and the Political

From 1857 to 1947 a third of the Indian Empire and a quarter of its population were not under direct British rule. In 1918 these states were ruled by 563 Indian 'princes'* varying in importance from the Nizam of Hyderabad, whose state exceeded in area, revenue and population many of the sovereign states which are now members of the United Nations, to the Talukdar of Bhadwa (population 1,401), who before ascending the throne kept himself beyond reach of want by working as a Guard on the Great Indian Peninsular Railway.

Few of these princes ruled states of great antiquity. The oldest were some of the Hindu kingdoms (e.g. Mewar, Jodhpur, Bikanir) in Rajputana. These by the early nineteenth century had been conquered and re-conquered by the Emperors of Delhi, repeatedly over-run by Mahrattas, and were rescued from extinction by the East India Company. Some states (e.g. Hyderabad and Rampur) had been provinces of the Mogul Empire, whose Governors broke away and set up on their own as the imperial grip relaxed. Others were created by the swords of Mahrattas (e.g. Indore and Gwalior) and Sikhs (e.g. Patiala) in the late eighteenth and early nineteenth centuries. In many cases the Company simply selected the most effective freebooters, confirmed them in possession of whatever tracts their armies were currently pillaging, and dignified them by the titles of Nawab and Maharajah (e.g. Tonk, Bhopal, Bahawalpur and Kashmir).

The forty most important states had entered into 'subsidiary treaties' with the Honourable Company. These, differing in details, were alike in their general effects. In, for instance, the treaty with the Maharana of Udaipur, the British Government undertook to defend the 'principality

*The more important Hindu and Sikh rulers were Maharajahs, Maharana (Udaipur only) and Maharawal (Dungarpur only). Lesser ones were Rajahs. Their consorts were Maharanis and Ranis.

In India proper, Moslem rulers were nearly all Nawabs, but the most important of all was the Nizam, of Hyderabad. On the Frontier they held a variety of titles, e.g. the Khan of Kalat, the Mir of Hunza, the Mehtar of Chitral, the Wali of Swat. Moslem rulers' consorts were all Begums.

and territory of the state', which implied a guarantee against both internal subversion and external aggression. The Maharana agreed to act always in 'subordinate co-operation' with the British Government, and to have no communication or understanding with any other state without the permission of the British Government. In return, the Maharana would always be 'absolute ruler in his own country and British jurisdiction would not be introduced into it'. Some states agreed furthermore to pay for contingents of the Company's troops to be stationed in their territories.

The princes gained from these treaties the Company's protection against internal and external enemies. The main advantage to the British was that at a low cost large areas which they did not wish to occupy were kept more or less at peace by more or less friendly rulers. Other advantages were frankly expressed by one of the greatest kingmakers of the early nineteenth century, Mountstuart Elphinstone: 'We must have some sink to receive all the corrupt matter that abounds in India, unless we are willing to taint our own system by stopping the discharge of it'; and by another, Thomas Munro: 'Among all the disorders of the native states the field is open to every man to raise himself; and hence among them there is a spirit of emulation, of restless enterprise and independence, far preferable to the servility of our Indian subjects.' In short, the states would provide employment for the best Indians and relieve British India of the worst. Munro wrote at a time when the East India patronage mattered in British politics, and the preferment of Jos Sedley to the Collectorship of Boggley Wollah might decide a close-run vote in the Commons. Eighty years later, when the British body politic had been purged of nepotism by the Reform Acts and competitive examinations for entry into the public service, Indians were still excluded from the highest positions in British India by racial prejudices lingering on from the Indian Mutiny of 1857, but not from the highest positions in the native states; an increasing number of able Indians made their careers in the states, often where one would least expect to find them – a Moslem Prime Minister in a Hindu state, or a Hindu in a Moslem.

Although the most important princes were by their treaties free to do as they pleased with their own, the promise of protection against internal enemies in effect gave the British Government a general and undefined interference-licence. The normal and natural check on autocracy is the fear of rebellion or palace-revolution. From this the princes were relieved by their treaties. In the words of a *Times* leader in 1853:

> . . . We give these princes power without responsibility. Our hand of

> iron maintains them on the throne despite their inability, their vices and their crimes. The result in most of the states is a chronic anarchy, under which the revenues of the states are dissipated between the mercenaries of the Camp and the minions of the Court.

That could have been so, but in general was not. For the corollary of freeing the princes from the natural consequences of gross misgovernment was that the British Government was under a moral obligation to ensure that gross misgovernment did not occur. In the words of the Viceroy, Lord Hardinge, to Gulab Singh, whom the British Government had set up as Maharajah of Kashmir:

> [the Government] can never consent to incur the reproach of becoming indirectly the instrument of oppression of the people committed to a prince's charge. If the aversion to a prince's rule should by injustice become so universal as to cause the people to seek his downfall, the British Government are under no obligation to force the people to submit to a ruler who has deprived himself of their allegiance by his misconduct.

So from time to time the British Government intervened in the affairs of a state, even to the extent of deposing a prince whose conduct was grossly cruel or incompetent, and annexing his state. The most celebrated case under the East India Company was the annexation of the Kingdom of Oudh, a prime cause of the Indian Mutiny of 1857.

In that year nearly all the princes sided with the British. When the Mutiny was over the Crown replaced the Company as direct ruler of two-thirds of India and indirect ruler of the princely one-third. Thereafter the princes would be handled with kid gloves: there would be, promised the Queen, no more annexations, ever. 'We shall respect,' she said, 'the rights, dignity and honour of Native Princes as Our own.' But she did not promise that no prince would ever be deposed, nor that there would be no intervention in their internal affairs.

So for the next ninety years there was a power struggle, generally polite and seldom coming to a head in the deposition of a ruler, between the princes who, standing upon the letter of their treaties, denied that the British Government had any right to tell them how to run their own affairs, and the British Government which insisted on its right to intervene in certain undefined circumstances – between the princes who said that the treaties were between equal and sovereign states, with one side voluntarily relinquishing certain defined powers, and the British Government which said, 'No. If it ever comes to a difference of policy or the interpretation of a treaty, we are the Paramount Power.' In the words of a letter from the Viceroy, Lord Reading, to the Nizam of Hyderabad in 1926:

> The sovereignty of the British Crown is supreme in India, and therefore no ruler of an Indian state can justifiably claim to negotiate with the British Government on an equal footing. Its supremacy is not based upon treaties and engagements, but exists independently of them and, quite apart from its prerogative in matters relating to foreign powers and politics, it is the right and duty of the British Government, while scrupulously respecting all treaties and engagements with the Indian states, to preserve peace and good order throughout India ... The right of the British Government to intervene in the internal affairs of Indian states is another instance of the consequences necessarily involved in the supremacy of the British Crown ... Where imperial interests are concerned, or the general welfare of the people of a state is seriously and grievously affected by the action of its Government, it is with the Paramount Power that the ultimate responsibility of taking remedial action, if necessary, must lie.

Other causes of friction hinged on matters of succession. The British Government maintained that an essential attribute of Paramountcy was that it should have the final say in these, and a prince should not be deemed to have ascended the gadi* until he had been presented with a Kharita, a formal commission from the Viceroy acknowledging that he was now the ruler of the state. This, it was argued, was an essential safeguard against disputed successions. Most princes had several wives, and there would be terrible instability if the youngest and prettiest could work upon a Maharajah to make her son his heir, disinheriting the eldest son of the Senior Maharani. In ninety-nine cases out of a hundred the succession was perfectly straightforward: except in Travancore and Cochin where it was matriarchal, it followed the ordinary rules of primogeniture. Some princes felt outraged that they should not be deemed to have inherited the gadi of their ancestors until the Viceroy had given his approval. The Maharajah of Dhrangadhara made his point when, at the ceremony of the presentation of the Kharita, the Resident (representing the Viceroy) expected to sit beside him, on the same level.

The Maharajah said, 'I'm terribly sorry, but I'm the anointed king, and he cannot be on a par with me. He may have the first seat on my

*Literally 'cushion', the throne of an Indian prince.

> right hand, above all my nobles, but one step below.' Everyone said, 'My God, they'll depose you tomorrow.' The Resident sat one step below and was quite happy. He could have insisted on his rights, but he was a very sweet man, Colonel Gaisford, and he agreed.

The kindred business of adoption also caused friction. For reasons which gave rise to unseemly speculation, many princes were unable to beget children. The problem was solved in a variety of ways. In one Hindu state where the heir turned Moslem, the Senior Maharani produced a son although His Highness was well beyond the age at which he was likely to be the father, and everyone closed their eyes to this improbability. The Mehtar of Chitral, after many years of childless marriage, was presented by his latest wife with a male child. Great as were the official rejoicings, they were somewhat marred by the more ribald elements of the populace surrounding the house of the Adjutant of the Bodyguard and serenading him with cries of 'Shabash,* Subadar Adjutant Sahib!' Even as a young man Maharajah Jagatjit Singh of Kapurthala had a stomach so huge and pendulous as to constitute an insuperable obstacle to the fulfilment of his marital duties, until the resourceful State Engineer constructed a special bed to accommodate it. Later His Highness underwent a slimming cure, with the happiest of results.

By far the most common method of surmounting this problem, after several wives had tried to no avail, was by adoption within the rules laid down by religion and custom, and it was as well that the British Government should have the power of ensuring that the adoption was within those rules. Some rulers changed their minds not once but many times, with grave danger to a state's stability.

The Indian princes' treaties were with the British Crown, not with the Government of India, which was involved only in that the Governor-General of India was also the Viceroy, representing the Crown. His men in the states, Residents and Political Agents, were from his own department, known before 1935 as the Foreign and Political Department, and thereafter as the Indian Political Service. In the words of a member of that service, Jack Bazalgette:

> This *corps d'élite* was directly responsible to the Viceroy for relations with more than six hundred semi-independent princes; it was responsible for certain areas of particular diplomatic delicacy not

*'Well done, congratulations.'

within British India such as the independent Tribal Territory of the North-West Frontier and Baluchistan; it provided the district administration of the North-West Frontier Province and Aden; and it staffed diplomatic and consular posts in Afghanistan, Persia, Arabia and Central Asia.

About two-thirds of the service was recruited from the Indian Army, one-third from the Indian Civil Service (the I.C.S.), with a handful from the Indian Police, and a few Pathans from the North-West Frontier Provincial administration for service on that frontier only.

'Politicals' thought a lot of themselves – as the Viceroy's special service, as holders of most of the interesting and glamorous, not to say dangerous, posts in and around India, far removed from the nitty-gritty of provincial administration, as being brainier than the Army, and as being more men of action than the I.C.S. Such are the imperfections of human nature, and so corrosive jealousy's effect on it, that their views were not altogether shared by the services from which they came. Some went so far as to categorise Politicals as soldiers averse to fighting and civilians afraid of hard work, who had absolutely nothing to do but shoot tigers and suck up to a lot of degenerate Rajahs. Army officers, however, who described their own life-style as half a day's pay for half a day's work, were in no position to charge anyone else with idleness.

Lord Linlithgow as Viceroy (1936-43) wanted to abolish the Political and transfer its functions to the I.C.S. as the best way of 'purging the Indian Political Service, with its large proportion of somewhat second-rate men, of its mediaevalism'. That, of course, reflected the I.C.S. view. Well, one can only say that in every service, profession or walk of life most people are inevitably second-raters. Even in the I.C.S. Even among Viceroys.

There was a certain rivalry, amounting sometimes to ill-feeling, between Politicals who came from the I.C.S. and those who came from the Army. The former felt that the latter had arrived by the back door, without going to Oxford, Cambridge or Trinity College, Dublin. Army Politicals resented the fact that civilians got a higher pension, and also most of the top jobs, because Army officers had to retire at 55, while civilians retired after thirty-five years of service, at about 58. In 1928, for instance, men from the I.C.S. held twenty-four out of the thirty-four 'selection posts'. They could, of course, have been more intellectually eminent than the soldiers.

Between princes and Politicals there was an ambivalent relationship depending largely on personalities. Every ruler sometimes saw the

Resident or Political Agent as the Viceroy's spy. 'Ask a Rajput,' says Tod in his *Annals and Antiquities of Rajastan*, 'which is the greatest of crimes. He will reply, "Forgetfulness of favours." ' To many princes whose Order had supported the British in adversity in 1857, 1914-18 and 1939-45, this seemed to be the besetting sin of the Political Department. But the Maharawal of Dungarpur, who had a highly developed political sense and was certainly no yes-man, told Charles Allen that he looked upon the Political Department not as an intruder but as a 'friend, guide and bulwark whose officers always had the utmost respect for the princes and saw to it that they were given due respect. There may have been black sheep among them, but on the whole they were sincere, honest and devoted to their job, and whatever advice they tendered to the princes was, I think, more often than not in their best interests.' Even when the Political Department 'acted in a high-handed way' and deposed a ruler, it was only after 'giving the prince a long rope, warning him, and then, when they thought there was no corrective, removing him very gently so that they never compromised his dignity'. Having removed him, they replaced him with his lawful heir.

'Whatever advice they tendered to the princes' – there's the rub. The Political was empowered only to give advice, not orders. Advice could be proferred tactfully so as not to cause offence, or otherwise. Sir Kenneth Fitze gives an example of advice being given in the most tactful manner on the most delicate of matters, a liaison between a Maharajah and a French lady of blemished reputation. Referring to the notorious case of another prince being blackmailed after being found in bed with such a lady, the Political Agent said in the most disarming and casual manner, 'I wonder if Your Highness is familiar with the case of "Mr A"?'

'I presume,' replied the Maharajah, 'that you are referring to poor Hari Singh of Kashmir.'

'Yes. I would not have referred to the matter had I not begun to discern a certain danger of Your Highness becoming a Mr B.'

It went down well, and the hint was taken.

Viewing the scene from a position on the extreme left, K.M. Panikkar wrote, 'The whisper of the Residency is the thunder of the state, and there is no matter on which the Resident does not feel qualified to give advice. The advice of the Resident is usually an order.'

The precise weight of a Resident's advice could never be measured: it depended on the personalities of ruler, Resident and Viceroy, and on the policy of the British Government of the day; over the ninety years between 1857 and 1947 the degree of interference waxed and waned. It rose to a maximum during the Pro-Consulate of Lord Curzon from

1899 to 1905. From 1919 to 1947, the period covered by this book, there was an almost pathological reluctance to intervene. Individual Politicals might feel a compulsion to poke a finger into the pie and leave a state better than they found it, but the Political was told, in his Manual of Instructions (1924), that 'He should leave well alone; the best work of a Political officer is very often what has been left undone.' So a ruler's misconduct had to be 'gross as a mountain, open, palpable' before sanctions were applied against him – first, perhaps, in the form of the Viceroy insisting that he employ ministers, British or Indian, selected by the Political Department; only in the last resort by the Viceroy compelling him to abdicate, with a generous financial settlement.

The change from the robust policy of Lord Curzon was the result of a change in the view taken by far-seeing people of the future of India. Before 1914, although some paid lip-service to more liberal aspirations, no one really doubted that the British would still be governing India by the end of the century. It was generally assumed, for instance by Kipling, that 'Kings' courts' were sinks of iniquity, 'Kings' justice' a travesty, life under the 'Kings' poor, nasty, brutish and short. The sooner they could be advised, nudged and bullied into mending their ways, the better. By 1919, however, the British were under pressure: few would have given them another fifty years. Any intelligent prince could see that if the British went his days were numbered; while the British, although they seldom openly acknowledged it, saw the states, flagrantly undemocratic, as impediments to progress towards Dominion Status or complete Independence. Princes and Britons, whatever differences they might have had, each saw the other as an ally in a rearguard action against the twentieth century. Unconsciously rationalising this, Politicals in particular saw the states not as sinks of iniquity but as examples of a form of government which was much better suited to Indians than Western democracy. It was argued, and with much justification, that Indians were happier in the states than in British India, a proposition which the previous generation would have denounced as infamous; that although taxes were in theory more severe, in practice they were mitigated by corruption and inefficient collection. Because social life in the states was more old-fashioned, there was more cohesion and mutual help in village life. Village solidarity was a check on bureaucracy, and there were in any case fewer bureaucrats. Because the rule of law, and of lawyers, was less prevalent than in British India, the moneylender had not such a stranglehold on the peasant. No prince would dare do anything to outrage his great nobles, who would protect their tenants against his encroachments. Indians liked pageantry: the spectacle of their Maharajah and all his nobles, clad in brocades and cloth-of-gold, with sword and shield, riding gaily caparisoned elephants through the capital, gave far more pleasure than the sight of a pallid English (or Indian) Commissioner speeding past in a car. Above all, it was argued, Indians liked their ruler to be easily accessible, to respond *promptly* to the cry 'Maharaj! A petition!' – not to be esconced in a distant office, surrounded by clerks and chuprassis* each expecting his cut from a petitioner, unable to make a decision without consulting some higher bureaucrat.

There were, admittedly, states where tigers were more important than official Blue Books, or where the budget might be unbalanced by the need to win an All-India Polo Tournament. A girl's – or a boy's – pretty face might change the direction of policy and overthrow a prime minister. Nevertheless, it was argued, Indians preferred their Maharajah with all his faults to the Collector with all his virtues. The case may have been over-stated by Politicals eager to justify their work and their service, but there was a great deal of truth in it. And for all the attention lavished on the shortcomings of some members of the princely order – much more entertaining than their virtues – most princes were decent men doing the best they could.

Congress politicians did not see them in this light. Nurtured in the theories, if not exactly wedded to the practices, of liberal democracy, they saw princes as worse even than the foreign oppressor, which tended to bring princes and Politicals closer together than they had ever been – except for a handful of princes who at heart were pro-Congress.

Of course in their dealings with the states the British Government used the carrot as well as the stick. Gun-salutes were a method invented by the British to mark the states' relative importance – from the twenty-one guns of the Nizam of Hyderabad to the nine of little hill rajahs: many princes would sell their souls to have a couple of guns added to their salutes. Decorations were eagerly sought: many a hospital and school has been built, many a tiger shot by many a Viceroy, in the hope that His Highness might be made a Knight Commander of the Star of India (K.C.S.I.).

Some, however, took all this with a pinch of salt. There was a rather pompous Resident, very meticulous in such matters. He, too, was entitled to a gun-salute, and before paying an official visit to Patiala made sure that he would receive it in full. Among Maharajah Bhupinder Singh's good qualities (he had several bad ones) was a sense of humour.

*Footmen, office attendants.

He gave orders that the Resident Sahib should have every gun of his salute, but that the guns should be loaded with only quarter-charges of powder, so that the salute went off in a succession of merry little pops like the opening of a row of champagne bottles.

The Maharajah of Dhrangadhara, asked if he would accept a Knight Commander of the Indian Empire (K.C.I.E.), replied that he would be delighted to do so if the King Emperor would accept the Shaktimat Order of Dhrangadhara. Nor was this cynicism about decorations and titles confined to the more sophisticated princes. Politicals themselves referred to New Delhi as the 'City of Dreadful Knights'; and George Kirkbride, on the analogy of the Babu describing himself as 'Failed B.A. Calcutta University', used to sign his letters, 'Failed C.I.E.'. The Assistant Political Agent in Fort Sandeman, Baluchistan, was Khan Bahadur Sharbat Khan, Afridi. Now 'Khan Bahadur' was a title awarded to Moslems – 'Rai Bahadur' to Hindus – for the sort of public services which would now be rewarded with a B.E.M., or even an M.B.E. One day the Agent to the Governor-General summoned Sharbat Khan's boss, R.H. Chenevix Trench.

'Trench,' he said, 'I'm afraid I must ask you to speak to Sharbat. He has deeply offended many loyal and eminent citizens by calling his dog "Khan Bahadur".'

Trench duly spoke to Sharbat, who replied, 'No problem. I'll change my dog's name. You can tell the A.G.G. that the thing is done.'

A few weeks later Trench was again summoned. 'You'll have to speak to Sharbat again, about his dog.'

'But he promised me he'd change the name.'

'*Exactly*. I've just heard him call the creature "Rai Bahadur".'

2

Young Politicals

Various motives moved men to transfer from the Indian Army and the I.C.S. Some had family connections with the Political and had heard from fathers and uncles of the interesting lives they had led; some noted that Politicals were paid more than soldiers. Walter Magor got engaged at the early age of 24, and was told by his Commanding Officer, 'in the nicest possible way, that subalterns of the Poona Horse were expected to spend their money on polo ponies, not on wives'.

Herbert Thompson, of the I.C.S. in Madras, was told by a senior Member of the Council, 'In your time this Presidency will become self-governing, and you will never be able to rise to the old heights of responsibility and power. You must therefore join the Government of India. Are you any good at finance?' Thompson said he was barely able to keep his own accounts. 'Well, then, you must join the Foreign and Political Department.' Peter Nicholson made the move when in Waziristan a dumdum bullet in the knee put paid to his chances of an active military career. Robin Hodson was semi-crippled for months in a lorry accident. In 1938 his Commanding Officer broke the news to him that if the Guides went on active service, he would have to be left behind at the depot. So he too applied for the Political. By far the most common motive was the feeling that the Political offered a much more varied and interesting life than peace-time soldiering or administering the same kind of district in the same province for twenty or thirty years, but with ever diminishing responsibility as provinces progressed towards self-government and the I.C.S. was Indianised. Yet most made the change with some regret. Thompson would miss Madras, and the subtle, sophisticated Indians of that Presidency. John Cotton, having passed the much sought-after, very tough year's Equitation Course at Saugor and with every prospect of becoming Adjutant of the 8th Cavalry, hated leaving them. A.J. Dring had thoroughly enjoyed his four years in the Guides Cavalry, played polo in the regimental team and made many friends who could not understand anyone ever wanting to leave the regiment. All those who had been in Gurkha battalions missed those 'grand little men'.

When it came to selection for the service, it was often said (not least by Politicals themselves) that there was none of this nonsense of merit about it. This is an exaggeration. I.C.S. candidates must have acquired merit by passing their departmental examinations, Army candidates by passing the examinations for promotion to Captain; both must, of course, have good reports from their provinces and regiments. There was merit in being more than competent in Urdu or Hindi, and preferably in a regional language – Gujerati, Punjabi, Pushtu. It was *very* meritorious to have a father or uncle in the service. Lastly (one admits it with a sense of shame), it was meritorious to be white.

The Political can be justly reproached for lagging behind other services in promoting Indians to positions of responsibility, which accounts in part for the hatred directed against it by nationalist politicians. The reason for this was that the princes, as Lord Reading informed the Secretary of State in April, 1921, were 'almost unanimous against the appointment of Indians as their Political officers'. Their relations, they felt, were with the British Crown, and should therefore be conducted through British officers. They believed that educated Indians, the sort who would pass examinations into the public service, viewed them with disrespect as anachronisms, and would not approve of or take seriously the ceremonial of princely rule. It could happen that a subject of a ruler would be taken into the Political, and in due course be in a position to exercise authority over his own sovereign. An Indian Resident might be tainted by the political opinions of his relations and friends. B.K. Kapur, a Hindu from a landowning family in the Punjab, was told quite frankly by Lord Willingdon during his selection interview that he must accept the fact that he would never be employed as Resident or Political Agent in a state.

This limited the scope of Indians in the service to thirty-eight 'superior' posts – on the Frontier, in Baluchistan, in the Secretariat, and as Secretary to First Class Residents. Three-quarters of these posts were on the Frontier and in Baluchistan, for which Moslems rather than Hindus or Sikhs seemed more obviously suited. So of the fifteen Indians in the service in 1939, out of a total of 130 officers, four were Hindus, one was a Sikh and the remainder were Moslems. Sankar Maitra, a genial and outsize Bengali, Cambridge graduate, in the I.C.S., applied for the Political. His application was not even acknowledged, and when the Chief Secretary of Assam asked how matters were progressing, Sankar Maitra replied with a good-humoured chuckle, 'Babus not wanted.' Nevertheless, some Hindu Politicals served happily and with success on the Frontier.

There was no examination or formal test for entry. Candidates were interviewed by the Foreign and Political Secretaries, the twin heads of the service, for general suitability and to give them the chance of expressing a preference for the states, the Frontier or the foreign consulates. Nearly all Politicals served in two of these areas, many in all three, but they naturally preferred one, and tended to specialise in it. 'We want,' ordained one Political Secretary, 'lean and keen men for the Frontier, fat and good-natured men for the states.'

The most dreaded test was luncheon *en famille* with the Viceroy and Her Excellency. This was a purely social occasion: no shop was discussed. The object was to make sure that Captain X or Mr Y was neither tongue-tied in the presence of important people, nor garrulous with liquor; that he used the correct knife, fork and spoon; and that he avoided the social quicksands which had yet to be charted by Nancy Mitford.

It was never as terrifying as one expected: Viceroys were men of the world, and it was part of a Vicereine's job to be nice to nervous young men. In trepidation Frank Pearson presented himself on the appointed day.

> The luncheon was small and pleasant. Afterwards I was summoned by an A.D.C. to talk with Lady Willingdon. She talked of the Lake District and told me she had spent her honeymoon on Ambleside. This was a great bond and the conversation flowed easily.

Hugh Rance underwent the ordeal with two other would-be Politicals.

> The story was that on these occasions the sweet was always cherry-tart, to see what the new entry would do with the stones. But on this occasion we, or they, were disappointed, as it was some harmless mousse. We did, however, have curry, and all three ate it according to Indian etiquette with *spoon* and fork. There were a few disapproving glances from one or two of the guests recently arrived from England, unaware of the local custom, but we survived with no adverse comments on our confidential reports.

Walter Magor of the Poona Horse felt no qualms, and unobtrusively put Lady Linlithgow at her ease.

> By the end of lunch I was getting on very well, talking to her about her racehorses, so that I hardly noticed when someone at my elbow said, 'Liqueur, Sir?' and, without looking round, I replied, 'Yes, please, I'd like a brandy.' To my horror the manservant put down the salver of liqueurs he was carrying and went out of the room, returning five

minutes later with a bottle which he proceeded to dust and uncork, and I was given my liqueur brandy.

My own ordeal was perhaps more agreeable, but more prolonged. In the autumn of 1938 I went on leave to Katmandu, in keen but fruitless pursuit of the British Minister's daughter there. On the way I stayed in New Delhi with the Foreign Secretary and was interviewed by the Political Secretary. Katmandu was hard to visit, permits were seldom given, and one had to walk from the railhead, baggage carried by an elephant. Shortly before my leave expired, the Minister asked if I would like to stay on an extra week to act as his unofficial A.D.C. for a Viceregal visit to the Maharajah combined with a week's tiger-shoot in the Terai. For more than one reason I jumped at it.

The camp was luxury. Even I had a huge tent to myself, with bathroom, electric light, carpets, armchairs. The Viceroy, Lady Linlithgow, his staff and our party all took meals together in a large mess tent, informally, though of course one changed for dinner. Lord Linlithgow, not the most genial man in the world, was in holiday mood, and in his dour way was rather amusing.

Soon after breakfast would come news of a tiger-kill. There were 300 elephants attached to the camp, 100 being used for each kill. We would clamber on to our steeds and ride out in single file through the jungle. About a mile from the kill we would file off, odd numbers to the right, even numbers to the left, to make a huge circle with the kill and, we hoped, the tiger in the centre. When the circle was complete we would close in until the elephants were shoulder-to-shoulder round a patch of jungle of about an acre. Then some small, nearly naked men would surround the area with a yard-wide strip of white cloth, to discourage the tiger from breaking out. Two or three tuskers would enter the ring to trample down the bushes and high grass until there was no cover left for the unfortunate tiger, and he would start trotting uneasily round the ring, in one case actually attacking an elephant, leaping at its head so that he broke the ring and escaped. The great man whose privilege it was to execute the tiger would fire, and there would ensue a volley from round the ring until the tiger fell riddled with bullets. The total bag for the week was sixteen tigers and three rhinos. *C'est magnifique, mais ce n'est pas le sport.* The Minister afterwards wrote to my father that I was an exceptionally bad A.D.C., which he did not hold against me. I dare say he was right: my mind was on other matters. With the Viceroy's three A.D.C.s in camp, my suit did not prosper.

After the interviews and the luncheon came the first posting. This was generally to be Personal Assistant to a Resident, but not in my case, which I will relate before telling the stories of more distinguished Politicals. I was ordered to join the service in October, 1939, but for obvious reasons the posting was cancelled. I had almost forgotten about it when, in January, 1946, I was told to report to the Political Secretary's office in New Delhi. There I was given my first task: to arrange the seating of the princes and their relations for the Victory Parade. I was provided with a table, chair, diagram of the seating, list of those attending, Table of Precedence – and told to get on with it.

It defeated me. I had no idea how to assess the relative importance of an illegitimate son of a fifteen-gun Maharajah and the legitimate second cousin of a thirteen-gunner, and the Table of Precedence was not very helpful. On the third day the Political Adviser himself, Sir Conrad Corfield, looked in to ask how I was getting on. I said I wasn't, and explained why.

'Let me have a look . . . H'm . . . yes, I see what you mean . . . I tell you what: we'll put all the names into a hat and draw lots for places. Then if anyone complains that he has been placed below the Maharajah of X, you can say, "But, Your Highness, you are above the Nawab of Y," and they really won't be able to kick up a fuss.'

Nor they were. The nearest I had to a complaint was from the Prince of Berar who knew my father well and whom I had met in London. 'Charles, I understand that you are responsible for these *extraordinary* arrangements. But give my love to your Pappy.'

Robin Hodson's first posting was as Personal Assistant to Sir George Cunningham, Governor of the North-West Frontier Province. He arranged his master's social functions, tennis and duck shoots, and accompanied him on tours through the settled districts and Tribal Territory. When Cunningham was temporarily replaced by Sir Arthur ('Bunch') Parsons, there was an additional duty for the Personal Assistant: carrying enough cash to pay compensation for goats mown down by his master's remarkable driving. Parsons was by repute a woman-hater, but always polite. Hodson spent an hour in great amusement listening to him evading Freya Stark's application to go to Chitral.

E.B. Wakefield was posted first to Ajmere as Assistant Commissioner. Being an I.C.S. man, he had already passed his law and revenue exams, and was proficient at district administration, but he had to pass a test, set by his Commissioner, E.C. Gibson, on Tod's *Rajastan** and to

**Annals and Antiquities of Rajastan*, a 1,000-page classic by James Tod, a Political Agent in the 1830s.

acquire that working knowledge of Rajput pedigrees which was regarded as necessary for a Political officer. He thought it was a great waste of time, and told the Resident so.

'Must I go through all this? It will take me weeks, and my work will suffer.'

'You mean I'll have to do your work for you?'

'Yes, sir.'

'Well, I don't propose to do that. I think you'll find the questions I set you will not be unanswerable.'

In the event, there was only one question. 'Tod says that Rajputs are a very gallant race. Do you agree?'

Answer, 'Yes.'

Passed.

Wakefield was put on to fighting a locust invasion. A locust lays 300 to 400 eggs and then dies. Two or three weeks later, the eggs hatch, and the 'hoppers' are vulnerable until they can fly. The essence of a locust campaign was to locate and destroy eggs and hoppers, and the key to doing that was accurate information. Eggs could be rendered infertile by flooding the ground in which they were laid. Slow-moving hopper bands could be destroyed by sprinkling poisoned bran in front of them, or by digging trenches across their route into which they would march like lemmings and could then be buried. Wakefield had an advantage over military commanders, in that the movements of this enemy were usually predictable; and the public was whole-heartedly on his side, Congress-wallahs and all. Not even the most jaundiced could blame locusts on the British.

A.J. Dring was thrown in at the deep end, his first posting, as Assistant Political Agent, North Waziristan, being 'to try to instil some sense of responsibility among the Khassadars in the performance of their road protection duties'. It was an uphill task. The Khassadars were tribal levies, armed with their own rifles, un-uniformed and unreliable. They were used to piquet roads and as escorts for officers, on the assumption that their fellow-tribesmen, not wanting to start a tiresome blood-feud, would not fire on them. But for the same reason they would be reluctant to fire on their fellow-tribesmen. They regarded themselves not as servants of the Government, but as servants of the Jirga, the tribal assembly, assisting the Jirga to implement the policy of the Government. The system worked moderately well in peacetime, but if the tribe was at war with the Government, the best that could be hoped for from the Khassadars was a dubious neutrality.

Dring's was a very unusual first posting. Johnny Raw's was more orthodox, as Personal Assistant to the Resident at Hyderabad. He was given little chance to develop his political and diplomatic talents as his duties were purely social – sometimes, he was inclined to think, anti-social.

I came straight from my regiment in Chitral, arriving at Hyderabad 2½ days later. A languid Second Secretary let drop that I had not been expected for another fortnight. I was taken to the Residency by that same individual who, seeing my bull-terrier lifting his leg against the most prominent sofa in the huge drawing room, informed me that my predecessor had been shunted back to his regiment, as being unlikely Political material, by the formidable Resident.

The latter's nickname suggested a toper, but he was relatively abstemious. He had a first class brain, with a fund of wit to match. Little of the latter was wasted on my lowly self, though in contact with him and his acidulous wife for much of the day. His interests were squash, golf and snipe-shooting, in which I was tactless enough to have the edge over him.

Apart from state occasions, comparatively little entertainment took place at the Residency, due largely to the reserved nature of the Resident's wife who (with great reluctance) put up with occasional mammoth dinner parties which served, on a bulk basis, to dispense with the normal round of smaller engagements. The after dinner excitement on these occasions invariably took the form of 'human halma'. Guests were seated in pairs round the vast salon (scene of my bull-terrier's indiscretion). It was then my duty to prise each man in turn away from his female partner, take him to another couple and introduce him to the lady, take the thus-created spare man to another couple – ad infinitum. Great woe was on my head if I inadvertently introduced a husband to his wife or made an introduction which showed that I was not *au fait* with current scandals; but much greater was my woe if I left the Resident's wife with a partner for more than the very brief time it took her to run through the gamut of her conversational abilities from A to B.

Fortunately my time took in the period of the Resident's recess for the hot weather at Ootacamund. With his wife gone to England, and a *locum tenens* installed, he was a changed man.

T.E. Brownsdon got on better with that formidable Resident, if only because he did not arrive accompanied by an incontinent bull-terrier. But he found the dinner-parties demanding occasions.

The Resident would give me an idea of whom to invite and of the menu. It was then my duty, when the acceptances were in, to arrange the seating plan. This was a tricky job in India where everyone had, and knew they had, a specific place in the order of priority, and woe betide the Personal Assistant who got it wrong. It was by no means unusual to receive a phone call or a letter after a function asking 'Why Mrs So-and-So was sitting above me'. Our bible was the Warrant of Precedence for India, an enormous document which laid down the exact order of precedence for every imaginable official in the country. We spent hours ascertaining that the Superintendent for the Opium Factory at Ghazipur was junior to the General Manager of the Rajputana Salt Resources.

Once the seating plan was approved and the menu translated into French (we had a special little book for this) the details were sent to our own printing press in the Residency Office and they were printed in beautiful gold lettering. The dining table was laid with official china and cutlery, every piece embossed with the rather smug motto of the East India Company, *Heaven's Light our Guide*. We had a most efficient butler, a Tamil, a spy in the Nizam's pay, and everything that happened in the Residency was immediately reported. But we took no action against him because it was better to know who was the spy than to sack him and then not know who was planted in his place.

One feels ashamed to relate D.H. Biscoe's first experience in the service:

My first appointment was as Personal Assistant (i.e. A.D.C. cum makee-learn) to the Resident at Baroda, an advanced state with a Legislature and a University. There was little work for the Resident and his Secretary, and none at all for the Personal Assistant. At Christmas we went off to some small state to shoot duck. I was deeply shocked by the arrogance with which the Secretary bossed the state guest-house servants around. I had not realised it was part of our custom to act so rudely, and it made me unhappy.

I think Biscoe was mistaken in charging the Political with habitual rudeness. The whole selection procedure was designed to exclude boors and bores; and although a few slipped through, I do not believe there were many. Critics charging us with excessive and sometimes insincere urbanity would, I think, be nearer the mark.

Of all debuts, the most pregnant with disaster was that of Leslie

Chauncey, as Personal Assistant to the Resident in Central India, Colonel Heale.

> It happened that when I arrived at Indore it was the Maharajah's birthday, and a message was left for me to change into shikar clothes and take my gun and join the duck-shoot at Malwa. I duly arrived, reported to Colonel Heale who told me to go across some shallow water and put up some snipe he had seen lodge there. This I did, but unknown to me the Resident hid himself behind some reeds. The snipe suddenly got up very low, and seeing no one in their line of flight, I let fly. Upon which there was a yell and a figure came out from behind the reeds and it was clear that I had peppered the Resident.
>
> Fortunately all the pellets were in his legs. (Nineteen, according to the Medical Officer who extracted them.) I had to break the news to Mrs Heale. It was difficult to know how to begin – 'It's all right, but I've shot your husband,' or 'I've shot your husband, but it's all right.' I chose the former. She was magnificent and called for champagne for us while the M.O. extracted the pellets. The Resident was equally fine, telling me that every dog was allowed one bite, and sent me out with the Political Agent, Malwa, next morning to 'shoot and regain my nerve'. We stood, on the P.A.'s insistence, back-to-back for this exercise.

The shortest service in the Political was that of Rupert Kilkelly of the Poona Horse. It terminated when, as Personal Assistant to the Resident for Rajputana, he sent an official invitation to a Miss Hoare, and spelt the name wrong. It was, they said, the only kind he knew.

John Cotton's introduction to the service was at first orthodox, as Personal Assistant to the Resident in Aden, welcoming and being nice to passing V.I.P.s, issuing passports and visas, handling cypher messages, acting as city magistrate, playing golf and polo. But in May, 1935, he was ordered to report for duty at the British Legation in Addis Ababa, an extraordinary assignment, since Ethiopia was no concern of the Indian Political Service. Ostensibly the posting was due to a loss of discipline among the Minister's Indian Cavalry escort, which consisted of a Daffadar and eight sowars,* all Sikhs, of Cotton's own regiment. He thought there might be more to it than that. Italian troop- and ship-movements, strident complaints of atrocities and border incursions, bellicose speeches from Rome and twitterings in the League of

*Daffadar: sergeant; sowar: trooper.

Nations, all suggested that Mussolini was about to launch his legions against Ethiopia.

Djibouti in French Somaliland, the terminus of the 500-mile railway to Addis Ababa, was even hotter than Aden.

> The down-at-heel Greek-owned hotels were full of journalists waiting, like me, for the twice-weekly train. I shared a room with a commercial traveller whose suitcases contained a set of British Army webbing equipment, of which he hoped to sell several thousand sets to the Ethiopian Ministry of War. The other Europeans were either journalists, or hoping to sell the Ethiopians something.

Addis Ababa, at 8,500 feet, was much cooler. Rain fell incessantly, transforming the few roads into quagmires. The railway was the only link with the outer world, for no transport plane of the day could take off at that altitude from the grass air-strip.

Cotton found the cavalry escort in poor shape, disgruntled by long absence from home, by idleness and by menial duties such as teaching the Legation children to ride. Being Sikhs, they reacted by quarrelling and intriguing among themselves, and some took to drink. They were delighted to find they were now to take orders from an officer of their own regiment, who spoke their language and knew their customs. Cotton worked them hard, made them clean themselves up, as well as their horses and their equipment, and had no more trouble with them.

But Cotton had been sent for another purpose. The Minister, Sir Sidney Barton, was worried that if war broke out and the Emperor's armies were defeated there would be a fierce anti-foreign reaction. There were 2,000 to 3,000 British subjects and British Protected Persons in Addis Ababa, who would flock to the Legation for protection. Could it be held against hostile mobs, rifle-armed tribesmen, defeated and mutinous troops?

It might seem odd that the Personal Assistant to the Resident in Aden should be called upon to advise the British Minister in Addis Ababa on military affairs, but there was no Military Attaché, and the arrival of a more senior officer might have alarmed the jittery British community and annoyed the Emperor, who never doubted that his raggle-taggle army would give the Italians a sharp lesson.

The Legation's military resources consisted of the nine cavalrymen with rifles, swords and lances. In the cellar were 100 service rifles kept for an emergency. The Legation with its officers, staff-houses, stables, gardens and tennis-courts was in a compound of about 600 acres, some miles out of the capital, dominated by a hill which was outside the

1 Elephants moving out for a tiger-kill in Nepal
2 J.R. Cotton (*centre*), District Magistrate of Abu, with his first tiger

3 The Peshawur Vale hunter trials, winter 1938. The Political team – Cunningham, Dring and Low.
4 A Political Agent moves house

perimeter. Cotton reported that it could not be held without at least a company of infantry, with extra mortars and machine-guns.

The Foreign Office saw no way in which British troops could be sent to a country with which Britain was at peace. British bureaucracy at its worst. So a wireless message was sent to New Delhi, and back came the answer that a Sikh company of the 5th/14th Punjab Regiment, with mortars, machine-guns, searchlights and 3,000 gas-masks, was being assembled at Bombay. Indian bureaucracy at its best.

The next problem was to obtain the permission of the Emperor Haile Selassie, a proud potentate who would reject with contumely any suggestion that his armies might be defeated, or might be unable to protect foreigners in his capital. Long and hard Sir Sidney argued, and at last the Emperor gave his consent, provided the company was brought in as inconspicuously as possible.

There was an anxious wait. Addis Ababa was packed with Special Correspondents and news-reel photographers of all nationalities,* who besieged the Press Authority for permission to proceed to the front; but none was allowed to leave Addis Ababa. For want of reliable, or even unreliable, news, they sat in their awful hotels, under dripping ceilings, typing out long and inaccurate reports. By day Cotton made secret arrangements with Indian contractors to house and feed the Punjabis. By night he frequented the sleazy bars and night-spots of the capital, hoping to pick up news from such as Evelyn Waugh, W.F. Deedes (later Editor of the *Daily Telegraph*) and the American, Knickerbocker, who in their turn were hoping to pick up news from him. In deference to the Emperor's susceptibilities they could not be given an inkling of what was afoot; but the French and Italian Military Attachés, despite congenital suspicions of *perfide Albion*, were helpful.

At last, early in September, there steamed into Djibouti the *Jehangir*, carrying a company of 140 Sikhs with three British officers, a Medical Officer and the vast quantity of extra equipment and stores. The Emperor, while realising that the operation could not be entirely shrouded in secrecy, was emphatic that it be kept as quiet as possible, lest wild rumours of an invasion by foreign troops rouse the populace to frenzy. The journalists knew something was up, but found it strangely difficult to get passes to go down the line. With French co-operation, the Punjabis and their stores were smuggled up the line in a special train

*Most of the British were, albeit grudgingly, *personae gratae* at the Legation. Not so Evelyn Waugh, who was on Sir Sidney and Lady Barton's black list for lampooning them in *Black Mischief* as the Envoy Extraordinary and his consort.

with closed shutters. There remained the problem of getting them secretly from the train to the Legation, the only passable roads being through the city.

The Minister persuaded the Emperor to order a curfew that night. When the troop-train arrived at Addis Ababa station at four in the morning, Cotton was waiting with a fleet of vans and lorries hired from Indian traders, in which the troops were driven rapidly through the empty streets to the Legation.

> We had pulled off a difficult operation. A day or two later the Press (less Evelyn Waugh) were invited to the Legation to see the smartly turned out Sikh sepoys going about their duties. No one had scooped the event, of which their editors had been simultaneously informed by the Foreign Office; and there was a good deal of sour grapes, with snide references to the panic measures of the British Minister, 'Barton's Folly'.
>
> Four weeks later I joined an immense crowd outside the palace. The great war-drum of Menelik was sounded; the Decree of Mobilisation was read by the Grand Chamberlain. The war started on time, just as the rains ended.

Cotton returned to India to continue his Political training. Events fell out just as had been predicted. With the defeat of his armies, the Lion of Judah departed to Surrey. The mob, the tribes and the defeated soldiery, in their rage and mortification, turned savagely on foreigners. But for 'Barton's Folly', there would have been wholesale massacre. The Punjabis defended the Legation and all who took refuge therein, occupied the hill overlooking it, patrolled the city saving hundreds from frenzied mobs and rescued the American Minister, staff and U.S. Marine escort just as their Legation went up in flames. Then the Italians arrived and restored order with a heavy hand.

For Cotton it was a remarkable introduction to a service which offered a career of infinite variety.

The 1920s and 1930s were years of increasing self-government for the provinces, of Congress agitation against the states, of Gandhi's Salt March and Fasts unto Death, and of attempts to make the princes join a Federation of India. But none of this was the concern of Personal Assistants, who were all struck by the importance attaching to shikar*

*Shikar: any form of field sport, generally shooting; shikari: one who indulges in shikar, or ghillie.

and protocol. The famous duck-shoots at Bharatpur, the sand-grouse shoots at Bikanir, were state occasions requiring the services of battalions of state forces, and state shikaris by the score. Invitations to them were eagerly sought by those who liked that sort of thing. Butts were arranged strictly according to precedence: the Great Man would fire off ten times as many cartridges as the humble Personal Assistant. It would cause the deepest offence to say to the Maharajah, 'Thank you, Your Highness, but I really don't want to shoot a hundred duck or five hundred sand-grouse.' And if the big day's bag fell short of average, there would be despondency at the palace.

To the cultivators, tigers were unmitigated disaster, killing in Gwalior or Rewa thousands of cattle a year, even if they did not turn man-eater. But to the ruler they were much more than Royal Game. They were a bait, attracting to one's state the Great and the Good (assuming one wanted them). They were a status symbol. It was a minor disgrace if a V.I.P. came to one's state, a tiger-shoot was laid on, and he did not get a shot. Whether or not he hit the tiger was immaterial: as soon as he fired, everyone within range fired too, and the tiger fell with a dozen bullets in him of which, it was axiomatic, the first had been fired by the V.I.P.

Apart from ringing a tiger with a hundred elephants, which was done only in Nepal, there were two principal methods of shooting him. The first, for important people, was a beat. A tiger would be located. The V.I.P.s would be safely established (according to precedence, the Top Person in the best place) in machans, platforms built in trees, or in stone towers, loopholed and machicolated. Hundreds of beaters would then drive the tiger towards the guns, while scores of 'stops' along the sides would prevent him from breaking out. The only skill involved was to organise the beat so that the tiger passed close to the Great Man, not at a gallop but at a slow pace, making an easy target. It was absolutely impossible for him to say, 'Look, I don't want to shoot a tiger, least of all from a fortress. Please let me out.' The gravest offence would be taken.

Alternatively one might 'sit up' in a machan over a tiger's kill and shoot him as he returned to it. One guest of a small state, not noted for his prowess as a big-game hunter, was surprised as he approached the machan to find the tiger fast asleep beside the kill, snoring loudly. To ensure success, the kill had been laced with opium.

If a state had no tigers, a panther was the next best thing. It was almost routine for the Political Agent visiting some states to be invited to shoot a panther. Mary Kirkbride, daughter of the Resident at Udaipur, was invited to sit up for the night with Keith Battye, Secretary to the Resident for Rajputana and (I hasten to add) a man of irreproachable character. Just out of school and very carefully brought up, she was surprised when the Head Shikari gave them a flask of neat whisky in case they felt cold; a lump of raw opium lest they feel disposed to cough; and, for more intimate needs, a chamber-pot stuffed (happy afterthought!) with grass to muffle the noise of its use.

Princely shooting camps were luxurious. A revealing light was thrown on them by the Maharawal of Dungarpur who came to stay with me in Kenya for a month's big-game hunting safari. My wife and I on safari lived fairly rough, sleeping on the ground, eating only basic food, taking no camp furniture or tents. For Dungarpur, however, we laid on tents, camp-beds, chairs, a table, even a red-and-white checked table-cloth.

'Mary,' said H.H., observing this splendour, 'you have made a great effort for me.'

'Well, Maharawal Sahib, when we remember the magnificent camps you are accustomed to, we think this is the least we can do.'

'But we only did that sort of thing for you! When my brother and I went shooting by ourselves, we took nothing but our bedding-rolls and a few chupattis and onions.'

Dungarpur used to shoot tigers on foot, stalking the animal as it lay up in the heat of the day and taking the shot at a few yards' range. Not many did that. The princes could not be blamed for the virtual extinction of the tiger. Records show that from 1900 to 1947 the tiger population in the states remained constant, while declining in British India due to the destruction of their habitat by encroaching cultivation and civilisation.

If shikar was important, protocol was the breath of life to many a ruler – a prop to his self-esteem, an assurance that he would be treated with proper respect by his own subjects and his fellow-princes, and a means (cunningly used) of scoring off a rival and even off the Resident. Where he and others were placed at dinner, how far down the palace steps he went to meet the Viceroy or, in Delhi, the Viceroy came to meet him, whether the Resident's elephant walked half a pace behind or half a pace in front of his in procession – all this was the subject of anxious concern. And if most Politicals regarded it all with cynical detachment, none could refuse to play. Some, indeed, (and their wives), took it very seriously. When Geoffrey Betham was Resident at Udaipur, a V.I.P. came on an official visit. After dinner Dorothy Betham took the ladies out to do whatever ladies do after dinner and automatically, as hostess, stood aside to let her guest into the bathroom first. Said the great lady graciously, 'Oh, pray no precedence in the bedchamber.'

It could be more than a game. Conrad Corfield paid an official visit to the new young Maharajah Yadavendra Singh of Patiala.

> When I arrived I was shown into the drawing-room – but no ruler. I waited for a quarter of an hour and then I thought, 'Well, this isn't good enough. He's trying it on.' So I said to the A.D.C., 'I've heard from His Highness that the garden is much improved lately. I'll just go and see it.' The A.D.C. said, 'Oh no, sir, he'll be here any minute.' But I said, 'No, I'd like to go.' So I went and walked away from the house as far as I could on what was a very hot morning, and I'd gone at least half a mile when His Highness came running up, pouring with perspiration and saying he was very sorry. The next time I arrived, there he was, standing at the bottom of the steps ready to greet me.'

That was a game two could play. A granddaughter of the Maharani of Baroda recalls accompanying her grandmother to pay a call on Lady Willingdon.

> There were my mother and my grandmother sitting in the back seat of my grandfather's Rolls-Royce, I on the jump-seat. The car stopped at the entrance of Viceregal Lodge and the A.D.C. came to open the door, but my grandmother said, 'Don't get down. Keep sitting.' We didn't understand, but we sat quietly while she said to the A.D.C., 'Where is Lady Willingdon?' She kept asking, 'Where is Lady Willingdon?' until he went into the house and out Lady Willingdon came. Then she said, 'Now you can get down.'

The rules regarding presents from rulers were extremely strict. Nothing more than fruit, vegetables and sweets could be accepted. A new Resident at Indore was presented with the usual basket of fruit at Christmas. Interested in some unusual fruits, he delved to the bottom where he found nestling 100 gold mohurs. Furious at being offered a bribe, he wrote an angry letter to the Regent Maharani, who replied apologetically: she had inspected the state records and found that 100 gold mohurs was always given to the Resident at Christmas. Was it not enough? Perhaps the Resident would indicate how much he considered suitable. Investigations disclosed that, year after year, the Resident's servants had pocketed this windfall.

Any present of value had to be returned politely to the donor. If this could not be done without giving offence, it was received with thanks and deposited in the Government Treasury, whence the recipient could select a gift of equal value to give the prince.

These rules were perfectly understood and strictly observed by all – except Lady Willingdon. She had the habit, notoriously, of admiring some trinket, perhaps a diamond brooch, and when the owner replied, *pro forma*, 'But, Your Excellency, it is yours,' taking him at his word. Her acquisitiveness was well known to her staff. One year they asked her what she and Lord Willingdon would like from them for Christmas. She thought for a while and replied, 'His Excellency, I am sure, would like a golf-club. And I would very much like an emerald necklace.'

It is extraordinary how Lady Willingdon seems to overshadow the Political/state scene in the 1930s. Dring was summoned to be interviewed for the post of Assistant Private Secretary to the Viceroy. Travelling in haste from the Frontier, he was obliged to borrow a respectable suit from one of the A.D.C.s. Said Lady Willingdon, shaking hands with him, 'I see you have Cecil's suit on.' He found the Willingdons were 'delightful to work with, and we had a very happy staff'. There were innumerable stories about her, mainly apocryphal. She had such a penchant for the colour mauve that the family motto was said to be, '*Mauve qui peut.*' But according to Dring it is not true that she had mauve lavatory paper. She could be thoughtful, helpful, kind. She was also very bossy and bullied many affluent rulers, and some not affluent, into building schools, hospitals, maternity homes and agricultural centres – or at least into laying their foundation stones. Occasionally she met her match. On a visit to Hyderabad she spotted that the Nizam was wearing a frayed and stained ribbon of the K.C.S.I. and the Resident was asked to tackle him about it.

'Did she say that?' exclaimed His Exalted Highness. 'Did she really say that? Wonderful woman, wonderful woman! The things she notices!'

But he never changed the ribbon.

Lord Willingdon was a grandee of grandees, but sometimes found his consort rather too much of a good thing and used to take comfort from half a bottle of champagne in mid-morning while the A.D.C.s (recalls Frank Pearson) restored their equilibrium with port and cheesecake. One day an exasperated A.D.C. exclaimed, 'I can't take her any longer! I'm going back to my regiment.'

Lord Willingdon, who liked dropping in on the A.D.C.s' room, overheard. 'My boy,' he said, 'I never had a regiment to go back to.'

The disgruntled A.D.C. stayed.

3

The Training of Politicals

Having spent some months in the humble position of Personal Assistant, the young Political from the Army had to pass the ordinary I.C.S. examinations in the Indian Penal Code, Civil Procedure Code, Indian Evidence Act, Revenue Law, Treasury Regulations, Excise Law and Local Government. (Those coming from the I.C.S. had already passed.) One studied for these examinations while actually working in a British India district as Assistant Commissioner and gaining practical experience of the subjects.

The most important part of the district training was in 'settlement', the assessment and collection of Land Revenue. It is most extraordinary, and a tribute to the sheer thoroughness of the Indian Administration, that, from the Khyber Pass to Cape Cormorin, every cultivable acre in British India was measured, mapped and assessed for the annual land revenue payment. From end to end of the country the same system was practised, though the technical vocabulary changed. Fair assessment and efficient collection were all-important: indeed in some provinces the Deputy Commissioner was usually called the 'Collector'. The actual money brought in mattered less than the need to show that the people must pay, each according to his means, for fair, but firm administration. A properly working revenue system was the hallmark of governmental efficiency. Moreover, by checking the revenue records personally, with the villagers who tilled the fields and paid the revenue crowding round, the district officer was brought into a purposeful contact with the people.

A 'settlement' (the term used for re-checking occupancy rights and reassessing revenue) took place in every district every thirty years or so. A district settlement took about four years to complete. Once his training was over, a Political would probably never have actually to do any settlement work; but if as Resident he was to persuade some reluctant Maharajah to settle his state on the same principles as in British India, he should have a working knowledge of those principles.

The principles of land tenure were inherited from the Moguls. The land belonged to the ruler, but the holder had proprietory rights, so long as he paid the land revenue assessed on it, and passed these rights on to his heirs according to Hindu and Moslem laws of inheritance. He was colloquially called 'landowner', but if he defaulted in his payments the King could resume possession of the land. Should there be a crop-failure because of floods, drought, locusts, etc., the revenue could be remitted or reduced for that year.

Thus the theory. Robin Hodson was instructed in the practice in Abbottabad District of the North-West Frontier Province. First, hereditary rights to fields, changes in ownership and tenancy rights were established by evidence on oath, given in public, and by reference to the Mutation Register in which all changes were recorded. Then, by simple triangulation on a plane-table, every field was delineated on a village map drawn with Indian ink on a large white cloth to a scale of 64 inches to a mile. 'In five days we measured 28 acres.' Five days to do 28 acres, and the whole of British India to do every thirty years or so! One is astounded by the magnitude of the task without any modern aids such as air photography.

Alec Redpath described the subsequent proceedings:

> The Settlement Officer and his staff recorded all titles to land – the soil classification, the sources of water, the yield of all crops on each field and average market prices over the past five years. From a gross valuation of the produce of each holding was then deducted the costs, leaving a net sum of which about a fifth was claimed by Government as revenue. Land Registers were kept up-to-date by the *Patwari*,* who entered changes of ownership in a Mutation Register. Appeals lay to the Deputy Commissioner, known in revenue matters as the Collector.
>
> Twice a year at harvest time the Patwari would visit the field and enter in the crop register the crop and its yield. These were spot-checked in diminishing proportions by the Tahsildar.*
>
> I never ceased to marvel at the dexterity and speed with which the Patwari, astride his pony, could handle the bundle of registers and cloth maps and identify fields . . . I found the Patwaris' entries remarkably accurate. Their estimates of crop failures – a quarter, a half, three-quarters, or total – I approved or altered after discussion. Wherever we passed we were joined by spectators who, uninvited, would join in the arguments, complaints, chit-chat and laughter, giving us unsolicited advice and useful tit-bits of local gossip.

Rance's Settlement Training was in Aligurh District, United Provinces.

*Patwari: a local revenue clerk; Tahsildar: a revenue assistant and collector.

The Settlement Officer was Khan Sahib Ahmed Ali, efficient and endlessly patient with the locals and with me. We travelled by elephants, ox-cart, riding camel, on horseback or on foot. The elephant was most satisfactory: we just sat sideways on a mattress tied on top of the animal, giving us an excellent view of the fields. The locals were able to keep up with us and say their piece as we progressed.

Every argument was put forward for a reduction in assessment. Rance and Ahmed Ali assessed a very good field – soil, irrigation, crops all first-class . . .

'But, Sahib, the monkeys from the jungle take half the crop.'

So the monkey factor was taken into account and a reduction made.

The key-person was the Patwari, nearly always men of integrity (they could hardly be otherwise since they worked under the eagle eyes of their neighbours and their work was subject to many spot-checks), and generally landowners themselves, which meant they could not be regarded by the villagers as faceless bureaucrats. The system was cheap, fool-proof and fraud-proof.

It was the contention of Politicals who came from the I.C.S. that their military colleagues knew less than nothing about revenue. The North-West Frontier Province was run mainly by military Politicals. Herbert Thompson, from the I.C.S. in Madras, was shocked by the cavalier attitude towards this vital matter of his first Deputy Commissioner, a Major, who made himself quite plain. 'It is,' he said, 'the duty of the rest of India to pay for this province.'

Whereas revenue and settlement work was *terra incognita* to the learner-Political just out of the Army, criminal law was not, for the same principles applied as in military law. He knew, or should know, the provisions of the Indian Evidence Act: he knew what value should be given to accomplice evidence, when hearsay was permissible, what constituted a leading question, and when such a question could be asked, and what use could be made of signed statements made to (and not infrequently by) the police. All this was, if not familiar ground, at least not entirely strange. He would not be quite lost the first time he sat down in Court as Third-Class Magistrate empowered to fine a miscreant up to 100 rupees or to sentence him to fourteen days' imprisonment.

Some features of the court would not, however, be so familiar. There was a helpful Court Clerk who knew a great deal about his own job and the Honourable Magistrate's. There was a Police Prosecutor, also knowledgeable and probably helpful. And there were the Vakils, or Pleaders, a cross between solicitor and barrister, the bogeymen of British India, reputed to be subversive, devious, mendacious, prepared to take advantage of every legal quibble and procedural error.

I did not find them so: nor, I think, did most learner-magistrates. Certainly they were not averse to spinning out a case, seeing it drag on day after day: that was their bread-and-butter. Nevertheless they were generally more inclined to be helpful to a beginner than to take advantage of his ignorance: 'With great respect, Your Honour, I submit that it would be more correct to proceed under Section . . .' You could identify the bad Pleader by his minions carrying fat, flagged volumes of case-law intended to intimidate the court and blind him with legal expertise. On the whole, though, I liked them, and was flattered that one or two seemed to like me. They used to take a walk with me after the day's work was done, never referring, even in the most distant manner, to a case, but chatting of this and that. It was my Court Clerk who disillusioned me. 'Sir, they want to give general public the impression that they are on good terms with you. Then more people will employ them.' Fair enough.

Most cases heard by Third- and Second-Class Magistrates were petty – cattle trespass, simple assault, pilfering, breach of municipal by-laws. Occasionally there cropped up something more interesting. Bazalgette in Dera Ghazi Khan heard a curious inheritance case:

> . . . three sons were quarrelling over the division of their father's property. The family were descended from a Moslem holy man whose tomb became a centre for pilgrimage, very lucrative for those who owned it for it was meritorious to give alms for its upkeep. Over the generations the family became more interested in money than in good works. When the case came up before me, the three brothers were literally fighting for possession of the tomb, each with his armed gang of supporters. I camped near the well for several days while I tried to sort out the claims and counter-claims, divide the inheritance according to Moslem law, and bind over the young men not to fight.

On the whole, though, this was by far the most tedious part of a young Political's training. One sat hour after hour in a court-room packed with sweating humanity, while the electric ceiling-fan languidly turned over the stale air, Each witness in turn told his story, probably quite untrue, in the local language or dialect; this was translated by the Court Clerk into Urdu, and written down in English, in long hand, by the Magistrate, a sheet of blotting-paper under his sweating hand, the ink running in the sweat-drops on the foolscap. It was a depressing thought that in many cases the only person in the court-room who did not know what had really happened was oneself, who had to decide whether the accused was innocent or guilty. How could one tell who was lying? Probably they were all lying to escape punishment, to get an enemy into trouble, to curry favour with authority, to earn a few rupees, or just out of fear of the police.

'Sir,' the Court Clerk might say during the midday break, 'watch their toes. If they wriggle their toes, they are lying.'

'There are two kinds of policemen,' the Deputy Commissioner would tell from his experience and wisdom, 'the honest and the dishonest. The honest policeman rigs the evidence to convict the man he knows is guilty. Probably it is the only way he can get a conviction. The dishonest policeman rigs the evidence to convict a man he knows is innocent.'

It was very satisfactory for the Magistrate when he *knew* he was right, especially if his decision resulted in an innocent man going free. Often that certitude came only from hearing a case, perhaps at great inconvenience, at the scene of the alleged crime. Redpath, under training, heard a man charged by a canal warden with stealing a canal-bank tree – quite a serious matter, for it might cause a breach in the bank and a flood of wasted water.

> The Prosecution claimed that the tree had been found in the accused's courtyard and taken out through the door. The case seemed watertight. But the defending Vakil pleaded that I visit the courtyard. I did so. The Vakil then called upon the canal warden and some locals to carry the tree into the courtyard. They could not do so: the angle of a wall made this impossible. Not Guilty.
>
> The effort to discover the truth was exhausting. But there were moments of satisfaction when I managed to unravel some tangled skein of falsehood. Often it was the ingenious and elaborate construction of the evidence which alerted one. The details, neatly dovetailed and graphically described, did not accord with fallible memories and different points of view. One developed a sort of human geiger counter enabling one to detect not so much the metal as the fact that it was flawed.

Congress Governments in the provinces, after the 1935 Government of India Act, introduced a new factor into the work of the courts. In Agra, wrote Rance:

> our City Magistrate, an able and honest Moslem, began to have his

troubles. Files dealing with cases of prominent Congress supporters were sent for by the Provincial Minister of Justice and never seen again: despite enquiries 'through the usual channels', nothing seemed to happen.

A mind-numbing experience for the Junior Magistrate was witnessing an execution. At sunrise a solemn procession proceeded from the condemned cell to the scaffold. The magistrate had to verify the condemned man's identity and then, before he was hooded, ask him if he had anything more to say, either to clear his conscience by a confession or of such a nature as to postpone the inevitable. One very experienced Pathan magistrate told me, 'If ever you have to witness an execution, read the judgment first, and you will feel better about it. No man is ever hanged except for the worst kind of murder: if there are any extenuating circumstances, he is transported.'

Another magistrate told Geoffrey Betham that he had witnessed over a hundred executions in Peshawur, where murder is as common as in Los Angeles.

'And how many of those men,' Betham asked, 'confessed to you at the last?'

'All except one.'

'Was he innocent?'

'Undoubtedly. No Moslem who was guilty would fail to confess in the last moment of his life to a fellow-Moslem.'

Quite a good testimonial to the Peshawur Criminal Courts.

Very boring training was that for the District Treasury, which consisted of three days working with each clerk until one could do his work, going through all the stages up to Treasury Officer – learning how cash came in, how it was accounted for, how to check the accounts, and at regular (and irregular) intervals counting the cash. Currency notes were stitched up in bundles and coins kept in bags of 1,000 rupees. The whole process, wrote Thompson:

> showed how facile sneers at red tape can be. Each collection of rupees weighed the same, so after counting a number in one bag, one weighed every other bag against it. In Madras bags were of strong net. This was because once upon a time an official had hit upon the bright idea of filling bags at the bottom of the pile with the equivalent weight of clinking metal. He retired to safety in French Pondicherry before the deficiency was discovered . . . It was unwise to assume that the packet of mint-new notes, stitched up and certified, were all that they appeared to be. One shrewd operator had unstitched a bundle,

replaced currency notes with lavatory paper, stitched it up again, pared the edges and restored the bundle to the shelf.

It sometimes fell to the trainees, as District Officer and Magistrate, to deal with a riot. The Moslem festival of Moharram was a dangerous time in places such as Agra, with a large population of Shiahs who on that day commemorate the martyrdom of the founders of their sect, Hassan and Hussein, grandsons of the Prophet. So at Moharram there were two potential flashpoints: between Moslem and Hindu, and between the two rival Moslem sects, Sunni and Shiah. Shiahs poured in from the countryside to march in procession between drums and bands and mobile shrines of the saints, shouting rhythmic, alternating, intoxicating cries of 'Hassan . . . Hussein . . . Hassan . . . Hussein . . .' and beating their own backs with whips and chains until the blood poured.

Their traditional route led past some Hindu temples. The problem here was no different to that in Derry and Strabane: did one let them follow that route, thereby perhaps provoking Hindus into attacking them; or did one prevent them following it, knowing that they would create an uproar at being deprived of their traditional religious observance? Usually they were allowed to follow the route, with a strong police presence and some magistrates around to read the riot act and authorise the police to open fire if necessary. The greatest danger was that they would form a huge, chanting, drumming mob outside a Hindu temple while temple bells indicated that prayers were in progress.

Rance was one of the magistrates in 1937, riding at the head of the procession on a skittish mare, staunch to pig and to mobs. Whenever they came to a temple, he discouraged the mob from forming up by passaging from side to side, reining back and plunging forward. So long as the bells were ringing, the crowd were so apprehensive of the mare's heels that they hung back; only when the bells had stopped did Rance lead the procession onward.

The pleasantest part of the training was the winter touring round one's sub-division. To Frank Pearson the winter tours were a joy:

> Out from headquarters and the stuffy office with bullock carts for camping equipment, a horse to ride, a gun for sport and food. In the early morning camp would be struck and the bullock carts moved on to the next camp. I would follow, stopping at villages en route. Talks with the elders. Check the revenue records and hear of any rural disputes. These were mainly about land boundaries and could be settled on the spot. Sometimes a case would be on my files for a local investigation, on the scene of an alleged crime or complaint. The

> main object was to keep in touch with the people and hear their problems. To hear and listen to problems is half the battle: few really expect them to be solved . . . And in the evening wander round with a gun for a brace of partridges or a duck for dinner.

Then, just as everything seemed to be going splendidly, there would be a sudden crisis. It happened to Dring on training in the Shahpur district of the Punjab.

> There was a disastrous flood in the Sutlej. The Deputy Commissioner was away, so I was left with many vital decisions to take. Railway embankments twelve miles from the river were washed away. Canals and road embankments had to be cut to let the flood water through, and a prison had to be evacuated.

The training and the work were nearly all concerned with rural India, the landholders and peasants. It was a weakness of the British in India that they did not pay enough attention to the city-dwellers, leaving them to the Congress agitators. It was natural – the villagers were so much nicer, and more grateful; but it was a mistake.

Finally there was Secretariat training, usually in the cool of Simla in the middle of the hot weather, a delightful working holiday for men sweating it out in Multan or Dera Ghazi Khan. In the Foreign and Political Department one learned how to handle official files, how to draft minutes, memoranda and despatches in clear, concise, accurate English. John Cotton was given the files of decided cases to study, involving decisions of accepted political practice.

> This was an instructive exercise as some of the cases had gone up as far as the Viceroy for decision. The minuting procedures of the Indian Government, which owed much to Lord Curzon, were laborious and time-consuming, but had the merit that no fact of importance was ignored. The culmination of the course was the presentation to us probationers of several files from which the minutes of the Deputy Secretary had been abstracted. We were then expected, on the basis of the original facts and of previous minutes, to produce our own reasoned and logical submission, which would enable the Foreign or Political Secretary to reach a decision.

Having passed all his examinations, undergone Secretariat training, passed a departmental exam on the history and background of the states, and learned the art of rapid encyphering and de-cyphering, the probationer found himself at the end of about three years a full-fledged member of the service. His next move was to buy a very expensive uniform, consisting of the mess-kit, an evening tail-coat with dark blue cuffs and facings; and the day-time full dress, which was not unlike that of the commissionaire of the Ritz Hotel, surmounted by a white topee with a silver spike. In the Dress Regulations of the service he might be surprised to read: 'Trousers will not be worn when ladies are present.' One was supposed then to wear white kerseymere breeches.

4

The Frontier

The North-West Frontier was the Indian Government's insoluble problem. From 1846, when it was taken over from the Sikh Empire, to 1947, when it became Pakistan's problem, about a third of the officers of the Indian Political were engaged in trying to find a solution.

Geographically 'the Frontier' meant, in general terms, the country between the Indus River and the international boundary with Afghanistan, known as the Durand Line.* The extreme north was inhabited by fairly tractable mountaineers known, inaccurately, as Dards; the extreme south was the land of the wild, nomadic but fairly tractable Baluchis and Brahuis. Between these extremes lived the Pathan tribes, who constituted the insoluble problem.

They were Moslems, reputedly fanatical but in some ways rather lax in their religion. (Many, for instance, waxed rich on usury.) By inclination and tradition, and in some cases economic necessity, they were traders and raiders rather than farmers. They were basic democrats, knowing no masters, least of all the Maliks (tribal headmen) with whom the Government must perforce negotiate. Authority resided, if anywhere, in the Jirga, the tribal assembly, in which every man was, in theory, equal: a Malik's power depended on his personality, his wealth, the number of his adherents – not on his being a Malik. This made Pathans very difficult to deal with, since any agreement reached with the Maliks was liable to be abrogated by the Jirga.

It might be thought that such people lived in perpetual anarchy. That they did not was due to their observance (strict in some tribes, less so in others) of the traditional code known as Pukhtunwali, which gave the Pathan certain rights, and laid upon him certain duties. The first duty was that of taking vengeance at all hazards (but in no hurry) for any injury or insult to oneself, one's family, section (clan) or tribe. Other duties were to give unstinted hospitality to a guest, be he Moslem,

*There were exceptions to this generalisation. Hazara District, counted as part of the Frontier, was on the left or east bank of the Indus. Hundreds of miles downstream parts of the Punjab district of Dera Ghazi Khan, and of Sind Province, were on the right or west bank.

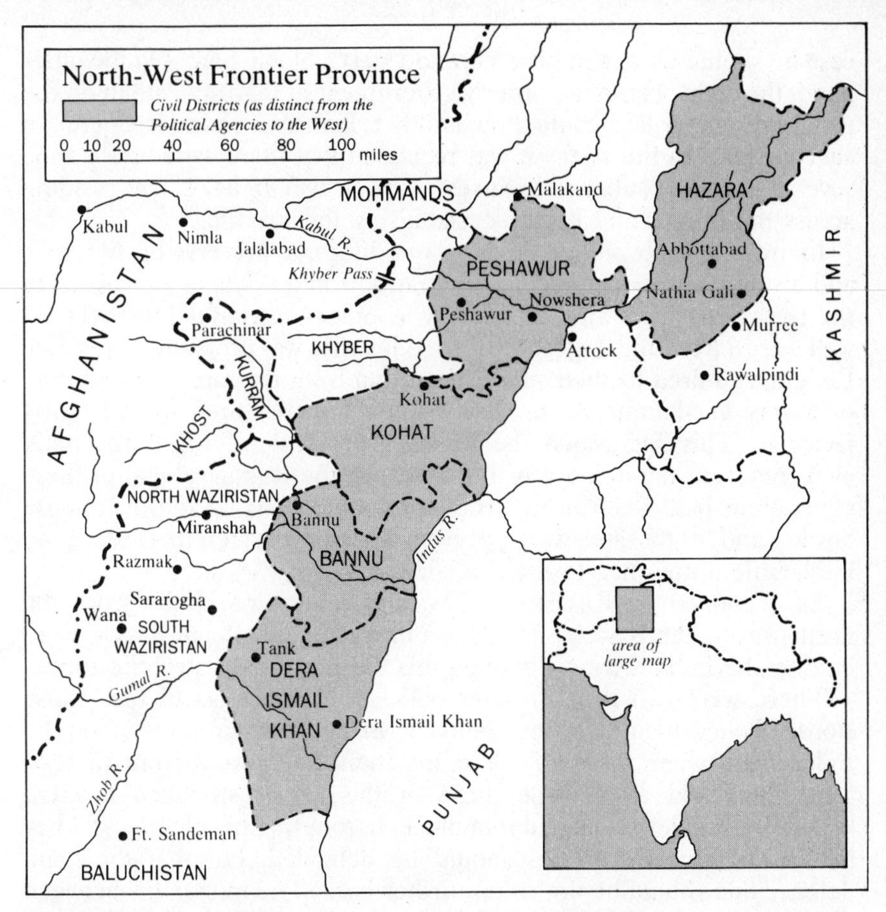

Christian or unbeliever, and to guard his life even at the cost of one's own; and to give protection and asylum to any who sought it. The Pathan's rights to hospitality, protection and asylum were the obverse of his duties.

Thanks to the Pukhtunwali code, hamsayas ('persons sharing the same shade') – fugitives from British justice or from another tribe, Hindu merchants, Sikh mechanics, Punjabi artisans, professional entertainers – could live and carry on their business with a fair degree of safety. And it was thanks also to the Pukhtunwali code that the Political Agent could generally go about his duties, without a military escort, in the wildest parts of the Frontier. He was the guest of the tribe, guarded by a tribal escort who were bound in honour to see that he came to no harm. And in any event, no Pathan, unless moved by an intolerable sense of grievance or the fiercest Islamic fanaticism, would fire at him in case he should hit one of his escort and start a blood-feud. On the other hand, the code obstructed orderly government in that any Pathan on the run from the police could find another Pathan in honour bound to succour him. In the 1920s it was reckoned that there were at any time several hundred outlaws, fugitives from British India, safely residing across the border and keenly destabilising the Frontier.

In order to carry out his Pukhtunwali duties, to preserve his life-style and his precious independence, the trans-Frontier Pathan was armed to the teeth, carrying a rifle as casually as others carry walking-sticks, as well as revolvers and daggers. By 1919 his rifle was probably a .303 Lee Enfield, acquired by theft, trade, desertion from the forces or in battle, or a very good imitation of that weapon manufactured in tribal rifle factories. This aggravated the Frontier problem, of which the main elements were the defence of India against the Russians, who in three generations had over-run the whole of Central Asia up to the Chinese border; and 'watch-and-ward', preventing the tribesmen from being too intolerable a nuisance to their neighbours.

As a counter to Russia, the invasion routes into India from the north-west – the Khyber Pass, Kurram valley and Bolan Pass – were held by the Indian Army, although this did not help control the tribes.

There were two rival Frontier policies. Protagonists of the 'Close Border Policy' held that it was better to meet a Russian invasion on the Indus plain where lines of communication, lateral and front-to-rear, were short and easy, while those of the enemy stretched through hundreds of miles of tangled mountains harbouring hostile tribes. They maintained that the passes should be defended, but that the main defence line should be drawn up further back. The mountains between the Indus valley and the Durand Line would then become a sort of human nature reserve, the denizens left to stew in their own juice until their conduct towards the peaceful plains-dwellers became too outrageous, when a punitive expedition would advance into the hills, kill a few men of the offending tribe, burn down their villages, destroy the terraces of their fields and then withdraw. This policy was also known as 'butcher and bolt'.

To Lord Curzon, Viceroy from 1899 to 1905, 'butcher and bolt' was quite unacceptable, unworthy of our imperial destiny. The alternative was the 'Forward Policy' of meeting the Russians well into Afghanistan and administering and disarming the tribes right up to the Durand Line. Fifty years' experience, including thirty punitive expeditions and two Afghan wars, seemed however to indicate that this was impracticable with the resources at India's disposal.

During Curzon's viceroyalty a compromise policy was evolved. Except for the garrisons of the passes, the army was stationed in the Indus plain; and the Frontier was divided into four areas.

In the north were small semi-independent Dard and Pathan States, ruled by potentates with such exotic titles as the Mir of Hunza, the Mehtar of Chitral, the Wali of Swat and the Nawab of Dir, with Political Agents to advise and supervise them. The fertile plains drained by the Indus and Kabul rivers formed the North-West Frontier Province, divided into six districts each run by a Deputy Commissioner exactly as in the other provinces of British India, except that the Deputy Commissioners (D.C.s) and Assistant Commissioners (A.C.s) were officers of the Political Department. Between the 'administered border' of the North-West Frontier Province and the Durand Line was Tribal Territory, ungoverned, untaxed, ungarrisoned (except at the passes), where Political Agents tried to discourage the tribes from their traditional pursuits and punished them when they became too outrageous. There was also Baluchistan, the pre-Curzon creation of a great Political officer, Colonel Sir Robert Sandeman. With meagre military forces, working through the tribal authorities themselves, he had extended a loose form of indirect rule right up to the Durand Line. There was controversy over Sandeman's policy. Some maintained that it was possible only in Baluchistan where the Baluchis, Brahuis and local Pathans were more under the control of their Sardars (chiefs) than further north; others, that the Baluchistan tribes were better behaved *because* of Sandeman's policy, which should and could be extended to the rest of Tribal Territory.

The top Political in Peshawur thus had a dual function as Chief Commissioner of the North-West Frontier Province; and as Agent to the Governor-General in relation to the states and Tribal Territory. The top Political in Quetta was the Agent to the Governor-General in Baluchistan.

Each Political Agent in an area where there was likely to be serious trouble had at his disposal a private army of battalion or brigade strength composed of Frontier tribesmen, led by officers of the regular Indian Army – a dangerous duty, for these poachers-turned-gamekeeper sometimes reverted to poacher and shot their own officers or the Political Agent. These units were known collectively as the Frontier Corps, individually as the Gilgit Scouts; Chitral Scouts; Khyber Rifles; and Kurram, North Waziristan, South Waziristan and Zhob Militias. Although trained and equipped as infantry and mounted infantry, they were not part of the Army and did not normally come under military command. Each corps was controlled by the local Political Agent. They were deployed in small forts, and their duties were to keep the roads open and to lend fire-power and muscle to the persuasion which was the Political Agent's main instrument.

Although the six districts of the North-West Frontier Province were governed by British Indian law, in Tribal Territory there was only the Sheriat, Islamic law, which lays as much stress on compensating the victim of a crime as on punishing the criminal, and accepts the principle of collective responsibility. Political Agents in Tribal Territory had recourse only to the Sheriat, as laid down in the Frontier Crimes Regulations.

When, for instance, it was known who had committed a murder, the Political Agent would refer the case to a small judicial committee of the Jirga who would pronounce a verdict and make recommendations as to sentence and compensation. Even if the culprit were in Afghanistan or took 'a hundred oaths of innocence', his family, clan or tribe could be made to pay a fine and compensation. If the Political Agent agreed with their findings, as he generally did, it was up to the Jirga to collect the fine; and to lend a sense of urgency to their deliberations, the Militia could arrest influential tribesmen and hold them as hostages, or impound their livestock, at their great inconvenience, until the money and rifles were handed over. These procedures were deplored by the legal profession, British and Indian, and by I.C.S. men in the provinces, but they were perfectly understood by the tribes and approved by Frontier Politicals.

Obviously such a people can best be pacified by giving them better things to do than murder and pillage. It was a chicken-and-egg situation: which came first, law and order or economic amelioration? To the British who governed India it was axiomatic that the essentials of government were law and order, good roads and low taxation: if these were achieved, prosperity would follow. In Tribal Territory law and order was never really achieved, so prosperity did not follow. Quite a lot was done to prime the pump of prosperity, in the way of wells, dams, irrigation schemes, rural co-operatives, schools, contracts for supplying Peshawur with timber and Army camps with meat and firewood, and for constructing and maintaining roads; but obviously not enough, as Pakistan, with ample U.N.O. and American funds, has shown.

Six months after the end of the First World War, when the disbanding Indian Army was at its lowest ebb in manpower, training, efficiency and military zeal, the Amir of Afghanistan declared the Jihad, or Holy War; his army invaded India, and from the Malakand to the Bolan Pass most of the trans-border tribes rose in rebellion. The Khyber Rifles was disbanded before it deserted en masse. The Waziristan Militias were not expected to hold their forts against invasion, since it was assumed that the regular Army would come to their aid, but in May, 1919, the Army could not do so, and the Militia were ordered to pull out. At the spectacle of the British on the run the tribal uprising flared up more fiercely, and thousands of Afridi, Wazir and Mahsud militiamen deserted with their rifles and ammunition. The Afghan regular forces were easily repulsed, but from the Khyber to the Zhob the Curzon structure collapsed like a card-house; and the Army, its ranks full of half-trained recruits, was faced with the most serious frontier war yet experienced, against Mahsuds and Wazirs armed with modern rifles and led by Militia deserters and men who had learned their trade in France and East Africa.

In the operations of 1919–20 two Politicals won D.S.O.s. The first was Major N.E. Reilly, Assistant Political Agent in Chitral when it was invaded by regular Afghan forces. There was only one regular battalion in Chitral, but Reilly mobilised and led in support of it the part-time, irregular Chitral Scouts, the Mehtar's even more irregular bodyguard, and a wild and woolly contingent of pagan Kafirs armed with bows. With these heterogeneous forces, six Afghan battalions were repulsed. The second was Major 'Bunch' Parsons. In Waziristan bombers were used for the first time, unreliable biplanes tossed about by thermals and hazardous in the extreme over these mountains. It was of the utmost importance that bombs spared the just and fell only on the unjust, but in no way could R.A.F. pilots distinguish between them. So Parsons, Political Agent, South Waziristan, guided, navigated and identified targets for the bombers. It became the practice on the Frontier, one of the rules of the game, to give the inhabitants of an area to be bombed a week's notice by the dropping of warning leaflets, so that they could clear out. The object was not to kill people but to inconvenience them, destroy their fortified towers, and prevent them grazing their cattle by daylight. The people themselves generally took refuge in caves which were flea-infested and extremely uncomfortable.

The new plan for Waziristan was to dominate it from within with regular brigade groups at Razmak and Wana, in fortified camps served by all-weather roads. The Waziristan Militia corps were disbanded and replaced by the Tochi Scouts (for North Waziristan) and the South Waziristan Scouts, still entirely Pathan in composition but not recruiting Mahsuds and Wazirs. After much bloody fighting the Mahsuds and

Wazirs of South Waziristan were forced to submit and a camp at Wana was established. The Chief Political Officer to the Waziristan Field Force, Steuart Pears, by brilliant political work persuaded the Wazirs of North Waziristan actually to co-operate in the establishment of a camp at Razmak.

In 1920 the Politicals began picking up the pieces. Among them was Major R.H. Chenevix Trench, Political Agent for Zhob in Baluchistan, with his headquarters in Fort Sandeman. Taking over in July, 1920, he was greeted by his capable Assistant Political Agent (A.P.A.), Khan Bahadur Sharbat Khan.

'You are English and I am Afridi. There are many things which you can do and I can't. But do not forget that there are many things I can do and you can't. Do not try to be like Sharbat.'

He found no trace of the loose, Sandeman-type administration. No taxes were being collected, as revenue assistants could not operate without a strong escort. The Wazir armies who had invaded Zhob in 1919 had returned home, but the country was infested with well-armed gangs of outlaws and Militia deserters who raided with impunity, carrying off cattle, camels, women and loot. Local Maliks were demoralised. Parties would not come to the Jirga courts when summoned, or abide by the findings of the courts if they did come. Fines were not paid. Raiders were neither resisted nor even reported. Important tribal Sardars were sitting on the fence, by no means convinced that the British meant to stay. Militia posts had been evacuated in 1919, most of the men deserting, with their rifles. But the deserters were being replaced by recruits from more reliable tribes, Pathan, Baluchi and Brahui, and gradually the posts were being reoccupied.

To the restoration of some semblance to law and order there were three obstacles: the Wazirs; the Suliman Khel, a tough, well-armed, predatory tribe of Powindahs (nomads), who migrated twice a year through the Zhob, in autumn down the Indus plains, in spring back to the highlands of Afghanistan, committing every kind of skulduggery en route; and local Pathans, notably Militia deserters.

The locals were the first to weaken. One by one the leading hostiles came in to Fort Sandeman to make their peace with the Government and return home with a clean slate. 'It goes against the grain,' wrote Trench, 'to let them off scot-free, but after all the object is a return to normal.' It does not seem to have gone much against his grain. One, a 'cheerful rogue, touched me two hundred rupees and a camel. As proof of his good-feeling, he told me he had twice had me in his sights but had refrained from pressing the trigger.' Another presented the Political

Agent with a beautiful astrakhan-trimmed posteen: 'It would not be fitting,' he said, 'to come in empty-handed.'

People began to consult the Political Agent about their problems. One was a tribesman who in the heady days of 1919 had bought from a plausible Mullah an amulet guaranteed to deflect bullets from the wearer.

'Whose bullets?' asked Trench.

'Yours, of course, Sahib.'

'Indeed. Pray proceed.'

To try it out, he had tied the amulet round the neck of his best fighting-cock, taken careful aim and blown the bird to pieces. 'Now, Sahib, I claim compensation against that rascal of a Mullah, who took my money under false pretences.'

'You must take your claim to the Jirga.'

The Jirga rocked with laughter at his tale. The simpleton, thinking that an amulet would deflect a well-aimed bullet! But with their new-found confidence, they awarded substantial damages against the man of God.

The Suliman Khel were a harder nut to crack. They killed an American geologist, and massacred a caravan of Nasars, another Powindah tribe, their hereditary enemies. Trench, with a Militia escort, followed them up and found the Nasar corpses, which were not a pretty sight: 'the Suliman Khel had gone out of their way to be unpleasant'. They raided the chrome mines in Hindubagh and got away with 250 camels. Worst of all, 800 Wazirs and Suliman Khel spent eleven days in British territory, dodging regular troops and Militia. They stole hundreds of cattle and camels, looted several villages, and got back into Afghanistan without losing a man. 'A little *suppressio veri*,' wrote the Political Agent, 'is necessary to keep on good terms with the soldiers. But the naked truth is that they were never hustled out of a walk.'

The Suliman Khel owed thousands of rupees in fines and compensation for their misdeeds, and had no intention of paying. They were induced to do so not by guns but by guile – Sharbat's guile. The most influential, he pointed out, spent the winter not shivering in tents, but comfortably in Calcutta, waxing rich and fat on usury and brothel management. The Calcutta Police obliged by arresting a round dozen and sending them up to Fort Sandeman, to remain there in durance vile until the tribe had purged its contempt. 'Imagine the disgust of these rich merchants! I tell them they are my guests: meat, tobacco, and no work. Their promises to settle if they are allowed back to the tribe would melt a heart of stone.' It was not quite what the framers of the Frontier

Crimes Regulations had envisaged, but neither was it quite *ultra vires*, and it worked.

The battle would be won if only the locals would resist raiders. 'We will do so, Sahib,' they said, 'if you will give us magazine rifles. We have only Martinis – the Wazirs will not let a man take a Martini on a raid.' But matters were improving. In July, 1921, a man came running into Fort Sandeman with news of a raid only eight miles away. Most of the Militia Mounted Infantry were on an operation in the opposite direction, only twenty were left to saddle up and ride off. But the Sherani Jirga were in session, and Trench put it to them that now was their chance to show their worth. 'They responded with alacrity, law-givers and litigants alike. Within a few minutes the court had broken up and sixty Sheranis, some mounted and some on foot but all with rifles, were following hard on the Militia's heels.'

The Suliman Khel purged their offences, but the Wazirs did not; and the Amir of Afghanistan, to destabilise Baluchistan, settled 700 Wazir families only a few miles across the border, well placed to raid. They were 'real die-hards, with a bitter hatred of us, every man and boy with a .303 Lee Enfield magazine rifle'.

They killed a veterinary officer and cut up a company of the 92nd Punjabis. Trench picked up some Mounted Infantry and riding camels and hastened to the scene of the fight. They met six wounded and naked Punjabis, gave them their riding camels and continued the chase. They met more wounded, sent them back on horses borrowed from a village and cantered on along the trail, but too far behind to stop the raiders getting clean away. The Punjabis had put up a good fight against some 300 Wazirs, until both British Officers were killed and the tribesmen rushed the survivors. Forty Punjabis were killed, twenty captured and eighty rifles lost. The prisoners were stripped and made to carry the Wazir wounded to safety, when the Sikhs and Hindus were decapitated and the Moslems released to find their own way home, naked.

Trench was posted temporarily to Quetta-Pishin, which he expected to be a rest-cure after Fort Sandeman. But within a few days of his arrival the Commanding Officer of the Punjabis drove up with news that two of his officers, out chikor-shooting, had been kidnapped. Trench, the Colonel and forty Punjabis piled into lorries and set off in pursuit.

> It was bitterly cold, freezing hard and a cruel wind. But we reached Migandi by ten o'clock in spite of a bad road, numerous breakdowns and practically no lights. I knocked up some villagers who told me that the raiders had passed through late that evening with two officers.

They gave me a note from the latter, Smith and Jones [not their real names], to the effect that they were unhurt and that their captors would be prepared to let them go if I released and sent to Haji Killa certain men whom I had in jail. They also laid down other terms on a liberal scale. The leader of the raiders was one Nadir who had come into prominence in the previous year. Well, there was obviously nothing to be done at Migandi. The raiders had a three-hour start and might have been anywhere in the hills to the north. It was pitch-dark and quite impossible to follow their tracks. So we started back and reached Pishin, half frozen in spite of our posteens, at one o'clock. I spent most of the night waking up people in Quetta with 'Clear the Line' calls. It gave me a quiet satisfaction.

In the morning the Agent to the Governor-General, Sir Armine Dew, arrived, six-foot-three of blazing fury, his beard bristling with rage. Not merely had the two idiots caused infinite trouble by being kidnapped, not merely had they disobeyed direct orders not to go into that area, but they had been poaching, chikor shooting having been closed there for a year. Meanwhile the most influential Maliks of Nadir's tribe had been gathered in. The first priority was to get back the two officers; but to accept the kidnappers' terms would set a very bad precedent, and there would be more kidnappings.

So we selected half a dozen of the Maliks, put the fear of death into them, and sent them off with orders to go to Haji Killa, get in touch with the raiders and tell them that unless they returned the prisoners unhurt, their relatives would swing, their villages would be burnt and the tribe ruined. I never saw men more frightened.

Meanwhile 'Smith and Jones' had been treated quite well by their captors. 'We are not Wazirs, Sahib, we don't mean to kill you. We only want a little money and our friends released from jail.' They were given food, riding oxen and kept going hard through the night, northward towards the Afghan border. During the next day Nadir and two others left the party to look up friends in a nearby village. There they were caught by Risaldar Khairo Khan of the Mounted Infantry, following the raiders on his own initiative, and Nadir was shot dead. The rest of the gang pushed on until four in the afternoon when, thinking they had out-distanced pursuit, they stopped at a house for refreshment.

Three very comely young women made tea for captors and captives alike, all sitting (girls included) chock-a-block round a fire to drink it. Khairo Khan and his men then came up and started shooting through

> the door and roof at 200–300 yards range. One of the girls who had a small baby went and hid among the cows, but the others merely moved out of the line of fire. The raiders then turned ugly and were about to shoot S. and J. when a local man rushed in between them with a Koran. He was dashed to the ground, but S. and J. guaranteed the raiders' lives and liberty if their own lives were spared. The raiders agreed, but made them sign a bond for Rs 2,000 before they were allowed to leave the hut and get Khairo Khan's men to cease fire.

It was with marked displeasure that Trench handed over Rs 2,000 to the raiders' emissary a few days later. That was the usual practice on the Frontier when a Government servant was kidnapped: pay the ransom, but recover it from the tribe later. It made kidnappers unpopular.

Trench returned to Fort Sandeman. The situation was improving. Local levies often resisted raiders, and outlaws could not count on receiving a warm welcome. Jirga awards were generally accepted, and tribal authority was being re-established.

> It must not be thought that the tribesmen as a whole are eager for the restoration of our control. They are not. They want our protection against the Suliman Khel and appreciate the levy service and other benefits they derive from us. But they like their freedom even more. For the time being, however, their hopes based on Kabul have received a check.

Fort Sandeman, where the Political Agent resided in 'Windsor Castle', a neo-Gothic erection perched on a hill, was considered safe enough for his wife and small daughter. May Trench was a competent water-colour artist. One day she was painting at Kapip, where in 1919 an army convoy had been annihilated. The ground was still littered with horse- and mule-skeletons and debris of battle.

> When my escort had gone for water, a small boy sidled up, handed me a note and scuttled away. Here was a mystery. I waited till I got home to read it. It was from an Englishwoman who said she had been abducted. The matter had to be handled carefully lest she get her throat cut. Dick waited till the men had gone to a fair and then surrounded the camp with Militia and brought her out. Her story was that she had come to Bombay to run a shop left her by her uncle. Having money to splash about, she had lost it all racing. She borrowed from a rascally Powindah money-lender who, when she could not pay up, had taken her back to the Frontier promising to

marry her. He broke his promise of marriage and kept her to do all the dirty jobs as well as teach English to the children. She was a silly little thing and I could well understand his not marrying her.

A few months later Trench left the Zhob in peace. His successor was shot dead in a road ambush.

5
The North-West Frontier Province

Politicals new to the Frontier were generally posted first either to one of the quieter Baluchistan districts (Sibi or Loralai) or to a settled district of the North-West Frontier Province. Herbert Thompson, from the I.C.S. in Madras, was appointed City Magistrate, Peshawur. Within days of arriving he found himself fighting a raging fire.

> When I reached the nearest gate of the city I saw the top window of a house just within the walls pouring out flames. A strong wind was blowing and as I looked the flames spread to the upper storey of a house to leeward. Confined within the walls of the city, development had been mainly upward. Houses were high and constructed around a sort of inverted scaffold of timber. Dried in the sun, that had the combustibility of tar . . . I saw a tongue of flame lick down one of the wooden supports with the speed of a blowlamp. The municipality's three fire-engines were soon overwhelmed. We called in a company of sappers whose enthusiastic captain used so much dynamite in trying to clear a blank space in front of the fires that he ran out of explosives.
>
> Dramatically, the wind swung round, and extinguished the fire by blowing it back towards areas already burnt out. I had been on my feet for fifty-four hours . . . Happily not a life had been lost, and I had thoroughly enjoyed the whole business, particularly the discovery of the power of a jet: directing it, I had demolished a twelve-foot high burning wall.

Thompson next applied his powerful mind to the Higher Standard Pushtu examination, obligatory for Politicals on the Frontier.

> For an hour before dawn each day a succession of young policemen were sent in to talk to me. I got them to tell me their folklore whilst I in return told them as many as I could remember of the adventures of the Wise Men of Gotham. These were a huge success and the simple, charming Yusufzais would break into laughter and shouts of 'Sha-

> bash!' I think I got closer to their philosophy of life by being able to match them with our ancestors in the reign of King John.

He spent as many as ten hours a day in court, with judgments to write up at home after helping his wife feed the twins. But there were breaks in the routine. When he was fairly proficient in Pushtu a police superintendent, Twinberrow, telephoned to ask, 'Are you on to come down to the city at midnight and disguise yourself as a Pathan? I'll tell you why when you arrive.'

> Of course I was on. For disguise all we had to do was pull on a pair of immensely baggy Pathan trousers, let down our shirt-tails and put on our heads ready-wound pagris . . . The plot was to capture the biggest drug-smuggler in the city, nicknamed Al Capone. An informer had undertaken to betray him if I came in person.

They waited for hours outside Al Capone's house, expecting a basket of hashish to be let down from a window for a carrier to pick up, which would be enough evidence for the prosecution. But nothing happened, so they returned to the Police Station where the sentry smartly presented arms. 'So much for our disguise!'

It transpired that the informer had shown Capone, through a slit in the shutters, the minions of the law squatting in the street outside, and threatened to reveal all unless his silence was bought. A few weeks later his body was found with a knife in the back.

Most of Thompson's cases were tedious. ('Imagine the waste of time when I had to wade through a whole year's accounts fictitiously created by Hindu merchants in alcohol who wished to establish a case of bribery against the only honest Excise Inspector'), but occasionally there was something more interesting, as of a man who had been taken to Moscow where he had graduated in a special university.

> He was charged with 'Waging war against the King-Emperor', for which I could sentence him to seven years . . . A leading member of the Peshawur Bar, Sardar Aurungzeb Khan, got him to plead guilty and, with help from me, extracted from him all he knew about that school for spies. I had then to decide on his sentence. The Sardar made a clever plea: 'As we are no longer at war with Russia, why should the court continue to wage war against my client?' Reflecting that I had before me not a big fish but a tadpole, I sentenced him to imprisonment until the rising of the court.

The next case was a different matter, a real traitor. 'I sentenced him to seven years. There was no appeal: the Russians did not waste their money on a spent spy.'

Much to his surprise Thompson was appointed District Judge, with unlimited jurisdiction in civil suits, about which he knew nothing.

> When the members of the Bar came to congratulate me, I made no bones about my ignorance. Aurungzeb Khan said, 'There are only two ways of learning civil law, at the Bar or on the Bench.' The President of the Bar assured me, 'We will not let you down while you are learning the job. After that, you must look after yourself.'
>
> I was lucky enough to have an early success. Two rich brothers, forest contractors, had fallen out. One of them bought a timber concession from the Wali of Swat. His brother then married his son to the Wali's daughter and persuaded the Wali to revoke that concession and transfer it to him. For years the logs floated down the Swat river and were held up at Nowshera by a court injunction, forming an enormous log-jam. I felt compelled to accept the argument that the transfer from one brother to another was a sovereign act of a ruler of an independent state, which could not be challenged in a court in British India . . . Of course it was unfair, but I often had to remind myself that my court was one of law, not necessarily of justice.

The relief from criminal cases was only temporary. Soon he was Sessions Judge, eternally trying cases of murder arising from blood-feuds. There was seldom any doubt about the verdict, but the judge had the discretion of awarding the death sentence, or one of 'transportation for life', which with remission for good conduct would mean about nine and a half years. 'I refused to follow a practice which had grown up of imposing only transportation. I argued that such a murder was deliberate and deserved the death sentence. Besides, if the death sentence were inflicted, the majesty of the law was capable of extinguishing the feud as a whole.' He had unusual evidence that hanging did deter. His court clerk happened to ask an acquaintance how his blood-feud was progressing. The man replied, 'I am waiting until this Sessions Judge goes on leave.'

Sentencing a man to be hanged for doing something which he thought to be his plain duty under the Pukhtunwali code was an awful responsibility for a 31-year-old Sessions Judge. Thompson tried 374 cases of murder and imposed 191 death sentences. Most Politicals would not have agreed with him.

There were lighter moments, such as the case of a British sergeant who played bold with the sergeant-major's wife. Believing herself to be pregnant, she claimed that he had raped her, and produced as evidence the brassière which, she said, had been torn from her shrinking person. The police investigation was carried out by an unmarried Assistant Superintendent. The case was heard by another young bachelor, who found the sergeant guilty. The appeal came to Thompson, who instantly allowed it. The barristers for the prosecution and the defence came to His Honour's chambers, much amused, to learn how he had been so certain. He replied, 'I spend all my time listening to lies told by your fellow-countrymen, so I ought to be able to spot one told by mine.'

'But *how*, Your Honour?'

Thompson explained to them. The lady, being of an economical turn of mind, had not liked to spoil the robust garment which she alleged had been ripped off her: she had carefully unpicked the shoulder-straps.

K.P.S. Menon was a Hindu, a Madrassi, a rare bird in the Political. His first posting was also to Peshawur, as Assistant Commissioner. If Thompson had been overworked, Menon enjoyed the softest billet he had ever known: there was so little to do that he and his colleagues during the cold weather used to hunt two mornings a week with the Peshawur Vale Hounds. A gregarious character, he enjoyed the gay social life of Peshawur – except in one respect: Indians were not allowed to become full members of Peshawur Club. Associate members, yes, able to use the club as they wished; but not full members with a vote in its running. Of course they rejected this insulting half-loaf. By 1930 Peshawur was about the only club which kept Indians out, other than a couple in Bombay and Calcutta, strongholds of 'boxwallahs' (European business men), who were two generations behind soldiers and civil servants in these matters. The reason for the Peshawur Club's obduracy was that by its constitution all past members had a vote on changing the rules. Scores of these, retired and living in England, did not see that India had changed since Kipling's day, and did not suffer the embarrassment of meeting every day friends and colleagues who were barred from one's club. However, there arrived in Peshawur a cavalry regiment which had Indian officers holding the King's commission. Its (British) Colonel informed the committee that unless all his officers could join the club as full members, none would: furthermore, he could not see his way to allowing his cavalry horses to be hired out for hunting. The rule was soon changed.

In Quetta there had been club trouble of another kind. There, Indian officers did join the club, but their wives never used it. May Trench, with the best intentions, persuaded three of the wives to accompany her there one quiet evening – whereupon Sharbat Khan upbraided these desperately shy ladies as whores flaunting themselves in a place reserved for men. Difficulties in this sensitive area were not all made by the British.

Another Political not over-burdened with work in Peshawur was George Kirkbride, who found time to whip in for the Peshawur Vale Hunt two mornings a week and to exercise hounds on non-hunting days. The country was not easy, intersected by formidable irrigation channels, sometimes two or three parallel cuts, separated by narrow banks. It was 'over – over – over', and only a good horse could do it. It was no joke being dumped in a freezing canal in mid-winter.

In 1929 there arrived in Peshawur the Simon Commission, appointed to devise means of bringing India forward on the path of self-government. For other provinces they recommended autonomy, but in the North-West Frontier Province they decided, on bad advice, that Pathans were neither capable of democratic self-government nor interested in it. They could not have been more wrong. Pathans were very politically minded, and knew far more about practical democracy than any other group in the sub-continent. The Simon Commission's negative attitude presented the opposition in the North-West Frontier Province with a target they could not miss. The opposition consisted of an organisation called the Servants of God, or, more usually, from their uniform, Redshirts. Its leaders were two brothers, Khan Abdul Gaffar Khan, a huge, extrovert rabble-rouser, adept at obstruction and propaganda but with no constructive ability; and Dr Khan Sahib, formerly Medical Officer of the Guides, far more able and pragmatic, eminently reasonable in private talk but apt to be carried away when facing an audience. The Redshirts embraced the non-violent philosophy of Mahatma Gandhi and murdered those who did not subscribe to it. In 1929 this dangerous organisation contrived a revolutionary situation in Peshawur in which an armoured car was incinerated, a despatch-rider hacked to death and Afridi war-bands mined the roads and invaded the Government Supply Depot.

The Afridis were pushed back into their mountainous Tirah, and a blockade cut them off from all economic contact with the plains, to their great inconvenience. A new Chief Commissioner was appointed, Sir Ralph Griffith, whom the Viceroy described to the Secretary of State as 'one of the younger men, and I think will do the job well. Poor Steuart

5 A.P. Low (*leading*), Assistant Political Agent, with Khassadars in Waziristan
6 Assistant Political Agent, Mohamad Yusuf Khan (*right*), and escort in South Waziristan

7 The Holy Man, the Shami Pir, having been bought off by H.A. Barnes, pictured on his happy return to Damascus

Pears* was really too old and the strain was altogether too much for him . . . Abdul Gaffar Khan is most truculent and his Redshirt movement will have to be squashed.'

The centre of Redshirt activity was the small town of Charsadda where the two brothers held mass rallies and uniformed parades, burning opponents in effigy, organising No Tax campaigns. There, in October, 1930, Captain H.A. Barnes was posted as Assistant Commissioner. He was accompanied by a wife and small baby. They had neither ice nor electricity. Incredibly, there was no barbed wire around their house, nor any security lighting.

Two attempts were made on Barnes's life. He made a point of always accepting a petition. A tribesman handed him a paper with one hand, and with the other drew a revolver and fired three shots at point-blank range. All misfired, and Barnes brought him down with a rugby tackle. The fourth cartridge, tested by the police, went off. The second attempt was at night, and this time Mrs Barnes was present.

> I was just coping with the ten o'clock feed (Barney in bed and feigning sleep) when I heard a faint scuffle on the verandah. I put the baby in his cot and peered out through the wire-mesh window screen, but could see nothing. Then a rifle shot rang out. The would-be assassin had been crouching on the verandah, where the guard saw him and fired. He got away but was wounded, and the blood trail was followed next morning. From then on it was considered unsafe for me and my baby to stay in Charsadda, and we were whisked off by Olaf Caroe, the Deputy Commissioner, to Peshawur, hating to leave Barney to manage alone.

Barnes was transferred to Peshawur, and Dring, a bachelor, replaced him at Charsadda. Prudently, Dring travelled by a roundabout route, but the grapevine worked too fast and he arrived with two bullet-holes in the bonnet of his car. His instructions were to show that the Government was still in business.

> Court work proceeded normally, as did the collection of land revenue on a reduced scale. The people as a whole were not surly or unfriendly, though of course I had to have a guard on the house and an escort on tour. The Lambardars [village headmen] were patchy, but the majority tried to function normally.

*He had a black-out, fell down a cliff and was killed at Nathia Gali, the hill-station for the province. In his time he had been a brilliant Frontier Political.

Soon the situation was back to normal, but Dr Khan Sahib and his brother had made their point: in 1935 the province was given limited self-government, and in 1937 full self-government with responsibility for law and order. The elected Provincial Government, labelled 'Congress', was headed by Dr Khan Sahib who made an admirable Chief Minister. He got on capitally with Griffith's successor, Sir George Cunningham, who became Governor instead of Chief Commissioner for the province, but remained Agent to the Governor-General in his relations with the states and Tribal Territory which were no concern of the Chief Minister.

On the whole, British and Indian officials rubbed along pretty well together, subject to human frailties. One can see in retrospect that there was too little friendly intercourse between the British and educated Indian non-officials, but rows were very rare. When they did occur, as often as not an officer of a British regiment was to blame, treating all Indians as wogs. G.H. Emerson, acting as Deputy Commissioner in Peshawur during the absence of the incumbent, had to sort one out.

> I arrived at my office to find a file of press cuttings about an incident between a Professor of the Islamia College and a captain of the Highland Light Infantry. The Professor had been driving a car along the Mall, and passed the Captain riding a horse. The Captain had used some very unfortunate language, which the Professor had understood. The result was a civil case for damages against the officer and headlines in the Press. Well aware of the possible consequences, I rang up the military headquarters and asked whether I could try to mediate. They gave me a free hand to secure terms which they would compel the captain to accept. I invited the Professor to discuss the case with me. He was very upset and said his friends had been urging him to get his story told in the Press as prominently as possible. I explained that we had no desire to defend the captain's behaviour, but must ask him to postpone the court case and cool the temperature. He accused me of trying to shield another Englishman, but I pointed out that if he had been an English professor, he would have complained to the Commanding Officer, and not rushed to the court and the media . . . He eventually agreed to accept a written apology handed over in my office by the captain, in the presence of a high-ranking military officer and myself.

After this deplorable incident, it is agreeable to record an adventure of A.N. Mitchell who was Deputy Commissioner, Nowshera, about the same time. He was touring his district on horseback, inspecting land records and enjoying a little hawking on the side.

At the foot of the hills there was a shrine commemorating a local saint. As I approached the mullah in charge invited me to enter. I replied that, as a Christian, I would much like to do so and to pay proper respect, but I was wearing a very tight pair of polo-boots which would take forever and a day to remove and put on again without the necessary tools. He smiled gravely behind his white beard, produced a cloth and with it dusted the soles of my boots. We then entered the shrine and prayed for some minutes.

6

Waziristan

Most Politicals in the North-West Frontier Province hoped to graduate to Tribal Territory, especially military Politicals who were not, perhaps, as well grounded as the I.C.S. entry in the nitty-gritty of district administration and thought that in Waziristan they would be untroubled by red tape and departmental rules. Tribal Territory was the *real* Frontier, Malakand, Khyber, Kurram, Zhob, above all Waziristan. Even Herbert Thompson, whose heart was in south India but who had been a fighter pilot on the Western Front, felt the old Adam stirring and hinted to his boss in Peshawur that he would like a posting to Waziristan. 'You are here to *work*, my boy,' was the reply.

The implication was unjust. Political Agents in Waziristan worked very hard, but it was a different sort of work to that in a settled district. A robust, practical approach, a first-class knowledge of colloquial Pushtu and a ready wit were more important than a detailed knowledge of the Indian Penal Code and the revenue law – and every Political liked to think that he had these qualifications.

The Political Agent was 'the man who stood between the soldier and his medal'. It was his job to settle trouble of all kinds – inter-tribal fights, raiding into settled districts, highway robbery, kidnapping, murder and mayhem – before it blew up into a situation which required the intervention of a brigade of regular troops. The forces at his disposal were the Khassadars (see p.16 and the Scouts . . . His reaction to any disturbances would be on a carefully graduated scale: first the Khassadars, then the Scouts; only as a last resort, the Army. He was naturally reluctant to ask for the Army, which would imply that he had in some degree failed. Moreover, any Political Agent tended to sympathise with 'his' tribes. The Political Agent, probably a captain or major, or a civilian, always seemed to be telling the Brigadier that he could not do this, that or the other because of the bad effect it would have on some set of unmitigated scoundrels the Brigadier had never heard of; and in normal times the Political Agent, representing the civil power, prevailed. Only if the Frontier blew up into a serious war did the military take over, when the Political was restricted to advise, and deplore.

This annoyed the Army. Simple soldiers said they really did not know

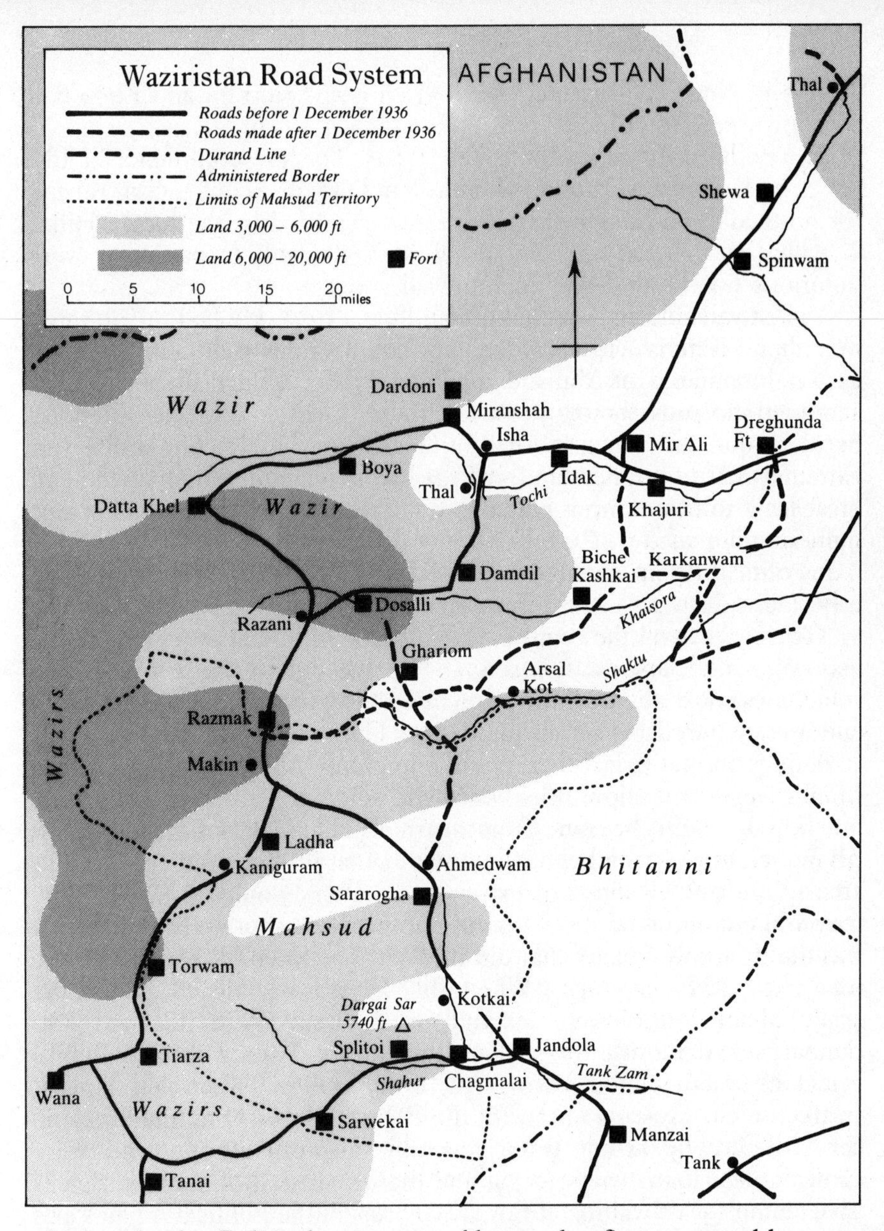

which side the Politicals were on. Almost the first story told to any subaltern on his arrival on the Frontier was of the Political who interrupted a military discussion on Mahsud casualties, 'You know, you're all wrong. We haven't lost nearly as many as you think.' Being so often at variance with the soldiers, it was just as well that the Political

Agents in North Waziristan, South Waziristan, Kurram and Zhob had their own private armies.

The Political Agent's job was dangerous. To show confidence in 'his' tribes he had to travel round without a military or Scout escort, relying for protection on Khassadars or gunmen provided by the local Maliks. Usually this was enough, but not always: Mahsuds in particular were notorious for flouting the Pukhtunwali code.

A most valuable art was that of handling a Jirga. He had no authority over them: if he issued an order, they could simply walk out. Sitting at ease before scores of Mahsuds or Wazirs (one did not address a Jirga standing) he must try to persuade them, often in the face of noisy heckling and salty repartee in the local dialect of Pushtu which was extremely hard to understand. A Jirga had to be argued into agreement, or at least into striking a bargain. Whether they would honour it was quite another matter.

A Political Agent spent a great deal of time talking and listening to tribesmen. It was a most important part of his job. He was the Government's, and the Army's, chief source of intelligence, depending mainly on his personal contacts and knowledge of the tribes – who sometimes spoke the truth and who never did, whether Sikandar Khan's tale was coloured by his dislike of Baz Gul, and so on.

Besides formal Jirgas there were numerous 'Allowance Jirgas' when Maliks were paid allowances which the soldiers likened to Danegeld, but which could be cut if not earned. The Mahsuds had thirty Allowance Jirgas, each held twice a year, generally light and even jocular affairs at which all kinds of extraneous matters would be aired. 'Why have you cut our allowances because of that lorry shot up last month? It was the dastardly Wazirs that did it.' 'Why has Sher Ali been given the road contract? It's my turn.' 'When will Mahsuds be enlisted again in the army?' There were even demands to be issued with the 1919–20 campaign medal for fighting against the British. Twenty or thirty Maliks would be waiting after each Jirga, every one of whom felt himself entitled to a long, cosy chat with the Political Agent. Such petitioners, liable to turn up at any time, generally the most inopportune, were known as malaqatis (mole-cats), and diaries are full of such entries as 'sixteen mole-cats waiting at Boya'. Not least of the Political Agent's arts was to get rid of them reasonably quickly without hurt feelings, but Mahsud and Wazir eloquence knew no fatigue and no time-factor, and was allied to an amazing ingenuity in argument. In the words of Olaf Caroe, only someone who has spent a long day with a Mahsud visitor 'will understand the exhaustion which comes from listening to his importunings, the effort required to meet his plausibility, even the struggle to match his wit'.

The only prediction one could safely make about a Mahsud was that his conduct would be completely unpredictable. G.H. Emerson, posted to Sararogha as Assistant Political Agent, South Waziristan, in the 1930s, had three Mahsud orderlies. For his first couple of months they drove him almost up the wall with their sheer bloody-mindedness.

> The day came when I could stand it no longer, and asked them to come to my room. I said that I had been used to my orderlies behaving as colleagues and friends, but here I had been given more trouble by them than by all the rest of the Mahsuds put together, and it did not amuse me. They laughed, and promised that I would have no reason in future to be angry with them, and they were as good as their word. In fact a few weeks later I was taken to task by them. The roads were not very safe, being subject to occasional attacks by bandits or malcontents. I was going between two forts accompanied by some Maliks with whom I wanted to discuss various matters. So I asked them to sit with me in the middle of the van, the orderlies being relegated to the back. On arrival at my destination, I was having tea when all three of my orderlies appeared. I had, they said, publicly disgraced them. 'How so?' I asked. Well, hadn't I removed them, my personal bodyguard, from the place of danger next to me, and invited *Maliks* to sit there? Considering that any bullet meant for me would almost certainly hit them, I thought this very moving and apologised.
>
> Some months later I was on my way back to Sararogha from the South Waziristan Scouts' headquarters at Jandola when I met a group of Maliks on the road. They obviously wanted to talk to me urgently, so I stopped and we exchanged the customary greetings. This done, they remarked casually that it was not a good day to travel.
>
> 'Why not?' I asked 'It's a lovely autumn day.'
>
> 'Yes, the weather is beautiful, but it is not a good day for a road journey.'
>
> Slowly the penny dropped. This was a plain warning that I ought not to go further, probably because there were outlaws in the area.

Reflecting that he would rather be a coward than a corpse, Emerson thanked them and drove back to the Scouts' headquarters at Jandola. He was slightly apprehensive that they might think he had not behaved with that intrepidity which became an officer of the Indian Political Service, but David Williams, the Commandant, said, 'Very sensible. No useful purpose is served by getting killed through obstinacy.'

To all generalisations about Tribal Territory, the Kurram valley was an exception. Elsewhere it was recognised that the tribesmen did not exactly welcome our presence: in the Kurram they did, indeed they had begged the British to come and govern them. The reason was that the local tribe, the Turi, were of the Shiah sect, entirely surrounded by Sunnis, and there is no enmity so bitter as that between Shiah and Sunni. Although they looked to the Sarkar* for protection against their enemies, no tribe was more capable of protecting themselves. They were true Pathans, Pushtu-speaking, governed by the Pukhtunwali code, but the 'trusties' of the Sarkar – analagous to the Campbells in seventeenth-century Scotland. The Kurram Militia, 1,200 strong, infantry, mounted infantry and two mountain guns, was mainly Turi.

In 1919, when Waziristan was evacuated and the Khyber Rifles, the Waziristan Militias and the Zhob Militia deserted in droves, the Kurram Militia drove back the invading Afghan regulars and then proceeded to invade Afghanistan. The security problem was therefore a simple one: preventing outsiders making trouble. So stout-hearted were the Turi villagers in their own defence that B.J. Gould, when Political Agent, Kurram, persuaded the Government to replace their ageing Martini rifles with new Lee Enfields. They were then able to see off all raiders.

Law and order – roads – low tax assessment. The Kurram valley had all three, including a land settlement giving the cultivators low rent, security of tenure and compensation for improvements. There was money for a school and medical services, and with the essentials thus secured the pump of economic progress could be primed. Edward Noel, Political Agent in the mid-1920s, was the man to prime it.

He was a great experimenter and, in particular, an expert on 'karezes'. The karez is a system native to Persia and Baluchistan of providing permanent running water in an arid country. There are families who for generations have studied and practised the art of making karezes. With an eye for the country and much experience, a place is chosen near the head of a valley where the run-off from the hillsides collects far underground. A shaft is sunk, just wide enough for a man to climb up and down, until water is reached in good quantities. Then – purely by eye, with no survey instruments – a tunnel is dug along the line which the underground water will naturally follow, with shafts sunk at intervals for ventilation and removal of the soil. Eventually the tunnel is near enough to the surface to be opened into a deep ditch; and at last the

*Government.

water reaches the surface, a regular, clean flow, which can be used for irrigation, for watering livestock or for any other purpose. Noel constructed the first karez in the Kurram valley and, having consulted various experts who said it could not be done, used it to power an electricity supply for Parachinar, the only town there.

In the 1920s there was a shortage of a drug used in the treatment of round-worms, because this was produced from a variety of artemesia believed to be grown only in South Russia, and the Bolsheviks had put an end to its export. Noel, who had served in South Russia, thought that the little dry shrub on which Turi sheep fattened might be this variety, and again he was proved right. Thereafter the export of artemesia to a pharmaceutical firm in Glasgow produced more profit for the Turi than the entire Kurram land revenue. They also did well out of pyrethrum, which Noel introduced.

With karez irrigation, improved strains of wheat and barley flourished; and around Parachinar every kind of temperate zone and semi-tropical fruit and vegetable – asparagus, strawberries, grapes, apricots – all seemed to grow bigger and better than anywhere else. The Turi tribesmen were the most prosperous as well as the most reliable on the Frontier.

In March, 1933, Barnes, sated with the fleshpots of Peshawur, was posted to Miranshah as Political Agent, North Waziristan. With an army rank of major, he was far junior to the brass-hats of the regular Army. Yet he, as the civil power, was the 'Grand Panjandrum for whom flags are flown and guards turned out'. There had recently been trouble, due to the Mahsuds and Wazirs invading Afghanistan to topple the Amir Nadir Shah. The Indian Government exerted itself to prevent this. To Barnes, who wrote to his wife on his arrival in Miranshah, it seemed the Army had shown up in its worst colours:

> sabre-rattling and trailing coats . . . within an ace of bringing about a first-class dogfight. The situation has cleared up miraculously thanks to George's* words of warning, which sent the lashkars† home with their tails between their legs. The only remaining trouble is to collect the fines and come to an agreement over compensation with the Afghans, who will submit colossal claims for damages which never occurred. This aftermath will fall to my happy lot.

*George Cunningham, Resident, Waziristan.

† Tribal armies.

But he enormously enjoyed himself in North Waziristan, where he had many old tribal friends from his service in the Tochi Scouts seven years earlier.

> We passed some Wazir encampments made of hair, utterly primitive, leading the life of 500 years ago. Some Maliks brought a sheep which I touched and 'passed on'. The result was the whipping out of a large knife and the sudden demise of the poor brute, after which we had to stay long enough to be regaled with grilled mutton. So we rode on under the sun with clean air and new scenery at every turn. Perdition take all office jobs and let me live like this!
>
> Dozens and dozens of my old pals have pushed in from all over the Agency to shake hands and smile reassuringly. Many of them joined in the last war and sheepishly acknowledge the fact. Day after day Maliks rolled in, some of them very old friends, who refused to be put off with a few minutes and demanded full details of all that has happened since we parted seven years ago. It makes the poor old mouth water to pay out Rs 500 a day to these woolly whiskered bandits . . . I have had friendly gossip with a couple of dozen first-class murderers, each with proudly recorded notches on his rifle. They are all positive that there are no signs of trouble and that even the fines we are now collecting will not lead to any serious ill-feeling . . . Oh Lord, this is a gorgeous life! Here is freedom and scope and interests that are little short of overwhelming. One lives the whole day and every day, and only lacks for having one pair of hands and one personality.

He paid a special visit to the Faqir of Ipi:

> the Archbishop of all the Mullahs, a gentleman of immense influence and a most insanitary appearance. On behalf of George I transferred Rs 500 to the old villain, and received in return a splendid assortment of vermin. Thence we rode across the Kurram river and inspected a water-channel Ambrose Dundas started in 1928 for a turbulent chieftain in the hope that it would help to domesticate him. He was almost boisterous when I presented him with Rs 1,000 for keeping his cut-throats in check.

Next day there was a Jirga to announce a fine of 250 rifles on a section which had joined in the Afghan rebellion. 'They were most indignant and produced a babel of sound, but it is quite easy to sit back and wait for the wave-lengths to get weaker, reannounce the terms firmly but politely and make a dignified departure.' After the Jirga no fewer than sixty-three 'mole-cats' were waiting with 126 petitions and complaints.

There was trouble with the military, in part a legacy of his predecessor K.C. Packman's 'dreadful vendettas with them', culminating in 'Packie', somewhat in liquor, sniping with his catapult at the General's house. The Military Engineering Service, responsible for the construction and upkeep of roads and army camps, liked to allocate contracts to entrepreneurs from British India. This Barnes vigorously opposed, for if fines were the stick with which he threatened the tribes, contracts were the carrots with which he rewarded them.

> The General and the C.R.E. [Commanding Royal Engineers] have been most truculent of late and have refused to accept our nominations. So we all gathered in conference, a galaxy of be-ribboned brass-hats, and poor little Barney. (The General is a pet and I love him.) The brass-hats started shouting me down, and he butted in and told me to deliver my speech. It lasted two and three-quarter hours (the conference, not my speech) and WE WON. It had never occurred to them to think of the tribesmen as monarchs of their own country and as people worth training in peaceful pursuits. But there is no answer to the argument that the Wazir can be trained up to the efficiency of the Pathan in British India, that the man on the spot can work at cheaper rates than the imported article, and that contented tribesmen are more economical than disgruntled gentlemen requiring endless punitive expeditions. 'Blast you, Barney,' says the General afterwards, 'for your ingenious arguments.'

But what really turned the scale was that Barnes had fought in two previous Waziristan campaigns, and the brass-hats had not.

The brass-hats' conference was hardly less of an ordeal than a spate of Jirgas, lasting all day for six consecutive days.

> What a grim prospect! A tribe will have been nursing its grievance for twelve months, subjecting it to hours of thought and ingenious preparation, and then shooting it off to the unfortunate Political Agent who has to produce some kind of answer impromptu in a few minutes. This goes on all day, and when the answers may mean a happy or a fractious tribe, justice or rank injustice, it is no laughing matter.
>
> Yesterday I did Jirgas from 9.30 to 6.15 – blarney, wheedle, threaten, joke and above all infinite patience. I had 113 Malaqatis, distributed nearly Rs 10,000 in allowances, and emerged whacked to a standstill. After each Malik has pocketed his pay, the petitions start,

hundreds of them. Eventually the tumult and the shouting come under some sort of control and we part good friends. There is a sort of second sight which a Political Officer develops for spotting the dud petition and flinging it out with scorn. This generally provokes a grin from all round the assembly. It is grand fun, and a lovely job.

In June, 1933, 'Bunch' Parsons took over as Resident, Waziristan, and Barnes's immediate boss. He was every Frontier officer's ideal of what a Frontier officer should be. He spoke near-perfect Pushtu in several dialects. Having served on the Frontier as Army officer, Scouts officer and Political Agent for twenty years, he knew his stuff. He was informal in dress and manner, having a distaste for pomp and circumstance which was not shared by all his colleagues. Should a red carpet be laid down for his august feet, he would walk in the dust alongside it. If a junior officer addressed him as 'Sir', he would reply, 'Kindly omit the honorifics.' Barnes enjoyed every moment of his first official visit.

In the few days he has had in the job he has laid his finger on all the inherent weaknesses – after that, no fuss but pages of notes and queries, simple to understand and to answer. A wish is not expressed as an overbearing command but as an obvious suggestion to be acted upon. What wouldn't one do for him? One sees so many examples of towering intellect and academic qualifications possessed by flabby-nerved creatures who cannot utilize it.

Obviously Parsons had an equally high opinion of Barnes, offering him the job of Political Agent, South Waziristan. 'Would I be willing to come? Do ducks swim? Do cats lap up cream? And does poor Barney turn down the best offer ever made him?'

It was a more exacting post than that of North Waziristan because it was concerned largely with Mahsuds, by common consent the most hostile, the most rapacious and the most faithless of all tribes. The Political Agent lived on a knife-edge. Any argument could end in shooting. Barnes's headquarters were in Tank, just within the administered border, so his wife could be with him during the cold weather. Long journeys, on foot and on horseback, were made by Barnes, with only Mahsuds as escort.

We left at 8.15 and did not reach Ladha until 6.45 p.m. It was strenuous physically but balm and healing to the mind. Every now and then we would come upon an encampment of Mahsuds grazing their flocks miles from anywhere. These fierce shepherds gave us a welcome that was most touching, and I wasted many spells of 5-10 minutes over a chat and a sip of ice-cold sour milk, all they had, but offered so royally. I and a tiny escort were handed on from one place to the next by friend and foe who sank all their differences for the occasion.

But in Mahsud country one could never close one's eyes to unpleasant possibilities.

I have decided that if there is to be any funny business [i.e. any shooting] the Maliks will share it, and propose to have the fattest and most influential trotting around me as conspicuously as possible. This is a new line, and judging by the cold reception it was accorded, there should be value in it.

Barnes was in his element in South Waziristan, and his wife – artistic, with a Royal College of Music degree in singing, moving before marriage in Quaker and Theosophist circles – made the best of Tank. The bungalow was fitted with long baths, the last word in sophistication; but the thunder-boxes remained. They acquired turkeys, hens, ducks, and a cow and calf. The children graduated from tricycles to bicycles and then ponies, accompanied on all their outings by an armed orderly who sometimes came in useful as a snake-killer. With irrigation and advice from Parsons, they made a cold-weather garden with roses, many herbaceous plants, magnolias, hibiscus, morning glory and scarlet-flowered bottlebrush trees. They had two tennis courts, but could make up a four only by roping in the nanny and the Pathan orderly, neither of whom had handled a racket before.

In Tank were the ladies of the Zenana Medical Mission: Dr 'Maidie' Sherburn; the matron, Vera Studd; and the Administrator, Ethel Hadow. Every year they treated hundreds of tribal women in childbirth, for eye-diseases and every kind of ailment. Dr Sherburn was a pioneer of plastic surgery, replacing many a nose sliced off erring wives by cuckolded husbands. They travelled freely in Tribal Territory, where no one would dream of molesting them.

They were wonderful women; but their very dedication made them occasionally an unmitigated menace, and when they converted to Christianity a Mahsud girl Barnes was furious. (His wife rather sympathised with them.) Proselytising was a breach of the terms under which they had been allowed to open their Mission. This might start a rebellion which would spread from end to end of the Frontier and shake even the loyalty of the Scouts. The Mahsud Maliks kicked up hell, and Barnes had to sort it out.

I rushed out to Ladha early this morning and have again spent the day there fighting to get this ugly show straightened out. The lashkar started dispersing, and there is a much cleaner atmosphere all round. The 'Mishes' will be back in Tank on the 10th, after which we can really get down to business. I will cut out the courtier and get down to clear-cut issues. I have it from Griffie* that they can be told to line up or clear out, and after all this heart-breaking trouble I am not going to have any song-and-dance from Sherburn. These last few days have been perfectly sanguinary. Things are better today, everyone seems to be sitting about waiting to see what will happen. What I worry about is the possibility of some fanatical outrage. You know my general view on missionaries: my present ones are quite unprintable. This show is going to be squashed, once for all.

When the missionaries returned to Tank he faced the dreaded task of tackling them on a straight conflict between their Christian zeal and his duty to keep the peace.

I found them dripping with sweat and looking so tired and out of place. Dreadful to think of what old Miss Hadow must go through, and Dr Sherburn was pale and thin as a rake. We got down to the old subject and it was just too unpleasant for me to dwell on now. I don't like that form of hysteria and don't know how to handle it. Anyhow there could be no dodging the issue and I told them as humanely as possible that there could be no alternatives and soft-soap this time, and left them as soon as it was obvious they understood. The girl was handed over next morning, and I then had three hours with the Jirga arranging her future.

The military presence was oppressive. Barnes was constantly out with brigade columns, showing the flag, preventing any outbreak, just warning the Mahsuds and Wazirs not to start anything. In a way he enjoyed this reversion to his youth and the atmosphere of the brigade column winding its way along the valley with the heights piqueted on either hand; but whereas the soldiers hoped there would be shooting, he hoped that there wouldn't, and worked hard to that end.

Fortunately he had the best possible Assistant Political Agent, R.H.D. ('Lotus') Lowis, one of the few who came into the Political from the Frontier Constabulary, a real Frontier expert, fluent in the Mahsud and Wazir dialects of Pushtu. Lowis, for his part, greatly admired Barnes:

*Sir Ralph Griffith, Chief Commissioner and Agent to the Governor-General.

'You know how convincing Barney is in English. Well, in Pushtu he is better still. He puts the most difficult things across in such a way that the Jirga can do nothing but agree. I'm inclined to get angry, which gets one nowhere.'

In 1935 there was trouble among the tribes north of Peshawur, necessitating two expeditions with a full division of troops. Among those killed was the Political Agent, Major A.N. Best, apparently trying to contact friends among the enemy to make peace. It was, wrote Lord Willingdon to the Secretary of State, 'a tragedy entirely due to his own impetuosity. A Political Agent should remain at headquarters and not career about with his levies in any part of the fighting area he pleases.' It could not be long, thought Barnes and Lowis, before Waziristan blew up. It wasn't.

A few months earlier there had occurred an event in North Waziristan which showed how wise Barnes had been to take so seriously the case of the Mahsud girl, even at the cost of the poor 'Mishes' hurt feelings. A Moslem student in Bannu eloped to Tribal Territory with a more or less willing Hindu girl, had her converted to Islam and renamed Islam Bibi, and married her. The girl's parents took the case to court – not to the Jirga because they were Hindus, but to a British Indian court. The case now took on a communal aspect with furious Moslem mobs demonstrating outside the Deputy Commissioner's house. He was an officer of the Political, Lieutenant-Colonel Evelyn Cobb, so renowned for his loquacity that the expression 'Cobbologue' passed into Frontier parlance. There are various ways of dealing with a mob – policemen with staves, reading the Riot Act and authorising troops to fire, and less draconic measures. (Lieutenant-Colonel Iskandar Mirza, when D.C., Peshawur, dispersed a mob by entertaining the leaders to refreshments, having laced the tea with a quick-acting laxative.) Evelyn Cobb's reaction to a mob was to climb on a chair and talk to it. And talk. And talk. First by ones and twos, then by dozens, the mob melted away until he found himself addressing only his orderly and a handful of policemen.

That, however, solved no more than the immediate problem. A very holy man, the Faqir of Ipi, raised the cry that Islam was in danger and every Moslem must rally to the Holy War. The magistrate in Bannu heard the case and ordered that until she came of age the girl must live with a respectable Moslem family in Bannu. Agitation then quietened down – until the Judicial Commissioner in Peshawur reversed the magistrate's judgment and ordered her to be returned to her Hindu parents. Later the Court of Appeal was to send her back, like a shuttlecock, to the respectable Moslem family, but in the meanwhile the Faqir's tribe, the Tori Khel Wazirs (Barnes's friends in 1933), rose in furious rebellion. Ironically, they were the 'fat cats' of Waziristan – none had benefited more from contracts, allowances, irrigation schemes and all the goodies of British rule. But they spent most of their money on rifles.

To teach them a lesson, it was decided in November, 1936, that two brigades would advance into their country and link up at Biche Kashkai in the middle of it, but in the event the operation was less than a brilliant success. One brigade had some stiff fighting but just managed to reach Biche Kashkai before dark. The other had even stiffer fighting and suffered heavy casualties, including many officers. By dusk they were still five miles short, but the brigadier unwisely decided to push on in the dark. They were ambushed, many of their horses (including the brigadier's) stampeded and were lost, and they eventually had to stop because they could go no further. At one time the Assistant Political Agent for North Waziristan, Captain Roy Beatty, who thought it his duty to move at the head of the column with the vanguard of Tochi Scouts, was crawling round a bush, revolver in hand, in pitch darkness, stalking the Scouts commander who was crawling round it, stalking him.

This was more than a minor operation: this was war. The General Officer commanding Northern Command took control of all military operations, and also, as was usual in such circumstances, political control of Waziristan, the Resident and Political Agents taking a back seat. A third brigade, with light tanks and additional artillery, was brought in, some Tori Khel villages were burnt, and by the end of 1936 the Tori Khel, disgusted at the paucity of support from other tribes, were ready to sue for peace and expel the Faqir of Ipi from their country.

But on February 6th, Captain Keogh, South Waziristan Scouts, was shot dead on the road near Ladha, and on the following day Roy Beatty was likewise murdered. The Faqir was in business again, and war flared up anew and a fourth brigade was brought in.

The murder of Roy Beatty provides a text-book example of the control of the tribe by 'political' methods, by the adroit use of the Frontier Crimes Regulations, with the minimum use of force.

The murderer was a Madda Khel Wazir named Zawel, who had been flogged by the Afghan authorities for robbery, taunted with robbing only Moslems and challenged to test his courage on a British Officer. Smarting under this treatment, he collected seven other Madda Khel desperadoes and laid an ambush for Beatty who was taking round the Khassadars' pay. Where a sharp bend in the road near Boya brought the car almost to a halt, a volley killed Beatty and two of his escort, wounding another Khassadar and the clerk. By the time the escort-lorry of Khassadars arrived, the gang had got away with Rs 32,000, three rifles and a revolver.

As soon as the news reached Miranshah the Political Agent, Captain G.C.L. ('Jogi') Crighton, arranged for the Scouts to pull in ninety eminent Madda Khel and told the Jirga to hand over the murderers – or else. Hearing where the gang were holed up, he got the R.A.F. to bomb that village (after the usual week's warning so that nobody was hurt and only property destroyed). He had a card up his sleeve. Three years earlier a hundred Madda Khel rifles had been taken as surety for a year's good conduct. The subsequent conduct of the Madda Khel had not been such as to justify the return of the rifles, so they were available as part of any bargain which might be struck.

No one imagined that the hostages would come to any harm, but their incarceration caused inconvenience to their families, who brought pressure on the Jirga to settle the case. So three minor members of the gang were brought to trial and acquitted after they had taken a hundred oaths of innocence. They said that Zawel and the other four were safe in Afghanistan, which was probably true. Forty of the hostages were then released, but fifty more rifles taken as surety for a final settlement. This, as a result of much bargaining, comprised a fine on the Madda Khel of Rs 25,000 as well as the return of the money which had been stolen, plus fifty more rifles. Most of the money was found by wealthy Madda Khel timber contractors; the hundred rifles taken in 1934 were accepted in lieu of the balance, and the incident was regarded as closed. But Zawel was in disrepute with the Madda Khel who had through his escapade lost 200 rifles and a lot of money: thereafter he kept a low profile.

It was an odd way to run a turbulent frontier, but it worked, more or less.

Meanwhile the Mahsuds, who blamed the Tori Khel for letting them down in the 1919–20 war, withdrew the skirts of their garments from these unseemly disturbances. A few hard men went north to have a crack at the British, but the bulk of the tribe stayed neutral. It was Barnes's task to keep them so. To this end he held a Jirga of the Dré Mahsud,* the entire tribe, under the walls of Sararogha Fort. He opened proceedings by telling them what they would have to pay as a fine for the murder of Captain Keogh within their tribal limits. This was ill-

*The Three Mahsuds, their own name for the tribe which is divided into three sections.

received, with much interruption. He went on to harangue them on the need to hand over the bad men known to be among them. There was a tumult of barracking – 'That's your job, not ours!' 'You're the Political Agent, aren't you? That's what you are paid for!' A back-row citizen with a voice like a bull bellowed, 'You're the Political Agent: haven't you got any balls?' It was a freezing morning. Barnes thrust both hands into his trouser pockets, groped around and shouted back, 'Well, I thought I had. But it's so bloody cold that now I can't find them!' There was a tremendous outburst of laughter, and the Jirga dispersed in high good humour, promising to do anything he wanted of them.

It was too good to last. On April 9th a routine convoy of forty-nine lorries and two private cars set off from Manzai to Wana. They had to pass through the Shahur Tangi, a defile three miles long, the road winding through between caves and culverts which gave perfect cover to riflemen. Lowis (in charge of the Agency while Barnes was on leave) had heard of a hostile named Konia Khel in the vicinity and of tribesmen apparently carrying out some sort of tactical exercise there. He and the new South Waziristan Scouts Commandant, Major P.R.H. Skrine, advised the Military against running the convoy that day. Their advice was ignored: the soldiers were confident that a convoy composed entirely of motor vehicles (no vulnerable mules and camels), escorted by armoured cars and two platoons of infantry with light machine-guns, would be in no danger.

At a quarter to eight in the morning, when the convoy was well inside the defile, lorries crawling up the steepest part, intense fire was opened on its entire length. Nearly all the officers, sitting in front of the lorries or in the private cars, were killed in the first two minutes. The infantry escort was slaughtered in the lorries. Vehicles slewed across the road, their dead drivers slumped at the wheel, forming impassable blocks. The armoured cars, immobilised between stranded lorries, could neither elevate nor depress their machine-guns enough to shoot at the enemy, who had chosen their positions with this in mind. All they could do was prevent the tribesmen rushing the lorries – except at one point, where they got in with the knife, killing and mutilating the wounded. A Medical Officer, Captain Durrani, a Pathan, heroically walked towards the tribesmen, holding up a Koran and calling on them to let him bring the wounded under cover. He was promptly shot dead.

On garbled reports of disaster, troops and Scouts hurried to the rescue. But the first to arrive was Lowis with a busload of Maliks and Khassadars from Wana. At Splitoi, the top or western end of Tangi, they found that the leading armoured car had extricated itself and three lorries. There was an old fort, abandoned by the Scouts some years earlier and intermittently used by Khassadars, but locked and empty that day. Lowis managed to climb in and found the telephone miraculously working, so was able to communicate with Chagmalai Post at the bottom end of the Tangi, where Skrine and three platoons of Scouts from Jandola soon arrived. Lowis put his Khassadars into two hills forward of Splitoi, where they were relieved about mid-day by Scouts from Sarwekai. Throughout it was a soldiers' battle, with regulars, Scouts, Politicals, Maliks and Khassadars arriving piecemeal and doing the best they could with little overall control.

More Maliks arrived and tried to remove their fellow-tribesmen by sweet reason. One, Koran in hand, was shot dead, and the remainder prudently withdrew, leaving their bus just where it contributed most to the blockage and confusion. More Scouts came from Wana, piqueted some hills further along the Tangi, and gave covering fire while tow-chains were fixed to two lorries, volunteer drivers installed to steer them, and the vehicles with infinite difficulty extricated. The third lorry was hit by a bullet in the petrol tank, burst into flames and made it impossible to do anything more to unravel the knot.

At this point, according to the *Official History of Operations on the North-West Frontier of India*, Lowis led his Khassadars straight down the middle of the road into the Tangi. Alas for heroics! In his own copy of the *Official History*, in his own handwriting, there is written in the margin, 'No I didn't.' It would have been very foolish to do so. There was some chance, now that a long day was drawing to a close, that Mahsuds would not fire on Khassadars of their own tribe; but if these were seen to be led by a Faranghi, they were certain to shoot him. So Lowis, after discussing the matter with them, sent in the Khassadars marching in columns of fours straight down the middle of the road. Not a shot was fired on them, and they occupied the caves, sangars and culverts from which the tribesmen had been firing. It was the Mahsud Khassadars' finest hour, and a great tribute to Lowis's personality and powers of persuasion. A few more lorries and wounded were then extracted, but most of the convoy had to stay in the Tangi all night, the survivors grouped round the armoured cars beating off repeated knife-rushes. By morning all was quiet, the enemy had disappeared and the casualties could be counted – over ninety, including seven officers. For the army it was a shocking disaster, but the Politicals and Scouts came out of it with credit. So, of course, did Konia Khel. Thereafter he was Public Enemy Number One.

When 'poor Barney' came back from leave there was no rest for him –

marching with the military columns, haranguing Jirgas to persuade them to keep the peace, and to expel local bad men and hostile lashkars, all through the hottest and most unhealthy months of the year.

> We (Scouts, Maliks, Khassadars and self) left Sararogha yesterday at a grim hour and plodded forward, slipping about and swearing until dawn. We got to the hills above Janata at 8 a.m., put up piquets and waited for the arrival of the column. Its head appeared about five miles away and we sat holding our thumbs and waiting for the first roar of guns and musketry to show they were engaged and that our troubles had started. I had about 400 Maliks and Khassadars out in an attempt to keep the country quiet, but there was the haunting fear of a swine like Konia Khel chipping in. However, none did, and next day I was busy arranging water supplies, local purchases, tribal piquets and the 101 things connected with a field column.

There arrived in Waziristan a mysterious visitor known as 'The Shami Pir'. 'Shami' means Syrian, or of Damascus, and Pir means a holy man, which was what he was, a grave preacher, with a noble beard and a sanctimonious air, a Sayid (descendant of the Prophet) and a member of the Gilani clan which is respected for its religious associations in every Moslem country. But the Gilanis were also thought to be pro-Italian, and favoured by Hitler. However, his preaching seemed innocuous. It was a pensioned Subadar of the South Waziristan Scouts, also a Sayid and so with an entrée into the Shami Pir's circle, who told Barnes what the holy man was up to – instigating and organising another Mahsud-Wazir invasion of Afghanistan in support of the anglophobe ex-King Amanullah. It was decided on high that he must be bought off, so after complex negotiations Barnes, alone and unarmed, with a suitcase of money, met him at a secret rendezvous. The Shami Pir went on his way rejoicing, having presented Barnes with a fine walking-stick. He was photographed in Karachi beardless, wearing a natty suit and pointed shoes, looking just like a Levantine tout with a pocketful of indecent postcards. His visit gave notice that the Axis powers had their eye on Waziristan.

In the middle of the Mahsud country was the large village or small town of Makin, its inhabitants balanced on the knife-edge of neutrality. In the centre of Makin there lived, in the usual fortified stone keep, a notorious hostile who was doing his damnedest to bring the Mahsuds into the war. General Hartley decided that the sappers must blow up his tower. But Barnes argued that this would have a very bad effect: it would be far better if his tower were demolished by his fellow Mahsuds, on the orders of the Jirga. So [wrote Lowis]

> Barnie and Aslam after a fearful argument got the Maliks to undertake to demolish the tower and bring in the bad man. Armed with this undertaking, he tackled Hartley who, after more argument, agreed. There was a full-scale Jirga near Makin, camp sniped at night, but Hartley took it well. The Jirga was an hour and a half late in producing their man, and there was more argument about burning the tower. But at last they burnt it. This was a great achievement on Barney's part. A hostile Makin on the lines of communication would have been serious.

Then came the day of Barnes's departure and a great farewell tea-party on his lawn in Tank. 'Who,' wrote Olaf Caroe, 'does not remember those farewell tea-parties when men who have made your life a burden for months and years all at once come round with fervent hand-clasps and wishing you God-speed – could it be with a tear in the eye? – almost make you believe that the burden was worth carrying.' Among the assembled guests was 'that swine, Konia Khel', Public Enemy Number One, sipping tea and nibbling sweet biscuits, perfectly safe under the Political Agent's safe-conduct.

Konia Khel *was* a swine, a pathological killer, hiring himself out for contract killings. The Pukhtunwali code meant nothing to him. Norval Mitchell, Assistant Political Agent, Sararogha, resented having to shake his hand when 'he thought it appropriate to visit me under safe-conduct'.

> I found a horrid fascination in looking at him. He was something under six feet tall, well-proportioned and lean. His complexion was of the light brown shade described in 'wanted by the police' notices as 'wheat'. His eyes were dark brown marbles with the whites showing all round. They were never still. Nor was he. He sat looking this way and that, the hands restless without the butt of a weapon to clasp, exchanging meaningless remarks until I could tactfully end the nonsense.

Some time later, officially at peace with the authorities, he arrived at Sararogha on the bus from Tank.

> Some friends told him that three blood-feud enemies were awaiting him in the bazaar. Konia Khel in a cold fury went from shop to shop

> with his rifle at his hip and his finger on the trigger. He came to a low door inside which the avengers were sitting. They shot him dead before his eyes had accustomed themselves to the dim light.

In a village called Karama lived a burly, ruddy-cheeked, hazel-eyed Mahsud Malik whose name was Shah Pasand ('Prince Charming'), but the tribesmen called him 'Colonel' for he had been Commandant of the Amir's Bodyguard in Kabul. Anticipating by some weeks the overthrow of his royal master, he had decamped with as many rifles and grenades as could be loaded on to an improvised mule-train and taken them into Waziristan. With those as his working capital, he had built a fortified tower and set up as a country gentleman. His antecedents were not such as to inspire confidence, but he was never detected in crime, and was outwardly co-operative with the Political Agent. Under political pressure he had agreed reluctantly to burn down the houses of three noted hostiles in Karama. It was Mitchell's job to see that this had been properly done, for the dense smoke billowing out from the village could have been from burning straw.

He went there with a Scouts officer, Captain Farquharson, a platoon of Scouts, and a young signals officer who asked if he might join them for the experience.

> On the outskirts of the village we were met by Shah Pasand and other Maliks. They were firm that the escort platoon should stay outside. I saw that the houses of the three miscreants were burning nicely and was taking leave of Shah Pasand when he insisted that we should partake of his hospitality. Refusal was out of the question, but by now I was really uneasy. The lanes were congested with Mahsuds armed with rifles and knives. They looked very cross, which was understandable. And now we had to go through a door into a courtyard, through the courtyard and up several steps onto the verandah of the house. The angry-looking men followed us in, sat down and filled the courtyard. There were more outside as the smoke from the burning houses wandered about in the windless air. Shah Pasand's household began handing out green tea, iced cakes and the conventional hard-boiled eggs. We were sitting ducks, and I thought we would soon be shot. I asked the Signals officer in a whisper whether his revolver was loaded, and the cheerful answer was, 'No.' I could see Farquharson's .45 Colt was loaded, but the holster was buttoned up. It really did seem as if we were for it. I remarked loudly that it gave me no pleasure to insist on tribal punishment for outlaws, while I cracked hard-boiled eggs on my knee and peeled and ate them. The

third egg was not hard-boiled and made a mess on my knee on impact. This raised a loud laugh which relaxed all tension, and away we went, after the proper exchange of courtesies.

Another Mahsud character was Honorary Captain Mir Badshah, a member of the Indian Order of Merit and of the Victorian Order, one-time A.D.C. to His Royal Highness the Duke of Connaught. A trim, soldierly man with a moustache but no beard and a patch over an empty eye-socket, he had had a brilliant record on the Western Front and in East Africa. Although loyal to the Government – sort of – he was intensely proud of being a Mahsud. In his eye, the Mahsud man was God's finest product, the Mahsud way of life was perfection. He was at variance with the Political Agent, Major Abdur Rahim Khan, a Pathan who did not have the good fortune to be a Mahsud, and rumour reached Mitchell that he had put out a contract for killing either the Political Agent or himself.

That sort of thing had to be taken seriously. I was quite certain where the attack would take place, and slowed down as we approached the place and took my pistol in hand. The three orderlies with me in the car protruded their rifle barrels through the windows. And there, stationary, was the car of the Assistant Garrison Engineer. I drew up beside it to pass the time of day. The radiator and windscreen were shot to bits. The only occupant was a dead man in the back seat.

The dead man was a Khassadar. They learned later that the Assistant Garrison Engineer had been wounded, but his Khassadar escort, following in a lorry, had fought off the attackers – a most unusual occurrence – and taken him to Sararogha.

Mitchell made it known generally that he thought the ambush had been set for him, at the instigation of Mir Badshah. This caused the Captain much concern, and he sent a message that he wished to swear his innocence.

The Post Commander and I went out to meet him. The meeting was cordial and he came to my quarters. There one of my staff brought a copy of the Koran wrapped in a silk cloth and the oath was taken. His reverence for the Book seemed to me profound and I found myself believing him. I am glad that we parted on good terms.

Mitchell often had to accompany a brigade column, and on one of these had a distressing experience. About a dozen hostile Mahsuds were cornered in a deep watercourse, where they stayed to fight it out.

> A British officer and two Punjabis were killed in an attempt to dislodge them, and their bodies remained in full view. I suggested that I negotiate with the enemy their surrender as prisoners-of-war. The battalion commander agreed, to recover the bodies. Negotiations proceeded and the enemy emerged, led by one of my Mahsud orderlies who had been my go-between. My orderlies relieved them of their weapons and they ran to me crying for mercy. They clasped my knees. They did the ritual clasping of the beard. I had guaranteed their safety but their guard, of the Punjabi battalion, was about to kill them. The guard drew in with bayonets fixed. The leading prisoner turned his back on me, drew a knife from his clothes somewhere, ran on to the leading soldier and killed him with a blow over the shoulder and into the heart. The prisoner turned in his tracks and found himself faced by the Colonel who had jumped in to stop the killing. The Colonel felled him with a right hook. They fell together. The Punjabis leaped to the Colonel's aid, and since he was on top of his man, probed with their bayonets past him into the enemy. One bayonet went through the Colonel's upper arm. Meanwhile the remaining prisoners were killed with the bayonet. I remember very clearly how not one of them raised a cry; how the soldiers stood back and fired shots into their bodies; and, as the enthusiasm ebbed, ran their thumbs up and down the bayonets to clean off the blood. It was a relief when I was able to leave this column.

Lest the Mahsuds treat it as a blood-feud matter, Mitchell was transferred to Peshawur. The Governor, Sir George Cunningham, raised a row over the slain prisoners and on the strength of Mitchell's report insisted on compensation being paid to their families. This, to the Mahsuds, settled the affair. Mitchell, therefore, returned to Waziristan. On his way to Sararogha he saw a party of tribesmen lined up across the road.

> I decided to receive whatever was coming to me on my feet, so I got out of my car and walked forward. 'They are here to thank you,' said my orderly. They came forward and embraced me, and I rather weakly sat down on the mudguard of my car.

Meanwhile in North Waziristan the war continued, with the Faqir of Ipi sustained by funds from the Axis legations in Kabul and, probably, from the Indian National Congress as well. Edward Lydall arrived in Miranshah as Assistant Political Agent, and within a few days was watching, from a prudent distance, his first battle: it was very like an

O.T.C. Field Day, except that the participants were not firing blank cartridges. A week later a friend in the R.A.F. invited him to take part in a bombing raid on the Faqir's cave headquarters. Lydall accepted with alacrity, although he had just consumed a heavy curry lunch. As the plane bucketed up and down, and the curry lunch likewise, he wished he had not come. Finally the pilot pointed down to a small hole on a hillside and put the plane into a steep dive. Lydall just made it to a window. He reflected afterwards that, although he had not done credit to his service, at least he had scored a nearer miss with his lunch than the pilot with his bombs.

His boss was Roger Bacon, bald as an egg, highly competent and unperturbable – until his old friend K.C. Packman arrived on ten days' leave. Let Lydall tell the sequel.

> Packie, having put himself on good terms with the universe by the absorption of some middle-morning gin, was taking a stroll round his old haunts in company with Roger and myself. Great was his pleasure, on passing the civil lock-up, to find that it contained many of his old tribal friends who had felt forced by the weight of tedium to shoot at the army or at us or by the laws of the blood-feud to murder their next-door neighbours.
>
> 'These poor fellows!' exclaimed Packie with rich benignity. 'There is no justice in the world.' He turned to the sentry on guard, another old acquaintance. 'My friend,' he said, 'give me the key.'
>
> The sentry hastened to comply and, flinging open the lock-up door, Packie addressed the inmates. 'My friends,' he said with radiant benevolence, 'I give you all your freedom.'
>
> And out poured a quite theatrically villainous collection of criminal types, fanning out over the fort and going to ground in the most improbable crannies. After lunch, Packie, feeling that he had righted a festering wrong, retired to bed to sleep if off, but Roger and I spent an anxious and exhausting afternoon winkling out his friends from their bolt-holes and replacing them one by one in the lock-up.

Next day Packie again made himself conspicuous, at a high-level operations conference which, as a mere visitor, he had no right to attend. A very senior R.A.F. officer held out at tedious length on how he would run the Frontier, until Packie, exasperated, said, 'Listen, chum, your job is to drive the f——g aeroplane.'

Nevertheless when his leave expired – not, in Roger Bacon's opinion, a moment too soon – he persuaded the R.A.F. to fly him to Peshawur. He boarded the plane amply refreshed and was gratified to see, when he landed at Peshawur airport, the Governor and all the top brass lined up in their best uniforms apparently to greet him. He advanced with dignity on the Governor, tried to take off his topi, got entangled in the chin-strap, nearly throttled himself, and settled instead for a deep salaam. At that moment the Viceroy's plane touched down. It was the Governor, Sir Ralph Griffith, who saved what promised to be a delicate situation. 'Packie!' he roared, 'F—— off!' And Packie, conscious of having been wronged, wandered moodily into the middle distance.

When next he applied for permission to visit Miranshah, Sir Ralph endorsed his application, 'No No No No.'

Packman was no clown. On leave he was unpredictable, but on the job he was an efficient and resourceful Frontier officer. One cannot quite visualise him as a Resident in Central India, but some of the less inhibited rulers would have got on well with him.

A pause in hostilities, a sort of half-time break, was the occasion for summoning to Miranshah the Tori Khel Jirga. The tribesmen, wrote Lydall:

> sat cross-legged in a semi-circle twenty or more deep. Along the base of the semi-circle, perched aloft on chairs, sat a General, Roger, the Tochi Scouts Commandant, the Political Assistant and myself. The tribesmen all looked tremendously fierce. Nevertheless they replied politely to Roger's traditional greeting, 'Never be tired.'
>
> Seeing in the front row an old friend who had been sniping at the fort three times a week, I wagged a reproving finger in his direction. This had the unexpected result of giving him a fit of the giggles . . .
>
> Roger opened with a short speech in Pushtu setting out the sins of the tribe. They were harbouring the Faqir of Ipi, they had kidnapped twenty-six Hindus and were holding them to ransom, they had wrecked bridges by placing beneath them unexploded R.A.F. bombs perched on the tops of bonfires, and they were perpetually sniping at the troops. The position was altogether unsatisfactory. What did they propose to do about it?
>
> For the rest of the morning lengthy speeches were delivered by the leaders, each point being emphasised with Pushtu proverbs and anecdotes. Why should they not harbour the Faqir of Ipi? He was a very holy man and a member of the Tori Khel tribe. And anyhow they were not harbouring him. The retention of Hindus was a purely commercial transaction, and nothing to do with us. As for the sniping, they had not invited us to build camps all over their country and so could hardly be expected to feel bound by the laws of hospitality.

Steam having been duly blown off, we adjourned for lunch, leaving a clear field for the wiles of the Political Assistant. He was soon at work, having persuaded my giggling friend to come, unbeknown to the others, and talk matters over quietly. The result was that my friend agreed for a consideration to refuse hospitality to the Faqir of Ipi, to return two or three Hindus who were with him, and to cease from bombing bridges and sniping forts . . . The rot now set in, and for the rest of the afternoon and evening the house of the Assistant was besieged by keen negotiators anxious to be in on the ground floor. As a result the plenary session next day was an altogether more genial affair. Lengthy speeches expressed benevolence and good intentions. Rifles were handed in as surety for good behaviour. Two or three Hindus were yielded up as an earnest of more to follow and with much handshaking the Tori Khel dispersed, pledged to be of good behaviour at any rate for a week or two.

Now was the time to win the tribesmen's hearts and minds by a programme of well-digging. They derived much pleasure from the spectacle of a perspiring sapper major wandering up and down holding a forked stick, which from time to time flipped up and hit him on the nose. Even better fun was to watch a gang digging where there was no hope of water, the diviner's marks having been moved the night before.

7
Baluchistan

Whatever Politicals may have thought of Waziristan, their wives greatly preferred Baluchistan. This was for various reasons: the danger was much less, so they could be with their husbands; in most places there was some European social life – in Quetta a great deal; and the climate was clement.

Except in Nasirabad.

This was a sub-division of the Political Agency of Sibi, 80 miles long by 5 to 15 miles wide, a finger of Baluchistan stretching from the hills roamed by Baluch nomads, eastwards almost to the Indus. The eastern end was irrigated in summer when the snows melting in the Himalayas caused the Indus to rise high enough to fill the canals. Where the canals petered out, the desert began, a flat, bare, mud '*pat*' (to rhyme with 'but') stretching to the foothills. It was without water, without shade, without life. The summer heat was lethal, the average annual rainfall 4 inches. But the mirages were splendid – lakes, palm-trees, domes, minarets. On the edge of the *pat* was the administrative centre, Jhatpat, a stark collection of offices, a Levy post, a jail and the houses of the luckless Indian officials who lived there. But right through the middle of the *pat* was a new canal system, a loop coming from and returning to the Indus.

Geographically Nasirabad was obviously part of Sind Province, and its canals were part of the Sind canal system. It was included in Baluchistan because many of the cultivators of the irrigated area were tribesmen from Baluchistan, and in May, 1933, G.C.S. Curtis was posted there as Assistant Political Agent and Colonisation Officer, to organise their settlement, and to arrange with the Sind authorities the division of the canal water. Curtis was just out of the Baluch Regiment and without any Political training.

First there was a law and order problem to be tackled. Law was dispensed by Baluch tribal Jirgas. A modicum of order was kept by local levies, provided by the Baluch chiefs, mounted on their own ponies and carrying their own swords and miscellaneous firearms. These were being set at naught by a bandit, Abdur Rahim Brahui, a ruthless and elusive character with the prestige of Robin Hood in that he robbed only the rich (no point in robbing the poor) and gave the proceeds of his crimes to poor Moslems, notably himself and his gang. To cope with this bad man, Curtis asked for reinforcements.

So there arrived at Jhatpat, after a ride of hundreds of miles from the furthest corner of Baluchistan, a platoon of the Chagai Militia, Baluchis and Pathans mounted on well-bred trotting camels, tough characters, hardened by skirmishes with raiders and arms-smugglers. Patrolling with them was a revelation to Curtis: there is no ride more comfortable than a good trotting camel with its swift and smooth action.

They patrolled day and night, padding silently over the *pat* and through the tamarisk bushes, arriving often at a village even before the dogs woke to bark. When the weather began to cool down, Curtis set out to inspect the crops, escorted by the Chagai camelry.

> I was conferring with the local revenue official when we heard shouting ahead and a fusillade of shots. We rushed into the crops. The officer of the levies beside me put his rifle to his shoulder and fired. There was a terrible cry and then silence. In a clearing there was a bedstead under a tree, an earthenware jug beneath it. On the ground behind was a prone figure, dead, and near him a large Mauser automatic. It was the redoubtable Abdur Rahim Brahui.

Curtis tackled the problems of settlement in the new canal colonies. The scheme had never been really thought out.

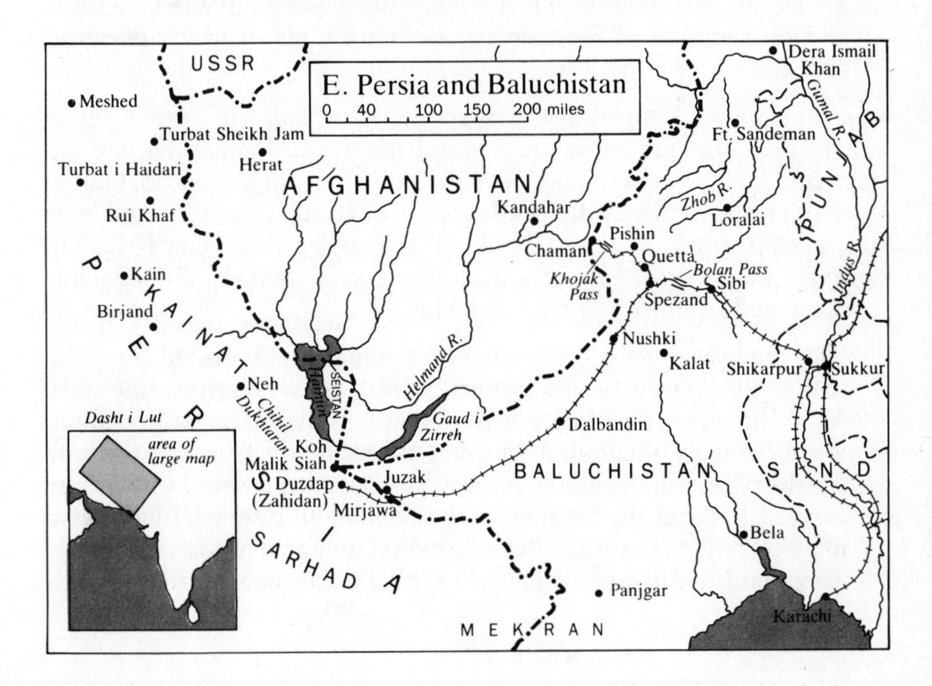

It was unreasonable to expect that men skilled in the care of sheep and goats in barren hills would in the twinkling of an eye be converted into arable farmers, masters of the husbandry of perennial irrigation. The financial terms of the grants must anticipate a degree of incompetence. There were many more applications than there was land. There had to be consultations with Political Agents to select the settlers on a clan and tribal basis, with due regard to tribal feuds.

A programme for taking possession had to be agreed, and arrangements made for advances of seed-corn and the provision of plough-cattle. The first to arrive were a barbarous procession of Maris and Bugtis [Baluch clans] driving sheep and goats before them. They declined to believe that they could survive without these, and when their first crop came through, turned them out to graze upon it. That would not have mattered so much. It was when they grazed their neighbours' crops that trouble began. The Bugtis were soon called to order by their chief, a striking figure of immense stature with cavalier ringlets and aristocratic features. But the Mari chief at the time was a minor: stern measures had to be taken to impress upon them the standards of conduct expected of them in their new home.

What the colonists lacked in skill they made up in energy. No time was lost in planting simple crops, the first-comers putting in barley, the late-comers millet. Pathans from the Quetta Agency succeeded in getting lucerne to grow. Trees were planted along the water-courses, and on the sites of the hamlets, the mud walls of which began to appear.

Curtis found keen pleasure in getting two blades of corn to grow where none had grown before. He did not live in Jhatpat (no one did who could live anywhere else) but eight miles away in Jacobabad, built in early Victorian times as the headquarters of General Jacob. It was now the headquarters of Upper Sind District, with which Curtis had to arrange the distribution of canal water, and smooth the relations between mild Sindis and wild Baluchis.

The shady avenues of trees which the soldiers had planted along the roads still survived. So did General Jacob's house. Here was the clock which the great man made with his own hands. Its great pendulum was weighted with a round-shot and its face showed not only the time but the phases of the moon. Nearby was his grave covered with a huge stone slab, the corners stained with the oil of little lamps. Lights were to be seen there occasionally: respect was still paid to the spirit of the man who laid the foundations of a settled existence in northern Sind.

Curtis lived in an old bungalow with immensely thick mud walls and a wide verandah. There were three or four Europeans in Jacobabad, enough to play squash (in temperatures up to 145°) and scratch games of polo on police horses. After exercise they bathed in a tank filled with lukewarm brackish water, swimming about holding a mug of beer.

He brought his new wife, Decima, to Jacobabad at the beginning of his second cold weather. They toured on 'well-mannered but cheerful horses', accompanied by a mixed pack of Salukis and 'a gaggle of Baluchis on their little mares, their baggy trousers ballooning out in the breeze. In the scrub at the edge of the *pat* dwelt a stout-hearted race of hares.' They rather liked Jacobabad.

Margery Hall, wife of H.P. Hall, with young children, didn't, from the moment they first approached it from the cool Baluchistan hills.

> Quite suddenly, as though a hot, stale, sweaty blanket had been wrapped round my head, the air got thick and oppressive.
>
> 'This is Jacobabad,' said Henry.
>
> 'Yes, I can smell it.'
>
> It was a sort of decay, and urine, and spices, the first two past the first stages of putrefaction, all inextricably mixed by sun and humanity.

There was electricity a few hours a day, to work the signals for the trains. Exhausted by this effort, it had no more energy to work the fans and lights. The bathroom had the usual tin tub, thunder-box and a hole in the wall to let water out and snakes in. There was no fridge. The water, flat and dead and boiled, gave the baby diarrhoea, until they imported better water from down the line in a padlocked container. All night one just lay naked under a mosquito net sweating, moving from time to time as one part of the sheet became sodden. The smell was worse at night, and could be countered only by drenching the pillow with eau de Cologne.

When Margery Hall ventured to inspect the servants' quarters, it was apparent that it was not the local custom ever to empty the latrine. Then they discovered that their driver, with whom the children played every day, was suffering (in common with 90 per cent of the population) with advanced syphilis; worse, the cook was discovered operating a brothel, at one rupee a go, in the guest-house; worst of all, the bearer was taken away by the police for buggering the kitchen-boy.

'How could he do it?' wailed Margery Hall to the ayah. 'How *could* he do it?'

'Vaseline, memsahib.'

Looking back on it all she reflected:

> The achievements of the men were nearly always very good and often beyond praise. But I think their wives had an equally difficult job to do. The men at least had their training, books of law and senior officers to advise. Wives rarely had anyone. They had problems to cope with that they had not even dreamed of, and they were always anxious for their children. Perhaps I wasn't clever enough, or perhaps I would have been better off with deafer ears or blinder eyes. I don't know.

Next door to Jhatpat was Sibi Political Agency, inhabited by Pathans, Maris and Bugtis who bred excellent horses, gave little trouble and as much as possible kept out of sight and out of mind, ruled autocratically by their Nawabs and visited by the Political Agent during his cold weather tours on horseback.

So respected was the tribal aristocracy that among the Maris an oath of innocence taken with one's hand on the Nawab's head was always accepted. Cases before the Jirga were sometimes settled by fire- and water-tests. The fire-test was to hold in one's hand a piece of paper inscribed with a verse from the Koran, allow a red-hot ploughshare to be placed upon it and walk ten yards. If a man did this, his case was taken as proved. For the water-test he had to swim to a pole in the centre of a deep pool, climb down it and pick up a handful of gravel from the bottom. If he was lying, his guilty conscience would prevent him holding his breath long enough.

Stock-theft was the most common crime. There were hereditary trackers, known as 'suragis', whose skill and rectitude were such that an assurance from one of them that he had tracked a stolen animal as far as the territory of a particular clan was always accepted. That clan then had either to pay up its value or to prove, by the evidence of another suragi, that it had been taken out of their area into that of another clan. Herbert Todd sometimes accompanied these suragis tracking, and was amazed at their speed, even in stony riverbeds or bare hillsides.

> I remember one astounding case of a tracker who was following a stolen cow when he suddenly stopped and pointed to some old hoof-marks and said they were those of a cow he had tried to follow a year earlier but had lost on the hard macadam road. We took him to the test of following up these ancient tracks, which he did, to the village where the cow was found.

The other crime to which Maris and Bugtis were addicted was

8 Quetta earthquake, 1935

9 D.H. Biscoe and J.C.E. Bowen, with Rover Scouts, extracting corpses from the ruins

10 The Agency Surgeon, R.D. Macrae (*right*), on tour in Gilgit, 1941

11 Nancy Kirkbride on tour in Hunza

wife-murder. Trench, as Political Agent, Sibi, addressed the Agent to the Governor-General on this matter:

> Custom among the Baluchis compels a husband to kill an adulterous wife and gives him no option in the matter. The theory is that her blood is not on his head but on that of the adulterer. In some cases she is butchered with an axe, in others she is beaten to death. The more usual method is to force her to hang herself with her own pyjama-cord. The mere accusation of adultery by the husband, unsupported by evidence, is held to justify his killing her and the alleged paramour.
>
> Every case is referred to the Jirga under the Frontier Crimes Regulations. If the husband has killed his wife but failed to kill the adulterer, the Jirga awards him blood-money, in the form of cash and a virgin, and invariably recommends that no punishment be inflicted on him.

The Political Agent could ignore the Jirga's recommendation and hand out stiff sentences for wife-killing. But if these were set aside on appeal, it would make bad worse.

> The temptations it offers to a husband are obvious. He can get rid of a tiresome wife and, if he plays his cards well, pay off old scores against some enemy.
>
> Tribal custom is the very basis of our rule in Baluchistan. But it is, I submit, possible to pay too much respect to it. We have now been forty years in this country and it seems to me that the time has come to purge custom of its more glaring abuses.

When Sibi got too hot, everyone – officials, shopkeepers, tribes – moved up the hill to Harnai; and when Harnai became too hot, up the mountain to Ziarat. May Trench described the start:

> Dick, as usual, had found it necessary to go on ahead, with such servants as he immediately needed. I was left to pay, pack and follow, with the children, the remainder of the servants, the office-staff, the animals – the children jolting along in a tonga; the baggage and George, the 'tame' tiger-cat, on camels; the rest of us riding camels and ponies.
>
> Dick's Afridi orderly, Taza Khan, usually a support, was shaking with malaria and quite useless. From the road came the shrieks of George who resented being shut in a box roped to the back of a camel.

'Why,' I asked Taza Khan an hour after dawn, 'have the camels not started?'

'The camel-men complain that the loads are too heavy. Furthermore,' he temporarily cheered up at the prospect of imparting really bad news, 'the Chief Clerk's wife and the wife of the Agency Treasurer have quarrelled and will not travel in the same camel-litter, and the best cow has been bitten by a cobra and will die . . . In fact I think I'm dying myself.' He flopped on to a charpoy and pulled the sheet over his head.

At this juncture the Malik of the local Pathans arrived. I explained our difficulties, but with the arrival of this large, authoritative man, these dispersed like early morning mist. A few words sent the camel-men scurrying on their way. The sick man took up his bed and walked. George stopped screaming. As for the two ladies, 'Tell them,' said the Malik, 'that if they won't go in the litter, they will have to stay behind, locked up together in the station waiting-room for their safety.'

The climate of Quetta, Loralai, Ziarat and even Fort Sandeman was delightful. The winters were frosty and bracing, the summers never really hot. Quetta was, after Aldershot, the biggest garrison-station in the Empire, and there was the Staff College too, so it did not lack social life, with polo-weeks, tennis tournaments, horse-shows and a good hunt. But those who wished to get away from it all could easily do so: mountains and deserts began only a few miles outside cantonment limits.

The Agent to the Governor-General presided over a Political establishment which reflected a more intensive government than in Waziristan, but less than in the North-Western Frontier Province. He had a First Secretary, an Under Secretary and a Personal Assistant. There was a Revenue Commissioner, for the people of Baluchistan were taxed on the basis of a simple land settlement. Outside Quetta justice was administered by Jirgas according to the Shariat, but the large population of Quetta itself was subject to British Indian law: there were magistrates, a Sessions Judge, a Judicial Commissioner, a Court of Appeal, with the usual attendant pleaders. The Political Agents of Sibi, Quetta-Pishin, Loralai, Fort Sandeman and Mekran in the far west had more executive powers than those in Waziristan, but the tribal Sardars really did have traditional, hereditary authority. The semi-independent state of Kalat, with its tributary Las Bela, was treated much as any other native state.

Trench's representations about wife-killing bore no immediate fruit, for in Baluchistan tribal custom was as the Ark of the Covenant: any attack on it was regarded as a breach of the promises made to the tribes by Sandeman forty years earlier. (Critics of the Baluchistan administration said that it purchased tranquillity at the price of stagnation.) But a few years later a friend of Trench's, Terence Keyes, approached the problem from another angle. As Political Agent of Kalat State (Maris and Bugtis were equally at home in Sibi and in Kalat) he tackled directly the tribal Sardars. The eyes of the world, he pointed out, were on them: if these horrid practices were known in London, Washington and Geneva, their faces would be blackened with shame. So they held a week-long Jirga, with no outsiders present, and agreed at last to alter their law. Thereafter no wife need fear that, if she were so much as nudged immodestly by a stranger in a crowd, her husband would take her to a lonely spot and kill her.

The nineteen-gun state of Kalat was inhabited by two tribes – Baluchis of Persian origin and Brahuis who were Dravidian. Their primitive nomad life-styles were similar. The state was not in the van of progress. Khudadad Khan, father of the Khan in Keyes's time, was an ogre, counting his toll of human heads as Rajput rulers counted tigers. He boasted to the Agent to the Governor-General that in his thirty-five year reign he had executed 3,500 of his subjects, give or take a few hundred. He had punished a minor theft from his Treasury by having the principal offender stoned to death, five women slain with the sword and two accomplices emasculated. He had caused his Wazir, the Wazir's son and the Wazir's father (aged 90) to be hacked to death. After which the Government said, 'enough is enough', and deposed him. In his son, the Khan in Keyes's time, eccentricity took another form: he combined a jackdaw-like love of hoarding useless objects with a paranoid fear of their being stolen. Thus he collected thousands of pairs of shoes but, to discourage theft, destroyed each left shoe. His numerous cars, their wheels removed, rusted away unused.

This was the man Keyes had to tackle on the delicate subject of slavery. Male slaves were generally employed in agriculture, the tribesmen not condescending to such menial occupation. They were allowed to keep about a third of the produce, but could neither bequeath property nor leave their masters who had absolute authority over them, short of taking their lives. Women slaves could be sold and owned whole or in shares. For example, a Mullah bought half the leg of a woman for Rs 25, then a full leg. Although the woman had a husband (not her owner), the Mullah was entitled to her first three children, and the owner of the remaining half-leg was entitled to the fourth. If there were several shareholders of a woman, they drew lots for priority in her offspring. A pretty, fair Hazara slave was forcibly betrothed to a negro slave 'with nostrils like a horse'. Her mother ingeniously put pepper in her eyes, which inflamed them, as an excuse to take her to Dr Holland, the eye-specialist in Quetta. From his consulting room she made a sudden dash to the Political Agent's office, and claimed sanctuary. Her owner then sold her to the Political Agent, who married her off happily to a drill instructor of the Hazara Pioneers.

The Khan said there was no slavery in Kalat State. In that case, said Keyes, there could be no harm in issuing a decree condemning it, and announcing that any slave who applied to the Political Agent could obtain a certificate of manumission.

A trickle of applicants applied – the men mostly of African origin, the women Persian – and departed with their freedom. Fingers pointed to a backwoods Sardar who was believed to be a leading slave-owner and dealer. Conrad Corfield, Keyes's Assistant Political Agent, was told to deal with him.

After a long desert journey Corfield pitched his tent beside the Sardar's camp. They spent most of the first day exchanging courtesies over cups of green tea, and on the second day Corfield mentioned in passing the subject of slaves. There weren't any, said the Sardar – perhaps a few discontented domestic servants, but no *slaves*. During the next two days a few old folk arrived, grabbed their certificates of manumission and departed. On the third day the Sardar hinted that perhaps the Sahib had other work and would be leaving soon? The Sahib said he was very happy and would stay a few more days. Finally, after a couple more days of manoeuvring, the Sardar accepted the inevitable and a stream of slaves reported for their certificates.

Corfield then departed. A little later, while he was on tour, two girls were rescued by his levies from a gang of slavers. They were Persians, one slim and beautiful, the other sturdy and handsome. They were exhausted and despairing. But what could he do with them? If he took them to Quetta they had no future but prostitution, and their parents would not now take them back. Corfield told the local Sardar to find two respectable husbands for them, and this was done: the beautiful girl was married next day to the Sardar's son, the handsome one to a corporal of levies.

Many of these manumitted slaves, discovering that freedom was not all that it was cracked up to be, returned to their former owners, as free labourers.

Edward Wakefield arrived with his family in Quetta in March, 1933, and was appointed Assistant Political Agent, Quetta-Pishin, with duties as varied as looking after the tribal levies, chasing stock-thieves, riding the Afghan Boundary to ensure that nobody had moved to Britain's disadvantage the boundary pillars, and keeping an eye on the caravans which every autumn brought down to the railhead at Chaman loads of dried apricots, peaches, pears, grapes, plums and walnuts. Each big Afghan orchard had its own pattern of saddle-bag, woven of gaily coloured goats' hair, and the packhorses had breastplates and breechings of the same material. The leading stallion of each caravan, who was supposed to have been to the Holy Places, carried round his neck a wooden, bell-like clapper. So long as this sounded, the caravan must keep moving; but any horse which presumed to pass him was savaged. To stop the caravan someone had to run alongside the leader and silence the clapper: otherwise the horses just forged ahead, shouldering aside anyone who stood in their path.

They made straight for the railway yard, where the fruit was loaded for Karachi. In the heat and dust lay huge mounds of fruit. Each horse in turn was led to the foot of a mound where a man stood on either side, back bent and hands on knees, to take the weight of the saddle-bags which were then cut loose and carried up a plank to the top of a mound where two more men, standing knee-deep in the sticky mess, cut the stitching at the bottom of the bags to let all the fruit out. The bags were then thrown into a heap to be washed in a mountain stream, and the men ran down the planks for more loads. All around sat the women and children of Chaman, packing the fruit into wooden boxes: they were paid nothing in cash but were allowed to eat their fill. It was a primitive, highly efficient assembly-line system, which might not perhaps have pleased a Health Inspector. From this medley of sweaty bodies, horse-dung, maggots, hornets and blue-bottles, the fruit eventually reached London and New York where it was sold in hygienic containers.

The station-master at Chaman was a fortunate functionary. 'There was always,' noted Wakefield, 'or could be contrived, a shortage of wagons. Only he could say which consignment went off first, which would be delayed for days or weeks.' The job was reputed to be worth £5,000 a year, and was customarily given to men with many years' exemplary service who were reaching the age of retirement. 'Great was their reward.'

One of Wakefield's oddest duties was to escort from Chaman to Quetta a banker recommended by the Afghan Government for special protection. He told Wakefield he was taking for sale in Bombay jewellery owned by White Russian aristocrats who had escaped to Afghanistan with this but no money. From the recesses of his garments he extracted a cigarette-box full of small, paper-wrapped packages, which contained a superb diamond necklace, a diamond bracelet, diamond earrings: diamonds were a Grand Duchess's best friends. Wakefield bought, at a jeweller's valuation, a marquise ring with an enamel centre surrounded by diamonds. In the middle of the enamel was the monogram, surmounted by a crown, of Nicholas II, Tsar of All the Russias.

Keyes's Khan of Kalat, the right-shoe fancier, had been succeeded by his eldest son, who was poisoned by the mother of his younger brother, Ahmed Yar. Ahmed Yar ascended the throne, and because of his youth and inexperience, Wakefield was appointed Wazir-i-Azam, Chief Minister, of the state. The Khan of Kalat administered through his Wazir only about a third of the State; the administration of the remainder was farmed out to tribal Sardars, a recipe for anarchy. Many state employees had not been paid for months, and had no resource but corruption: the outlying treasuries were empty. Slavery, 'abolished' in 1927, was again rife. Prisoners languished untried in jail. Even the horses of the famous Kalat stud were starving: there was no money to buy feed.

The state's finances were restored to health in a fortuitous manner. By one of the unpredictable convolutions of international trade, there was a boom in imports to India of Japanese silk. The import duty on silk in British India was 66 per cent, in Kalat 5 per cent. So huge quantities of silk were brought to the Kalat port of Pasni and smuggled overland into Sind. Happily the Chief Customs Officer at Pasni was an honest man. Wakefield doubled his salary and promoted him: such are the advantages of autocracy. The Government of India protested at this intolerable situation, and protested again; but Wakefield, like other Politicals lent as Ministers to states, was the servant of the state, not of the Indian Government. Not until the Kalat Treasury was well replenished did he, as a goodwill gesture, raise the Kalat import duty to the Indian level.

The process of regularising Kalat's finances was painful to many who prospered from chaos. One of these Sardars worked on the Khan, a likeable but vacillating young man, to order his Wazir to tour the Kachi district, down at the coast, in the middle of the hot weather, and inspect the flood irrigation system. The Sardar then himself advised Wakefield, 'If His Highness makes the suggestion, don't go. The heat is killing.

Even I have never been there in summer. No Sardar has. Send your Revenue Assistant but don't go yourself.' Either, he reckoned, the Faranghi would disobey the Khan's order and be discredited, or he would obey and ruin his health, perhaps even die. Had His Highness been available, Wakefield might have suggested that he go in winter, but the Sardar had thoughtfully persuaded His Highness to take a little holiday.

> I spent a week in Kachi inspecting earthen dams built across the dry river beds. It was a week of horror. The worst day was the one on which we rode from Gandava to Bhag, some thirty-five miles across a treeless, shadeless plain. We set off long before dawn and reached Khududad, nineteen miles on our way, before the sun became really tyrannous. There were some trees and a well. We watered our horses and rested a while in the shade. When we resumed our journey the sun was scorching, searing . . . A horse collapsed, then another. When there were still four miles to go, our party of eighteen had been reduced to ten, and I began to wonder whether I myself would complete the journey. I touched my horse's withers. They were burning hot, too hot to rest my hand on. The track swayed up and down. Was this hallucination? I didn't know. And then I began to feel myself swelling as though my body were a balloon being pumped up . . . I felt myself being inflated and knew I would soon burst. And now I saw the tall houses of Bhag, raised by a mirage high above the level of the horizon. In my mind I debated the only question which seemed to matter – 'Can I get to Bhag before I burst?' I did get there, but only just. I do not think I could have lasted another quarter of a mile. The horse which had carried me so bravely died within an hour of our arrival. Other horses and one man died on the way . . . The doctor in charge of the State dispensary at Bhag told me that the thermometer on the verandah registered a shade temperature of 135 degrees. He expressed surprise that any of us had survived the journey . . .
>
> 'I am sorry,' said the Khan, 'that I had to ask you to carry out such an unpleasant task, but the Sardar made the suggestion. Now you have shown that you really care for my interests and those of my people.'

Wakefield's wife, Lalage, became honorary trainer to the Kalat stud, which won many races under her supervision. With their daughters, Imogen, aged four, and Xanthe, aged two and known as 'Bold One', they lived in Quetta; with Kalat problems under control, they could relax and enjoy the racing, hunting and social life.

Despite its pleasant climate, Quetta was notoriously unhealthy: malaria and intestinal diseases were rife, cholera always threatening. After a large Army exercise had to be brought to a premature end because so many of the troops went down with malaria, General Karslake, General Officer commanding the Western Command, Sir Norman Cater, Agent to the Governor-General, and the newly arrived First Secretary, B.J. Gould, decided that something must be done about it. With the medical staff, they launched a full-scale campaign to improve sanitation and eliminate the anopheles mosquito. Draconic measures were taken to make the civil population use latrines; all vegetation in and around the city was sprayed regularly with insecticides; and all still water was sprayed with oil to cover it with a film through which mosquito larvae could not breathe. Military units were lectured and trained in these matters, sometimes with unforeseen results, as when some ingenious Indian cavalry soldiers were discovered to be preserving a breeding-ground of the anopheles mosquito in order to win the monthly competition for the largest number of dead larvae. Some of the lectures fell on stony ground. The officers and N.C.O.s of a British battalion sat for a full hour while an expert explained to them the life-style of the anopheles mosquito. They were then invited to summarise it in a few words. Up spake the Sanitary Lance-Corporal, not the brightest star in the military firmament: 'Sir, the tiddlers in the *pani* grows wings.' And he was dead right.

But the campaign had an effect. At Sir Norman Cater's garden party, with sticky cakes galore, it was remarked that there was something missing: what could it be? Then realisation came: there were no flies. And the hospital attendance figures showed a gratifying decline.

During the hot weather most people in Quetta slept out-of-doors, but the night of May 30–31st, 1935, was unseasonally cold, so nearly everyone went to bed in their houses. At three minutes past three in the morning there was a violent earthquake, and within forty-five seconds the entire city, the civil lines and the R.A.F. lines were flattened. Wakefield described in a letter to his mother-in-law his personal experience, which was typical of thousands.

> At about a quarter to one in the morning, I was woken up in pitch blackness by an indescribable roar of noise. I had time, so Lal tells me, to say, 'My God, what's that?' before the crash came; but to me it seemed I had hardly woken from a deep sleep and had half turned towards Lal, when the whole world collapsed. Everything tumbled on

me – beams, rafters, bricks, mortar – from above and from both sides. I was surprised, when all this falling of the house had stopped, to find myself alive. I called to Lal, but she could only groan in reply, asking how I was. I told her that I was unhurt and she then said that there was a big beam across her back, that hurt her frightfully, and she could not move. I then struggled desperately to move, but could not manage to. My head was wedged between two rafters, and the beam that was across Lal's back was also across my thighs . . .

The only part of my body that I could move was my right hand, and I tried to move such bits of bricks and plaster as I could touch. But the danger of that was soon apparent, as some plaster was dislodged and almost filled the small breathing-space that was left . . . Working again with my hand, more cautiously, I managed to free most of my arm and gradually cleared a space by Lal's head so that she could breathe more easily. My anxiety then was to get the beam off Lal's back, which was causing her agony: it seemed immovable . . . Meanwhile I heard Nurse (from a great distance, it seemed) shout for help, and I also heard Bold One crying, but no sound from Imogen.

After I found it quite impossible to free myself or help Lal, I simply lay still, and we waited. After about ten minutes I heard the sounds of people moving; I shouted, but got no reply. Nurse also shouted and it seemed that people answered her. After that, things are confused in my mind. I remember feeling relief that Bold One had got away, with Nurse, though how I knew they had been pulled out, I cannot say . . . I shouted again, and eventually a voice replied from the infinite distance. Gradually the voices came nearer, and eventually communication was established with our rescuers, one of whom pattered prayers to Allah incessantly. Then the worst period of all followed. I could not move at all: everything was pitch black, and Lalage was silent, in great pain and possibly dying. The rescuers made no headway; they had no light and no implements, and could only guess where we were . . . At last they got to the beam lying across me and Lal. They tried to move it – and failed. I urged them, with entreaties, to try again; and again they failed to move it . . . I had the last horror of feeling that Lal and I could not even kill ourselves.

Eventually the rescuers (a sweeper, a driver, a levy and a prisoner from the lock-up behind our house) tried approaching us from a different direction . . . And now a light appeared, a candle [which] showed them where we were and how we were lying . . . And now I got terrible, excruciating cramp in my neck, but not a muscle could I move to relieve it. At last they got my head and Lalage's free, and

> after that I was able to show them how to get Lalage out. They cleared all the rubble away from the upper part of her body and legs, took some of the strain off the beam across her and drew her out by the shoulders . . . It was another ten minutes before I was got out.

Imogen had been killed instantly; Lalage was badly injured, but recovered. Nurse and Bold One were unhurt.

About half the population of the city, civil lines and R.A.F. lines were killed in that terrible forty-five seconds or died of their injuries or of suffocation – some 25,000 to 30,000 in all. Fortunately the military cantonment was hardly shaken, and within minutes units were organising for rescue work by the headlights of cars and lorries. Daylight disclosed what looked like a huge rubbish-heap, some two miles square, with only a few of the wider roads identifiable. By six o'clock areas had been allotted to units and a Relief Headquarters set up in the grounds of the ruined Quetta Club.

In reading the official report on the weeks that followed (compiled by the Assistant Political Agent, Captain L.A.G. Pinhey), one is struck by the efficiency of the measures taken to rescue, feed, heal and shelter the living; to dispose of the dead; to evacuate as many as could be evacuated; to keep order and prevent looting; and to restore life to the ruined city. At first it was mainly a military operation; several Political officers had been injured, and their subordinate staff decimated; the Quetta Police had been almost wiped out. But the Army had suffered no damage; only the Army had the organised manpower, the equipment, the transport, the technicians and the medical officers that were needed; and the Army's Mobilisation Stores containing large stocks of food, tents, blankets and medical supplies. So Martial Law was declared, General Karslake took charge, and the Staff College students formed and officered an emergency police force. The Agent to the Governor-General was so shaken that he retired from the scene; 'Bunch' Parsons replaced him, acting also as Earthquake Commissioner, taking control when Martial Law was lifted; and other Politicals were drafted in for the many jobs to be done.

The most pressing task was the rescue of those still alive. In the days before bulldozers (though these could hardly have been used safely) this could be done only by muscles, picks and shovels. Work continued day and night, soldiers and civilians working side by side. After three days, in that hot weather, the smell of corruption was so dreadful that the city was closed except to working-parties, and ringed with a barbed-wire fence. By June 7th it was reckoned that none could now be left alive in the ruins; about 4,500 had been extricated and treated in emergency hospitals staffed by Army doctors and volunteer nurses.

The Royal Corps of Signals re-established communication with the outside world. Tented camps were set up for refugees who were fed on Army rations. All stray cows were collected into an improvised dairy farm, and their milk distributed to those most in need. In the first few days some 5,000 people were sent down the repaired railway line to Sind. Police and military patrols kept out looters, who were further discouraged by grenades dropped into the underground karezes leading into the city.

There was the obvious danger of a cholera epidemic, so everyone was inoculated. Blocked karezes were opened up to supply drinking-water, which had to be sterilised. Anti-malarial measures were resumed. Hundreds of tons of fly-attracting rubbish were burnt; latrines were dug, and even used. It is a tribute to the efficiency of all concerned and the good sense of the public that there was no epidemic.

There was the dreadful task, more dreadful every day, of disposing of the dead. This was done by a specially raised Labour Battalion and a heroic band of Rover Scouts, volunteers from the Punjab. Hindus, Sikhs and Moslems, they lived and worked side by side and ate out of the same dishes. They were joined by two young Politicals, Biscoe and Bowen. Those employed on this nauseating work were provided with gas-masks, leather gloves, overalls and hooks for hauling out the decomposing corpses. These were removed in lorries and, after a brief, gruesome inspection to see if the men were circumcised, sorted into Moslems for burial, Sikhs and Hindus for cremation. About 15,000 dead bodies were disposed of in this way. The remainder still lie buried where they died.

After thousands of tons of rubble had been removed, Quetta was rebuilt – at first crude mud-and-wattle huts, then temporary, prefabricated buildings, finally permanent buildings. A Relief Committee was set up, and Biscoe and Bowen were taken away from their corpse-disposal duties to adjudicate on claims to salvaged property. Through the Viceroy's Relief Fund, money poured in from all the provinces of India, all countries in the Empire and many foreign countries. The earthquake, commented Pinhey in his report, 'was a great leveller: wealth and position tumbled to the dust and were "equal made with the poor crooked scythe and spade".' It was decided, in assessing compensation, to follow the principle of returning a person roughly to their status quo before the earthquake, neither better nor worse off. Thus 'a tailor would be provided with a sewing-machine; a dentist was enabled to purchase the necessary apparatus; a tonga-owner was provided with a tonga and horse'.

When it was all over, 'Bunch' Parsons, now Sir Arthur, succeeded Cater as Agent to the Governor-General. During his tenure of office there was posted to Zhob a most unexpected Political Agent, K.P.S. Menon, the Hindu Madrassi who had previously been in Peshawur. He was a remarkable man, at the start of a distinguished career. He liked serving on the Frontier, spoke good Pushtu and had excellent relations with the British officers of the Zhob Militia, his 'private army', and of the regular units in his Agency. But not with the Brigadier, twenty-two stone of self-indulgence and cunning, but a good soldier, a very competent archaeologist and a wonderful shot. Menon wrote of him:

> We began by being on the most friendly terms. One day, however, I received a telegram from him saying, AREA COMMANDER ARRIVES FORT SANDEMAN TOMORROW. WISHES TO SEE YOU IN INSPECTION BUNGALOW AT 11.00 hrs. This sounded like an order and I resented it. I immediately sent a reply: POLITICAL AGENT WILL BE GLAD TO SEE AREA COMMANDER IN WINDSOR CASTLE AT 11.30 hrs. The Brigadier regarded this as an affront, broke off all relations with us and refused to permit the Army horses to take part in the races. During this crisis I was pleased to find that all the military officers in Fort Sandeman were on my side. I reported this incident to Sir Arthur Parsons, and his reply was, 'Well done! That is how I used to treat the Finance Department in Delhi.'

Menon, like everyone else, had a tremendous admiration for Parsons.

> I knew him first in Delhi when he officiated as Foreign Secretary. He came into the Secretariat like a breath of fresh air into an over-heated room. And the air which he brought with him was the crisp, clean, bracing air of the Frontier. Bunch Parsons was a wiry, well-preserved man in his early fifties. There was nothing flabby about his mind, either, which was keen as a razor. It could cut through all obstacles to the heart of a problem. As soon as Bunch came to the Secretariat, files which had been pending for months, and even for years, began to move quickly. Even the Finance Department had a proper respect for him. They knew that he knew his mind; they also knew that he could speak his mind with devastating effect . . . As Benedick said of Beatrice, he spoke poniards, every word stabbed . . . His predecessor was always carefully dressed, and we never dared to appear before him in grey flannels and a tweed coat. Bunch wore nothing else, and

when he became Foreign Secretary, we followed his example. If on any day he saw us in a decent suit, he used to say, 'Ah, lunching out again!' In Baluchistan we always went about, as Bunch did, in mazri* shorts and a shirt.

There were no difficulties in the Fort Sandeman Club, of which the Political Agent was ex-officio President.

The British officers decided to take the risk and were glad to see that I did not keep my wife in purdah or scorn a drink. Anujee, however, continued to be a teetotaller, and whenever she appeared in the Club, our friends would shout, 'Waiter! A strong glass of water for Mrs Menon!'

The tribesmen at first resented the idea of a down-country Hindu ruling over them, and protested to Menon's predecessor, who advised them to wait and see.

They were relieved that I did not wear a loin-cloth or put a caste-mark on my forehead, and that I could speak Pushtu as fluently as any British sahib.

They were, however, puzzled by his daughters, indubitably dark-skinned, but wearing jodhpurs and galloping about on their ponies, unveiled, like brazen Faranghi hussies.

To Parsons Baluchistan seemed very slack. Abetted by Menon, he went through it like a dose of salts. A surprise inspection of the Zhob Militia disclosed that its lorry-tyres lasted half as long as those in Waziristan, though the Zhob roads were much better. By a singular coincidence, the Motor Transport Jemadar – soon to be the ex-Motor Transport Jemadar – was cousin to the garage-proprietor in Fort Sandeman.

It was discovered that the levies (corresponding to Waziristan Khassadars) were not handed their pay direct: it was given to the Maliks who were supposed to pass it on to them. When this was rectified, the roads were better patrolled and safer, but the Maliks resented being deprived of what they had come to consider a legitimate perk. Promotion in the levies, it seemed, was hereditary, irrespective of merit. The adjustment of this matter, too, caused resentment.

I [Menon] strove to reduce the monetary hardships caused by the

*Mazri was the coarse, black-flecked, grey cotton, of which Frontier Corps uniforms were made.

> reforms by persuading Parsons to increase the regular allowance of the Maliks. At the same time I explained to them that in the long run these reforms would work to their own interests: disaffection always throve on legitimate grievances . . . Gradually agitation died down, and when I left Fort Sandeman, I was happy to receive a letter from Parsons saying I had left the Zhob a better place than I found it.

But there was a tragic sequel. Menon's successor was 'Barney' Barnes, expecting an easy ride after South Waziristan. One day a disgruntled levy, passed over for promotion, came into the Political Agent's office and shot Barnes dead. He was the third Political Agent in Zhob to be murdered in thirty years. Menon was saved only by the quick wit of an office orderly who disarmed a tribesman riding up the road with murderous intent. And by pure chance he postponed a journey from a day on which a notorious outlaw was waiting in ambush for him. He was sorry to leave Fort Sandeman, where he had been an undoubted success, and everyone was sorry to see him go. On the day of his departure:

> the Sardars and Maliks escorted us to the border of the Zhob Agency, embraced us in the Pathan style and bade goodbye to us with tears in their eyes. I little dreamt that a time would come when, if I wanted to go to Fort Sandeman, I would have to apply for a visa from a foreign government.

8

The Northern Frontier Agencies

Further north, relations with the Khyber Pass tribes, of which the Afridis were the most powerful, were the responsibility of the Political Agent, Khyber, who lived in Peshawur. Except when the Afridis invaded Peshawur in 1930, it was not an onerous post. For forty years no Government servant, except Afridis on leave, had set foot in the mountainous Tirah, heartland of the Afridis; so long as they did not obstruct traffic through the Khyber Pass, from which they made handsome profits, the tribe was left very much to itself. Relations with the tribes north of Peshawur, of which the strongest were the Mohmands, were a small part of the work of the Deputy Commissioner, Peshawur. So long as they did not bother us, we did not bother them. Only when their behaviour was completely unacceptable, as in 1935, was a punitive expedition sent in. It was really the 'butcher and bolt' policy of the nineteenth century.

Further north the Political Agent for Dir, Swat and Malakand, and his Assistant Political Agent in Chitral, had an enviably easy time. The Nawab of Dir, the Wali of Swat and the Mehtar of Chitral ran their states more or less efficiently (the Wali, most efficiently), and the Politicals could spend a good deal of time playing the local variety of polo and shooting partridges. There was a small enclave of British territory which they governed directly. When the subordinate staff complained that this laid too heavy a work-load on them, B.J. Gould solved the problem by reducing the subordinate staff.

Gilgit, further north still, was 'far-flung', which gave it an aura of romance. It contained the highest fort in the British Empire, at over 19,000 feet, on the Mintaka Pass leading into Chinese Turkestan. It bordered also on Afghanistan, and was separated from Russia only by a strip of Afghan territory five miles wide. Its tribes, Dards and Kanjutis, were not unlike Pathans, but less treacherous. Until defeated in a hard little campaign in 1890, their raiding parties had been the terror of Central Asian caravans. Since then they had been fairly law-abiding, give or take a few score blood-feud murders every year; and they seemed to appreciate the benefits of the loose indirect rule which the British exercised through the rulers of six little kingdoms.

Legally the Gilgit Agency was part of Kashmir State, and up to 1935 it had been a sort of condominium, with the British Political Agent responsible for relations with the kingdoms, and a Kashmir Governor ruling directly the country in the immediate vicinity of Gilgit town, known as the Gilgit Wazarat. In 1935 the Kashmir military and political presence was withdrawn, though its notional sovereignty remained, and the Political Agent was responsible for the entire Agency. It was about 100 miles from north to south and 140 miles from east to west; bounded on the north by the Hindu Kush range and the Pamirs, on the east by the Karakoram Range; on the south by the main Himalayan Range; and on the west by Chitral State and the independent Tribal Territory of Darel and Tangir. It contained eight peaks over 24,000 feet, including the beautiful killer-mountain of Nanga Parbat (26,650 feet).

The Political Agent had his private army, the Gilgit Scouts, of battalion strength, all local tribesmen. Unlike other Frontier Corps they were never in action before 1947, but they played quite an important 'cloak-and-dagger' role in 1917–18. A number of Germans, employed on the China coast, showed great enterprise in trekking right across Central Asia to make trouble for the British in Afghanistan or join Wasmuss, the German equivalent of 'Lawrence of Arabia', in Persia. The Chinese Government, while not exerting themselves to stop them, had no objection to the British trying to do so. The Political Agent therefore stationed a patrol of Gilgit Scouts in the Pamirs, the Roof of the World, in Chinese territory. The havildar in command heard news of a party of Germans making their way through the oases fringing the Gobi desert. In disguise, he intercepted them and, posing as their guide, interpreter and friend, undertook to lead them across the Afghan frontier. Instead, he led them across the Indian frontier, produced a revolver and put them under arrest. He deserved well of the state. To have got so far, they must have been brave and resolute men, who could have done much harm to the Allied cause.

For the journey from Srinagar to Gilgit one had to divide all one's possessions into 80-pound loads, packed in special boxes fitted with rings for slinging on ponies' pack-saddles. It was a fourteen-day journey, riding or walking, fourteen to fifteen miles a day. Nights *en route* were spent in rest-houses infested with bed-bugs.

George Kirkbride, Political Agent, made the journey in 1934 accompanied by his wife, Nancy, his 8-year-old daughter Mary, and his two boys, Mike, aged six, and Tim, aged four. The boys, Mary recollects, were carried in a sort of basket, slung on poles and carried by two porters.

It was jerky and uncomfortable; and although it was freezing at night, the days were hot. My brothers fought incessantly, much to the annoyance of the porters who every now and then went on strike because of the disturbance within the basket.

The first part of the journey was over the 11,000-foot Tragbal Pass and down a glorious valley to the Kishenganga river where flowers and forests abound. I can still in my imagination see the thick white bark peeling off the trunks of the birch trees and smell the foxy scent of codonopsis underfoot. Then on to much harder country with little vegetation save a strong-smelling artemesia, where the valleys were like chasms and, if they did flatten, were stony and bare. The rivers we forded were fiercely flowing and very cold: sometimes pools fringed with tamarisk and willow made pleasant places for our lunches of corned beef sandwiches and dark, nutty chocolate. Another pass we crossed was the 14,000-foot Burzil. To negotiate this before the sun made the snow too soft, we left the bungalow at four in the morning, when it was extremely cold, and we children complained a good deal. At the top the sun appeared and we posed for photographs beside the little hut which soared high above our heads on stilts. This was a shelter for mail carriers during winter when there were 20 feet of snow on the pass. After that we descended over an alpine meadow, serenaded by marmots, until we found a nice place for breakfast. At every village we were greeted by the village band which turned out to meet the new Political Agent. The headmen and elders said polite things, the band was deafening and we children skipped all over the place, a thorough nuisance. The people brought us flat basketware dishes of tomatoes, cucumbers and apricots; there is no fruit in the world so delicious as the Himalayan apricot.

And so we went on, always surrounded by snow-peaks, at one point a glimpse of Nanga Parbat. Often the roads wound up and down steep mountainsides, narrow, rocky and uneven, with a drop of several hundred feet to the torrent below. In some places landslides had carried the road away and a makeshift path had been made of sticks and brushwood. At one point we crossed the Indus, ponies and all, in a large, flat-bottomed boat; at another crossing the ponies had to swim while we were ferried over on a raft made of inflated yak-skins. At last, to the accompaniment of yet another band, the Rajah of Gilgit and many notables, a Scout Guard of Honour, much saluting and hand-shaking, we arrived.

Everyone who served in Gilgit loved it, but it is not a beautiful place. The valley of about six by two miles is fairly stark, and the surrounding mountains are very ordinary except for a glimpse of the shining cone of Haramosh away to the east. There was a certain amount of forest on the mountain to the south of the valley. In the valley were tiny terraced fields, stone walls, stone and mud huts, little apricot orchards and earth roads edged with Lombardy poplars and irrigation channels . . . There was a one-street bazaar, a hospital, the Scouts headquarters and parade ground, polo ground, tennis court and an ancient mud-brick fort. I loved the bazaar – the politely curious people, spicy smells, cheap Japanese toys, rolls of pretty silks and chintzes. Our bungalow was built of stone with a roof of mud tiles. It was almost smothered in climbing roses, including a wonderful Banksian. Our schoolroom opened on to a sunny verandah where pigeons coo-ed and made a lot of messes.

George Kirkbride's young and attractive sister came out as governess to the three unruly children, but not for long. She was soon snapped up by the nicest of the Gilgit Scouts officers and married by her brother, on his lawn, in a bower of Banksian roses and spiraea under a huge chenar tree. The happy couple then galloped off on their honeymoon, sandals tied to their ponies' tails.

The stables behind the house were a source of endless interest, because sheep for the household were butchered there. We were not allowed to watch the butchering, but stared goggle-eyed at the subsequent dismemberment. The head groom was tall, stately and black-whiskered. We were in great awe of him. His underling was a gloomy little man from Nagar (Nagar people are reputed to be gloomy because theirs is the shady side of the valley) but we liked him more because he was sympathetic when things went wrong, as they frequently did for me, for the ponies were quite unschooled. But we did love them, and they were our only form of transport. It was perfectly safe to ride and walk wherever we liked, accompanied always by one of my father's orderlies, Alif Khan. He was far more than our shadow – he was our friend, guide, playmate and guard. If we fought too much, bullied the dogs, spat, teased the servants, or flogged our ponies, we respected his very severe reprimands. There was never any question of us pushing the servants around. The only time my brothers were really beaten was for playing leapfrog over Alif Khan, a devout Moslem, at his prayers . . . At the bungalow gate was a little house occupied by the Gilgit Scouts guard, who turned out with a full salute whenever my father appeared, even when he was only pottering in the garden; but for us and our mother merely came rather languidly to their feet . . .

Polo was one of our chief entertainments. Himalayan polo, played on a long, narrow ground with a wall along each side, is a ferocious affair, with each team's band egging on the players to further ferocity. It was great fun to watch. We sat on canvas chairs on a lovely carpet under an awning, with all the local grandees. My mother dressed up and wore a hat – ties for Mike and Tim and white socks for me. We were most interested in the game when it became really vicious and I, a girl, could not help noticing how incredibly good looking were most of the players in their crisp white shirts, baggy breeches, embroidered waistcoats and kuis. (The kui is a long cylindrical bag of white or beige tweed, rolled up all round until it forms a beret-like hat.) At exciting moments the bands played faster and faster, louder and louder.

'Heb' Todd, Political Agent in the mid-1920s, had come to the Political via Probyn's Horse in Mesopotamia and the Bagdad Police. He was the best polo-player in the service, and his style was much admired in Gilgit, but he was surprised by some features of the local game. There was general agreement that the teams should consist of about six players, and that they should, ideally, be equal in number. But the chukkars were of no fixed length, continuing until a goal was scored. The captain of the scoring team would then gallop down the field holding the ball in his left hand beside his pony's off-side ear: on reaching the half-way line, he dropped the ball and hit it in mid-air with a terrific underhand swipe at the enemy goal, a ploy known as the 'tambuk'. There were no rules against crossing or foul-hooking. A particularly admired trick was to hit the ball at the side-wall, catch it on the rebound and then gallop full-tilt through the enemy goal while the other side tried to drag one to the ground. The best ponies were imported from Badakshan in Russian territory, well-bred, Arab-looking little animals. They galloped hardest when their own band was playing fortissimo.

Brown trout had been introduced to several of the local streams. In Todd's time, with ample feed in virgin water, they grew very large, and it was not difficult to catch half a dozen of a pound or more in a days' fishing. There was good chikor-shooting, and those with superabundant energy could stalk the huge-horned wild goats, markhor and ibex. Todd even shot one of the enormous *ovis poli*, Marco Polo's sheep, which occasionally strayed from the Pamirs into the highest Gilgit pastures.

Summers in Gilgit were hot, and the Political Agent used to migrate to a small wooden house in the Naltar valley, two days' trek away.

> The second day we climbed steadily up and up a narrow valley for about fifteen miles with the air becoming cooler all the time, through trees and flowers, until we suddenly rode over a dusty little pass and there laid out before us was Naltar – Paradise! There were forests of cedar, juniper and pine, alpine flowers, wild roses, an edible wild rhubarb, grassy alps, tumbling streams. The mountains that confined our valley ran up to 16,000 feet and were topped with snow. Avalanches rumbled intermittently during the day. There were ibex and markhor and red bear to be seen on the hillsides, and no other human beings except a few nomadic Gujar shepherds . . . We spent most of the day roaming with Alif Khan or building dams in the streams which would then collapse and release a glorious torrent down the hillside. Sometimes we camped at the head of the valley where there was a tiny ice-cold lake, crystal-clear. We were allowed, rather unwisely I think, to float on this on Lilos.

The Europeans in Gilgit were the Political Agent and Assistant Political Agent, two or three Scouts officers, and the Medical officer, with their families. The doctor treated many patients who had been carried for days across the Hindu Kush or the Pamirs, from Afghan, Russian or Chinese territory. There were a fair number of visitors. In the Kirkbrides' time these included Peter Fleming and Ella Maillart, who had trekked all the way from China; and the irrepressible Packman, on his way back from being Consul-General in Kashgar. (He made a pass at Nancy Kirkbride.) Alec Redpath, Assistant Political Agent in 1939, entertained Eric Shipton, on his way back from hitherto unscaled peaks in the Karakoram, and a rosy-cheeked young man who successfully posed as Ella Maillart – greatly to the annoyance of Shipton who laid on a party for 'her'. Redpath was able to show Sir Aurel Stein a rock inscription commemorating the digging of an irrigation canal in the sixth century. A Turki sericulturist arrived, who started to teach the locals the theory and practice of silk-worm breeding and the production of silk, but then departed with all his fertile silk-worm eggs and left them with the infertile ones. He knew his stuff, all right.

Occasionally a plane would come in from Risalpur, a hazardous performance when machines could not fly high enough for safety but had to zigzag along valleys. Some pilots did not find it as terrifying as the four-mile ride from the airstrip to Gilgit, clinging to the pony's mane. Then, recalls Mary Kirkbride, there would be 'a couple of riotous days, with rough wild games for the boys and possibly a broken heart for me'.

The Political Agent was not overwhelmed with work. He considered it no great disadvantage that for much of the year letters took several weeks to and from his departmental superior, the Resident in Kashmir; and even in summer the telegraph line was often broken. He seldom interfered with the patriarchal sway of the hereditary Mirs of Hunza and Nagar and the Rajahs (not, strictly speaking, hereditary, though succession generally passed from father to eldest son) of Yasin, Punial, Kuh Ghizr and Ishkoman. An occasion when action had to be taken was when several hundred Yasin tribesmen marched on Gilgit to complain against their Rajah. Redpath, with half a dozen policemen and a platoon of Scouts in reserve, stopped them and sent them home; and then conducted in Yasin an enquiry into their grievances – excessive taxation, forced labour and so on. The matter was settled by the old Rajah accepting a golden handshake and being replaced by a kinsman of the young Mir of Nagar, who at home played the part of the wicked uncle but was perfectly satisfied with the new arrangement; as were the Yasinis.

The Political Agent was Sessions Judge, the Assistant Political Agent was District Magistrate, and below him were the Tahsildar and Naib Tahsildar who also had magisterial powers. They dispensed British Indian justice, within the Gilgit Wazarat. Redpath at first thought how nice it would be to have no crafty pleaders to trip him up, but soon found that he missed them: *he* now had to look up precedents and authorities instead of having these politely pointed out to him. Redpath was also in charge of the small police force, not a very onerous task. Stock-theft and the diversion of irrigation water were the most common offences; and the Gilgit Scouts were there to deal with incursions from Tribal Territory or across the Afghan or Chinese borders. Once he had to arrest and deport a turbulent mullah who was agitating, not without reason, against the treatment of his Moslem subjects by the Hindu Maharajah of Kashmir. The mullah and Redpath parted the best of friends. But the man of God was soon in disrepute with the tribesmen whom he had assured, with all his ecclesiastical authority, that if they dug deep enough at the places he indicated, they would strike water. They didn't.

In theory crimes committed within the Gilgit Wazarat were tried by the courts, and crimes committed outside by Jirgas. In fact there was a good deal of flexibility about this. A tribesman from independent Darel pursued his wife and her lover to Gilgit, hacked off their heads and paraded through Gilgit bazaar, swinging the heads by the hair and boasting of acting like a true Moslem. He might have appeared before

Redpath's court, but was handed over to the Darel Jirga and warned never to show his face again in Gilgit lest the 'Mulki Sahib' (the Assistant Political Agent) change his mind.

Jirgas were composed of men whose power depended on prestige, not their prestige on power; they knew the facts and background to most of the cases, and they had to live with their judgments, on which depended their good name and repute.

Redpath was particularly concerned with agricultural matters.

> The best cultivated land was on the alluvial fans where tributary streams joined the main rivers. Rainfall was negligible. Irrigation depended on mountain streams and melting snow and glaciers. The fields were irrigated by water-channels known as kuhls, taking off miles upstream to follow the contours along the hillside at gentler gradients than the parent stream. The local people were very expert in the construction of kuhls, and could estimate with uncanny accuracy at what point upstream the head of a kuhl should be located. One Gilgit kuhl, about eleven miles long, started in one valley and finished in another, after negotiating with a U-turn the long spur between them. In Hunza there were even longer kuhls, some tunnelling through foothills and negotiating precipices at vertiginous heights. The initial alignment of a kuhl, avoiding unstable hillside and inaccessible rock-faces, was selected by local experts standing on the opposite side of the valley shouting instructions and gesticulating to those marking the line. They knew instinctively what gradient was needed to produce a steady flow of water without scouring or silting up the channel. Wooden conduits on cantilever supports driven into crevices were used to traverse rock-faces. Willow-cuttings were planted on kuhl-banks: when these took root, they helped to bind the construction. Several kuhls were constructed by the Public Works Department with proper survey instruments, but these proved less satisfactory than those of the local experts.

Redpath constructed a portable wooden flume which could measure the amount of water passing through a kuhl. With this he hoped to ascertain how much water per acre was required by rice, wheat, barley, maize and fruit-trees. All this was already well known to the elders, but the ritual performances by the 'Mulki Sahib' and his myrmidons provided the locals with endless amusement. He kept a stock of explosives for heavy work in the construction of kuhls, the breaking of boulders and the opening up of new land.

> I sometimes had to settle disputes about grazing-rights, ill-defined but allegedly hallowed by custom. One day I was persuaded after a long ride to climb thousands of feet to a hamlet high on the slopes of Rakaposhi where the parties set me on a bed in a shaded grove of mulberry-, apricot- and apple-trees. They fed me with the most delicious apples and called up a giant with hands like hams to massage my calves and thighs by gripping them so fiercely that I could have yelled with pain. It was bliss when he stopped, and I felt so refreshed that I climbed another thousand feet to a col where, I was assured, I could examine the disputed boundary.

Forestry was another of his concerns. There was a qualified Forest Ranger to deal with experimental nurseries, seedlings, young plantations and culling; but the protection of young trees from goats, the closure of areas to grazing and felling, were the 'Mulki Sahib's' job, and much resented as an encroachment on villagers' rights.

The great event of the year was the Jhalsa, when all the Mirs and Rajahs came in, with their nobles and retainers, to pay tribute in gold-dust washed from local rivers to the representative of the King Emperor and, with reluctance, to the representative of the Maharajah. In return they received presents such as a rifle or a saddle. At the Jhalsa was held the great polo tournament of the year, with rivalry between teams of Hunza and Nagar, Yasin and Punial, so fierce that on occasion the Political Agent had to call a halt lest there be killing. At the end of it the losers had to dance before the winners, a custom which might with advantage be adopted at Cowdray and Smith's Lawn.

The remoteness of Gilgit and the paucity of specialist staff made Politicals there jacks of all trades. Of all Frontier stations, Gilgit was most fun. Officers there were widely envied, except perhaps by their more ambitious colleagues.

9

The States of Rajputana (i)

It was customary in the Indian Political Service for officers in one department to declare that their colleagues in another had nothing whatever to do. Thus Politicals in the states used to say that Politicals in Tribal Territory were virtually unemployed, if not unemployable, while Johnnie Raw, a Frontier Political whose brief experience in the states was under a Resident who failed to establish a satisfactory rapport with him, writes of those concerned with Maharajahs and Nawabs, ceremonies, Darbars and tigers:

> From all one has heard and from what one occasionally gleaned from some friend or acquaintance in the states, nobody, but nobody, had anything like a hard job. The most arduous occupation was the production of a letter that was 'perfect' in all respects. This takes a long time, as you know, especially when a potential split-infinitive obtrudes and the ghastly decision has to be taken whether the offending adverb is to precede or succeed the infinitive, or whether (an alternative hardly to be contemplated) it should, in the most unusual and unavoidable circumstances, end the sentence. It was the making of cruel decisions like this that drove so many to drink.

Raw's was an extreme view, not to be taken without a pinch of salt. It depended on what one meant by 'work'. The job of the Agent to the Governor-General in, say, the Rajputana States resembled in some ways that of an ambassador. Is it 'work' for an ambassador to dine with the head of the state to which he is accredited? It is unlikely to be unalloyed pleasure. Was it 'work' for a Political to spend a day shooting with a Maharajah? It probably was a pleasure, if they got on well together, but it was work too. Good rulers, with nothing to hide, had no doubt about this: they wanted the Agent to the Governor-General or Political Agent to visit their states two or three times a year, and baited the invitations with sport. The Maharawal of Dungarpur, a good ruler of a medium-sized fifteen-gun Rajputana state, explained: 'We all played that game. If a ruler had the Resident for a whole day, the opportunity would arise of putting the state's case for all sorts of things – perhaps a linkage with a British Indian canal system, or the loan of a Forest Officer or land settlement expert; or gaining his sympathy in a dispute with a neighbouring state.' The first duty of a Political officer, as laid down in his Manual of Instructions, was to 'cultivate direct, friendly, personal relations with the Princes with whom he works'. Perhaps that could be done better while shooting or playing tennis than by writing him 'perfect' letters.

Good rulers gave the Resident very little work, apart from semi-social and ceremonial occasions, and advice when it was asked for. Bad rulers gave him a lot of work. During the years 1912–30, as a reaction against the autocratic, interventionist style of Lord Curzon, it was the policy of the Political Department to let well, and even not so well, alone. But the necessity remained of intervening if misrule became so flagrant as to provoke grave discontent, even rebellion, in a state: the government could not be placed in the position of supporting a cruel or grossly incompetent ruler against his outraged subjects. But to establish that the grievances were genuine, and to make a convincing case for imposing a strong Diwan on a bad ruler, or even compelling him to abdicate, required from the Resident a great deal of detailed work, long reports, awkward interviews and investigative tours during which the ruler and his officials would do all they could to divert them from murky corners, and prevent the victims of misrule from complaining to him.

A number of Politicals worked in and for states as Diwans, Finance Ministers or in other capacities. This might be during a prince's minority, or because of a prince's misrule. The work might be interesting, with much responsibility and power; but it was hard, not least because the Diwan was working with colleagues and subordinates who might not be up to British Indian standards and would certainly be unaccustomed to British Indian ways. Furthermore, he might be at variance with the Resident and Political Agent, for his loyalty was to the state, theirs to the Government of India. During a prince's minority he must act with financial prudence, so that the young man should not be in the red at the very start of his reign, but at the same time avoid accumulating money for him to squander as soon as he had control of it. The Diwan had to strike a balance between ruling the state as well as he could, and not altering its essential character: he must not Europeanise it.

Up to about 1912 princes were discouraged, indeed forbidden by their treaties, from dealing with one another except through the Political Department. But they were linked by blood, marriage, common interests and the telephone. They really could not confine their conversations to family affairs and tiger-shooting, and so, in 1921, there was set up the

Chamber of Princes, presided over by the Viceroy. It consisted of 108 rulers of states of eleven guns or more, sitting in their own right, and twelve representing 127 states of nine guns or fewer. A small Standing Committee did such work as there was to do.

The Chamber had no power, even over its own members. Being purely advisory, it was little more than a sounding board for the princes' grievances against the Political Department. The larger states were resentful at having to debate against, and perhaps be out-voted by, the small fry. Hyderabad, largest of the states, never joined the Chamber: Kashmir, Mysore and Travancore joined but soon left it. But for princes who were well educated, articulate in English and furnished with committee skills, it provided a stage on which they seemed more significant than the importance of their states warranted. The Nawab of Bhopal, the Maharajahs of Bikanir, Patiala and Alwar, the Jam Saheb of Nawanagar ('Ranji', cricket captain of Sussex and England) all enhanced their public images by dominating debates about nothing in particular and being elected by their fellow-princes to the prestigious office of Chancellor to the Chamber. But when they collectively tried to establish some definition of Paramountcy, a matter on which they all felt very strongly, they did not get far: the last thing the Political Department wanted was to define this invaluable all-purpose concept. A committee was set up to report on the working of Paramountcy. Great was the rulers' pleasure when they learned that it was to be chaired by Sir Harcourt Butler, who they assumed would accept their point of view that Paramountcy derived from a contract made between equally sovereign states, a contract that had been grievously extended and abused by the Political Department over the past hundred years. To put their case they engaged a British barrister, Sir Leslie Scott, and an American, whose fees alone exceeded £100,000. Great was their disappointment when the Butler Committee, while soft-soaping princely rule in general, and agreeing that Paramountcy could not be transferred from the Crown to the Government of India, accepted the Political Department's contention on the main issue that Paramountcy was not an arrangement between equals but had been imposed on the states, *de haut en bas*; that any extensions to it had been sanctified by usage and the general benefit; and that it was incapable of definition. 'Paramountcy,' the princes were informed, 'must remain paramount.'

One useful procedure emerged from discussions in the Chamber. It was manifestly unfair that a ruler could be compelled to abdicate, or to hand over the running of the state to his son or to ministers chosen by the Political Department, without any form of enquiry by his peers. It was agreed that a ruler against whom such action was contemplated could demand that his case be referred to a panel of ruling princes for enquiry and recommendation. In fact this was seldom done: an erring prince would not want his dirty linen to be washed by members of his order. But the threat was useful: 'Either you quietly accept His Excellency's advice, or there will have to be a formal Enquiry.'

Indian nationalists in the nineteenth century tended to regard the princes as potential allies against the British. By 1919 that view had changed. Nationalist leaders had all been nurtured in English-speaking schools on the Liberal Interpretation of History: Kings = bad; parliaments = good, especially parliaments in which Liberals can be sure of a majority. The princes, they believed (not without reason), were cherished by the British as rivals to the politicians and as obstacles to India's advance to independence. The Indian National Congress did not openly operate in a state against its ruler: they may have reflected that such a course might lead to more unpleasant consequences to themselves than would agitation and civil disobedience in British India. Instead, they set up within the states political parties known generally as 'Praja Mandals', ostensibly composed only of subjects of the state, and loyal to the ruler, but in fact directed by Congress leaders in the neighbouring British Indian provinces. So during the 1920s, with Paramountcy being exercised less onerously than in the past, the princes saw Political officers less as interferers, more as protectors.

Perhaps the most interesting posting for a Political officer was to the Rajputana States. Most of the rulers were pretty good, some very good, and most were gentlemen of character and charm. States were of viable size, with populations ranging from 2.5 million (Jaipur) to 630,000 (Kotah). Only one was much smaller in population, the desert state of Jaisalmer (population 76,000). They were comparable in size to largish districts in British India, which experience had shown to be of the optimum size to be run by one man. (Districts in the United Provinces averaged about 1 million, the largest being 3 million.)

The Agent to the Governor-General, or Resident, Rajputana, was stationed at Ajmere during the cold weather and at Mount Abu during the hot. He had under him the Political Agent for (six) Eastern Rajputana States, and the Residents (a courtesy title: their real status was Political Agent) for Mewar (Udaipur), Jodhpur and Jaipur, each of whom conducted relations also with several smaller states.

Leonard Reynolds was Resident at Jodhpur just after the First World War, during the minority of the Maharajah, Umaid Singh. Regent of the state was the boy's uncle, Sir Pratap Singh, a Rajput Bayard, *chevalier sans peur et sans reproche*, back from commanding the Jodhpur Lancers in France and Palestine. He was fluent in Hindi, Urdu and Persian, erratic in English, but could read not a word in any language because he considered literacy to be the accomplishment of babus. He used to say that he had only two ambitions, to die for the King Emperor in a cavalry charge, and to chase the last Moslem out of India. He was far from being the traditional wicked uncle of boy-rulers, but did rather overshadow his young nephew, so Lord Curzon made him fill the vacant throne of the smaller state (fifteen-gun) of Idar. He greatly preferred being the *éminence grise* in Jodhpur, but Lord Curzon said firmly, 'To Idar I have sent him, and in Idar he will remain.' Lord Curzon was wrong: Pratap Singh (who had a private line to Queen Victoria, Edward VII and George V) was soon back in Jodhpur. He never married, lest his legitimate sons become Pretenders to the Jodhpur throne, but had two famous sons, Hanut Singh and Abhey Singh, the best polo-players in the world. Their status in Jodhpur was that of well-born slaves, for their mothers, although of good Rajput stock, were concubines, not wives; they owned nothing, not even the magnificent polo-ponies which they trained and rode in India, England, France, the Argentine and the United States. Pratap Singh made the Jodhpur polo-teams the best in India. He sometimes used to watch practice chukkars, standing among the saises with a blanket over his head, to see which young nobles did not bother to turn up to practise when word went round that he was not watching from the stand.

During his school holidays the young Maharajah was always in and out of the Residency. One year Lady Reynolds had a Christmas tree for the Railway Eurasian children, and the boy Maharajah happened to turn up.

> He has never seen a Christmas tree and was delighted with it, taking toys from it and giving them to the children. Some disgruntled Brahmins decided that he had been induced to take part in Christian rites and sent a petition to the Viceroy against my husband, saying that he had pig-like eyes in an arrogant face and I was the devilish Eve sitting beside him.

Maharajah Umaid Singh was a Biggles fan, and, as soon as he was old enough, took his pilot's licence and bought two light planes. It was more than an expensive hobby. He constructed an airfield near his capital which was used regularly by Imperial Airways and brought useful revenue to the state. In the Second World War it was a pilots' training centre.

Among the Reynolds' social ordeals was to be photographed between two large tigers held by servants on chains. 'They smelt horrible.'

Reynolds went on to Jaipur as President of the Council of Regency during that Maharajah's minority. When the boy, always known as 'Jai', was twelve, he was married to a Jodhpur princess. After the splendid ceremonies, the processions of elephants, the bridegroom wearing a wonderful pearl headdress, he went straight back to school and his princess came to live in what was now her own palace in Jaipur. There she was extremely bored, so Reynolds gave her a pianola; this her attendants sabotaged, although she loved to play, because music-making was for the lower orders. It wasn't much fun being a married child-princess with a husband away at school.

At an early meeting of the Council of Regency Reynolds opened a file concerning the remuneration for the wet-nurse of the latest palace baby, born of one of 'Late His Highness's' widows.

'I suppose this is all right,' he said, 'if it is the custom. How much is she paid?'

'Eight rupees a month.'

'Well, anything customary must of course be paid. Is that all?'

'Not quite, Sahib. The same for her husband, and clothes for them both, and food from the palace kitchen.'

'Oh well, as it is only for a short time, I suppose we must pass it. For how long is it customary to pay these allowances?'

'For seven generations, Sahib.'

'Late His Highness' left over 400 wives of sorts.

When Jai grew up, he too formed a famous polo-team. He trained as a soldier and fought on the Frontier, but was not allowed to go to the Second World War. In the Indian Army List he ranked as a Captain, indicating that he was a real soldier, unlike all those princes who held exalted, but purely honorary rank. He married *en troisièmes noces* a beautiful and accomplished lady with a rare talent for public relations. His former tutor came on a visit and was invited to breakfast in the princely bedroom, where he found His Highness cosily sitting up in bed between his three Maharanis.

He was a good ruler, but had trouble with a rebel baron who shut himself up in his castle and defied his liege lord in the matter of his son's education. A battalion of the Jaipur State Forces besieged the castle for three months; and Walter Magor, Under Secretary to the Agent to the Governor-General, was sent to exercise his diplomatic skills and raise the siege without bloodshed. This he did, for everyone concerned was anxious to end a situation which was farcical and embarrassing. Some months later Magor was most hospitably entertained by the rebel baron, now restored to favour, and regaled with the Rajput drink, 'Asa', said to be distilled from partridges and pearls and best taken after trickling over a very large piece of ice.

To the British public the most familiar Rajput ruler was Maharajah Ganga Singh of Bikanir, who had been a member of Lloyd George's Imperial War Cabinet, and had attended the Versailles Peace Conference. He *looked* the part, with his burly figure and bristling moustache. His repute was, perhaps, higher outside than inside his state, but one great work he did. Appalled by the horrors of a local famine, he had used all his influence, and his contacts as A.D.C. to the King Emperor, to have a diversion to his state from the Jhelum canal system in the Punjab. This he extended year after year so that the barren desert changed into rich, green, wheat-growing prairie. His bait for Viceroys and such was the famous Bikanir sand-grouse shoot, with the bag counted in thousands. His state was so efficiently run that cadets of other Rajput houses used to be sent to Bikanir for administrative training. But it was the efficiency of a benevolent despot, who deprived others of power and influence until he was the sole ruler – not quite appropriate to the twentieth century, at least before Mussolini's time. Walter Magor accompanied the Agent to the Governor-General on a tour to Bikanir for the Maharajah's Golden Jubilee: the Viceroy, Lord Linlithgow, was also there.

> One day we waited half an hour for His Highness to arrive for luncheon. He came, and apologised jovially, 'So sorry to keep you waiting, Your Excellency, I've just been sacking a brace of Ministers.' There was a banquet the last evening, and as one of the junior guests I had to be content to eat off silver plate: only the top forty ate off gold. An A.D.C. came to tell the Maharajah that the Viceroy's special train was waiting, to which the Maharajah replied, 'Tell the Station-master that His Excellency will be ready to leave in about an hour's time.' So much for railway timetables.

Although no Indian state had any genuinely democratic institutions, few rulers could emulate Bikanir and enjoy absolute power. He who tried to govern without the support of his nobles would soon find himself in difficulties, with the Resident asking awkward questions. Bikanir, however, as a personal friend of the King, was virtually untouchable: he could have got away with anything, and it is perhaps to his credit that he did not take more advantage of this.

Among Rajputs, Maharana Fatteh Singh of Udaipur had more prestige than all the other rulers put together. In 1920 he had ruled for thirty years. His nineteen-gun state, properly called Mewar but more generally known as Udaipur after his capital city, was neither large, rich nor powerful. His prestige stemmed from the descent of his Sesodiah clan from the Sun (other Rajput clans were descended from the Moon) and from the long, desperate struggle of Mewar against the Moguls. Their ancient capital, Chitor, had stood two lengthy sieges, each ending with a sortie of every man and boy able to bear arms, dressed in saffron robes of sacrifice, all of whom were killed, while their wives, sisters and daughters walked in procession into the great burning ghats below the castle. Thereafter the House of Mewar, alone among Rajput families, never gave a princess in marriage to the Mogul.

Fatteh Singh was a pale-faced, fork-bearded aristocrat with charm and dignity. He had refused, pleading illness, to attend Lord Curzon's Darbar lest he have to take precedence behind twenty-one gun parvenus like Hyderabad and Baroda. He had consented to go to Delhi for the Coronation Darbar of 1911, and had paid a courtesy private visit to the King Emperor, for whom as a fellow monarch (albeit of somewhat recent provenance) he had quite cordial feelings; but had again pleaded illness when it came to the public ceremonies. While other princes in Delhi flaunted their magnificent pavilions with silken hangings and Persian carpets, themselves and their nobles splendid in brocades and pearls, carrying swords with jewelled hilts and scabbards, Fatteh Singh and his nobles wore the same white jodhpurs and coats as they wore at home, their plain-hilted swords in black leather scabbards. In his reception tent, a rather shabby marquee, the furniture consisted of two bent-wood chairs for himself and any visitor who might call. Few presumed to do so: rulers of lesser lineage, such as Pratap Singh of Kashmir (twenty-one-gun) would have given their eyes for an invitation. His life-style was spartan and frugal. He had a horror of running into debt and would never borrow money. His full names, titles and decorations, in Hindi, Persian and English, would take up three or four lines of a large envelope; but an envelope thus addressed would be returned by the Udaipur Post Office, 'Addressee unknown'. The proper way to address it was to 'Himself, Udaipur'.

It was customary, almost obligatory, for a prince to keep scores of nautch-girls, but Fatteh Singh was a man of the strictest morals, devoted to his Maharani. He was also far too kind-hearted ever to sack these ladies. So year after year on state and social occasions these elderly coryphées tottered through their dance routines, sere and withered as irises in December, to the polite approbation of bored nobles.

He was rigidly conservative. The state's motto, 'Let the old never be blotted out, let no new thing ever come to pass', might have served for his own. He sacked one Diwan for introducing Girl Guides into the state. In 1920 he presided, as the apex of society, over the world's last completely feudal state. His chief nobles had their hundred or more villages apiece, and their castles along the frontier for the policing and defence of the realm. At fixed intervals they rode into the capital with their contingents of horse and foot for their spells of feudal service, each with his sword at his side, his shield slung on his back, his bard singing the glories of his line. Rajputs of lesser degree held their lands from the great nobles, rent-free by virtue of military service. Wealthy religious foundations held great estates: one 'Abbot' was striking his own coinage, in defiance of his liege lord the Maharana. At harvest time troops of horse would ride out with lance, automatic pistol and straight cut-and-thrust sword, to protect the crops of their Jat tenants against the wild, jungle-dwelling Bhils. 'My blood, drop for drop, against your sweat,' expressed the feudal bargain. Should they kill a Bhil, they left it where it lay, no questions asked.

One cannot emphasise too strongly the liking and admiration in which Maharana Fatteh Singh was held by the Agent to the Governor-General, the Viceroy, the King Emperor himself. An agonising dilemma therefore faced the Agent to the Governor-General, R.E. Holland, when he realised in 1921 that the state was shockingly misgoverned. In the words of Donald Field, the Resident at Udaipur, 'His Highness's dignity, courtesy and charm are famous, and his character in many ways admirable. Unfortunately his disposition is such that all state business withers at his touch.'

The basic trouble, as Holland reported to the Political Secretary, Sir John Wood, was that the Maharana would delegate not the smallest detail of administration; but although he worked very long hours, day-in, day-out, taking time off only for shikar, he was too old at 72 to see to everything himself. His officials, underpaid and unsupervised, were tyrannical and corrupt. The Customs Department was notorious for mismanagement and extortion. The Court of Wards, supposed to manage the estates of minors, was a gold-mine for those who worked in it. Educational services were almost non-existent, and there were only thirteen ill-equipped dispensaries to serve 1.25 million people. The Public Works Department was useless, and the roads appalling. The

12 The Mir of Hunza's palace at Baltit

13 The Maharao of Bundi's palace, Rajputana

14 Maharana Fatteh Singh of Udaipur

judicial system had almost ceased to function, because the Maharana insisted on reviewing himself hundreds of petty cases. There were 30,000 cases pending, and prisoners were held in jail for years without being brought to trial. Begar – compulsory, unpaid labour on public works – was grossly abused by minor officials. There was widespread damage to crops by wild animals, but the Game Laws would have earned the approval of William Rufus. The most urgent need was for a property land settlement, with rents assessed in cash to replace a medley of ancient and obsolete feudal dues.

All this had resulted in agrarian troubles, including a No Rent campaign by Jat tenant farmers. The nobles were exasperated beyond endurance by His Highness's harassment for petty details of ceremonial observance. A First Class Noble was punished for a sneeze at a Darbar by the excision from his estates of two villages. Discontent might well blow up in rebellion, in which case, wrote Holland, 'The Government cannot support with force an administration so wholly incompetent and out of touch with the needs of the people.' The whole situation was a gift to Congress agitators. 'A really good case against a state like Udaipur would be a powerful weapon in their hands.'

What should be done about it? The Political Department could not announce publicly the reasons for any action it might take against so renowned a figure as the Maharana. To do so would discredit the whole princely order, and undermine the Department's argument – indeed its very *raison d'être* – that the benevolent autocracy of the princes suited Indians better than Western democracy. Other rulers were quietly sounded. The Maharajahs of Bikanir and Alwar thought that the Government must intervene. The possibility was considered of persuading the Maharana to accept an experienced British Diwan to re-model the whole administration and redress the people's grievances; but this would have been very galling to His Highness, and aligned on his side an incongruous partnership of his fellow-princes, Congress and the vernacular press.

The matter was brought to a head in the spring of 1921 by a Bhil rebellion, when the Maharana was obliged to ask H. Wilkinson, who was then Resident at Udaipur, for the help of the Mewar Bhil Corps, a para-military force controlled by the Agent to the Governor-General. Sir Robert Holland visited the state and offered the astonished and outraged Maharana the choice between a Commission of Enquiry into the administration, or of retaining his title and honours, but handing over the detailed administration to his eldest son, Maharaj Kumar Bhupal Singh, an able little man but a cripple paralysed in both legs, generally known as 'Bapji'. Under strong protest, the Maharana chose the latter alternative. At the same time, also with the greatest reluctance, he consented to employ an experienced I.C.S. officer to conduct a land settlement of the state. The choice fell on C.G. ('Jack') Chenevix Trench, brother of R.H. ('Dick') Chenevix Trench, who was then Political Agent at Fort Sandeman. He was not a member of the Political Department but was, his brother assured him, 'temporarily promoted to the Elect'. He came on a two-year contract, nearly resigned after nine months, and stayed for thirteen years, learning more about Udaipur than had any other European.

Holland took this firm line with great reluctance.

> I had always hoped that things would not come to a head in his lifetime and that his subjects would bear the yoke until he had been gathered to his fathers . . . Subjects of Indian states will stand a great deal from their rulers because the sentiment of loyalty is so strong. When they rebel it is because their patience has been strained to breaking-point. The prestige and influence of the Maharana of Udaipur is greater than that of any other prince because he is 'the descendant of the Sun' and 'Diwan of Eklinga', i.e. Regent of God on earth. The rebellion of his people was therefore of deep significance. It was very repugnant to me as an old friend of His Highness and a great admirer of his many remarkable qualities, to have to recommend stringent action against him, but there was no alternative. I do not believe he will take it much to heart. He has the iron-bound complacency of one who is God's Regent. So long as he can preserve the atmosphere of mediaeval adulation in which he lives, he will regard everything else as a passing show, remembering that his ancestors endured far worse things at the hands of the Mohammadan invaders.

Holland was wrong on one thing. His Highness did take it very much to heart. First he offered Holland (indirectly, through a banker) a large bribe to let him off the hook: 'My respect and sympathy for His Highness has been materially lessened by this.' Next he obstructed, craftily and ceaselessly, the reforms which Bapji and Trench were trying to introduce.

Although he was supposed to have resigned the government to Bapji, he retained massive negative powers. Minor officials were still terrified of him, and dragged their feet in any measure of which he signified disapproval. According to Wilkinson:

> His Highness has wielded absolute power for many years and is determined not to part with it . . . It is a matter of common knowledge that his influence is paramount, though the Maharaj Kumar [Bapji] does not admit it. His Highness does not regard the settlement as final and hopes that his powers will be restored to him. The feeling is abroad in the state that his hope will be fulfilled, with the result, as the Maharaj Kumar has informed me, that officials hesitate to take any action in furtherance of the Maharaj Kumar's plans for improvement, knowing that they would render themselves the objects of His Highness's displeasure hereafter.

His methods of obstruction were clever. He demanded to see a certain class of revenue file before action was taken on it. It seemed a reasonable request: how could it be refused to one who was still, after all, the Maharana? 'But,' wrote Wilkinson, 'at a moderate estimate these files will number 20,000 to 30,000. It is obvious that what he wishes to do is to retain all the files and block the very important enquiry which is now taking place.'

Trench ascertained that all the miscellaneous feudal dues supposed to be paid by the cultivators to their liege lords amounted to four times the Central Provinces' Land Revenue; but they were simply not being paid, to the great distress of the landlords. There were over 8,000 files on arrears pending for orders. There was no proper registration of revenue cases, so that reminders were either not sent, or were ignored with impunity. But a cultivator, chosen at random or the object of an official's spite, could be ruined by the demand for several years' rent in a single payment. Congress agitators made the most of this. As one First Class Noble, almost ruined by the No Rent Campaign, complained to Trench, 'The cunnings, who fear to meet me face-to-face, are playing higgledy-piggledy on my backside.' The chaos was most lucrative to officials who declined to work hard to clear arrears.

The Maharana constantly petitioned the Viceroy for the restitution of his ruling powers, insisting that all the charges against him were fabricated by agitators. At the same time he fought his son, 'that cripple' as he habitually called him, on two fronts. During the cold weather Udaipur, a famous beauty spot, was visited by many influential people – peers, Members of Parliament and revered English Establishment figures. By deploying all his charm and providing for them panther- and duck-shoots and other entertainments, he built up a powerful lobby in England. The Secretary of State for India was bombarded with letters demanding that justice be done to this grand old man. At the same time he instigated and financed a vicious campaign against 'that cripple' in the vernacular press. Most Rajput princes thought that the Maharana, doyen of their order, had been harshly treated. Ignoring his loyalty to the Crown, his lifetime of unremitting diligence, the British were guilty of the worst crime in the Rajput calendar: 'Forgetfulness of favours'. Was he extravagant, immoral, sadistic? Far from it. Then why render miserable the last years of his life? As for Bapji, lending himself to the persecution of his own father, could anything be more abominable?

This went on for years. In 1928 Trench wrote to Holland, who was by then Political Secretary:

> I should like to do a little agitation on Bapji's behalf. We know the trend of agitation at home in favour of H.H. Out here the stream of calumny and obscene abuse of the son has redoubled and Bapji's nerves are beginning to feel the strain. Some of the vernacular papers are simply too disgusting to read – marriage of a cripple and so forth. His own order is against him, pillorying him as an unnatural son who goes against his own father. His only friends are the 1.25 million state subjects, for whom it will be a black day if the old man is ever given back his powers. Even now that terrible old man wrecks everything he touches. There is an excellent scheme for providing pure water for Udaipur City, quite cheap. For months H.H. has been refusing his sanction to the work, not caring a pin if his subjects die of cholera or rot with guinea-worm. He delays settlements of land-grants, his private informers torture and extort. Bapji is certain that the most disgusting paragraphs in the press were paid for by his father.
>
> Bapji is not a debauchee, nor a spendthrift, nor an incompetent noodle, but a hard-working, canny little man who does his best under great difficulties. He has pulled off quite a respectable programme of reform and wants to do more. H.H.'s lot are having it all their own way in the propaganda line. The idea that his subjects wish to see his powers restored is sheer myth.

Yet to put Bapji's case in public, and counter the Maharana's propaganda, would do the states and the princely order an infinite amount of harm, and Congress a great deal of good.

Holland forwarded Trench's defence of Bapji to the Permanent Secretary to the Indian Office with a covering letter: 'Trench is absolutely reliable and is doing devoted service to Udaipur. He is the only European in the state in the position to know the whole truth.' The Permanent Secretary minuted to the Secretary of State, 'If it were possible to restore the Maharana's izzat* (without restoring any of his powers) it would probably be popular with the Rajputana princes. But this account of the old man's behaviour does not encourage one to be sympathetic.'

Nevertheless the land settlement was producing results. With land revenue assessed in cash, and with all the curious feudal dues abolished, the cultivator could grow what he pleased and what suited his soil, not what was forced on him by custom such as lucerne for his lord's horses, to say nothing of first fruits, three days' free ploughing of his lord's land and free carting of his lord's hay. Trench could write in 1928:

> Revenues for the year are a record and much wheat is exported. The new market and town of Bhikwam is booming. My new cotton, the Government Economic Botanist says, is the finest in India, burst bolls as big as oranges. Bombay traders are badgering me for a monopoly. Nothing doing! We are working up to 10,000 bales a year.

After several requests for the restitution of his powers had been refused by successive Viceroys, the situation was resolved by Fatteh Singh's death in 1930.

As Maharana, Bapji ruled well, and 'Heb' Todd found the post of Resident at Udaipur the easiest and most pleasant in the service, which it had not been in the 1920s.

The Resident at Udaipur had no problem states. His main concern, in many ways, was the ceaseless stream of visitors during the cold weather, on official business and on leave, colleagues and friends and unknown friends of friends. For six months he and his family seldom had the house to themselves. And what a house it was! Very old, white-washed, thick-walled, cool and airy, with large bedrooms, and all mod cons installed for a visit by the Prince of Wales. It was set in a superb garden. At the start of the garden year in October there were cannas in profusion, several kinds of hibiscus, allamanda with clean and clear yellow flowers. Then came asters, flowering cork-trees and potato-trees. At Christmas the roses were at their best. In January the annuals were all in flower – hollyhocks, candytuft, phlox and many more. In March the rust-coloured, purple and red Bougainvillaea put up a terrific show of colour, with babul trees, flame-of-the-forest, sky-blue jacaranda, scarlet-flowered bottle-brush trees, pink cassia and gold mohur trees.

There were five tennis-courts in the Residency garden. Tennis was a

*Honour, the respect in which one is held.

game of which Udaipur Rajputs were passionately fond. Twice a week it was open house at the Residency, and the Sardars arrived in their white jodhpurs, tunics down to the knee and small, tight Udaipur turbans, each carrying a curved sword in black leather scabbard, followed by a bearer with his tennis-racket. Changing sword for racket, tucking shirt into jodhpurs, they would play a terrific game. Bapji liked watching. He suffered from bladder-trouble, and when he had to be carried away to relieve himself, the games stopped until he returned.

Udaipur was one of the sights of India. The Maharana's snow-white palace towered beside Pichola lake (not so snow-white close to); Jagmandir, the little island palace on Pichola where the Mutiny refugees were accommodated and guarded, was a gem; and most visitors wanted to see the ancient, ruined, haunted fortress-town of Chitor.

In his role of pseudo-Political, Trench was invited to the seventeen-gun Rajput state of Bundi, to arbitrate a dispute between the Maharao and a land-development syndicate. He found Bundi:

> a very beautiful and sinister little capital, huddled in a red-hot valley, with a marvellous honey-coloured fort and palace on one side, the town on the other, and a lake in between. In age and prestige the Maharaos of Bundi come very near to the Maharanas of Udaipur, but the formality of Udaipur is wanting here, which is refreshing. The Maharao drops in for a drink in the evening and goes out with only three or four attendants. He is a good naturalist and a great shikari, but the tigers which he meets on his evening drives he never shoots. They come to within a mile of the palace and swarm like hares in a Wiltshire preserve. Imagine a bustling small town about the size of Godalming and three tigers not a mile away, any number a little further off. None of them man-eaters. The ruler is a very decent fellow, but drinks two bottles of gin a day and has a liver the size of a horse's. I saw no signs of worse-for-liquor. His predecessor's portrait in the palace is remarkable, an extremely handsome savage, pure Greek type, with long forked beard and almost white face. In one of the last suttees ninety-four wives were burnt with the ruler, all of whose portraits are carved on a pillar in the royal burning-place. They took their last bath in a garden pool, then descended into a masonry pit roofed over with sandalwood logs. If suttee were permitted today, hundreds of women would follow their example . . . I am being used as a pawn. They and we have been dead cuts for 160 years, three Bundi rulers having killed three of our Maharanas, by treachery, on hunting excursions along the border, while we have killed only two of

theirs. So they are one-up. But both now want to make friends, so my being here will be used as a pretext for their Maharao writing to our Maharana thanking him for lending my services, and so start rolling the ball of friendship. The real snag is whether he should make a two-handed salaam to our Maharana or a one-handed one, and the records of 300 years are being searched for precedents. But the very idea of our Maharana going down there for a tiger-shoot turns our hair grey. The old madness might seize some Bundi fanatic. At the last fatal meeting the Maharao speared his guest from behind as they rode out to a beat. It comes over them just like that.

Touring in the early 1920s was often by trotting-camel, a swift and comfortable ride. Sometimes when riding across the desert one would hear a sound like a cricket. But it was not a cricket: it was the ghost of a bulbul (singing bird) which sang there long ago when all the naked desert was green. Less often one marched beside the Hamrikab, that ghostly rider who keeps pace with the traveller, mile after weary mile. The padding of the cushioned feet, the creak of the harness, the heavy, honey-sweet odour from the black patch of sweat exuding from behind his camel's ears – one could hear and smell it all. Trench had a superb riding-camel named Aganbot. One day he and the Resident decided to cut miles off a long ride by man-handling Aganbot down a steep escarpment. A stout, nine-foot plank with a long rope attached to each end was slung round his neck so that it hung across his chest, and six strong men were detailed to hang on to each rope. Then came the agonising business of lowering the ungainly beast down the cliff.

'Oh, my darling!'

'Oh, my uncle!'

'Proceed with extreme caution, my pearl!'

'The she-camels await thee at the bottom . . .'

Then, as he gave a lurch, the most appalling aspersions on the chastity of his female relatives, past, present and to come. When it was all over he was shaking like a jelly and had to be restored with smelling-salts, in his case asafoetida.

Touring by rail, horse and camel gave place inevitably to touring by car. It was the Agent to the Governor-General, Residents and Political Agents who did most of the touring: the Agent to the Governor-General's understrappers (Secretary, Under Secretary and Personal Assistant) were employed mainly on the dogsbody jobs in Ajmere and Mount Abu – court work, revenue, general administration. How much they were taken out on tour depended on the personality of the Assistant to the Governor-General – and, no doubt, of the understrapper.

Alex Redpath was lucky: his master, Sir George Ogilvie, took him about a great deal. He was 'captivated' by these ancient Rajput States.

> Some had traces of sophisticated town-planning and scientific research. Raja Jai Singh III of Jaipur in the early 1700s planned beautiful buildings, wide thoroughfares and a complicated series of structures for observing and recording astronomical measurements and predictions which modern astronomers find accurate and far-reaching. The Rajput princes were proud of their heritage.

At Jaipur too was the ancient fortress of Ranthambore, perched on a precipitous rock with a steep path zigzagging up it. One ascended by elephant, the sagacious pachyderm feeling every step with the tip of his trunk; and descended, probably, on foot.

> It was a delight to see Jaysalmere, a remote desert-city dominated by a fort perched on an ochre-hued jurassic escarpment. The battlements, almost secular Gothic in style, consisted of 101 massive, linked, crenellated towers. Inside were the palace and state apartments, and below the ramparts, the town. The first sight of the fort rising ethereally out of the desert with a hazy rose-tinted sunset behind was unforgettable. It was the only Rajput state which had never been conquered by the Moguls, and had in the fort a priceless collection of Jain religious documents taken there for safety.

But Redpath had a social conscience, and was shocked by the extravagant ceremonial and hospitality in a land where there was so much povery. 'The disparity between rich and poor and its tacit acceptance by Indians of all levels seemed to be rooted in the caste system and in feudalism.'

To what extent did a Resident or Political Agent on tour really see a state 'warts and all'? John Cotton doubts whether a touring officer ever saw anything which the ruler preferred to remain unseen.

> Any tour in Rajputana or Kathiawar was most carefully stage-managed. The ruler was always present in person in the capital, and outside it some high state official would act as conductor. I remember being told when I went with Lothian to Bikanir that the hygienic, well-staffed and well-equipped hospital had been carefully filled the day before with hand-picked and grateful patients. The object of this deception was to get more money, not for His Highness but for the hospital. The Jam Saheb of Nawanagar was an artist at handling

> visiting Politicals. There was always a full programme of shoots, golf and cricket matches, tennis tournaments, picnics and state banquets, but I do not remember ever visiting the harbour and docks to look at the dhow traffic.
>
> As to how the Resident learned what was going on, in Kathiawar he was kept pretty well aware by Indian Deputy Political Agents who were an astute band of men and toured continually. There must have been mischievous, self-seeking informers. I fancy rulers themselves were not averse to telling tales about their fellow-rulers.

One seldom, said Cyril Hancock, got good news of what was happening, but bad news travelled like the wind. Although lent officers, and freelance officers serving the states, saw their principal loyalty as being to the state, there were many who did not consider it disloyal to keep the Resident informed if things were going really badly. But Residents had no regular spies, which perhaps explains how it was sometimes not realised how badly a state was being ruled until it either went bankrupt and had to ask the Government to bail it out, or the ruler's subjects rebelled.

The Maharawal of Dungarpur, however, gave a rather different picture.

> There was nothing that a Political officer could not do or demand on visiting a state. What he did not know about the public and private life of a ruler was not worth knowing. He was constrained by good manners, usage and sufferance. Good manners apart, Political officers were usually reasonable.

Clearly the practice varied from state to state, and according to personalities. Dungarpur would have nothing to hide: some rulers would.

Ajmere contained the holiest Moslem place in India, the Dargah Mosque. It attracted hundreds of thousands of pilgrims, and the Chief Commissioner in the North-West Frontier Province used to send his spies there to learn what was happening on the Frontier. Lady Reynolds describes an extraordinary scene:

> Money having been given by some rich pilgrim for the poor, huge cauldrons were filled with boiling rice, meat and spices, and men jumped in to dish this out. Their arms and legs were bandaged to prevent scalding, and with the dense steam rising it was like a scene from Dante's *Inferno*.

At Mount Abu, the Assistant to the Governor-General's summer headquarters, pleasantly cool at about 4,000 feet, Lady Reynolds experienced:

> frequent noisy earthquakes, but they did no harm. There was a beautiful lake and often a family of otters were to be seen swimming fast behind one another and making a great swirl like a long sea-serpent. I sat up one night with the Magistrate for a supposed panther kill. We sat on the ground, in a hollowed-out cactus-bush. After a long wait there appeared close to us a tiger. There was nothing we could do but let him have his noisy meal and depart, for tiger-shooting there had been banned by the Maharao.

For the cold weather, while the Resident and Secretary were in Ajmere or on tour, the Under Secretary remained in Mount Abu, monarch of all he surveyed. John Cotton, soon after his marriage, had an impressive string of titles:

> District Magistrate, Civil Judge, Chief Forest Officer, Chairman of the Municipal Committee, Secretary of the Gymkhana Club and the Golf Club . . . The Civil Station, covering an area of about sixteen square miles, was an enclave, leased to the Indian Government by the Maharao of Sirohi whose territories surrounded it on all sides. In addition to the Resident's mansion, it contained the offices of his considerable staff located in a huge and sombre building known as 'the Bastille'. The bungalows of the officers and many small palaces belonging to various ruling princes of Rajputana and Kathiawar, who normally spent the hottest months with their families and retainers there, dotted the valleys and hilltops of the enclave. It was not the climate, or the scenery which attracted them to Abu. A ruler without a palace there would lose face with his fellow-princes who might, moreover, steal a march on him with the Resident.
>
> I was virtually a Rajah of my small demesne. Apart from the interest and variety of the work, the great interest was the shikar, big game and jungle-fowl, a strong-flying bird and good eating. So we lived well and enjoyed ourselves.
>
> The peasants round Abu were plagued by tigers and panthers. They came to me with piteous prayers to rid them of these pests. But the tigers which caused the damage probably came from the surrounding forests of Serohi state. If anyone had a duty or claim to shoot a tiger in Abu, it was probably the Maharao, and he could not be bothered. However there would come a time when the susceptibi-

lities of the ruler could no longer be tolerated, and the Resident would give permission for a tiger to be shot. For my single tiger I must have spent at least thirty nights sitting up over the kill of the night before, a cow or a hill pony. The thrill of listening to the rustling of animals moving in the dark – deer, jackals, hyenas, porcupines, was quite unforgettable. Every noise seemed to be made by the king of the jungle, but the only certain indication was the tearing and eating of the carcase.

10

The States of Rajputana (ii)

As has been said before the great majority of princes were decent men ruling their states as benevolent despots, loved and revered, whatever their shortcomings, by their subjects. Such princes gave no trouble to Political officers: when they wanted advice, they asked for it, and very often took it; and they were glad to show whatever the Resident or Political Agent wanted to see on tour. But the bad and eccentric rulers, a small minority, took up far more of the Politicals' time, and are of course far more interesting to the readers of this book. Of these, the Eastern Rajputana States Agency seemed to have more than its share.

The ruling family of Bharatpur (seventeen-gun, population 0.5 million) was not Rajput but Jat. The fort of Bharatpur was reputedly the strongest in India, and had stood many a siege by British and Indian armies, its mud walls, twenty feet thick, absorbing 18-pound cannon-balls as a lump of putty might absorb pebbles, without cracking or crumbling. 'Go, bully Burtpore!' was the taunt addressed to paladins of the East India Company by stay-at-home critics who well knew that all attempts to 'bully Burtpore' had ignominiously failed.

The ruling family had a reputation for instability and eccentricity. Maharajah Kishan Singh succeeded his father who, probably insane, was deposed for murder in 1900. He was invested with full powers in 1918. His tutor, E.H. Gibson, wrote of him as being somewhat immature and wildly extravagant, but slowly improving. In 1923 the Agent to the Governor-General, R.E. Holland, reported that he was without any vicious propensities but with a hyper-active brain, always in a whirl of excitement, heading for a nervous breakdown. He was addicted to bizarre leather uniforms for his guard; every motor in the state service – lorries, shooting brakes, runabouts, limousines – had to be a Rolls-Royce. He had spent, as a gesture which should never have been allowed, some 18 lakhs*, nearly half the state's annual revenue, on the Prince of Wales's visit. His expensive toys included eighteen Purdey guns and rifles, an electric canoe and a private jazz-band. In 1925 he had a spectacular spending-spree and bought six Rolls-Royces, six Arab

*A lakh (100,000 rupees) was worth about £7,500.

polo-ponies and the entire stock of saddlery in the Army and Navy Stores. He bought African lions and South American jaguars to turn out in his jungles. Yet because he saw fit, as an economy measure, to sack the Chief Engineer, his state suffered disastrous floods and a breakdown of the irrigation system.

Extravagance, and an inability to distinguish between the Privy Purse and the state's exchequer, was common among Indian princes. Traditionally, and still in the eyes of many, there *was* no distinction. Maharajah Kishan Singh of Bharatpur exhibited that trait in an extreme form, bordering on insanity.

He was always secretive about his state's finances, telling Holland that the revenue was about 55 lakhs and the expenditure 53–4 lakhs. In fact the revenue in 1924–5 was 37 lakhs, and the expenditure 78 lakhs. Holland reported that he was borrowing money at a ruinous rate of interest and heading for personal and public bankruptcy. Yet the pay of the state employees was months in arrears.

In August, 1926, S.B.A. Patterson, Holland's successor as Agent to the Governor-General, reported serious misrule in Bharatpur including the misappropriation of flood relief money. The administration was a scandal, the roads and irrigation in ruins. He recommended that, under threat of a Commission of Enquiry, the Maharajah should be given a suitable allowance and withdraw from all participation in state affairs, leaving Lieutenant-Colonel Lawrence of the Political Department to take over as Diwan, ruling in the Maharajah's name. His Highness procrastinated, argued, pleaded in tears with the Agent to the Governor-General, who offered him Kenneth Fitze as an alternative to Lawrence. But no, His Highness would prefer even Lawrence to Fitze. So the Viceroy, Lord Irwin, relented and offered him instead, as Diwan, a clever Brahmin, Pandit Hari Kishan Kaul, C.S.I., C.I.E., 'able to move on equal terms in the best social circles'.

A Diwan from outside, imposed on a reluctant ruler, was in a position that was bound to be difficult, even impossible. Foreseeing trouble, the Viceroy wrote to the Secretary of State:

> I have been much concerned with the affairs of Bharatpur. I told the Maharajah that I was gravely disturbed at the accounts which were reaching me of his financial state and I most earnestly wished he would put all his cards on the table and allow us to help him get straight. He evinced the utmost willingness to do whatever I told him. He always has a great polo gymkhana tea in each Simla season and he asked me which date would suit me to be his guest. I told him that

until his finances were cleared up, I did not think I could properly encourage him to spend his money on my entertainment, and I advised him to abandon it for this year. This he did with good grace but I suspect a heavy heart . . . The tragedy is that he has the best duck-shooting in India!

Lord Irwin came to the reluctant conclusion that 'the young man is really off his head as a result of some hereditary disease . . . The other princes regard him as a very dangerous black sheep.'

All might yet have been well, but for the Maharajah's favourite and toady, one Raja Kishan (not to be confused with Maharajah Kishan Singh and Pandit Hari Kishan Kaul), a former bugler in the state forces who had been exalted to the post of Chief of Staff.

In May, 1927, there was a shooting affray at the house of this unsavoury character during which a man named Mokhan Singh was killed and a woman named Kutti wounded. The Diwan decided that an Enquiry should be held by a European Superintendent of Police from outside the state. His Highness agreed to this, but it was generally assumed that he would do all he could to obstruct proceedings, that witnesses would be bribed and intimidated and that the local police would be unhelpful.

All this duly happened, but in August the Political Agent, Lieutenant Colonel Pritchard, reported the findings of the Enquiry. There was a moral certainty, but no absolute proof, that Raja Kishan had shot both the woman, Kutti, and Mokhan Singh, who was Raja Kishan's pimp but had lately been somewhat dilatory in this role, and that a woman whose body was found in a nearby well had been killed by Raja Kishan or on his orders. The police had partly burnt the body and clothes so that she could not be indentified, but a post-mortem showed she had been tied up and killed before being dumped in the well. Finally, it seemed that His Highness knew these facts all along.

A month later Pandit Hari Kishan Kaul resigned because of accusations by Raja Kishan that he had 'fixed' the enquiry. After a tearful interview with the Viceroy, the Maharajah agreed in December to banish Raja Kishan and accepted a European Diwan somewhat thicker-skinned than the sensitive Pandit. The choice fell on an officer known throughout the Political as 'Drunken' George McKenzie, a tribute to his first name, Duncan, rather than to his life-style; just the man for a job requiring firmness of character. There then stepped on to the stage the dapper figure of Sir Leslie Scott, a barrister who specialised in representing Indian princes against the Political Department. He warned the Maharajah against 'a clique within the state which is hostile to Your Highness and will make capital out of any concession'. Was not His Highness intending to introduce a brand-new, democratic Constitution with an elected Legislative Assembly and Cabinet? Were not elections due to take place almost any day now? Then let His Highness refuse to accept any conditions imposed on him, but wait until after the elections and consult his Legislative Assembly. Grasping at a straw, the Maharajah on February 13th, 1928, told the Political Secretary that he needed more time for consideration.

The Political Secretary minuted on a file for the Viceroy:

> His Highness now proposes to delay acceptance of the conditions on the amazing pretext that the concurrence of his subjects is in some sense necessary. Sir Leslie Scott and his friends seem to look forward to good times when the 'case' against the Government of India has been won.

Thus briefed, Lord Irwin fairly blasted the unhappy Maharajah:

> I have read with considerable astonishment Your Highness's letter of the 13th February. In your letter of the 29th December you promised to abide by whatever advice I offered, and my letter of the 31st January conveyed the advice that Your Highness was already pledged to accept. If the arrangements indicated in my letter prove insufficient to enable Mr McKenzie to proceed promptly and effectively with the rehabilitation of your state, I shall be reluctantly compelled to advise other methods for Your Highness's acceptance.

The Maharajah capitulated – or pretended to. Irwin promised that if McKenzie's work was not obstructed, 'I can assure Your Highness that it will be my desire to do everything possible to maintain your prestige as ruler in the eyes of your people.'

But obstruction continued unabated. The Political Agent, Pritchard, wrote on April 22nd, 1928:

> His Highness's disclaimers of obstruction cannot be taken seriously. Were he to be given chapter and verse it would only provide him with the opportunity he is seeking to add to his protestations of innocence and to explain the purity of his intentions – in other words, adding to the volume of mendacious statements with which this file is already burdened.

The Maharani, a spirited lady, now joined in the game. Lengthy, daily interviews with Her Highness, angry, tearful, wheedling, turning on all her charm, brought even 'Drunken George' near to the end of his tether.

The Assistant to the Governor-General thought the Maharajah should be excluded from the state, 'and no further consideration given to a prince who has throughout shown himself so entirely destitute of any shred of honour and good faith'. But the Political Secretary thought the case was not quite so clear and heinous as to justify banishment.

The Maharajah now took to hobnobbing with his evil genius in exile, Raja Kishan, holding parties in his honour which officers of the state forces had to attend on pain of a court-martial if they refused. His obstruction grew more blatant: he censured McKenzie for sacking a corrupt official, and appointed that official his A.D.C. In September, 1928, there was another viceregal blast, albeit addressed to 'My Esteemed Friend': no self-respecting officer, wrote Lord Irwin, could under present circumstances consent to serve as Diwan in Bharatpur. The Viceroy's considerable patience was exhausted: the Maharajah must live at least 100 miles outside the state and abstain from all participation in Bharatpur affairs.

With witnesses no longer in fear of the Maharajah, Raja Kishan was brought to trial, found guilty of kidnapping, extortion, rape and buggery, and sentenced to seven years. But Her Highness won the last trick. 'She seems,' wrote Pritchard, 'to have made away with the greater part of the motor transport of the state, and it would certainly seem reasonable to require her to give up three of the five Rolls-Royces in her possession.'

The pathetic Maharajah sunk into a decline and died, probably of consumption, six months after his banishment. Characteristically, Lord Irwin visited him on his death-bed: 'he was a pitiable sight and could not speak above a whisper'. A few months later his Maharani, that spirited lady, died too. The Maharajah's four sons were sent to England for their education, and his two daughters remained in Bharatpur.

In 1932 McKenzie was succeeded as Diwan by Cyril Hancock. Aged 38, a mere Captain, he seemed to some too junior to be the autocratic ruler of a state with a population of half a million. But he had plenty of varied experience behind him: four years in Mesopotamia with the 114th Mahrattas, winning an M.C. in the last battle of the war; Secretary to half a dozen Residents in Western India; Assistant Private Secretary to the Viceroy; Secretary to the Agent to the Governor-General, Rajputana. He spoke perfect Hindi with no trace of a 'sahib's accent', and he looked forward eagerly to his new job. The Assistant to the Governor-General impressed on him that he would be 'first and foremost a servant of Bharatpur State and must not hesitate to protect the rights of the local people against claims from British India'.

He found that McKenzie had drafted a constitution. It did not contain any unsettling element of democracy: 'minority administrations' were not allowed to change the essential character of a state. But it was written, and so gave the subjects rights which were not solely dependent on the ruler's whim. There was a Council of Administration, with Minutes properly kept by a secretary. His first duty was to allocate to the members their portfolios. The most important were R.L. Batra (Revenue) and Colonel Sanpat Singh, a Jat (Home Member). Hancock was lucky in the members chosen by his predecessor, all competent and honourable men. He allocated to himself Finance, Forestry, law and order, and command of the Bharatpur Infantry Battalion which he meant to bring up to something near the perfection of his beloved Mahrattas.

> At our first Council meeting . . . I told them that whenever a subject required the individual opinion of each of us, I would start by obtaining the views of Mr Batra. After a few weeks, having noticed that each member always agreed with him – as also did I – I told them that thereafter I should start from the most junior and work upwards. The result was the same. I learned that the eldest daughter of the late Maharajah, known officially as the Senior Bibiji Saheba (by name Kusum, aged 17), was refusing to marry the person to whom her parents had affianced her when she was an infant, an unprepossessing, very fat young man whom she loathed from all the accounts she had heard and from all the pictures she had seen. Here was a hot potato and my success or failure as Diwan depended on the manner I handled it . . . Wisdom lay in selecting one confidant who could be trusted, who had experience of zenana practices and who would guide me in the basic principles of the Hindu religion and on the recent history of the ruling family. Fortunately he was available in Colonel Sanpat Singh, to whom I confided my plan of placing myself *in loco parentis*.

The two princesses, having during their parents' lifetime enjoyed a fair degree of freedom, had been relegated to the strictest purdah. They could go out only in their Rolls-Royce limousines of which the windows had been darkened so that they could see through a glass darkly but no lascivious eyes could peer in. They must have been feeling lonely and abandoned by all except their female servants.

Sanpat Singh and I discussed her case from every angle and it was obvious that . . . the Bibiji could not be forced into an unsuitable match, and that I should be compelled . . . to intrude behind the purdah and make a deal with the young lady. I was to remind Kusum that the Council was responsible for maintaining the high reputation of the Bharatpur ruling family and that we could only agree to break off the engagement if she would agree to marry, without undue delay, a suitable young Jat boy of good family of her own choice . . .

Accordingly I arranged a meeting in the palace where Kusum and I sat on a sofa after I had breezed in as though we were old friends. She covered her face with her sari so that I had no idea what she looked like. I said I would from time to time bring photographs and other relevant details of suitable families until eventually we would be certain to find a boy agreeable to the high honour of an alliance with the Bharatpur Darbar, and meanwhile we would cancel the current betrothal. She was a sensible girl and agreed . . .

I met Kusum about once a fortnight and found her becoming less and less shy. On her second visit she showed the tip of her nose and gradually, interview after interview, she gained confidence until she looked at me, her veil lowered, full in the face . . .

Within three of four months our search succeeded. There followed the interminable customs and ceremonies of a Hindu betrothal and marriage. Most important was the comparison of the horoscopes of the aspiring bride and bridegroom. Eventually Kusum with a large party of relations and servants and escort could proceed by special train to the bridegroom's home town. I met Sanpat at the station to make sure all was well. There I was told that Kusum was indulging in a fit of nerves and inclined to back down. Whereupon I pretended to be incensed, and prepared to marshal sufficient force to put her back into her carriage, should she open the door and attempt to scamper back along the red carpet to the palace. It was a trial of wills and wits in which I held the stronger cards; the guard blew his whistle, the engine wheels started to turn and to a strong smell of incense and smoke from the engine's funnel the trainload of optimists started on its journey.

For the wedding itself, Sanpat could not tell me at what precise time of night the happy couple would be declared man and wife – only a Brahmin priest could do that – but he thought that by about 2 a.m. the crucial stage would be reached. He suggested that I watch the ceremony through a window until he could break away from his duties to give me the word. I could then return to my cottage satisfied.

All went according to plan.

It was a common phenomenon that Political officers in Hancock's position, servants of a state, often became 'More Darbari than the Darbar'. His relations with 'Heb' Todd, the Political Agent, could have been awkward, as Hancock did not encourage Todd to go about the state without his knowledge and consent. But they got on well together. During an interregnum between Political Agents, Hancock was instructed to act as Political Agent. In this capacity he used to report on his own work as Diwan, 'always in the most glowing terms'.

His main job was to restore the state's finances after ten years' profligacy. There was one feature of Bharatpur which Hancock and his Bank Manager found equally gratifying: no Income Tax. The main income of the state was from land revenue, which depended on a complicated irrigation system falling every year into worse disrepair since 'Late His Highness' had sacked the State Engineer as his only economy measure.

> Taking advantage of the downward slope of the ground, previous rulers had constructed a series of high parallel dykes ('bunds') across large tracts of country to hold the flood waters of the river Chambal and the rainwater of each monsoon. These bunds were intersected every two or three miles by masonry aquaducts slotted and grooved to hold strong wooden planks to control the flow of water to huge squares of silted land . . . It was the first duty of the Chief Public Works Officer to ensure that the earth works and masonry sluices were kept in perfect condition . . . The revenue staff assessed the value of the crops of wheat, barley, oilseed, sugar-cane etc. for the annual revenue collection . . . During August each year the level of monsoon water in the fields fell gradually by evaporation and the manipulation of the sluices by the irrigation staff, so that ploughing and sowing the silt at one end of a square could take place while the other end was still under ten feet of water . . .
>
> Good rains fell during my six years in Bharatpur; and the Agricultural Institute of the Punjab produced an improved strain of wheat. During my first winter, in some villages only one head of grain sprang from one seed of wheat, but by my third winter most cultivators saw up to eight or ten dark green sturdy shoots springing from each seed.
>
> With good monsoon the state's finances improved and we were able to repair roads and plant roadside trees; restore the irrigation system; repair the hospital and schools; buy a couple of elephants and train them for shikar and ceremonial duties; purchase and train four waler horses; and restore the palace and Bharatpur fort.

During his first cold-weather tour Hancock created consternation by touring on horseback instead of in a swift motorcade. Candidates for the Revenue Department were informed that horses were available for them and they would be expected to follow the Diwan Sahib closely. All went well until the Diwan Sahib started to trot. Then there was a series of bumps, followed by riderless ponies whizzing past. But he took no notice, riding steadily on as though this was the sort of thing they must expect in the Bharatpur Revenue Department.

The famous duck-shoot was revived. Surplus water from the irrigation system drained into a swamp known as the Ghana, some ten square miles in extent and three or four feet deep. Throughout the winter, duck came in from Central Asia: it was the best duck-shoot in India, and during Hancock's time the Viceroy, Lord Linlithgow, invited himself for a day there. It was the Diwan's job to arrange it. Normally Viceroys were placed in a special butt where birds flew low and they could, without great skill, make a creditable bag; but Hancock knew Linlithgow to be a first-class shot who would appreciate really high birds, rather than the teal which passed back and forth like agitated bees. He placed the Viceroy accordingly. Shooting started with a bugle call at 10 a.m. and was stopped by another bugle call for lunch. By that time the Viceroy had 'shot some forty single birds by shooting to a high standard which it was a joy to witness'. For the afternoon His Excellency was placed where the shooting would be easier and he could make the sort of bag expected of a Viceroy . . . assisted by Hancock's own shikari who was instructed to pick any wounded birds in the vicinity and credit them all to His Excellency's bag. 'Thus reputations are earned.'

Hancock's initial appointment was for four years, but it was extended to six. When he heard the news, 'I threw my topi in the air with delight for that was above all others the decision I had hoped for.'

In 1936 the young Maharajah designate, Indu, arrived. From his point of vantage as Member for Forestry, Hancock had ensured that the elephants he bought were staunch to tiger and the waler horses to pig. With such manly diversions, and training in administration, law and revenue, he hoped to make Indu a better ruler than his father had been. Despite all his father's shortcomings he noted a genuine bond of affection between subjects and the young prince. He also noticed that Indu was developing a swollen head. One day:

> I found the young man in a kind of trance, flatly refusing to obey his tutor's instructions. This called for a bellow from me such as I had received on the square at Sandhurst, coupled with the threat that

unless Indu came instantly to his senses I would report him to the Viceroy as being unfit to be invested with the powers of a ruler.

The bellow was effective for the moment, but Hancock began to wonder if he would really be able to make a man of Indu. Nobody had seen fit to warn him of the instability in the Bharatpur ruling family.

There was in the hills a small, very holy temple, to which pilgrims came for a sip of holy water issuing from the mouth of a carved stone cow. One year, there was consternation: the water ceased to flow. Clearly the gods must be very displeased with Bharatpur. Following an unusually rapid decision by the Council, out drove the Diwan in his Austin Seven to view the scene of the disaster. During a thirty-mile drive, he noticed very little undergrowth along the roadsides, and flocks of goats vigorously destroying what little there was. There are advantages in autocracy: within a day all goats were banned in the valley of the temple, and next year the holy water was again in full flow.

There was little crime in Bharatpur, but one notorious dacoit (armed robber) had committed several murders and there was a price on his head. He was caught, condemned to death and lost his appeal. When the death sentence was confirmed and the case sent back to the Council:

> I had only one question to answer, 'What is the tradition of the state in such matters?' After some research in the archives, the answer proved to be 'death by public hanging'. My duty as the servant of the Bharatpur Darbar was simple: to say that he must be hanged outside the walls of Bharatpur fort. The sentence was carried out in the presence of an enormous crowd . . . He was a brave man. As he mounted the scaffold, he harangued the crowd, saying, 'Brethren, do not grieve for me. I have committed many sins and am about to receive the proper punishment.' I did not think that my duties required me to witness the ceremony.

So ended what were, perhaps, the most enjoyable and interesting years in Hancock's long service.

The halcyon decade when the Political Department let well alone in the vast majority of states and the princes almost ceased to regard Politicals with suspicion, ended with the first Round Table Conference which met in London in 1930, mainly on the inspiration of Lord Irwin, to speed India to Dominion Status. Nearly all the Indian political parties and interested groups attended, except the most important party of all, the Indian National Congress, which boycotted it. Without Congress, which wanted only an independent, unitary state dominated by itself, the

Conference had no difficulty in deciding that the best constitution for a free India would be a federation in which the Hindu majority, the Moslem minority and the states could be accommodated. A representative party of princes attended, advised by Sir Leonard Reynolds who was then Agent to the Governor-General in Rajputana. Before even arriving in London they agreed, under the influence of Bikanir, that the states would favour a Federation, and would play a full part in it. But Reynolds doubted that they had really thought out the implications.

They had not. They thought that by federating they would free themselves from the gyves of the Political Department. But the more they studied the matter, the more they realised that in a Federation they would lose at least as much of their independence as they had lost through their treaties with the Paramount Power, and probably a lot of their income. Defence, foreign affairs, posts and telegraphs, customs and excise, railways, air transport – there seemed no end to the list of subjects which would be reserved for the federal Government. In the Second Round Table Conference, in which Congress took part, they began to see very clearly that any future federal Government was bound to be dominated by Congress, so they might well be exchanging King Log for King Stork, and their early enthusiasm waned.

There were other, even less welcome, considerations. Would it be possible for a Federation to accommodate a large number of mediaeval autocracies when its most powerful units would be democratically governed? Would not the princes have to accept a degree of democracy lest an unsympathetic federal Government impose it on them? Finally there was the daunting difficulty of amalgamating into a few viable units innumerable petty states, each proudly independent but too small to take its place in an all-India Federation.

In so far as the princes had a collective view of Federation, they did not want it. Why should they change the whole nature of their rule to oblige a bunch of subversive politicians? They were getting on perfectly well as they were, and their people were perfectly content. Did the British really mean to go, or were they just pretending? By procrastinating and playing hard to get, might they not obtain better terms? Finally, their treaties, which guaranteed their independence, a guarantee which had been repeated again and again from Queen Victoria onwards, were with the *Crown*, not with the Government of India, still less with the British Government. In the last resort, the King would not let them down.

It was the view of the Government, expressed through the Political Department, that the princes *must*, in their own interest, join an all-India

Federation. They had no viable alternative: they could not stay out in the cold. For the first half of the 1930s, however, little was done to press this view on the princes. Individual Residents would, if their opinion was asked, give it. But Political officers too had their own opinions about Federation. It is one thing to preach to order, even to be intellectually convinced of the validity of the sermon; quite another to preach with fervour in the knowledge that the more persuasive the sermon, the sooner one's service and career will come to an end. Years later the Maharawal of Dungarpur said, 'Never for one moment did we believe that most Political officers in their hearts believed in Federation.' All the more, perhaps, did the princes resent being nagged about it.

The argument was to continue through the 1930s, especially after 1935 when the Government of India Act brought matters to a head. But from the very beginning it made relations with articulate, politically-minded princes, whose lead on Federation others would follow, much more difficult. They had to be handled with kid gloves.

Such a man was Maharajah Jai Singh of the fifteen-gun state (population 750,000) of Alwar. He was extremely able. Indeed, Edwin Montagu as Secretary of State noted, 'There is no Indian as intelligent as he is. I would rather have him at the Imperial Conference than anyone else.' Lord Willingdon considered that he, the Jam Saheb and Bikanir formed the 'intellect and leadership of the Rajput princes'. He was an articulate, indeed a compulsive, public speaker, equally convincing in writing and on committees. He hd an instinct for politics, and considerable charm. He had been a good Chancellor to the Chamber of Princes and was the sort of prince that the Viceroy used to consult about less satisfactory princes. His attitude to Federation could be crucial.

He had overweening pride in his Rajput blood and zeal for his Hindu religion. He could not abide the defiling touch of leather – or of an Untouchable as, to strict Hindus, all Europeans must be. He disliked shaking hands with them and habitually wore cotton gloves to greet even royalty, thus giving deep offence to Queen Mary.

Conrad Corfield as Assistant Private Secretary to the Viceroy, Lord Reading, heard rumours that Alwar cared more for his tigers than for his subjects; and, on tour with the Viceroy, saw the sites of deserted villages which the Maharajah, like William Rufus, had enclosed in his hunting preserves.

> So far as I could see there was no official discussion about the state administration. The whole atmosphere was that of a country-house party. Was the Maharajah's rule being protected from prying eyes for

personal reasons? I began to wonder, and stored this away in my mind.

The Maharajah was a man of ungovernable temper. He had poured petrol over, and set a match to, a polo-pony which let him down in a tournament; and B.J. Glancy had an unpleasant interview with him during which Alwar picked up a heavy metal ash-tray and slowly crushed it in one hand, like a matchbox, an exhibition of demonic power which physically frightened Glancy. He was rumoured to have peculiar sexual predilections, and to provide boys for the entertainment of his guests. Opinion about him among his fellow-princes varied. Some thought him a great Indian patriot, which in a way he was; others thought him mentally deranged. One Rajput boy was sent to him for training in administration, and very quickly ran back home. The Maharajah was not, in short, a nice man. But he was almost a genius, albeit an evil one. As a personal compliment to him, the Political Agent attached to his state had been withdrawn, and his state was included in the Eastern Rajputana Agency.

Successive Viceroys knew – if not exactly liked – him. Lord Irwin wrote to the Secretary of State:

> Alwar came to see me a few days ago and made me a present of a beautiful double-barrelled rifle which he had had engraved with his – but fortunately not my – name. I was rather embarrassed as to how to extricate myself from this position. Later in the day I returned it to him saying that I had only recently reissued orders about Government servants taking presents from ruling princes. He was anxious to explain that of course he knew all about the rule but did not think it reasonable that what was a personal mark of friendship should come within it, and said that he had made a similar present to Reading who did not think it necessary to raise the point. Although friendship may justify it in one case – though not, I am bound to say, in the present case as between Alwar and myself – it would seem to land the Viceroy in great difficulty.

His subjects were mainly Hindu, but included a minority of Meos, a hardy Moslem tribe recruited into the army, noted for keeping the feasts of both religions and the fasts of neither.

In December, 1932, an unruly mob of Meo rebels was alleged to have fired on a detachment of Alwar state forces who in self-defence fired back, killing and wounding several Meos. With memories of Amritsar still fresh, an incident of this kind was shocking headline news. (Nowadays it happens every week and rates hardly a mention on a back page.) The Meos, it seemed, had grievances, to which Congress and the vernacular press gave ample publicity. They were assessed for land revenue at about double the rate in British India with no remission in years of poor harvests. Agricultural land was constantly being taken from them to extend the Maharajah's hunting preserves. They complained that, with no Political Agent accredited to the state, they were at the mercy of a ruler who hated Islam.

By January the situation was out of hand, and a small party of Alwar infantry was lucky to escape from an angry Meo mob. The Maharajah could not be persuaded to ask for British Indian troops to restore order, but they were sent in nevertheless – a battalion, a squadron of cavalry and some armoured cars. At the same time, Ibbotson, an Indian Civil Servant from the United Provinces, was appointed Special Commissioner for the disturbed area to investigate and report on the causes of the trouble.

He found that the story of the Meos opening fire from a range of fifty yards on the troops was a fabrication. The soldiers' wounds were superficial and probably self-inflicted. The holes in their uniforms had indeed been made by bullets and shotgun pellets, but (as was obvious from the powder-burns) from a range of a few inches. He found ample evidence of torture by the state police. The favourite method was to place the victim face down, his body supported by his arms as though he was doing 'press-ups', his shins in shallow slots in a heavy beam. Another beam was then placed on top of this, crushing his shins, and on this his torturers sat while putting the question to him.

The Maharajah reluctantly agreed to the retention of Ibbotson and a senior officer of the Indian Police to clear up the mess, but a Political Department minute initialled by R.I.R. Glancy warned:

> After the employment of our troops, it is fundamental that the Government of India must accept responsibility for the redress of grievances and the maintenance of order. To save the Maharajah's face, the British officers to be employed will be described as his servants; but they must be protected against his vagaries. His proposal to engage them on the basis of a month's notice on either side shows how the wind blows.
>
> So far we have no assurance as to the powers they will exercise. There is a very great danger that the Maharajah will pick a quarrel with the British officers, as he has always done in the past, and take them at a disadvantage owing to failure to specify their exact powers.
>
> As to the military adviser, there is the very strongest objection to

him moving about with Alwar troops or directing their movements at times of disturbance. He might be saddled with the responsibility for shooting down a crowd of cultivators. His duties are confined to training.

The Maharajah's obstruction of Ibbotson was constant and ingenious. On February 10th a Political Department telegram informed the Secretary of State:

> He has refused to agree to conditions which were considered essential by Ibbotson and which were pressed by the Viceroy and Home Member at personal interview with His Highness on 6th February. We are now convinced that we cannot hope for his co-operation and that no officer can carry out pacification while the Maharajah and his present Prime Minister remain within the state. We have therefore decided to present him with an ultimatum to the effect that either he must leave the state at once and ante-date his intended visit to Europe, giving Ibbotson full power to carry out administration under title of Prime Minister, or that we shall take over administration of Alwar as an act of state and require him to live outside until we consider he can be allowed to return. Before, however, conveying these orders to the Maharajah, in order to give the princes generally no cause for complaint, the Viceroy will consult two or three ruling princes.

Two days later the Viceroy, now Lord Willingdon, amplified this in a private letter to the Secretary of State, Sir Samuel Hoare.

> We have delivered to him an ultimatum. He is so clever and such an astute manoeuvrer that the only thing to do is to go straight at him. We must insist on restoring order in the Meo area, and I am inclined to think that he is perfectly terrified of an English officer coming into the state and finding out the facts.

Three princes were consulted – the Nawab of Bhopal (Moslem), the Maharajah of Bikanir (Rajput) and the Maharaj-Rana of Dholpur (Jat). On their advice the proposed ultimatum was modified. The Maharajah need not leave Alwar before his planned visit to Europe in May, but he must immediately dismiss and banish his Prime Minister, Girdhari Lal, and accept a British Prime Minister in his place, as well as Ibbotson as Special Commissioner in the disturbed areas. To this the Maharajah had to agree.

The choice for Prime Minister was Arthur Lothian, a tough,

independent-minded Scot, and Francis Wylie was also brought in as Finance Minister. Both were members of the Political Department. They arrived in Alwar while the Maharajah was still in Delhi, and Lothian reported to George Ogilvie, Agent for the Governor-General, on his first meeting with the Maharajah.

> His manner was quite courteous but he showed that he was annoyed by our having come in spite of his attempt to delay us until after his return from Delhi. He said he had been particularly anxious to be present himself to introduce me and instruct me in my new work, and that I would not get the proper spirit or atmosphere in his absence. He said Girdhari Lal had served him well and was being made a scapegoat. He went on to say that the bond between himself and his Prime Minister was a curiously personal and flexible one, and that it was therefore essential for him to get to know me and for me to get to know him thoroughly. He wished his Prime Minister and himself to be in constant touch. He then said that the Government of India had commanded him to give the Prime Minister his confidence. Confidence, however, was a psychological thing that could not be commanded. Either it came or it did not. It could not be given by order. I said that while perhaps the psychological confidence to which he referred could not be given by order, nevertheless all the external manifestations of that confidence could be given.

The Maharajah then put his case at length. His subjects, he said, were not more heavily but, on the contrary, much more lightly taxed than in British India. The trouble with the Meos was communal, not agrarian: his Hindu subjects were perfectly content. It was entirely the work of Congress agitators. He could have dealt with it himself, without Special Commissioners and British Indian troops.

In a private letter to Ogilvie, Lothian gave more details:

> I close this report with a brief account of His Highness's personal equation, for he is a very extraordinary character. The Maharajah is now about 53 years of age, and has always kept himself very fit physically with the result that he looks younger than his actual age. Perhaps the main defects in his character are his gross extravagance and his overweening arrogance. As regards his extravagance I have made a rough estimate of the expenditure of the ruler which suggests that it amounts to well over half the total income of the state, and would note that 9 lakhs of unpaid bills are now pending against the state, mostly for articles ordered by His Highness. If he plays tennis, a

table displaying anything from ten to twenty rackets has to be set out in front of him; so with guns when out shooting; his office table is festooned with gold fountain-pens in racks like those one sees in a stationer's shop window.

As regards the Maharajah's arrogance, he cannot bear not being in the centre of every picture. In his own state this is natural enough, but he pursues the same policy elsewhere by staging spectacular late arrivals, the wearing of clothes of the most conspicuous possible hue and headgear of extraordinary shape, and by making speeches on any and every occasion. When to his arrogance there is added a vindictive, capricious and cruel temperament, his officials and attendants never dare put up any proposals which are unpalatable to him. He is currently reported to thrash his A.D.C.s. Be that as it may, and it is quite in keeping with the strain of cruelty in his character, there is a cringing, frightened atmosphere among the members of the Maharajah's staff such as I have never seen in any other state.

I was not sent to Alwar as Censor Morum so I have hitherto refrained from any reference to this aspect of his life. But to complete the picture of conditions in the state, it is necessary to bear in mind that the moral atmosphere of the place is mephitic. The people around the Maharajah have an evil, brutalised look such as I have seen nowhere else. One incident which happened a couple of years ago will give some idea of what goes on under the veil. The Alwar Darbar pressed for the extradition of a man from a neighbouring Rajputana state as a deserter from the Alwar Bodyguard; but the other Darbar flatly refused, because the Alwar Bodyguard was not a military unit at all but was well known to be recruited for another more personal purpose.

Against all this, however, there is something to put on the credit side. He has probably the acutest brain of all the Indian princes. When he cares, he can make himself the most charming host and companion. To see him at a shooting party beguiling the company with story after story of interesting experiences he has had, makes one regret all the more that there is another altogether different side to his character, the Dr Jekyll to his Mr Hyde.

The Maharajah's description, to Lothian, of the relations between himself and his Prime Minister, Girdhari Lal, as 'curiously personal and flexible' moved the Foreign Secretary, Ronald Wingate, to unseemly verse:

Recent intensive researches by Wylie and Lothian show
How little of H.H. of Alwar the Indian Government know.
The state may be bankrupt and ruined, the ryots may suffer and groan,*
While the ecstasy fond of the personal bond is enjoyed by the P.M. alone.

In April Lothian departed, handing over to Wylie who was (wrote Ogilvie) 'an officer possessing a combination of firmness, tact, patience and courtesy rarely met with in one individual. He seems to enjoy his verbal battles, sometimes ranging over hours, with His Highness.' The Maharajah, through various agents, proceeded to stir up Hindu communal hatred against Meos, and the Hindu shopkeepers staged a week-long strike allegedly in protest against Ibbotson and Wylie's favouring of Moslems. The Maharajah, to evade responsibility for communal disturbances and to make plain where his own sympathies lay, departed on pilgrimage to the Hindu holy city of Benares. He returned clad in a pilgrim's white loincloth and with a large jar of holy Ganges water which he carried in procession to a temple, followed by a mob of Hindus in a state of religious excitement. George Ogilvie, the Agent to the Governor-General, wrote to the Political Secretary:

> Next day a sort of religious Darbar was held in the palace followed by a procession in which the Vedas† were carried on elephants through the streets of the town . . . The impression that the public have undoubtedly gained is that His Highness has ranged himself on the side of his Hindu subjects in resistance to the alleged pro-Mohammadan activities of Wylie and Ibbotson. Wylie received visits from various prominent Hindus of the town who were genuinely alarmed at the new developments.
>
> His Highness was evidently in a condition bordering on hysteria. He was dressed in white and wore a coarse yellow pugree printed all over with 'Ram'‡ in Hindi. He appeared to be in an ecstasy of religious emotionalism and during my talk with him he frequently shed tears and lifted his hands in the attitude of prayer. His mukat, which he has made his own peculiar headdress for many years, has been discarded and placed, surrounded by a circle of rose leaves, on the mantelpiece in his study under an illuminated picture of Shri Ram. By this he meant to convey the idea that he had placed his

*Peasants, cultivators.
† Hindu holy books.
‡ God; Hindu deity.

kingship in the hands of God. He wore no shoes at night and covered his shoulders with a large handkerchief printed in Hindi with the names of God. He has banished from his table all meat, eggs and wine and ate the coarsest vegetable food served on platters made of leaves stitched together, of the pattern used by vendors of food at railway stations. Ganges water was his only drink. During meals his conversation was almost exclusively confined to interminable religious discussions . . . By the third day, however, the religious pose was beginning to wear thin . . . his dress showed a tendency to return to normal and he began to revert to his normal mentality.

Attention was now directed to the finances of his state which, wrote the Viceroy to the Secretary of State, were 'as bad as can be'. The State Treasury contained about Rs 4,000 (£300), and to pay public servants their salaries for April a cheque had to be drawn on His Highness's personal bank account, putting that in the red. State debts amounted to 40 lakhs (£300,000). With luck some 7 lakhs might be recovered in land revenue during the next six weeks, and then no more until the late summer harvest. To keep the state going a loan of 40 lakhs was necessary, but various wealthy states which had been approached for a loan had refused to oblige unless it was guaranteed by the Government of India.

The state, in short, was spectacularly bankrupt, and could be rescued only by the Government of India, which could therefore impose on the Maharajah any terms it wanted. The terms suggested by the Agent to the Governor-General were that a British officer be in effective control of the state's finances until the loan was repaid; and that His Highness leave the state for at least a year. If he refused these terms, a Commission of Enquiry would be necessary, followed inevitably by his deposition. But, Ogilvie pointed out, a Commission of Enquiry, by drawing public attention to what the Government had allowed to go on under its very nose, would embarrass not only His Highness:

> Interest in Alwar affairs has of late been very widespread. The revelations which would be made public would be such as to provoke the horror of the whole civilised world. They would draw down a storm of criticism not only on the whole system of princely rule, but on the policy of the Government of India under which such misdoings have been possible for a quarter of a century. To let loose such a storm would give a tremendous handle to the growing agitation of irresponsible politicians against the states and might shock the feelings of the princes, already sensitive to a fault of criticism,

> however true and moderate, in such a way as to *prejudice seriously the chances of Federation* [my italics].

To the Government's immense relief, His Highness agreed to go quietly, or at least as quietly as lay within his character. But Willingdon complained to Sir Samuel Hoare:

> I am having a terrible time with Alwar . . . He has tried to procrastinate, declaring that certain days of departure which I had suggested to him were inauspicious days; and finally I got a wire this morning to say that he had settled to go to Benares and become a sanyasi, or holy man, and live there until he was allowed to go back to Alwar. About half an hour afterwards I received a further communication that he had changed his mind and was going off this evening. I must say this has been a most difficult job to tackle. I am quite sure we were right to do so, but he is as cute as Gandhi.

Although exiled from his state, Alwar had no idea of passing into obscurity. On board ship he tried to persuade the Captain to speed up and get to Genoa a day early so that he could entertain Mussolini to a banquet in celebration of his (Alwar's) birthday. He was then reported to be sitting on the doorstep of the Vatican demanding an interview with the Pope. To the fury of King George V, who had a testy temper, he got himself invited to a Garden Party. His last appearance in the Willingdon–Hoare correspondence was a year after his departure from his state.

> He left his daughter Baijilal in charge of the notoriously immoral Miss D'Cruz whom Wylie had to dismiss. H.H. hates his daughter and treats her with great cruelty, striking her head against a wall when she annoys him. The child is suffering from congenital syphilis for which H.H. is most unlikely to arrange treatment.

But on Willingdon's final departure from India, Alwar asked if he might be present at the farewell. Frank Pearson was the Viceroy's A.D.C., and had been warned that Alwar might try to take revenge:

> I moved along the line of princes introducing them to H.E., and as we approached Alwar the tension mounted. I introduced him and, as he shook hands, he stood erect and said, 'Your Excellency, I am sorry to say farewell, but you can leave India knowing that everything you have done to me was entirely justified.' A devil, but a great man.

He died in 1937.

11

The States of Central India

Adjoining Rajputana were the Central Indian States, fifty-eight of them varying in size and importance from Indore (nineteen-gun, population 1,325,000) and Bhopal (nineteen-gun, population 730,000) to Banka Pahari (area 5 square miles, population in 1931 1,326, no guns at all). The Resident (or Agent to the Governor-General) was stationed all year round at Indore, the wealthiest of the states with textiles and light industries. There were Political Agents for the Bhopal Agency (ten states), and Bundelkhand Agency (thirty-three states) and the Malwa Agency (thirteen states). Indore and Rewa enjoyed direct relations with the Resident. Most of the princes were Rajput, but three (including Indore) were Mahrattas and a few (including Bhopal) were Moslems of Afghan or Pathan descent, whose ancestors had carved out little kingdoms for themselves during the chaotic period before the Company established its rule in Central India.

These states were not as interesting as Rajputana. Except for Bhopal, there were no rulers of the calibre of Bikanir, Jodhpur, Jaipur or, in his sinister way, Alwar. There was no hot-weather hill-station like Mount Abu. The Residency area, leased from Indore State, was flat and unattractive, containing the Residency and officers' bungalows, the Daly College for princelings, the lines of the Malwa Bhil Corps, the Club, and the Thuggee Jail, built by the great Sleeman who suppressed the Thugs.

However, Central India has its quota of eccentric rulers. Prominent among these was His Highness Tukojirao Puar, Maharajah of the little Mahratta state of Dewas Senior (fifteen-guns, population 83,000). That he had a more varied emotional life than most of us was due to his marriage, at an early age, to a lady named Akka Saheba, sister of the Mahratta Maharajah of Kolhapur. She was a termagant, but also rather a tragic figure, her personal life blighted by the fact that she had not been born a man. In 1910 she produced a son, the Yuvraj Vikram Singh, after which she went back to Kolhapur whence she never returned. E.M. Forster in *The Hill of Devi* made out that Tukojirao was persecuted by a bully of a Political Agent. In fact, it was his wife who bullied him. The Yuvraj Vikram Singh lived with his father in mutual hatred, and

15 R.A. Lyall (*second from left*), Commissioner Ajmer, and L.W. Reynolds (*second from right*), Resident Jodhpur, with Maharajah Pratap Singh and his three sons (two of whom became the world's highest handicapped polo-players)

16 The Chamber of Princes, March 1942

A contrast in styles:
17 The Viceroy, Lord Willingdon, visits Kotah State in 1935
18 Political Agent North Waziristan, K.C. Packman, at an informal tribal Jirga

idolised his mother whom he had hardly seen. He married a very nice girl, daughter of a minor Mahratta chief. His father was beastly to her: his own life having been made a misery by his wife, Tukojirao took it out on his son and daughter-in-law.

In December, 1927, Vikram had had enough. He ran away from Dewas and arrived at the Indore Residency, twenty miles away, in a semi-hysterical state. To the Resident, R.I.R. Glancy, he poured out his woes. His father had humiliated him by demoting him in the army; and was bent on poisoning him. His father, having failed to seduce Vikram's wife, had denounced her as a wicked girl and chased her out of the state. The blame for all this lay with his father's latest mistress, a dancing-girl who had recently produced a son and was determined that he should be Maharajah. Here, commented Glancy, were all the elements of a classic zenana intrigue.

The situation was delicate, as the Government was pledged by treaty not to give shelter to discontented relatives of the ruler. The proper course was for the young man to return to Dewas and for his father to treat him decently. Vikram was persuaded, reluctantly, to see his father, and came away from the interview sobbing bitterly, his father having taunted him with being illegitimate. He wanted to go to his mother in Kolhapur and there work for his B.A. degree.

Glancy did not regard Kolhapur, virtually governed by the Akka Saheba, as a suitable place for a young prince's upbringing.

> But I regard any place as better than Dewas where revolting immorality, misrule and hypocrisy are the order of the day . . . The Yuvraj has at times a marked resemblance to the Maharajah, and I do not believe for a moment the story of illegitimacy. I hope the Yuvraj will be allowed to live with his wife, who will be a steadying influence.

Meanwhile Vikram continued his studies, while staying with the Under Secretary, 'the society of young men being probably more desirable for the Yuvraj than our own'. But it could not be a permanent arrangement, if only because of that clause in the treaty. The real answer was for Vikram to return home, with a proper allowance from his father and with his wife allowed back to live with him. Glancy wrote to the Political Secretary:

> I am in possession of strong evidence of the father's design on his son's life, possibly sufficient for a Commission of Enquiry. If the Maharajah insists on impossible conditions for his son's return to Dewas, I will tell the Yuvraj that he can go where he wishes and he

will then go to his mother at Kolhapur. Attempts by other Chiefs to arrange a compromise have failed.

In the event, the Yuvraj went to Kolhapur, on an adequate allowance from his father, and there took his B.A. degree at the Rajaram College in 1932.

In 1933 an audit disclosed that the Treasury was almost empty, the state owed debts amounting to 15 lakhs plus 4 lakhs in arrears of pay to its employees, and state cheques were being bounced by the bank. The Maharajah solved many of these problems, especially his own, by decamping to French Pondicherry with which India had no extradition treaty. Before making his getaway, reported the Resident, His Highness distributed lavish gifts, jewellery, grants of land and elephants to his favourites. He then collected all the ready cash in the Treasury and, 'having consummated the complete bankruptcy and ruin of his state, took his departure with a light heart'.

Four years later he died in exile and was succeeded by Vikram Singh, who had developed into an excellent young man. He ruled his little state well, joined up in 1939 and had a 'good' war – not on someone-or-other's staff, but up front, as an ordinary company officer in an ordinary Mahratta battalion in the Western Desert. He returned to resume the government of his state and to pursue his passion for pig-sticking, riding like a demon but with an uncanny knack of guessing what the boar would do next – as I know, for I often rode with him, or rather more often, in his wake.

Another problem state in Central India was Jhabua (eleven-gun) where the Maharajah was unable to distinguish between his own private expenditure and state expenditure. His rule was a perpetual tug-of-war between himself and his nobles; when he was in the ascendant he extorted from them, and they from the peasants. He had changed his Diwan twenty-one times in twenty-nine years. He had two extremely expensive hobbies, fast women and fast cars: the former were uncounted, indeed uncountable; the latter numbered five, plus many slower, to cover precisely eleven miles of metalled road in the state. The only efficiently run state service was the provision of excise liquor to the Bhils. Glancy, the Resident, got his kinsman, the Maharajah of Ratlam, to 'speak to' the ruler, who was persuaded to accept restrictions on his powers, that is to say, virtual government by the Political Agent for five years. The restrictions were removed, and he was as bad as ever. So he had to go.

The Maharajah of Indore, whose Mahratta family-title was Holkar, was also named Tukoji Rao. He had a mistress, a ravishing Moslem dancing-girl named Mumtaz Begum. Perhaps she found palace life restrictive, perhaps she pined for the bright lights, or perhaps she just wanted a change. At all events she ran off to Bombay and became the mistress of a wealthy businessman named Bawla. Holkar was consumed with jealousy and rage, and all the talk of the palace was how to get even with the bitch.

Late one evening in 1925, in the fashionable Bombay suburb of Malabar Hill, a gang set on Mumtaz Begum and her protector, trying to abduct her. Two British officers who happened to be passing came to their help. In the ensuing fracas Bawla was shot dead, one officer was wounded, and Mumtaz Begum had her face slashed.

This was a scandal which could not be hushed up, for the press were on to it and would not leave go. Bawla's murderers, it transpired, were Indore palace bravoes, one on the pay-roll of the Indore Police and a favourite of the Maharajah. No one doubted that Holkar approved of the attempt to recover or punish his erring mistress. The question was, had he ordered or connived at it?

The Resident made his investigation for the acting-Viceroy, Lord Lytton, who reported to the Secretary of State.

> I have not the slightest doubt that the Maharajah gave orders that Mumtaz Begum be brought back to him. I am equally certain that he never contemplated the murder of Bawla, but he sanctioned the mutilation of Mumtaz Begum by his agents in the event of their failure to capture her. The cuts on her face were not accidental and appear to have been caused in an attempt to cut off her nose.* No one would have dared to mutilate the mistress of the Maharajah without his express authority. The mutilator was the trusted servant of His Highness.

The Maharajah was then offered the choice of a Commission of Enquiry or 'voluntary' abdication. After consulting the two best lawyers in India, Holkar chose to abdicate.

He had been a good ruler. Everyone was sorry for him, and the details of his abdication were arranged, so far as possible, to spare him pain. At the Darbar on the appointed, auspicious day, his son, Yeshwant Rao Holkar, was seated on the gadi. His father advanced towards him, marked his forehead with the red mark of a Maharajah Holkar, withdrew five paces, turned about and walked out.

*The traditional punishment for a woman's adultery.

The ex-Maharajah then departed on a long tour of the United States, and returned from Hollywood with a beautiful American bride. They settled down quietly in Indore and caused no trouble, never intriguing, never setting themselves up as a rival power-centre. Urbane and dignified, in a quiet way rather amusing, 'Former His Highness' was part of the social scene, despite the embarrassment sometimes caused by the ban on Political officers calling his American wife 'Your Highness', and her refusal to be called anything else.

The family had a reputation for eccentricity. Tukoji Rao's father used to amuse himself by harnessing a team of high-caste bankers to his coach and driving them round Indore race-course. But Tukoji Rao's son, the new Maharajah Yeshwant Rao Holkar, was an excellent, enlightened ruler who did much to develop the industrial economy of his state. He even introduced a Legislative Assembly, which was *elected* – albeit on a somewhat restricted franchise. Charles Allen, in *Lives of the Indian Princes*, alleges that, having been educated at Oxford, Yeshwant Rao hated England and the English. If this is so, he disguised his feelings, and was a great social asset in Residency circles. John Biscoe recalls:

> Indore was an advanced state with a young ruler and a very pretty wife whom he adored. They loved to entertain informally in a small house, not the palace, where after we had all been to the pictures in the cantonment town of Mhow, nine miles away, we would foregather and His Highness would put on an apron and become the barman.

Opium in India was a Government monopoly. Among Redpath's duties as Under Secretary in Indore was that of Deputy Opium Agent.

> Opium grown in controlled areas was processed in government factories . . . and sent to a distribution centre in the Residency Area. Here sealed packing-cases containing balls of opium – the size of cricket-balls, looking like hard brown fudge, smelling of something quite indescribable and packed in sawdust – arrived periodically to replace outgoings. I had to check these cases into the security-locked, police-guarded warehouse. Every Monday I opened the warehouse and, in my presence, four coolies, each wearing only a skimpy loincloth, opened a case and brushed the sawdust off the balls of opium. Next, various quantities of opium were weighed, packed and sealed for despatch to the state authorities who were responsible for supplying their drug licensees. The coolies were searched before they departed and the warehouse was locked for another week, giving me time to recover from the nauseating smell of opium. On the advice of a *soi-disant* expert, I mulched the soil

round my roses and hollyhocks with the slighly impregnated sawdust which had been brushed off the opium balls. The effect was astonishing: the plants grew and flowered outrageously, then withered. Surely there was a lesson to be learned from this phenomenon. Perhaps they needed another 'fix.'

Years later, in 1946-7, there was a problem caused by American servicemen in India developing a drug-addiction. Huge quantities of opium were smuggled down the railway to Bombay for export to the United States, to be processed into heroin and sold at a 5,000 per cent profit. The Under Secretary in Indore, who was then myself, tried many cases of opium-smuggling, and the Railway Police became adept at spotting suitcases with false bottoms, tea-urns used for purposes other than brewing tea. But the big fish were never caught: only the small fry, such as the man who was given ten rupees in Delhi by a man he had never met before, and asked to carry a box to Bombay and hand it over to a man who would identify himself by flourishing a red cloth. If they kept their mouths shut, their families would be looked after; if they 'grassed' their principals, the consequences would not be so pleasant.

For touring, Central India was not a patch on Rajputana. The ancient, ruined fortress and city of Mandu was worth seeing – temples, battlements and palaces all overgrown with jungle like the 'Cold Lairs' of Kipling's *Jungle Book*. But there was not much else of interest. I recall a tour to the small Moslem state of Jaora (thirteen-gun, population 100,000). The morning was, as usual, spent by the Resident laying the foundation stone for a – hospital? – dispensary? – primary school? – I don't know, and it really does not matter. Close by, under a heap of dry grass, was a foundation stone laid by his predecessor a year earlier. Surely it must have been to the Nawab of Jaora that a cynical Resident remarked, 'Your Highness really should collect all the foundation stones that have been laid in the past ten years and use them to pave the palace courtyard.' Through the late afternoon and evening, in company with the Nawab and a dozen bored courtiers, we lined the banks of a muddy little river, fishing for mahseer with lures designed, made and coloured by His Highness himself in a palace workshop. The fishing was poor, but the Nawab a Compleat Angler, and no courtier who valued his place would plead that he had not the patience for it. At night there was a banquet consisting not, as we hoped, of Indian and Persian dishes, but, disastrously, of course after course of 'European' food prepared by a cook borrowed at great expense from the nearest railway station restaurant.

Derek Harrington-Hawes describes a grisly tour to some small states in the Bhopal Agency, in company with the Resident, Kenneth Fitze, and their respective wives.

13.Feb. We arrived at Narsingarh in time for a very welcome cup of tea. Police whistles blew, guns boomed, bands played and soldiers (?) presented arms on our arrival. Mr Fitze then inspected one of the lousier Guards of Honour and was brazen enough to express satisfaction at their smart appearance. The guest house was comfortable. We played some card-game with a pack of cards that were *so* indescribably filthy that we hardly dared touch them . . .

15.Feb. Narsingarh to Kurwai. We left after breakfast, but not before the usual distribution of Itr and Pan* – ugh! From Sehore we took the train and travelled in some comfort in the saloon. At Bhopal I had much pleasure in teasing the unpleasant Head Clerk from the Agency Office. He had come down to the station in the hopes of doing an oil to the Resident, but I got hold of him first and sent him off to buy two newspapers. By the time he got back, Mr Fitze was out of sight, in the saloon . . . After dinner our host tried to show us *Gay Divorcee* but the attempt was only partially successful. The Fitzes made it plain that they wanted to go to bed as soon as possible, so the picture was shown at twice its normal speed and a whole reel was left out . . . We seem to spend all our time on tour longing for bedtime.

16.Feb. Kurwai. The day was devoted to the inevitable reception by the Begum-Mother in the fort. The old lady was as charming as ever and regaled Mother Fitze with her usual stories, but she might as well have saved her breath as Mrs F. could not understand a quarter of what was said. Like so many 'domiciled Europeans', Mrs F.'s knowledge of the vernacular is wilfully limited. After dinner Mr Fitze started the usual cricket-game on the billiard table, which was not a great success.

17.Feb. Kurwai to Kilchipur. On arrival at the palace we passed a group of very obvious dancing-girls. Mrs Fitze asked her host brightly, 'And now I suppose we are going to meet the bride', pointing at the most bitchy of all the nautch-girls. Curtain! Who but she could mistake a no-caste Mohamadan dancing-girl for a Rajput royal bride? Dinner followed, and some rather raucous singing by the 'bride of Kilchipur' and her girl-friends.

*Itr, atar of roses; Pan, betel-nut and spices wrapped in a vine leaf.

18.Feb. The easiest day of the tour . . . At the end of dinner we were asked to drink the health of the Nawab 'who is not only a great ruler but a great gentleman'. Says you: says who? . . . The singing girls were much saucier this evening, encouraged by our intoxicated host. Just as things were beginning to look really cheerful, Mother Fitze swept us off to bed.

The reek of Itr on pocket-handkerchiefs – packing suitcases at 11 o'clock at night – listening to Mrs F. and Mr F. and family – driving miles in hot clothes on uncomfortable seats – making polite conversation to half-witted Diwans and private secretaries – trying to retort to Mrs F.'s facetiousness without being cheeky – eating endless meals – keeping bright and cheerful in any circumstances – lighting cigarettes and carrying coats – collecting garlands – and so on, and so on without end.

Rewa (seventeen-gun, population 1.5 million) was one of the largest states in Central India; also one of the least developed, consisting mainly of jungle inhabited by aboriginal Bhils and a unique breed of near-white tiger. Its Rajput Maharajah, Gulab Singh, was intelligent, and could have been a good ruler during the brief periods which he could spare from tiger-shooting. Although young, he was one of the old-fashioned sort, telling Fitze quite frankly that his ancestors had come to Rewa as conquerors, that he regarded the state as his private property, its revenue as his private income, and saw no reason to defer to democratic fads or to consider for one moment the welfare of his subjects. He had an unfortunate history of being at variance with officers lent by the Government of India, and of indulging his sense of humour at their expense. The following story is Fitze's:

During one of my visits I found the officer in charge of the state Army in a state of extreme indignation which had led him to proffer his resignation. He was an outstandingly spruce young Indian captain, borrowed from a crack cavalry regiment, a fervid devotee of the cult of spit-and-polish but lacking perhaps in the faculty to adapt himself to the requirements of his present situation. The death, after many years of dignified leisure, of the favourite charger of the late Maharajah was regarded by His Highness as a suitable opportunity to show his respect for his revered father by ordering that the animal should receive a state funeral. A pit was dug in the centre of the parade-ground and surrounded by an impressive parade of troops. The interment was to take place at 4 p.m. and His Highness was to be present in person to pay his last respects. Punctuality was never one of his virtues, the heat of the summer afternoon was overpowering, and

> long before the aroma from the venerable war-horse was quenched by its consignment to the grave, the breach between the ruler and his Commander-in-Chief, standing stiffly with drawn sword amidst a swirling cloud of bluebottles, had become irreparable.

When, therefore, Conrad Corfield was offered the post of Adviser to the Maharajah of Rewa, he did not expect an easy time, but he accepted with alacrity what promised to be a job full of interest. He was surprised to find the capital thirty miles from the railway, which made a wide detour round it. The reason for this was characteristic of this state: 'Late His Highness' would not allow trains to pass close to his palace carrying passengers who might be eating beef.

Trouble was in the wind. Corfield was put in the picture by the state's Inspector General of Police, a competent Sikh. The administration, said Santokh Singh, was archaic, the cultivators over-taxed, the townsfolk disgruntled because of the lack of any urban development and the landowners, known as Pawaidars, who should have been the main support of the Maharajah, were angry and disloyal because he had invaded their hereditary rights. It was a situation made for exploitation by Congress: the local Praja Mandal was active, Allahabad (home of Pandit Jawaharlal Nehru) was close by, and Congress agitators passed freely between the state and the United Provinces.

> I asked Santokh Singh how soon he thought the explosion would come. He replied blandly that he would let me know in good time . . . With his help I prepared a plan to restore the ruler's authority. The basis of the plan was to act before the pot boiled. The Maharajah, however, was afraid of public criticism outside the state if he acted before there was an explosion . . . I said I was only his Adviser and would, of course, accept any different plan he wished to propose. But I pointed out that if my plan were adopted and failed, I took the blame: if it succeeded, he got the credit.

In the event the Maharajah sanctioned Corfield's plan, but asked that he be given notice of 'D-Day' so that he could be far away, tiger-shooting.

The Pawaidars were reminded that one of the written conditions of the grant of each one's estate was that he should be loyal to the Maharajah. Should this condition be breached, the Maharajah could cancel the grant. The Pawaidars' zeal for revolution waned.

The plan was to arrest the plot-leaders just before they staged their revolt. But where could they be confined? To put them in the local lock-up would invite riots, perhaps even an attempt to storm the jail and release them. Corfield learned of an ancient fort, deep in the jungle, which he examined on the pretext of an interest in archaeology. It was just what was wanted – remote and, with a little barbed wire, secure.

Santokh Singh, who had his man on the Praja Mandal committee, learned the date of the revolt, and during the preceding night all the leaders were taken quietly out of circulation. The mob which assembled in the morning to storm the bastille dispersed for lack of leadership.

Then the constructive work could start: the Pawaidars' and cultivators' legitimate grievances were to be settled, the state opened up with roads that were planned for purposes other than to facilitate His Highness's shikar, the administration trimmed of sinecures and purged, more or less, of corruption. The Maharajah's willingness to take his Adviser's advice waned day by day.

> His authority had been re-established, so why not relax? Each time we met I saw a question flitting behind his eyes, 'Is an Adviser really necessary? . . . How can I get rid of him without a fuss?'

He tried the elementary tactics of summoning his Adviser for consultation and then keeping him waiting for hours. Corfield riposted by taking a crime-novel to the ante-room and, when he was at last told by an A.D.C. that His Highness would soon be ready for him, begging the A.D.C. not to hurry His Highness since he had reached the most exciting part of the book.

After that they got on better. Only over police pay was the Adviser defeated. He maintained that a constable paid only Rs 15 a month had to accept bribes to feed his family: police pay should be doubled. 'Not so,' replied the Maharajah. 'A policeman will take in bribes a sum equal to his pay. If I double his pay, he will double his bribes.'

Corfield in his innocence assumed that once the Maharajah had approved some worthy project, such as a bridge over the Chambal river to make the southern part of the state accessible, and its cost had been included in the state budget, the battle was won. Far from it. No money could actually be spent without another order from His Highness ordering the work to begin; and if the money had not been spent by the end of the financial year, it passed through the state reserves into the Maharajah's private bank account. So His Highness had a vested interest in approving some development project, having money set aside for it – and then not authorising the work to start. This was the fundamental obstacle to any progress.

From the Rewa officers Corfield met nothing but friendliness and co-operation. Sometimes, indeed, too much. He was no horseman, but in Rewa he started playing polo. After a while he could hit the ball quite often on the off-side, occasionally on the near-side, and began to pride himself on his progress. Great was his mortification, on a visit to the Rewa Officers' Mess, to see a notice requesting players not to ride the Adviser too hard as his seat on a horse was not very safe.

While Corfield was in Rewa, his wife met with a hunting accident in Ootacamund, which proved fatal. Living alone afterwards, he felt in need of a hobby and bought a cine-camera. He thought his children would be amused by a film of a dancing-girl and her musicians, and arranged for one to perform against the suitable background of the old palace.

> A few days later I emerged from my bungalow in the cool of the evening to find her awaiting me, accompanied by her 'managers'. Covering her face with her sari, she presented me with some ears of corn, which I blushingly accepted. Then, with a hurried exchange of courtesies, I leapt into my car and was off . . . I learned afterwards that seeds of corn were emblems of fertility.

The Maharajah could not bring himself to sign Corfield's rules setting out the privileges and duties of the Pawaidars. Month after month he procrastinated, until one evening, when they were having a friendly drink together, Corfield asked for a few days' leave to go to Delhi.

'Who are you going to see there?'

'The Political Secretary, Your Highness.'

'I see . . . Well, I hope you have a nice time.'

The rules, duly signed by the Maharajah, were delivered to his bungalow that evening.

When Corfield's two years were nearly up, the Maharajah presented him with a gold cigarette-case, which he duly returned. A few days later they went to Delhi together, for separate interviews with the Viceroy. Lord Willingdon asked Corfield what he thought of the rule forbidding government servants from accepting presents. Corfield replied that if the present placed one under no obligation, he did not see that it mattered.

'Just my view,' said Lord Willingdon. 'Would a gold cigarette-case put you under any obligation to your Maharajah?'

'Not a bit, after all I've done for him.'

'Then here it is,' said Lord Willingdon, handing it over . . . 'Let's open it and see if it's real!' They did, and it was.

12

The States of Gwalior, Baroda and Gujerat

The three great Mahratta chieftains who had over-run Central India, plundered Rajputana and humbled the Mogul were Holkar, Scindia and the Gaekwar. Their descendants were the Maharajahs respectively of Indore, Gwalior and Baroda.

Although geographically in Central India, Gwalior was not one of the 'Central Indian States': the Maharajah Scindia enjoyed the felicity of a Resident all to himself. Gwalior was a twenty-one-gun state, with a population of 3.5 million. Its ruler in the 1920s was, in Cyril Hancock's words, a 'chubby little extrovert with a reputation for practical joking', improbably but loyally named George Jivaji Rao.

Occasionally he was the victim rather than the perpetrator of a joke. The Gwalior jungles were full of tigers; the jungles of the neighbouring small state of Datia (fifteen-gun, population 158,000) had none. But the Maharajah of Datia kept one tigress in a cage which, when she was in season, he used to have placed in his jungle near the Gwalior border, with the result that all the nearby Gwalior tigers crossed the border into Datia. Scindia was not amused, especially when he had invited some V.I.P. for a tiger-shoot.

In Datia, as a laudable economy, the duties of Chief Justice (@ Rs 150 a month) and Inspector of Dancing Girls (@ Rs 500) were performed by the same person.

Lord Reading visited Gwalior, accompanied by his Assistant Private Secretary, Hancock. Reading was an agile lawyer, but no sportsman and a poor shot. However, a tiger-shoot there had to be. Hancock writes:

> We reached camp on the last day of March, 1924, when it was already getting warm; and when my mosquito-net was lifted next morning so that I could drink my early-morning tea, the contents of the cup fizzed into activity when the sugar proved to be Eno's. Other surprises followed at formal meals, such as trick soup-plates spilling their contents. Much hilarity followed until news of a tiger arrived.

All was then hustle and bustle. A beat was arranged which would cause the tiger to swim a narrow river just below a tall tree in which the Viceroy would be esconced. But a breeze made the tree sway and Lord Reading flatly refused to venture up the rope-ladder. So he awaited the tiger standing on the river-bank, flanked by two trusty marksmen. The tiger duly reached the river, started to swim across, was missed by His Excellency's first barrel and wounded by the second. He turned back and disappeared into a ravine. The Viceroy was then escorted back to camp and operations to despatch the beast were commenced.

The tiger was despatched, and was very properly proved to be of immense size . . . indeed, a great deal larger than any other tiger ever measured or imagined. Arguments about the correct way to measure a dead tiger – in a straight line from nose to tail or along the curves of his back – were bandied back and forth in the correspondence columns of *The Field*, and allegations were made that several inches of the measuring-tape had been stuffed into the tiger's mouth. But young Hancock, who knew a thing or two, kept his own mouth shut, and Lord Reading's tiger remains a record.

'George' Scindia may have been a 'chubby little extrovert' who enjoyed simple jests such as inviting an immaculate A.D.C. to sit down on a freshly painted bench, or causing the electric train on which the decanters were circulated after dinner to shoot past a guest who was known to be 'fond of his port'; but he was a conscientious ruler who established cotton, leather, pottery and engineering industries in his state, and a proper land revenue system. Like Harun-al-Rashid he loved to walk about in disguise, talking with the humblest of his subjects, and thus learning what really went on and where the shoe pinched.

His Darbar was wholly traditional, with the Mahratta Sardars sitting cross-legged on the carpet, each with his sabre across his knees; and among them the present head of the Filose family, descended from the Italian military adventurer who had served the Scindia of the 1820s, also sitting cross-legged but wearing top-hat, striped trousers and morning-coat.

The Gaekwar of Baroda (twenty-one-gun, population 2.5 million), Maharajah Sayaji Rao, was the third great Mahratta prince and a far cry from his freebooter forebears. His state was rich and advanced, as was he in his Privy Purse and his political opinions. In the Coronation Darbar, while other princes were gorgeous in silk and jewels and gold-hilted swords, he appeared in white, hand-woven khaddar, the garb of Congress activists, and saluted the King Emperor with a nod and a jaunty twirl of his walking-stick. His support for the war-effort had been less than whole-hearted, and he was addicted to employing in his state foreign, even American, experts, rather than those of the Island Race. His son at Oxford was reported as being intelligent, wealthy, anti-authority and revolutionary material. However, by the 1920s he had achieved respectability, if not absolute trust; in his views on Congress agitators he seemed to be sound; he bought a stud-farm in Kildare and was a successful owner on the English and French turf.

Before 1933 his and neighbouring states had been in political relation with the Government of Bombay, not with the Indian Government; but in that year this arrangement was changed and they were brought under the wing of the Indian Political Department. The Gaekwar did not, like Scindia, enjoy the undivided attention of a Resident, but had to share him with eleven smaller states, mainly Rajput, of which the largest was Rajpipla (thirteen-gun, population 200,000). The Secretary for the Resident for Baroda and the Gujerat States also acted as Political Agent for fifty-six pocket-handkerchief-sized states, all of which were non-salute, as well as the Dangs, an aboriginal jungle tribe resembling the Bhils.

Baroda was run very much like a province of British India, and quite as well. It had properly differentiated departments, a revenue settlement like the Bombay settlement, a regular judicial system of subordinate, District, High and Appeal Courts; and a Legislative Assembly composed of non-officials, including an elected element. The local government was based on the traditional Indian village panchayats, grass-root democracy which Indians understood. There was compulsory, free primary education, several high schools, and the Baroda University College. There were light and heavy industries, notably textiles, a well-run railway producing considerable revenue for the state, experimental state farms and agricultural institutes. Baroda, in short, was admirably run, and consequently a trifle dull from the Political's point of view.

It was Hugh Rance's first Political posting, as Under Secretary to the Resident, Lieutenant Colonel Leslie Weir, although he had had no preliminary training in court work or civil administration.

> As well as being Under Secretary I found I was also a First Class Magistrate, with powers of up to 2 years' imprisonment, judge of the Small Causes Court, and Cantonment Magistrate. As a Company Commander in the army I had been limited to sentencing an offender to 10 days' C.B., so I found my new powers somewhat intimidating. I was just twenty-four. In Baroda Cantonment there was a European population of about sixty, including British officers and families of the

5th/7th Rajputs, bankers, missionaries, Europeans in the Baroda state services and us in the Residency.

Baroda was a well-run state, due, I think, to the high standards set by the Diwan, Sir V.T. Krishnamacharia, a Madrassi. We saw a good deal of him in the Residency, and he was a charming and most able man.

(In parenthesis, the Maharawal of Dungarpur wrote that what Rajput and Mahratta princes most resented from the Political Department was being nagged into employing Madrassi Diwans.

> Baroda, Udaipur, Jodhpur, Jaipur, Bikanir and Gwalior were all more or less pressed into having Madrassi Diwans. These Madrassis were vegetarians, teetotallers, detested games and the nicer things of life; they had no ear for music and hated to attend the princely Darbar. They were sullen and self-centred. They may have been able men, but one and all betrayed their masters and made common cause with the Congress leaders. For this they were richly rewarded by Nehru.)

An agreeable feature of Baroda, and indeed of most states, was the absence of religious bigotry. In this Hindu state all communities joined joyfully in the great Moslem festival of Mohurram, the Gaekwar, his family and the Diwan riding in the procession on elephants.

With the Abdication Crisis secret telegrams proliferated, and Rance spent many hours coding and de-coding them:

> On the night before the Abdication became public, I sat up until the small hours decoding Top Secret telegrams, only to see them printed word for word in the newspapers next morning. The Europeans in the Station were deeply shocked, but most Indians could not see why the King had to go. 'Mrs Simpson was only a woman, so why all this fuss?'

This was doubtless the reaction of the Maharajah of Rajpipla, a cheerful young man whose Christmas parties were great fun. 'He had a penchant for European ladies of uncertain background, and one never quite knew whom one would meet in his household.' He did not let affairs of state weigh heavily upon him, and owned a Derby winner, Windsor Lad. His taxpayers smarted for it.

A tour to Cambray, a small Moslem state, took Rance and Weir to one of the places in which the East India Company was first allowed to set up a 'Factory'. On the Old Factor's House was the date, 1611 – long before the English had any idea of conquering or ruling India.

M. Worth was in Baroda at the same time as Rance, but one step up, being Secretary to the Resident. In this capacity he acted as Political Agent to the small Gujerat States:

> all with insignificant revenues mostly appropriated by their rulers. I remember counting the money in the Treasury – a Chubb safe – in one state in the presence of the ruler and his Chief Clerk. The safe was found to have 8 annas in excess of the balance shown in the account book. This was too much for the clerk, who fell off his chair in a faint. An enquiry revealed that the money in the safe had been supplied by the local moneylender and that the clerk had miscalculated the amount.
>
> Another small state, Sachin, had a Moslem ruler with three very beautiful wives, who were not in purdah. The first, having failed to produce a child, had been sent back to Lahore to find a second. This one too had failed, and had been sent back to Lahore to find a third, even prettier, who was also unable to have a child. Later I mentioned the sad state of these lovely girls to the Jam Saheb of Nawanagar. He told me to watch the column of Births and Deaths in *The Statesman*. Sure enough, an announcement of the birth of a son and heir to the Nawab of Sachin duly appeared, to be followed a month later by a notice of his premature death. The Nawab's virility was thereby vindicated.
>
> While I was in Baroda the Gaekwar died. I had to accompany the Resident to commiserate with the Maharani and her daughter. As we knew that neither lady was unduly distressed by the death of His Highness, we were not impressed by their lamentations, especially when the younger Maharani gave me a wink when thanking us . . . We had chairs placed for us by the funeral pyre so that we could make sure the Maharani did not commit suttee. As there was no likelihood that she would do any such thing, we were able to leave as soon as the pyre was lit.

For two months in summer Worth and his family were able to escape the muggy heat of Baroda and 'recess' in Mount Abu. On the way their train passed through Bombay Presidency, in which a Congress Government had introduced Prohibition. Worth had a couple of bottles of whisky in his suitcase, which he was reluctant to open for the inspection of the Railway Police. Argument was becoming heated when he was rescued by 'Sardar' Vallabhai Patel, the 'Iron Man of Congress', who was Home Minister in the Bombay Government, responsible for enforcing Prohibition. They breakfasted together on the train, which by then had passed out of the Presidency. The Iron Man produced a large hip-flask, poured himself a generous peg of whisky, offered it to them, and remarked that, outside Bombay, he could drink what he liked. On another occasion, reproached for smoking a cigar when Congress was promoting a boycott of foreign goods, he replied blandly, 'I'm burning foreign goods. What's wrong with that?'

Leslie Chauncey, when Political Agent, Gujerat States, was confronted by the most delicate of problems. The ruler's mother, widowed young, had an unwanted baby by one of the men about the palace. There was every likelihood that the ruler, if he heard of this when he came back from school for the holidays, would have his mother murdered. What to do? Chauncey and the Diwan arranged for the baby to be taken care of by a convent in southern India. For absolute secrecy, the Diwan himself took the child there. He returned, a shadow of his usual robust self.

'Sahib,' he told Chauncey, 'I am loyal to the Government. I would do anything to help – except go through that again. The Mother Superior and the nuns refused to believe that I wasn't the father.'

13

The Punjab States

Of all the Indian princes Bhupindar Singh, Maharajah of the Sikh state of Patiala, came closest to what the world thought an Indian prince should be. Born in 1890, he was an enormous man, bearded, bull-chested, and pre-eminently a military figure, though he probably never heard a shot fired in anger. Highly articulate, albeit with a somewhat caustic tongue, he was elected Chancellor to the Chamber of Princes year after year from 1926 to 1930. He was a crack shot, a good all-round cricketer and a fine, aggressive polo-player: his Patiala Tigers was one of the half-dozen best teams in India. His state was very fertile, and rich with railway and canal revenues. With a population of 1.6 million sturdy Jat and Sikh cultivators and a seventeen-gun salute, it was by far the most important of the fourteen Punjab states. He was, of course, anathema to Congress politicians, and their dislike was heartily reciprocated. He spent money in princely style, like water, and had tremendous presence. By common consent, he was the top Sikh in all India and, as such, not a man the Government would wish to have as an enemy.

He had an insatiable appetite for women, of whom his zenana contained a large number, and was unscrupulous in his methods of procuring them. The author of a scurrilous anti-state pamphlet wrote that different people have different ways of starting the day: the Englishman with bacon and eggs, the Frenchman with coffee and rolls, 'His Highness with a virgin'. If, as is probable, he was thinking of Patiala, he was not quite right: virgin, wife or widow – it was all the same to Bhupindar Singh, provided she was comely and preferably, though not necessarily, willing.

In 1929 there was published a book of some 200 pages entitled *Indictment of Patiala*. Supported by many witnesses and much circumstantial detail, it alleged, inter alia, that the Maharajah:

1. Procured the murder of a relative by marriage, Lal Singh, in order to have his widow.
2. Procured the abduction of innumerable women whose husbands were murdered, imprisoned on false evidence, or compensated from state funds.

3. Quarrelled with two of his A.D.C.s over a dancing-girl. A few days later the A.D.C.s were murdered.
4. Imprisoned a state official for failing to supply him with nubile hill-girls.
5. Made indecent proposals to his young step-mother, who was compelled to flee to British territory.
6. Forced a 12-year-old girl who died from his attentions.
7. Pursued, caught and had burnt alive four Rajput girls who escaped from his zenana.
8. Raped the daughter of a European Minister in his state.
9. Punished recalcitrant women by putting red pepper up their vaginas.
10. Set up a bomb-factory in his palace grounds.

B.J. Glancy, Agent to the Governor-General for the Punjab States, was asked for his opinion on the *Indictment*. He replied on October 6th, 1929, that it was neither necessary nor desirable to set up an enquiry: there was 'no evidence in our records to support most of the charges against His Highness'.

The Viceroy, Lord Irwin, disagreed, and wrote to the Secretary of State, Colonel Wedgwood-Benn:

> The problem of Patiala is causing me great concern. The indictment of his administration which has been published is not, I am afraid, something we can pooh-pooh or quietly smother. For here are statements very grave in character made by people who have come forward publicly and professed their willingness to stand cross-examination. Moreover the authors of the Patiala volume have been clever enough not to advance the material as proved, but as material that constitutes a *prima-facie* case for enquiry. I do feel very grave difficulty in either the Government of India or His Majesty's Government refusing to enquire in any way. The best thing would of course be that Patiala should himself prosecute, but this I have reason to believe he dare not do. This is tantamount to an admission that the charges are not altogether ill-founded, and if this is the deduction I am back at my difficulty that we cannot afford to sponsor an administration which has laid itself open to an attack that it dare not meet. I propose to ask Patiala to come to see me in the next day or two and have a very frank talk with him on these matters.

Patiala was open to attack on another front that autumn. He had to admit that his state, potentially so wealthy, was bankrupt, mainly owing to his personal extravagance, and had to ask the Government of India to come to his rescue with a loan. (The Nizam of Hyderabad, disapproving of Patiala's life-style, had already refused to do so.) The new Agent to the Governor-General, FitzPatrick, examined the state's finances and found it needed a loan of nearly two crores (£1.5 million). His Highness, reported FitzPatrick, was transcendently loyal and generous. His unique position in the Sikh community recommended him for special consideration.

> Patiala is a very valuable asset to the Government of India and the Empire, and by saving the state and its ruler from bankruptcy and consequent discredit, we shall be gaining valuable political results and getting good value for our money.

He recommended a loan at 5 per cent, well below the current market rate, on the security of the state's canal and railway revenues. The Government turned down his recommendation. Patiala was a rich state, His Highness must economise, budget for an annual surplus for a few years, and employ a British Minister of Finance until the state was on its feet again. To this the Maharajah reluctantly agreed.

He assented also to an official enquiry into the allegations contained in the *Indictment of Patiala*. One might have expected that a former Chancellor of the Chamber of Princes would have demanded an enquiry by a panel of princes in accordance with the procedure agreed between the Government and the Chamber. But Patiala, knowing his man and sensing his sympathy, asked for the enquiry to be held by the Agent to the Governor-General.

FitzPatrick found that there was no bomb factory. (No one ever supposed there would be.) There was no proof of His Highness's complicity in the murder of Lal Singh, but the principal witness had 'escaped' from Patiala custody and the convicted murderers had been let off very lightly by the Patiala court.

> As to all those stories about women, these should be seen in the light of the custom of a bride coming to the house of a ruler to bring with her young girl attendants to serve the double purpose of attending on the Maharani and providing distraction for her husband, and thus preventing second marriages or recourse to public women should the Maharajah be of an amorous or roving disposition . . . His Highness does not deny youthful indiscretions, and is willing to make monetary amends.

The Maharajah's conduct, wrote FitzPatrick, was indefensible on moral grounds, but there was no proof of the graver charges against him.

Sir Gilbert Laithwaite, Permanent Secretary to the India Office, minuted drily on the file:

> The tone of the Agent to the Governor-General's report suggests that he has been anxious to whitewash Patiala. Mr FitzPatrick's report contains a number of peculiar and unpleasant features and there are sufficient weaknesses in the Maharajah's position and in the conduct of his private affairs to afford his enemies an excuse for mud-slinging. The statement made by the Agent to the Governor-General in his summing-up, 'There is nothing in the evidence to prove that His Highness has been in the habit of taking the wives of his subjects and sardars for immoral purposes', is of interest so far as it goes.

So Bhupindar Singh, with the help of FitzPatrick, weathered a storm which would have sunk many a lesser ruler whose attitude to Federation was not so crucial. For a couple of years he kept a comparatively low profile, but in 1934 and 1935 he was re-elected Chancellor to the Chamber of Princes. 'I am very sorry,' wrote Lord Willingdon to Sir Samuel Hoare in February, 1934, 'to have Patiala as Chancellor of the Chamber of Princes. Such a stupid man.' And in the following year, 'Patiala is the most unreliable man I know. Either a great fool, or the slipperiest customer that ever existed . . . The Chamber of Princes under Patiala is fast becoming a decrepit organ.'

But His Highness's organ, under the care of a French specialist in these matters and stimulated by variety which is the most potent of aphrodisiacs, was far from decrepit. In 1937 he was being threatened with exposure in the press by the outraged Anglo-Indian husband of a lady he had stolen.

It fell to Wakefield, as Secretary to the Agent to the Governor-General, to deal with this delicate problem. The only solution, he thought, was financial, and he consulted the Maharajah's Private Secretary, who shrugged his shoulders and said, 'You know what His Highness is like.'

'How much can he pay?'

'Very little. He has not yet paid for his last two cars.'

Wakefield next tackled the husband, who waxed very indignant at the idea of being bought off. He wanted to see the seducer *punished*. But how, asked Wakefield, can a Maharajah be punished in his own state? He could hardly be tried by his own court. It might, however, be possible to persuade His Highness to pay a sort of fine, a *voluntary* fine, for his disgraceful conduct – say Rs 10,000 which would naturally go to the injured person; not, of course, to buy him off, but to punish the man who had done him wrong. Well, replied the husband, if you put it that way . . .

Wakefield's superior, the Agent to the Governor-General, was Sir Harold Wilberforce-Bell, a remarkable man whom Wakefield's three predecessors had not found congenial. He was, like many men small of stature, most concerned with his own dignity. He ranked in Lahore below the Governor of the Punjab, so he would never attend any social function at which the Governor might be present; but above the Commissioner of Lahore, so he instructed his Secretary to ensure that his dhobi* always had the use of a flat stone *upstream* of the flat stone used by the Commissioner's dhobi. He was a snob. He had not been to one of the major Public Schools, but a copy of the *Eton College Chronicle* was always prominent on his desk. If, opposite the name of any caller in his Visitors' Book, he saw the magic word 'Landowner', his eye lit up, his Personal Assistant was instructed to bring him *Debrett* or *Burke's Landed Gentry*, and uniformed chuprassis hastened away with invitation cards.

He was a terrific stickler for etiquette and for wearing the correct garb for every occasion, and thought nothing of sending his Secretary or Under Secretary back to change if he was improperly dressed. Brook Neale, his Personal Assistant, countered this by ordering from a bazaar tailor exact replicas of his master's suits, so that he could appear in a garb which Wilberforce-Bell could hardly fault. Neale did not remain long in the Political.

Sir Harold deemed it his special duty to defend the prerogatives of the Royal Family. No Indian prince could, he insisted, sit on a 'throne': there was only one throne in the Empire and that was occupied by the King Emperor; Indian princes sat on gadis. Indeed, the very word 'prince', when applied to the chiefs or rulers of Indian states, he regarded with disfavour. Attending gundog trials in Kapurthala State he spotted a notice outside a luncheon-tent – 'For Royalty only'. Wakefield was instructed to tear down the offending board.

He was a bully, but unlike most bullies, he was no coward: the bigger his opponent, the more he relished a row. He even took on Patiala. The Maharajah won the first round on points, the affair of the pop-gun salute (see p.10). But Wilberforce-Bell came out fighting from his corner for the second. Most rulers displayed over their coats of arms a crown, some an arched crown. But an arched crown, Sir Harold

*Washerman.

insisted, impinged the Royal Prerogative. He used to examine with a magnifying glass the crowns atop letters from Maharajahs and Nawabs and, if one was arched, dictate a stinging rebuke. On this issue he gave battle, and Patiala eventually gave in. However, Sir Harold met his match in the Maharajah of Kapurthala, who wrote to him from Paris. There was a crown on top of the writing paper, and the crown, Sir Harold saw with pop-eyed indignation, was arched – but the paper was that of the Hotel King George V.

Although in some degree a figure of fun, Sir Harold was a very formidable, efficient officer. There was no one who could better be trusted to enforce on some obstructive Darbar an unpopular Government policy. But he was not loved.

He gave Wakefield special responsibility for the fifteen-gun Moslem state of Khairpur, the 24-stone Mir of which was so spectacularly extravagant that on his shopping-sprees to Bombay and Calcutta his Finance Minister used to dog his footsteps, cancelling his orders as he left each shop. His son, who succeeded to the gadi in 1935, was not exactly deranged but just a trifle off-centre, and was comfortably established well away from the capital, while a capable Finance Minister tried to restore the state to something near solvency. He and Wakefield brought in a Hindu accountant with a harsh metallic voice to suit his abrasive character, who examined and classified ten years' accumulation of unpaid bills, the biggest being for jewellery. He recovered much of this from the former and existing Mirs' wives – not without difficulty – and returned it to the shops. He rejected many claims, compromised on others, and in two years got matters more or less straight.

Wakefield's next special job was as President of the Council of Regency of the thirteen-gun Sikh state of Nabha. The former Maharajah had been banished after almost going to war with Patiala. He died in exile, and his heir, who had been educated in England, came out to be trained in administration before assuming full powers.

Wakefield found that his predecessor as President of the Council had been an efficient administrator, but over-fond of imprisoning people who caused trouble for 'bringing the Darbar into hatred and contempt'. Wakefield had a jail delivery of those who had really done no more than complain and criticise, and then turned to the delicate problem of the hair and beard of the young Maharajah, Pratap Singh.

His hair had been shorn and his beard shaved while he was in England. This was a terrible thing, uncut hair and beard being one of the outward and visible signs of a Sikh's faith. There was a terrific uproar about it, not confined to the Akali Sikh fanatics, while Congress propagandists accused the British of forcing this desecration on the innocent young man. He and his mother protested in vain that he had done it only on the advice of a Harley Street specialist in order to cure a skin-rash, and declared that he would rather abdicate than grow a beard. There could hardly have been a more unpleasant storm in a tea-cup.

Wakefield took him aside for a long heart-to-heart talk.

'Are you,' Pratap Singh asked defiantly, 'ordering me to grow a beard?'

'No. I'm asking you as a friend.'

'In that case, I will.'

He duly ascended the gadi, making Wakefield his Diwan.

Wakefield got on well with the new Maharajah, and flattered himself that he had not an enemy in the state, even among the Akalis. There he was wrong. Sikhs are notorious intriguers, and it is almost impossible to befriend one without making enemies of others. He had befriended the most upright and capable member of the Regency Council, who obviously had ill-wishers.

Wakefield fell very ill, with bouts of nausea and a jaundice-yellow face. A German Jewish doctor took specimens and ordered him to go away, immediately, to a cooler climate; so he took leave and went up to Simla. He got better but did not resume his duties as Diwan because he was posted elsewhere. Years later he again met the doctor, who told him that he had been slowly poisoned with antimonium. Wakefield had been sent to the hills not to get him out of the heat, but to get him out of Nabha.

An Indian prince did not assume full ruling powers until he had been invested with them by the Agent to the Governor-General, representing the Crown. Jack Bazalgette as Under Secretary to the Agent to the Governor-General, Punjab States, officiated at the investiture of the Rajah of the Sikh state, Faridkot. Although this was a mere eleven-gun state, the investiture was quite a spectacle.

> The Hon'ble the Resident (or Agent to the Governor-General) and his staff were received at the border of the state by state officials, while the Rajah himself drove out three miles to meet him and conduct him to the Guest House. The guests had an hour to clean up and change before the Mizaz Pursi or 'Enquiry after the health' call was to be made.

For this ceremony the Under Secretary met His Highness at his car, the Secretary standing at the top of the stairs leading to the reception hall, and the Resident exactly at the edge of the carpet. All sat down. The Secretary offered to His Highness, and the Under Secretary to His Highness's staff, Itr and Pan. After a few minutes' formal conversation, His Highness asked permission to leave, and was escorted to the edge of the carpet by the Resident, to the top of the stairs by the Secretary, and to his car by the Under Secretary.

Two hours later the Resident paid a return call to invest His Highness with ruling powers. He was escorted by state cavalry along a route lined by thousands of people to the palace, where there was a Guard of Honour, a band and a Royal Salute.

> [The Resident] and the Rajah sat on gilt chairs at the end of a room, with the Resident's staff down one side of the green and gold carpet, the Rajah's staff down the other. Behind, all around and in the gallery above were crowds of guests wearing long brocaded coats and turbans of every colour.
>
> After a few minutes' chat the Resident read a message from the Governor-General (the Viceroy) and made a speech, summing up the history and status of Faridkot, and looking forward to the rule by His Highness.
>
> The Secretary intoned His Highness's full names and titles, the Resident took him by the hand, conducted him up to the gold-carpeted dais, sat him on the golden gadi, placed a string of jewels on his turban and the Sword of State in his right hand, declaring, 'By the powers invested in me, I declare Your Highness invested with full ruling powers.' The bands played the state anthem and the guns fired a salute of 11 guns.
>
> Each ceremony had its appropriate uniform for Political Officers. For the Mizaz Pursi we wore 'undress uniform', a dark blue frock coat buttoning up fairly high but allowing a black tie and butterfly collar to show, a sabre in a gilt scabbard. For the investiture we wore Levee Dress, a dark blue jacket rather tight up to the neck, velvet collar and cuffs, black breeches, white silk stockings and a court rapier.

No wonder the Army, the I.C.S. and non-officials sometimes smiled.

14

Jammu and Kashmir

The twenty-one-gun state of Jammu and Kashmir had a problem, the essence of which was that three-quarters of its 3.5 million people were Moslems, while its ruler was a Hindu Dogra Rajput. This was because in 1846 the British Government had the unhappy inspiration of rewarding the Rajah of Jammu, Gulab Singh, for his support in the Sikh War by selling him Kashmir. Whereas in most states the ruler, however unsatisfactory in the eyes of the Political Department or Indian Nationalists, was sustained by the loyalty of his subjects, the Maharajah of Kashmir evoked that loyalty only in Jammu, where Dogra Rajputs formed a large majority. In the eastern part of his state, Ladakh, the scanty population viewed him with indifference, being Tibetan in race, language, religion and life-style; while over all the rest of his dominions the Moslems, an overwhelming majority, abhorred him as an interloper imposed upon them. The sale of Kashmir to Gulab Singh was one of the few really disreputable deeds done by the British in India, bringing its nemesis 100 years later. The Police and the state forces were composed mainly of Dogras, good fighting material but heavy-handed with those they despised; the civil administration was in the hands mainly of a class of Brahmins known as 'Kashmiri Pandits', competent but notorious all over India as devious and venal. (Pandit Nehru was one.) The Moslem population was thus in a perpetual state of resentment, which from time to time erupted in rebellion. Kashmiri Moslems were a timid race; but in the feudatory state of Poonch the people were tough Punjabi Moslems, much recruited into the Indian Army.

To add to the ruler's problems, the state of Jammu and Kashmir was enormous – 85,000 square miles, most of it inaccessible except on foot; it had common boundaries with Tibet, China and Afghanistan, and was separated from Russia by a strip of Afghan territory only a few miles wide; and two passes leading into it from the north were practicable for modern armies.

Its ruler in the early 1920s was Maharajah Pratap Singh, a tiny man who habitually wore an enormous turban, so that he resembled a mushroom. He had had a chequered career. In 1884 he had almost been debarred from the succession because of what was believed to be his mental incapacity and his 'habitual indulgence in the most degrading of vices'. (By this, the Resident meant the life-style which we are now expected to regard as normal.) However, in the following year he succeeded to the gadi but under humiliating restrictions, being compelled to defer always to a Council of which the President was his capable younger brother, whom he naturally hated. He had sired only one son, who died in infancy, and was compelled by Hindu custom to adopt the son of that brother, who thereby became the Yuvraj or Heir Apparent, Hari Singh by name. He would rather have adopted almost anyone else.

However, in 1905 his ruling powers were restored; he became in succession a Grand Commander of the Indian Empire (G.C.I.E.), a Grand Commander of the Star of India (G.C.S.I.), a Lieutenant-General in the Army; he was addressed as the Viceroy's 'Esteemed Friend'; and he abandoned pederasty in favour of cricket, year after year heading the state batting averages, largely because whenever he was caught or bowled the umpire used to call, 'No ball!'

Apart from the general undesirability of a Moslem population being ruled by a Hindu, his state was quite well run. During his long reign communications were greatly improved; an up-to-date revenue settlement was completed; irrigation and hydro-electric schemes introduced. There was a High Court with properly qualified judges, and an adequate system of primary and secondary education. His state forces did well in the East African campaign. The Vale of Kashmir was fertile and well-cultivated; there were lively textile and timber industries, and a flourishing tourist-trade, Kashmir being a favourite summer holiday ground for Europeans and Indians. Nor was the tribute which he paid annually to the British Government unduly onerous: it consisted of two Kashmir shawls of the finest wool and three silk scarves.

His heir, Hari Singh, was in 1919 a burly, heavy-jowled young man of 24, likeable, intelligent and reasonably well educated. The main trouble was that the Maharajah, his uncle, had never given him anything worthwhile to do. His English tutor described him as a promising young man in a very difficult situation because he had only about an hour's work a day as nominal Commander-in-Chief of the state forces, no friends, and was kept in a state of repression and aimlessness.

In Kashmir for the first post-war season was Captain Charles Arthur, an Irishman with a temporary commission in a cavalry regiment – good-looking, amusing, with a fund of improper stories inimitably told. He made a great hit with the friendless young Yuvraj, who was determined to take him as A.D.C. on his forthcoming Grand Tour, despite warnings from the Resident and the Political Secretary that

Arthur had an indifferent report from his regiment both as an officer and as a gentleman. However, there was nothing specific against him, and the Viceroy, Lord Chelmsford, eventually said, 'Oh, let the boy take whom he wants.'

At the Victory Ball in the Albert Hall in November, 1919, Hari Singh was picked up by a most attractive lady named Maudie Robinson. She moved in the best circles where, indeed, R.H. Chenevix Trench, on leave, met, fancied and played bridge with her. But he had a keen nose for a rat, and smelt one when she gushed, 'You must know *dear* Hari Singh! He wants me to spend the summer with him in Kashmir, but they are making difficulties in Delhi. You *will* help, won't you?' When his wife, not so easily enchanted, said rather crossly, 'Well, if she is so marvellous, I suppose we had better call on her in London', Trench replied, 'No, I think we'd better not.'

This was fortunate. A call at her little house in Shepherd Market would have blighted a promising Political career, since it was being watched both by the police and by private detectives. Maudie and Hari Singh had spent a week in Paris, and were tucked up in bed in the St James and Albany Hotel when into their room burst a large Englishman shouting, 'Now I've got you!' Maudie (who afterwards complained that he came in too soon) exclaimed, 'It's my husband!' And next morning Captain Arthur, who was the organiser of the coup, persuaded the appalled Hari Singh that unless he paid Robinson hush-money to the tune of two cheques (one post-dated), each for £150,000, the scandal would be such that he would never be allowed to succeed to the gadi of Kashmir.

Fortunately for the Kashmir taxpayer, before the second cheque was presented the gang quarrelled over the swag, and Robinson boldly took the Midland Bank to court for negligently paying out the first £150,000 to the wrong person.

So it all came out, headlined in the English papers. In an attempt, wholly unsuccessful, to conceal poor Hari Singh's identity, he was referred to throughout the case as 'Mr A.'. There was a hilarity about the proceedings, much appreciated by the British public. For instance, mention was made of Mr A. presenting Mrs Robinson with a silver model of a 'certain object' as a memento of a happy occasion. The nature of this object was not disclosed in court, but was written by the Judge on a piece of paper which was passed round the male members of the jury only. Naturally this was the subject of much ribald speculation, and the Bond Street jewellers which had made the 'object', feeling that they were getting a bad name, insisted on its nature being revealed. It was a model of a safety-razor. Mr A., like most Oriental gentlemen, found a lady's pubic hair very off-putting.

Everyone knew who Mr A. was, but there was no thought of excluding him from the Kashmir succession. After all, many a prince, perhaps even many a Secretary of State, had been guilty of youthful indiscretion. The Secretary of State for the day, Lord Birkenhead, wrote to the Viceroy:

> I am extremely sorry for this young fellow. Like another, he fell among thieves, and there was no better Samaritan available than Captain Arthur. Having paid so much, he got so little for it – not even privacy for his squalid amour. I was a little alarmed by a phrase in your letter which indicated that the hero – or victim – of this conspicuous melodrama might come to England within the next year. My earnest advice to you is to keep him away for two or three years. If he were to visit this country in the next twelve months every placard in England would display the simple announcement, 'Mr A. arrives', and thereafter the young man would know no privacy from reporters.

Naturally Hari Singh was subjected to a good deal of ridicule, and was known as 'Mr A.' for the rest of his days. On the whole he took it well, and showed surprisingly little rancour. It did not, as it well might, make him an anglophobe: he employed a British Chief Private Secretary, G.E.C. Wakefield;* and his relations with British visitors to his state was always good. (Sometimes very good: one lady's nickname was 'Mr A.'s chota hazri'.†) But he had a feeling of resentment against the Political Department, as one would against a friend who gave good advice which one ignored, with the worst consequences. Sir John Wood, the Political Secretary, blamed at first for allowing Hari Singh to take Captain Arthur, was able to demonstrate that he had strongly advised against it, but his advice had been over-ruled by the Viceroy, Lord Chelmsford. According to Lady Reynolds, Captain Arthur was a distant cousin of Lady Chelmsford.

Hari Singh still had to wait several years before his uncle died, and his position was an unenviable one. Wakefield describes the first Council meeting which he attended.

*A freelance engineer, surveyor and general trouble-shooter, who had a most distinguished career in many states. Not to be confused with his namesake in the Political Department, Edward Wakefield.

†Early-morning tea.

> I was sitting behind Rajah Hari Singh to help him if need arose, but that was not to be. The old Maharajah made me go and sit beside him at the head of the table and I was converted into a Council Secretary. The Council was assembled before His Highness entered. He always shook hands with me and that handshake became the barometer of his feelings. If he gave me a hearty shake of the hand and continued to hold my hand as he walked to his seat, all was well. Sometimes I was given only a couple of fingers to shake; at other times my hand was merely aggressively touched; then we knew trouble was in the air. There were frequent clashes between the Maharajah and his strong-minded nephew and heir. As soon as a clash occurred Hari Singh would scribble on a piece of paper, 'I have a headache, I must go', or some such sentence, and, rolling the paper into a ball, would push it across the table to me.

In 1925 he became Maharajah. According to the Resident, Evelyn Howell, he engrossed all the power to himself and Wakefield, took no advice, and deliberately held the Resident at a distance.

Although not classed as a First Class Residency, Kashmir was a posting much sought after. The Resident spent the winter in Sialkot, a pleasant cantonment conveniently close to Jammu where the Maharajah wintered; and the summer in Srinagar and Gulmarg, so he enjoyed a delightful climate all year round. Receiving reports from the Political Agent in Gilgit, and the Joint Commissioner for the Central Asian Trade Route in Leh, his work had a Central Asian international dimension: he was on the sideline of the 'Great Game'. He could tour on board his houseboat, or on foot or horseback, his baggage carried by ponies or porters, or over snowbound passes by yaks. His summer garden was as fine as the Udaipur Residency garden in winter. He had excellent bird-shooting and could cast his fly in beautiful streams for large brown trout.

Nor was he overwhelmed with work. But he had one duty which could be onerous, not to say embarrassing: by special request of the Kashmir Darbar, he had to see that the hundreds of European summer visitors behaved themselves. Some did not, regarding a Kashmir season as a sort of Saturnalia during which the ordinary rules of conduct and morals could be ignored. When a visitor's conduct became too outrageous, or when the Darbar reported that one had impiously imported beef in the shape of a packet of Oxo cubes, then the Resident had to act as chucker-out. One lady established herself semi-professionally at Nedou's Hotel in Srinagar. The Resident, H.V. Cobb, described her as an adventuress, immoral, and constitutionally incapable of telling the truth. He asked her to depart. To this she made a spirited rejoinder, announcing that he and his Secretary had made improper proposals to her and demanding a written apology posted on the board of the Kashmir Club:

> Failing which I shall complain to the Viceroy and enlist the services of my grandfather, General G——, in Simla to obtain the fullest enquiry into your conduct and your suitability for holding your present position.

Of course she was bluffing, and when her bluff was called, she departed.

Soon after Hari Singh came to the gadi, Howell was complaining of snubs and discourtesy from the Darbar in minor matters. He quite politely and properly asked for information on malaria prevention, on observance of Armistice Day, and on the dismissal of a Moslem Magistrate in Poonch who had had a distinguished career in the Indian Army. He was told to mind his own business. He took it up with the Prime Minister, Sir Albion Banerji I.C.S., and received a reply which (he informed the Political Secretary, Sir Charles Watson):

> is I think to be construed as a somewhat grudging and ungracious reply on the part of His Highness for his rudeness. After I read it, I laughed and said to Sir Albion, 'Then I take it we may now regard the incident as satisfactorily closed.' He laughed and agreed . . . Since then His Highness has gone out of his way to render a small act of courtesy, which seems to show he bears no malice.

But Hari Singh still needed very careful handling, the carrot more than the stick. In 1928 Howell again wrote to Watson, recommending that the ruler be made a G.C.I.E., the second highest award given to Indian princes.

> If merit is to be the governing consideration, I do not think that His Highness, for all the real efforts he has made for the welfare of his people, has yet earned it. But merit cannot be the sole consideration. Expediency must be taken into account. Kashmir is likely to be ruled by His Highness for the next thirty years or so and if an immediate award is going to make him discharge his duties in a manner more satisfactory than he otherwise would, then it should be given whether actually earned or not. So far as I am aware, there is no ruler of an Indian state comparable to Kashmir who is not a G.C.S.I. Many

whose status is far below His Highness are both G.C.S.I. and G.C.I.E. The withholding of at least the inferior of these dignities is probably already regarded by members of his order and by His Highness himself as a reflection on him. There is a very real danger that if an honour is not bestowed in the near future His Highness will regard himself as a recognised black sheep. It is moreover desirable before His Highness goes to England, which he may be doing this year, to show publicly that the unhappy 'Mr A.' incident is closed.

His Highness deserves credit for being alert, receptive and energetic, but he is not a good administrator, though the general standard of administration in the state still remains high. Surrounded by every sort of temptation to indolence and vice, he in general lives simply and works hard, if somewhat intermittently, devoting undeniable ability and energy to the welfare of his subjects. There are however certain reservations. The first relates to His Highness's attitude towards the Residency. I believe him to be so moved by his experience of Residency control in his early years as to be now almost obsessed with a passion for independence . . . It is his fixed policy to exalt himself at the expense of the Government of India and its representative . . . My personal relations with His Highness have been pleasant enough, and he has on occasion gone out of his way to show friendliness and courtesy. The policy nevertheless remains.

Howell's representations bore fruit: a G.C.I.E. in 1929 and a G.C.S.I. four years later. Meanwhile, however, through no fault of Hari Singh's – except in that his great-grandfather had been imposed by the British Government on a people which did not want him – his state was rent with communal frenzy. For at last the Kashmiri Moslems had found a leader, a charismatic rabble-rouser named Sheikh Abdullah, a friend and political associate of Jawaharlal Nehru. It was an incongruous alliance, the Kashmiri Moslem and the Kashmiri Pandit, but they had a common enemy: Sheikh Abdullah hated the Dogra Rajput, and Nehru hated the Maharajah.

The trouble started with Moslem newspapers in the Punjab trying by a vicious press campaign to destabilise Kashmir. The consequent demonstrations were orchestrated by mullahs preaching in Srinagar mosques, and the Moslems, far more fairly governed than they had ever been before, remembered all their old grievances and took to rioting, arson and strikes. In a frenzy of defiance they even slaughtered cows, and Dogra soldiers slaughtered them, killing and wounding several dozen. Over 100 rioters were sentenced by the courts to be flogged. In

Poonch, where the people were tougher, the trouble was more serious. Armed Moslem gangs, including many ex-soldiers, attacked police-stations, more gangs came in from the Punjab, and again the state forces had to open fire, and went on firing rather longer than was necessary. There were the customary allegations of Moslems forcibly circumcising Hindus, and of Hindus raping Moslems. Sheikh Abdullah was arrested, but the trouble did not die down until, at the Maharajah's request, a battalion of the Rifle Brigade was brought in.

The violence was suppressed, but the agitation continued. Sheikh Abdullah was released, and formed the Kashmir Moslem Conference, allied to Congress. These events put Congress in a dilemma. At heart, though not in its public utterances, Congress was anti-Moslem. But it was also anti-Maharajah; so what should be its policy when Moslems and Maharajah were at loggerheads? Under pressure from Nehru, Congress put its money, a great deal of money, on Sheikh Abdullah and kept the pot boiling. The Kashmiri Pandits were also in a dilemma. They had always looked upon the Maharajah as the dispenser of bounty and sinecures but now he was under an attack led by the most distinguished member of their caste. They tended to side with Congress, a serious weakening of the Maharajah's position. The Government, of course, had to support the Maharajah; but every European who had ever spent a month's leave in Kashmir and talked with Kashmiri servants, boatmen, pony-men and shikaris thought that the Moslems were in the right.

The Maharajah was not an anti-Moslem bigot. His closest friend, Military Secretary and Number 2 in his polo team was a Moslem from Hyderabad. He was the captive of history. In affairs of state he identified completely with the Dogra Rajput. On them alone could he rely, and he was under overwhelming pressure from them to keep lesser breeds in their proper place, as a subject people.

The villain of the piece, reported Lord Willingdon to Sir Samuel Hoare in 1931, was the Prime Minister, Hari Kishan Kaul. As the Diwan imposed by the Political Department on the spendthrift Maharajah of Bharatpur, he had been well-meaning but not sufficiently robust for the situation. But in Kashmir he was a Kashmiri Pandit, on his own ground, emotionally involved and very anti-Moslem. 'The Maharajah is doing quite well,' wrote Lord Willingdon, 'and if only we could get rid of the Prime Minister, that would make an enormous difference.' The Maharajah did brace himself to sack Hari Kishan Kaul, and accepted instead Lieutenant Colonel E.J.D. Colvin of the Political Department. He also, like any Government which does not know what to do, set up a

19 & 20 C.P. Hancock and the Maharajah of Bharatpur riding in state processions

21 The Nizam (*centre*) and Members of Council, Hyderabad. R.H. Chenevix Trench is on the left.

22 State banquet at Hyderabad

Commission of Enquiry. This was chaired by another very distinguished Political B.J. Glancy, who recommended in 1935 that the Maharajah promulgate a new constitution to meet Moslem grievances. The dilemma was insoluble, however: if the proposed Legislative Assembly was to be representative, it could not be entrusted with power because it would be basically hostile to the regime; if it was to be entrusted with power, then it could not be representative. In the event, it was representative, more or less, but powerless. Kashmir, despite the efforts of a ruler who was neither weak, incompetent nor repressive, was in no state to meet the crisis of independence and partition in 1947.

The Under Secretary to the Resident was ex-officio British Joint Commissioner (in partnership with a Kashmir Joint Commissioner) for the Central Asian Trade Route, spending each summer in Leh. It was a job which many British officers would have given their eyes for, and many more their eyes to avoid. It was essentially his responsibility to keep in good order the bridle-path which ran – or, rather, crawled and zigzagged – from Srinagar over the 12,000-foot Zogi La Pass to Leh, then over three more passes between 17,000 and 19,000 feet to Yarkand. The post of Joint Commissioner was created to encourage the caravan trade between Srinagar and Yarkand, a gambit in the 'Great Game' of the nineteenth century; but by the 1920s the trade had diminished to practically nothing. However, the route had still to be kept up. There were rest-houses every sixteen miles or so, and a system by which village headmen provided transport (ponies, porters or yaks) at fixed rates for merchants and travellers. For all this the Commissioners were jointly responsible.

In 1939 Leslie Fry crossed the Zogi La in the dark, long before the sun began to melt the snow and start avalanches. He took fifteen days to reach Leh. He noted the condition of the road, bridges and rest-houses, chatted up the village headmen and the High Lama of the monastery of Lamayuru Gompa; and eventually came in sight of Leh, some three miles from the Indus river, an oasis in brown desert with poplar and juniper trees, approached between long walls of stones all inscribed with the Buddhist prayer, 'O Mani Padma Hum' ('The Jewel in the Lotus'). In the wide central high street leading up to the castle, he inspected a state forces Guard of Honour, was garlanded by notables, and at last reached the modest whitewashed Residency.

Seven hours' march from Leh was the famous monastery of Hemis Gompa, of which the High Lama was the equivalent of an archbishop. There Fry watched the annual devil-dancing, an allegorical play depicting the struggle for man's soul between the forces of good and evil. A clay model of man is flung into a fire and gleefully poked and prodded by monks wearing bestial devil-masks, the forces of evil. It resembles the more dramatic representations of Hell in Italian Renaissance art, and is accompanied by screeching pipes, clashing cymbals, thumping drums and bellowing trumpets. After two days of this there is a sudden, dead silence, and in comes another set of monks wearing benign, smiling masks, who put the devils to flight and rescue man from the flames of Hell. The whole affair lasts three days, but Fry thought that honour was satisfied after he had watched for a couple of hours.

At a ceremonial call on the Rajah of Ladakh, Fry was regaled with brick-tea thickened with barley-meal and a melting lump of rancid butter. He presented the Rajah with some saffron, highly prized in lamaistic rituals, and a chromium teapot-holder; and received in return a sand-coloured jade cup.

Beyond Leh the trade route divided, one branch going direct to the Karakoram over the Khardong and Sasser La Passes, the other over the Chang La, the Changchenmo plateau and the salt-plains of Lingtsi Kiang. Both routes were liberally strewn with the bones of baggage animals. They met at the foot of the Karakoram, which they crossed on their way to Yarkand.

First Fry had a look at the Chang La route. The climb to 19,000 feet was very difficult and two of his ponies failed to make it; but he was rewarded at the top by a fine display of alpine flowers between the snow-drifts. At the foot of the pass they camped beside a lake and pressed on next day northwards along a tributary of the Shyok river. But not for long. Two bridges had been washed away and the river was too deep to ford. Since to rebuild them would be the work of many days, if not weeks, Fry writes:

> I had to give up any idea of reaching Shyok which for this year will have to go uninspected. I climbed a precipitous hill from which I could see across the river to the road to Shyok. It seems all right.

Back he went to Leh, and a few days later set off on the direct route to the Karakoram over the Khardong La. He was provided with a riding yak to cross the pass; but he was no yaksman, and soon got off and walked. They arrived at Khardong village after a 27-mile march over a 17,600-foot pass, not bad going. And so on, for ten days, he walked and rode about the dreary, snow-streaked wastes, up and down zigzag paths across steep scree, crossing rivers by fording, by rope-bridges or by inflated sheepskin rafts. He resisted what to some would have been an irresistible temptation to go on to the Karakoram and peer down into Chinese Turkestan.

> There is little point in going further. The track continues to the Karakoram in much the same dilapidated condition as it is from the Shyok to this unnamed and desolate spot, and my looking at it won't improve it.

The Central Asian connection added a unique flavour to the work of the Kashmir Residency. Derek Harrington-Hawes was Secretary when there came a report from Lhasa, via the Political Agent in Sikkim, of a Mongol horde, 20,000 strong, pillaging their way across Tibet towards Leh. They called themselves 'Kazaks'. No one in Srinagar had heard of Kazaks, but he found in an atlas the word written across an otherwise empty space in Russian Turkestan, north of the Gobi Desert.

Because it was not possible for a company of Kashmir infantry to stop them crossing a 300-mile border, the Kazaks were reluctantly allowed to come to Leh, having been relieved of their swords and ancient rifles. Sheepskin-garbed, fur-hatted, high-booted, they emerged on their shaggy ponies and pitched their yurts on the plain below Leh. Most of the citizens had fled, but those who remained enjoyed rich pickings. For the Kazaks had no disposable property other than their thousands of sheep, and no idea of the value or purpose of money. It was child's play for a Kashmiri official to fine a Kazak five rupees for breach of some law of which he had never heard, and then buy his sheep at four annas each so that he could pay the fine. There arrived in Leh an Indian trader to recover some bolts of cloth which, he said, the Kazaks had taken from him in Tibet; but he was told that since the offence, if any, had been committed in Tibet, his remedy was to apply to the Courts in Lhasa. The Kashmiri officials were not going to share their treasure-trove.

The horde could not stay in Ladakh: there was little enough grazing for the Ladakhis, none for 500 horses, fifty shaggy, two-humped camels, and 17,000 sheep. The Tibetans would not let them back, and it was too late in the year for them to cross the passes back to Central Asia. After many telegrams had passed between Leh, Srinagar and New Delhi, they were told they could settle in Hazara District in the North-West Frontier Province.

Harrington-Hawes, accompanied by a trader from Kashgar who spoke Turki and Kirghiz, met them on their way through Kashmir. The wanderers' felt yurts were scattered over some 200 acres with their horses, camels and sheep. The women were collecting firewood and bringing water, the men sitting outside their yurts in the winter sun. As

Harrington-Hawes arrived, they formed a friendly ring around him.

The men were short and thick-set. None wore beards, though some had a few scraggly hairs on their faces and thin black moustaches. They did not a stroke of work, and would catch and saddle a pony rather than walk a hundred paces. The women wore long coats of coarse tweed, pyjama-like trousers of the same material and white head-dresses like a nun's. Round their necks were stitched pre-Bolshevik roubles. The Khan Padshah (king) came from his tent to greet me. He wore a hat made of purple brocade, lined with leopard-skin. He led me into a yurt where we sat on brightly-coloured rugs spread on the ground.

He told the story of his people's wanderings. The Russians had tried to break down their tribal structure and put an end to their nomadic life-style. Any who resisted were killed, so five years ago he had led his people southwards to seek a new home. They crossed the Little Gobi Desert, but could not settle with the Chinese Tungans despite being fellow-Moslems. They moved on to Tibet, where they were persecuted. Then they heard of the English, and of Calcutta, which would suit them nicely. Now all their troubles were over.

Although well treated in Hazara, they pined for the free life of the steppes, and were eventually allowed by the Chinese to trek back over the passes and 1,000 miles east to Urumchi. How many survived, and whether the wanderers found what they were seeking, may never be known.

It was the sort of situation for which the post of Joint Commissioner had been created; but the year after Fry held it, the post was abolished, as no longer necessary.

15

The Faithful Ally

The twenty-one-gun state of Hyderabad, with a population of 14.5 million and an area nearly the size of France, was a giant among Indian states. Its founder had been the Mogul Emperor's Governor of the Deccan, who by 1724, with the weakening of the imperial authority, had made himself virtually independent. He could trace his descent from Abu Bakr, the first Khalifa of Islam: and the Nizam in the 1920s, Mir Usman Ali Khan, was directly descended from him. The Nizam was not 'His Highness' but 'His Exalted Highness' and Faithful Ally of the British Government.

Hyderabad had a unique atmosphere of sophistication, combined with racial and religious tolerance. K.P.S. Menon, the Madrassi Hindu, who served there as Under Secretary to the Resident, felt inclined to:

> shed a tear over the disappearance of Hyderabad from the map of India. Hyderabad used to have a character of its own. It was the last repository of the Moghul tradition. Indeed a favourite adjective which was on everyone's lips was Moghlai. The hospitality which the Nawabs and nobles dispensed was truly Moghlai; so was the standard of personal living. Moghlai, too, was the friendship between Hindus and Mussulmans in the city of Hyderabad; there was no religious or communal trouble. Sometimes the term Moghlai was used in a less complimentary sense; if you arrived late at a function, you would laugh it off by saying it was just an example of Moghlai punctuality. Yet this state, where the Upper Tenth lived so elegantly and luxuriously and in complete forgetfulness of the hardships of 90 per cent of the population, could not possibly survive in an independent India; and if I were to shed a tear over its eclipse, it would be a very idle tear.

For all its wealth, strength and apparent stability, there was a basic weakness in the state: the Nizam and the ruling class (though not, admittedly, all the senior ministers and officials) were Moslem, but over 90 per cent of the population were Hindu. This, as in Kashmir, made it impossible for the Nizam – even had he so wished, which he did not – to set up any sort of legislature which was both effective and representative.

He *had* to rule as an autocrat, and the only question was, how benevolently?

There was a running sore in the relationship between the British Government and its Faithful Ally. In 1798 the East India Company had made a subsidiary treaty with the Nizam which provided, *inter alia*, that he would pay for a force of 6,000 infantry and 9,000 cavalry stationed within the state, officered and controlled by the Company, primarily for the defence of the state against Mahrattas and others, but available to act with the Company's forces in times of war. This force became known as the Hyderabad Contingent. In 1852 its pay was badly in arrears and the Government took on the responsibility for maintaining it. As security for these expenses, the rich Hyderabad province of Berar (known generally as 'The Berars') would be administered by British officials; but the Nizam retained titular sovereignty over it. In 1902-3, since its original purpose, the defence of Hyderabad, no longer had any validity, the Contingent was absorbed into the Indian Army, losing its special character. Berar might well at that point have reverted to Hyderabad, but the Viceroy was Lord Curzon: the Nizam was persuaded to lease it in perpetuity to the British Government, which in due course merged it into the Central Provinces, though the Nizam was still its titular sovereign. But the arrangement rankled, and the Nizam Usman Ali felt that his father had been the victim of sharp practice. Berar had been taken by the British Government to pay for the Hyderabad Contingent; the Contingent no longer existed; so Berar should be handed back to Hyderabad. It was as simple as that. The British contention was that the people of Berar, nearly all Hindu, had become accustomed since 1852 to the blessings of British administration, and could not now be handed back to the tender mercies of the Nizam. It was an argument not entirely compatible with that so often advanced by Politicals – that Indians *preferred* princely rule.

The Nizam Usman Ali was a very strange character. The most common fault of Indian princes was extravagance. He, often described as the richest man in the world, was grotesquely mean. He was mean in appearance, wearing the clothes, the greasy tarbush, the three-day beard of a seedy shopkeeper. He was mean in his private life, begrudging his children every penny. He used to sell at exorbitant prices, to officials who dared not refuse to buy, baskets of fruit from his gardens, bundles of old clothes and worthless bric-à-brac. The symbolic tribute, 'nazar', paid to Indian rulers on special occasions two or three times a year by officials and nobles, he made into a major source of income, demanding larger and larger nazars many times a year, from more and more of his subjects. He sold appointments and promotions, and cut to the bone the salaries of officials who then had to resort to bribes and perks. He was by nature autocratic, resisting the smallest restrictions on his personal rule. Yet he had his good points. He was no debauchee, reducing the number of palace concubines from 300 in his father's time to about thirty – enough for any reasonable man, and cheaper too. He combined intense loyalty to the Crown with intense dislike of nearly all the Crown's representatives.

'Lean and keen men for the Frontier, fat and good-natured men for the states.' These were exemplified by Sir Lennox Russell, Resident at Hyderabad in the early 1920s, pre-eminently a states man, and Sir William Barton, by temperament, physical characteristics and experience a Frontier man, who took over as Resident in 1925.

In response to the mild remonstrances of Sir Lennox, the Nizam had agreed to rule through an Executive Council with an (Indian) President from British India. But as all the members of the Council were his nominees, it was hardly a check on his autocracy. When Sir Lennox suggested that nazars were making him unpopular, the Nizam retorted that they were purely voluntary, and were indeed a gratifying tribute to his popularity. In any case, Sir Lennox was not his mentor. In 1924 the Nizam had what Sir William Barton later described as 'the temerity' to suggest that the baskets of fruit which the Resident customarily received on festive occasions should be commuted for an annual cash payment. It may have been a studied insult, though it was certainly the sort of arrangement that the Nizam, had he been Resident, would have jumped at. Barton related with relish several other slights to his predecessor, which he regarded as part of a deliberate campaign by the Nizam.

It was hardly a propitious time for the Nizam to revive the old claim, arguing that by retaining Berar in 1903 after the Contingent had been abolished, Britain was in breach of a treaty between *two sovereign powers*, the United Kingdom and Hyderabad, and hinting that he might appeal to the League of Nations about it. The Viceroy, Lord Reading, responded with a sharp rap on His Exalted Highness's knuckles, setting out that definition of Paramountcy (see p.4) which, coming from a former Lord Chief Justice, was no doubt constitutionally correct, but was deeply resented by all Indian princes; especially, of course, by the Nizam who was brusquely told that the Paramount Power could do what it liked, anywhere in India, including Hyderabad, which had no special status. Smarting under this, he was in no mood to be co-operative with Barton.

The man from the Frontier, resolute and uncompromising, loathed the Nizam, who in turn detested him. Barton bombarded the Political Secretary with denunciations of the Nizam. Despite warnings, the forced sale of valueless stuff continued; officials of the Revenue Department, the Customs and Excise, the Court of Wards, were mere instruments of the Nizam's cupidity. A diseased sheep was slaughtered in the palace garden and its flesh sold at the price of best mutton to the palace staff. The Nizam was 'undoubtedly an interesting problem for the alienist'. All these abuses had paralysed the administration, and 'even those who had been ardent supporters of the Nizam have fallen into complete despair and privately beg for the intervention of the Government of India'. Barton earnestly advised the Viceroy, Lord Irwin, not to invite the Nizam to Viceroy's House: his habits were dirty; and because he never had a bath, his physical proximity was disagreeable.

He recommended very firm action by himself, backed by a stiff personal letter to the Nizam from the Viceroy. Nazars should be reduced to token payments on two or three Moslem festivals a year. The sale of appointments and promotions must cease. The Nizam must rule through his Executive Council which must be strengthened by three Government of India nominees in key positions. After long argument, the Nizam agreed to these terms, but with every intention of evading them.

(In order to discount the element of personal dislike between Barton and the Nizam, it is proper here to quote, out of chronological order, the comments of Barton's successor, Sir Terence Keyes.

> When I was taking over from Barton, he amplified his written notes by still stronger condemnation of the Nizam and all his ways, and by insisting on the necessity for watching every move made by him or by any of his satellites and of nipping in the bud any attempt to weaken Council Government or regain any personal control. I gained the impression that the only things that stood between Hyderabad and chaos were the unceasing vigilance of the Resident, and the devoted services of the lent officers.
>
> There is much in Barton's description of the Nizam with which I am not in agreement . . . His miserliness in money matters is extreme, though nearly all the grotesque stories about it are untrue. His passion for control impels him to interfere in the domestic affairs of all the nobles. When it distorts his really great affection for his children, it is perilously close to insanity. I suppose the person he loves most in all the world is his daughter, Shahzadi Begum, but for her his love is a ghastly incubus. He won't arrange a marriage for her.

He always makes her sleep in his bedroom, and when he travels she sleeps in his compartment. She has complained that when it is cold they have only one dirty, threadbare blanket between them. When, during investigations into thefts in the palace, it was discovered that she had stolen large sums and given the money to one of the Nizam's concubines to smuggle out of the palace to her father, it was also alleged that she had unnatural relations with this concubine. The Nizam was so upset that he told me nearly the whole sordid story, and sent a trusted man to tell me the rest. Shahzadi wrote to me that she had been beaten to a pulp; but the Nizam said he had only made her sit down and get up fifty times, twice a day. He made an opportunity for me to see her after this, and she hadn't a single bruise on her shoulders or arms . . .

His control over his sons was also intense. It is said that they were never allowed to have a bath without his permission, and as he is obviously not an advocate of diurnal ablutions, and they were afraid to ask him, they didn't get many baths. They say they only had one towel between them and no sponge. It was our intervention on behalf of his sons which the Nizam disliked more than anything else. His rage at Lord Reading's rather contemptuous rejection of his claim to the Berars had been an absolute obsession for some time, but the Berars were remote, and the sting had lessened. Lord Irwin's insistence on Council government rankled for a bit, but he did realise the necessity for some change of policy, and he had a great respect for Lord Irwin. He could not, however, reconcile himself to losing control over his sons . . .*

Strangely enough he is very jealous of his reputation as a keeper of promises; and, I believe, can always be made to honour his bond; but he is an unblushing liar in negotiations, or in narrating a case, and totally unashamed when bowled out . . .

I have seen nothing of 'that leprous growth' which Barton said nothing could remove – 'the love of power for the opportunities of repression and tyranny which it offers' . . . I have always tried to get at him before he committed himself: it is terribly hard to make him go back on himself. I have tried to persuade him to act as if on his own initiative. He once said to me, 'I want your advice, and will generally take it; but I don't want these people to know.'

For all his unpleasant characteristics, and he is in many ways mean

*The Nizam's two legitimate sons, the Shahzadas Azam Jah and Muazzim Jah were sent on a prolonged tour of Europe with an English tutor.

and sordid, I have a real affection for the queer little creature. He has distinct powers for good, a quick sense of humour, an unexpected capacity for friendship, and a pathetic craving to be liked and understood.

There is one matter to which I think the Government of India has paid too much attention – the taking of nazars by the Nizam. To anyone who has been in Persia this is a comparatively venial affair, and is it really any concern of ours?

Whether Keyes or Barton was the more correct in his assessment of the Nizam, the former's observations show how close the relations between a Resident and even the prickliest of rulers could be.)

The two key members of the Executive Council on which Lord Irwin insisted were Sir Akbar Hydari, I.C.S, as Finance Member, and R.H. Chenevix Trench as Member for Revenue, Police and much else.

Fresh from Baluchistan, where he had been Revenue Commissioner, Trench at first found the atmosphere of intrigue oppressive and the work uncongenial. It was also extremely laborious, being conducted largely in handwritten Arabic script. He was a First Class Interpreter in Urdu, but found hours of poring over the script very hard on his eyes, and the Urdu so full of Persian and Arabic words as to be at first most difficult.

If I had known what I was to be up against, I think I would have preferred indigent obscurity in Baluchistan. However, I must make the best of it. My first task is to get to know the men in the departments for which I am responsible – Revenue, Customs, Excise, Police, Courts of Wards, Famine, Settlement. If I can only oust the knaves and get in good men, I shall have done much. But it is a big If.

As an example of what one is up against, H.E.H. sent a firman* that the Superintendent of his Irregular Forces was being relieved of his job for misconduct, and that I was to provide for him at equal pay in the Revenue or Police. I sent for the fellow to have a look at him. He drove up in a Rolls-Royce! I rather liked him!

A friend from Quetta, the Parsee businessman, Sir Ardeshir Marker, came down to Hyderabad where he had various concerns and asked Trench how he was doing.

'Everything would be all right if only I could get rid of three Nawabs.'

'Who are they?'

*An edict by the Nizam of Hyderabad.

'Nawabs Rishwat (Corruption) Yar Jung, Khushamat (Flattery) Yar Jung, and Sifarish (Nepotism) Yar Jung.* Tell me, Ardeshir, you know Hyderabad much better than I do, how can I oust these three Nawabs?'

Sir Ardeshir had to confess that he did not know how it could be done.

At first Trench was housed in a horrible bungalow, riddled with vermin and snakes, with a most evil atmosphere, which his family called Cesspool Cottage. There his Goan cook, commonly known as 'Borgia', whom he had brought from Quetta as a precaution against poisoning, was bewitched.

> If you could see the poor little man, you would realise how quite respectable people came to burn witches alive. He howled night and day, keeping everyone awake, talked gibberish, tore off all his clothes, went for the other servants, tried to set alight to the beard of his friend the syce when he was asleep. The syce reported, 'I had to tie him to the mare's leg all night and we lay one on each side of her.' Fortunately the mare is very understanding! The servants – Christian, Moslem and Hindu – were unanimous that a spell had been cast upon him. They showed me weird marks near his quarters and coloured powders on the ground with fingertip prints in them.

The office stenographer knew of a very good exorcist. He turned out to be on the establishment of the City Police, and much in demand since black magic was rife in Hyderabad. He did his best to drive the evil spirit out of 'Borgia', but failed. A Catholic priest with a high reputation in these matters was then called in, and was equally baffled. Finally the cook was sent to Goa, to seek a cure in the Cathedral of St Francis Xavier. He returned some months later, cured and in his right mind, and resumed his job.

Meanwhile Trench's protests about 'Cesspool Cottage' had borne fruit in the allocation to him of the Revenue Member's proper house, spacious and elegant with a large garden and tennis-court, in the suburb of Begumpet. He began to appreciate the extraordinary, attractive character of Hyderabad.

> Here you meet a society of Indians which you come across nowhere else; wealthy, well-bred, with vast estates, courteous manners and no sense of inferiority. The President of the Council, for instance, (Maharajah Sir Kishan Parshad), is an amateur artist, while the

* Yar Jung was a title or appellation of honour conferred by the Nizam.

> Political Secretary dabbles in English verse. They all make me very welcome.

But for all Sir Kishan Parshad's charm and culture, no one gave a more vigorous shake to the Pagoda-tree.

> Great fight in the Council this morning when we all tried to persuade the President to agree to the reduction of the military guard furnished over his residence from 118 of all ranks to 20 or 25. We pointed out that a permanent guard of that strength practically destroyed the efficiency of the battalion which has to furnish it, and that he already has 400 of our Irregular troops attached to him (mainly Arabs, whom he employs in his gardens), not to speak of 350 servants of sorts – *all* at state expense. It was to no purpose: his prestige would be affected if a man were withdrawn, etc., etc. Considering that the old gentleman (for whom I have the highest respect, though not as an administrator) draws about £1,000 a month pay (no Income Tax), and enjoys an estate from the state worth about £40,000 a year, I thought his attitude was a little unreasonable.

An agreeable feature of Hyderabad was its religious tolerance. Hindus took part in the processions at the Moslem festival of Mohurram; Moslems lit candles and splashed people with coloured water at the Hindu festival of Holi. Both observed Christmas with their Christian friends. In this ecumenism Sir Kishan Parshad (a Hindu) set a fine example. Of his four wives, two were Hindu, one was a Sunni Moslem and one a Shiah Moslem. The children were brought up according to their mother's faith. Could tolerance go further?

Trench was impressed by the standards and efficiency of the Hyderabad Civil Service.

> I spent all morning on a small Board for the selection of probationary Tahsildars. We find we get better results by arbitrary selection than by open competition. The main points we look for are academic qualifications, personality and family claims. The lucky candidates start on a salary of about £15 a month. (The same as a subaltern in the British Army.) We had about 130 up for 8 vacancies. Many of the lads we saw were L.L.B.s while all were B.A.s of sorts. Some had been captains of their College football teams, or prominent Boy Scouts, or had done well in their Officers' Training Corps, or had been head of their College Union; one had been heavyweight boxing champion of Aligarh University.

As Revenue Member he was ex-officio on the Boards of several companies in which the state was a big shareholder. This took him down frequently to Bombay where it was:

> a great experience to meet Indian men of business. One of our Directors is a cousin of Gandhi; another of Saklatvala, the Communist M.P., a particularly good chairman and a nice fellow. Their younger wives and daughters are mostly out of purdah, very attractive and well educated. If we stay thirty years more in India, all our subalterns will be marrying them.

Hyderabad society was sophisticated, elegant, racially intermixed and great fun. It was also very snobbish. There were many mixed marriages, though, for the Nizam considered it his duty to employ Europeans who married Moslems. Most of these marriages were happy and successful, but there was one couple whom May Trench had heard of but never met. She asked her friend, Masuma Begum, 'Why haven't I met the Hassan Ali Khans?'

'My dear,' replied Masuma Begum, 'I don't think you'd really find much in *common* with them. Poor Hassan was studying in London and is M.L.D.'

She thought M.L.D. must be some academic qualification, and asked what the letters stood for.

'Don't you know? Married Landlady's Daughter.'

It was not only the lent officers who were welcomed into Hyderabad society. K.P.S. Menon was enchanted by it, though not blind to its faults. Arriving as Under Secretary to the Resident in 1925, he watched Sir Lennox Russell's 'philosophic unconcern' at the rapid deterioration in the Hyderabad administration, and the power-struggle between Barton and the Nizam.

> Between autocracy and paramountcy, between the Nizam and the Resident, now siding with one and now with the other and carrying tales to both, stood the nobles of Hyderabad. They were men of enormous wealth and lived at the height of luxury. The most cultivated among them was Maharajah Sir Kishan Parshad, who was a scholar of Persian as well as Sanskrit, as proficient in the Koran as in the Gita. There were other personalities too, each notable in his own way: Sir Amin Jung, who had one of the best private libraries in India; Sir Iman-ul-Mulk and his son, to whom must go the credit for reverently preserving the precious sculptures and paintings in the cave-temples at Ellora and Ajunta; Sir Nizamat Jung, scholar, poet

and politician, who built a house on the bank of Hussein Sagar lake on the model of his old college at Cambridge; Sir Farid-ul-Mulk, a Parsee, playing bridge all day with someone holding the cards for him because he was too frail; and Sir Salar Jung, a great collector, whose house was full of rare china, Satsuma bronzes and Sèvres porcelain, old Persian carpets and pictures, marble statuettes and chandeliers from all parts of the world, and such historical relics as a Dresden dressing-table belonging to Marie Antoinette, a Sèvres porcelain piece presented by Louis XVI to Tippu Sultan in 1788, a dagger, studded with emeralds and rubies, belonging to Nur Jehan [whose tomb is the Taj Mahal], and a Holy Koran autographed by the Emperors Jehangir, Shah Jehan and Aurangzeb. There was no other city in India which could boast such a galaxy of cultured, idle and versatile men.

To these he might have added a Member of Council, Nawab Wali-ud-Dowlah, Eton and Oxford, able, indolent and equally charming drunk or sober. When in his cups he used to sing the Eton Boating Song and/or shoot a .22 rifle with unerring aim at silver rupees (or, preferably, gold mohurs) tossed into the air. For Menon:

> Hyderabad was a new world. I have never seen anything like it. All the forces of a waning empire were there – autocracy, feudalism and paramountcy – and, through them all, was breaking in a new, faint voice, the voice of the people.

The voice of the people, faint in Menon's ears, rang loud and clear in Trench's house, where a frequent dinner-guest was Mrs Sarojni Naidu, 'India's Patriot Poetess', equally esteemed in Hyderabad society and in the Congress hierarchy. Dining there after a propaganda and fund-raising tour of the United States, she said, 'And do you know, Sir Richard, when I gave a recital of my poetry at Chicago and spoke of British oppression, they cheered me to the echo and hundred-dollar bills showered on to the platform.'

'A tribute,' he replied gallantly, 'to your beauty and charm, not to your intelligence.'

She almost threw something at him. He could always get a rise out of her.

With her lively daughter 'Bibi' Trench's relations were more complicated. He rather fancied her, of which she took full advantage. For instance, she obtained his permission to work on famine relief, and then made speeches giving the simple villagers the impression that they were enjoying the bounty of Congress, and disparaging the famine relief work of the Nizam's Government which had provided all the food, money, transport and personnel. Soon after this coup, May Trench was choosing guests for a dinner-party. 'Bibi?' she suggested.

Her husband showed signs of discomfort. 'I am afraid, my dear, that Bibi has been behaving rather badly. Perhaps she had better not come here in future.' So Bibi's name was struck off the list.

A few weeks later, 'May, we don't seem to have seen anything of Bibi for a long time. Why don't you ask her to dinner?'

Mrs Sarojni Naidu was rather a friend of Trench's mother-in-law, Mrs Pocklington, a redoubtable traveller known from one end of Asia to the other (but only in the best circles) as 'Mrs Pock'. They were both very social, and great chatterers. One day (it was the sort of improbable thing that happened in Hyderabad) they attended some kind of committee meeting to discuss women's education. The Chairperson, highly gratified at Mrs Naidu's presence, said, 'I hope we can have a few words from India's Patriot Poetess on a subject that must be very dear to her heart.'

'Oh no, I don't want to speak.' Then, wickedly selecting the most public-spirited bore present, Mrs Naidu added, 'Mrs Rustomjee knows far more about it than I do.'

Nothing loth, Mrs Rustomjee rose ponderously to her feet, clutching her voluminous notes.

Sarojni Naidu turned her back on the platform and resumed her cosy chat with 'Mrs Pock'. Above the voice of Mrs Rustomjee, booming away in her best platform manner about female Teacher Training, could be heard with painful clarity that of Indian's Patriot Poetess, 'And why do you think *she* never married?'

She took a cool view of Gandhi, whom she called 'Mickey Mouse'. It did not escape her acid tongue that when he travelled, with ample publicity, third class on the railways, a whole carriage was reserved for him and his entourage; and when as a gesture of humility he spent a few days in a sweeper's house, it had first to be swept and garnished and all mod cons installed. 'If you only knew, Sir Richard, how much it costs Congress to keep him in holy poverty.' It was an excellent joke, and like most excellent jokes, it bore repetition. She seems to have repeated it a good many times. She was not the only prominent Congress politician who regarded Hyderabad as a sort of rest-centre in which, provided they kept their noses clean locally, they could recuperate from their labours in British India.

Hyderabad was of course a despotism, but a fairly relaxed one, relying less on brute force than on outwitting its enemies. When Ghandi announced his intention of paying the state a visit, there was discussion in the Council on whether he should be allowed in.

'If we keep him out,' said Trench, 'it will look as though we are afraid of him, and will give him a legitimate grievance. Far better let him in. Besides, it will be interesting to see who his chief supporters are.'

So it was agreed.

Congress sympathisers then announced a hartal* in his honour. Trench, whose portfolios included the Police Department, used to invite the Commissioner of the City Police, an old, fat, cunning Hindu named Venkatram Reddy, to a working breakfast every Thursday.

'What are you doing about the hartal?' he asked.

Venkatram Reddy replied, 'I have told the Chamber of Commerce that I think a hartal is a very proper mark of respect to the Mahatma. The Police will co-operate by sealing all the premises which are closed, to prevent looting. You see, Sir Richard, if the Police seal the premises, the owners will have to apply to the Police to have them re-opened. And *that*,' the Commissioner thoughtfully rubbed together finger and thumb, '*that* might perhaps be rather expensive. I do not think there will be a hartal.'

There wasn't.

There were hundreds, if not thousands, of domestic slaves in Hyderabad. All the nobles, including all the Hyderabadi Members of Council, owned them. But when Trench urged the Council to abolish slavery in the state, he was met by a firm *non possumus*. The difficulty, he was told, was that slavery had already been abolished, by a firman some years earlier. To abolish it again would serve no useful purpose; it would merely draw attention to its continuance and imply that His Exalted Highness's firman was ineffective. The only support Trench got was from the younger nobles, who complained bitterly that slaves were quite impossible to discipline or control. No matter how idle, dishonest or quarrelsome a slave, you could not sack him, because he had nowhere else to go; you could not sell him, because no one would buy; you could not fine him, because he owned no property and received no wages; you could not even beat him because he would immediately lodge a complaint with the nearest magistrate and you would be charged with assault. Female slaves were even more unmanageable, and a *very* bad

*A one-day general strike and closure of business premises, owned mainly by Hindus.

influence on the children. The whole situation was intolerable. So slavery was quietly phased out.

Although he had – as will be related – one keen disappointment, Keyes greatly enjoyed his time in Hyderabad, as would any man who feels he has succeeded in a very difficult task. His main achievement had been to coax the Nizam out of his sulk. Indeed, Lord Willingdon was perturbed that Keyes's relations with the Nizam were too close. Keyes, he reported to the Secretary of State, 'is a very able man but can't recognise that his business isn't to run and do things through the Nizam himself, but through the Nizam's Council. He has unfortunately got the Nizam very much in his pocket.' It was a far cry from the days when the Resident and the Nizam were at loggerheads.

Besides his concern with major political issues, the Resident administered certain areas leased by the Hyderabad Darbar to the Crown. These comprised the Residency Area of several hundred acres with gardens and bazaars, and an area about the size and shape of the Isle of Wight for the accommodation and training of the largest garrison in central and southern India, a cavalry brigade, an infantry brigade, gunners and ancillary troops. This included the large town of Secunderabad with some 180,000 inhabitants. Over these the laws of British India applied, with the Resident holding Governor's powers. He delegated most of this work to his staff.

In Barton's time, K.P.S. Menon, in addition to his secretarial work, was District Magistrate for Secunderabad and the other administered areas, Railway Magistrate, Superintendent of the Residency Bazaars, Manager of the Residency Gardens and Registrar of Births and Deaths.

> Sometimes I would write a letter from myself as Superintendent of the Residency Bazaars to myself as District Magistrate, complaining of the inadequate sentences imposed by myself in my magisterial capacity for the municipal offences committed in my jurisdiction. Or I would write a letter from myself as Under Secretary to the Resident to myself as Superintendent of the Residency Bazaar complaining of the perpetual noise in the bazaar which disturbed the Resident's sleep.

As Magistrate he tried two sensitive cases in which the Nizam took a personal interest. The first concerned a bequest of 15 lakhs (£112,000) left by an old widow to her nephew. Under Hyderabad law, if anyone died intestate, his property passed to the Nizam, who frequently caused the law in such matters to be bent to his advantage. The nephew had therefore moved into the Residency Area, thus bringing the case into

Menon's court. The Nizam maintained that the will was fraudulent, and the widow had died intestate. Indirectly it had been hinted to Menon that 'the Nizam is the richest man in the world, and the future of a man who wins his favour is secured for ever. He is also the most powerful ruler in India, and the man who incurs his displeasure is finished.' Undeterred, Menon found that the will was genuine and the nephew was entitled to the 15 lakhs. At this the Nizam, he heard, flew into a towering rage.

The other sensitive case concerned a brother-in-law of the Nizam, charged by the British Indian police in Secunderabad with negligent driving which caused the death of an old woman. Menon considered that the prosecution evidence was not sufficient and acquitted the accused. 'The Nizam was pleased with the verdict. "Menon is a just man," he said. And with this princely bouquet in my official buttonhole, I left Hyderabad.'

Jack Bazalgette was Personal Assistant to Keyes, and had an enormous liking and admiration for a man who in middle age took with equal zest to contract bridge and pig-sticking. His duties were mainly social.

> One needed a good memory for faces and names. I had to introduce some hundreds of guests at a Garden Party for the Viceroy. It was my own friends, with whom I was on Christian name terms, whose surnames refused to come to my tongue.

The ex-King Alfonso of Spain, who had recently abdicated, came to India dead-set on shooting a tiger. The Viceroy asked the Nizam to invite him to Hyderabad, putting His Exalted Highness in a great tizzy, for he was equally parsimonious and superstitious, and one way or another he felt the royal visit did not bode well for him.

'What can I do? What can I do?' he asked Sir Terence. 'Everyone knows how infectious is ill-luck. Here is the King. He's lost his throne. His number is 13. What else? What else? If I have him to stay, surely I will catch his ill-luck and, who knows? Who knows? I may lose my throne.' Sure enough, fifteen years later, he did.

Keyes therefore put up the royal visitor at the Residency, whither the Nizam sent his two sons to convey his compliments. King Alfonso was a great raconteur and soon had Azam Jah and Muazzim Jah rocking with laughter. They must have told their father as soon as they got home, for the phone rang: a call from the Nizam to ask if His Majesty would come and see him. Bazalgette relates:

> Sir Terence was tied up in conference, so I was detailed to

accompany the King. It went well. Alfonso told some of his stories and soon had the Nizam laughing his head off. 'You must come to dinner! You must come to dinner!' But here his parsimony asserted itself. There were fifty dinner-guests, and only one bottle of champagne between the lot.

For the King's entertainment, Prince Azam Jah laid on a performance of the Rafai sect of Arabs, belonging to the Nizam's Arab Irregular Legion, demonstrating their ability to control the flow of blood and perhaps pain. It is not a pretty entertainment. The men gouge out their eyes until they hang on their cheeks. They stick knives through their cheeks, their tongues and even through the gullet, after pulling forward the windpipe and throat. Finally one bangs an iron tent-peg into the top of another's skull, bashing it with a stone until it is firm. It was no easy job to shake it loose and pull it out. In all these penetrations there is no blood-flow, though I noticed that they press on certain centres and massage the wound very hard after pulling the knife or tent-peg out.

Alfonso's one previous experience of tiger-shooting, in another state, had been disappointing. He was conveyed in a Rolls-Royce to the jungle where he saw to his dismay the Maharajah awaiting him with three Guards of Honour – cavalry, infantry and irregulars – and three military bands. Swords, lances, bayonets flashed in the sunshine; Royal Salutes and National Anthems were played, and the King thought there must be some misunderstanding: there could not be a tiger for miles. But there was. No sooner had he been established, with loaded rifle, in a commodious tree-house than a rather ragged, unhappy-looking tiger was seen walking slowly towards him, peering anxiously from side to side as though looking for a way out. 'Shoot! Shoot!' everyone shouted, and the King obediently shot, aiming well away from the animal. But like an echo to the sound of his rifle, a dozen more shots rang out, and the tiger fell dead. Loud were the congratulations and champagne corks popped. 'I couldn't have hit a hair of its tail,' said Alfonso afterwards. 'The wretched animal was in a netted lane.'

Hyderabad shoots, recalled Bazalgette, were very different.

We drove some miles into the jungle and then walked a mile or more. Dead silence. Each of the guns found a machan, a string bedstead tied into a tree, and climbed into it. No scraping of boots or snapping of twigs. Get comfortable and keep still. Don't move. Flies and midges buzz and bite. Don't scratch. Then, far away, there is a faint shout and a shot, the signal for the line of beaters to start, not loud at first. The tiger has killed this morning, eaten his fill and is having his after-dinner nap. They don't want to scare him. Beaters gently tap the trees, an occasional shout, a bang on a drum or a tin can . . . Gradually the noise increases. This disturbs the tiger's siesta so he decides to move . . . No, not that way; those villagers are too noisy. The other way? No, there are noisy villagers there too. So he goes this way, as it seems quiet. Thus the tiger is gently honked in the direction the Chief Shikari has chosen, to bring him quietly to the machan where the guest of honour may have the best chance of a clean shot.

The noise intensifies till the line of beaters reaches us. No tiger. 'He was coming along very nicely,' we are told, 'until he reached that bend in the path a hundred yards ahead of you. Then something alarmed him, and he broke out to the side.' Alfonso had brought an old friend who sneezed at the critical moment.

Alfonso had one last tiger-hunt, also unsuccessful, and then had to hurry to catch his train for Delhi. He was a Field Marshal in the British Army, so at the station were the General, a Guard of Honour and a band. He was late. At the last moment the King's car roared into the station and he got out, covered with grease and mud from changing a punctured tyre. 'Royal Salute! Present Arms!' The band crashed out the Spanish National Anthem and the King took the salute, inspected the Guard, chatted to the General without batting an eyelid. Afterwards he said, 'I'll give George a good laugh over this when I get back to London. I bet none of his Field Marshals has ever taken a salute in such a mess.'

Marriages were arranged between Azam Jah and Princess Durrashewar, daughter of the ex-Sultan of Turkey, rather a coup for the Nizam (cost what it may!); and between the younger Prince, Muazzim Jah, and her cousin, Niloufer. To break the ice for them, the Resident invited both newly wed couples, and the Nizam, to a small dinner-party attended only by his family and personal staff, including his Secretary, Conrad Corfield, who wrote:

When they arrived it was clear that the Nizam was bubbling over with pride in his daughters-in-law. He had good reason. Niloufer was the loveliest creature I have ever set my eyes upon. Her violet eyes and blue-black Circassian hair were enough to ruin a man's appetite, and I was to sit next to her. I hardly ate a thing as I gazed surreptitiously at her perfect features, her creamy complexion and the dimples on her cheeks while she lisped the English she had only started to speak three months before. When I pressed her to have a chocolate with dessert, she looked across the table at her husband and said, 'Please, no. He say I already too fat.' I couldn't see anything wrong with her figure myself.

Durrashewar, who married the Nizam's elder son, was not so beautiful but more regal. She was used to being called a Serene Highness, but her husband was not even a Highness, as this title was reserved for ruling princes. He wouldn't like it if she was accorded a title higher than his own, and she didn't like the idea of dropping her previous title. Fortunately a new agreement was being negotiated which accorded her husband the title of Prince of Berar, so she became a princess.

It was a compliment which pleased everyone, and cost nothing.

Bazalgette's fiancée, Jo, came on a visit and the Chief of Police invited them to watch the annual fire-walking ceremony by a Hindu weaver with magical powers. A huge pile of wood was set alight, and when after a long time it was reduced to ashes, the weaver arrived.

His acolytes raked out the great heap of seething white embers, glowing in the dark, to form a level mass about twelve foot square and a foot deep. After prayer, the weaver walked firmly through, while his acolytes danced around him.

'Come on,' said the Chief of Police, 'if you want to come through. I always go first before the mob stamp through and spoil it all.'

Well, if he could walk through, why should not I? He and I went through the fire together. The heat above my knees was intense and I had to put up my hand to shield my face, but below my knees it was cool and the embers crunched like walking in snow. When I got back, Jo demanded to go too, so we went through hand-in-hand.

How was it done? The great wood fire had made much ash. Ash is a low conductor of heat. Heat rises. Cold air rushes in from all sides and cools the ash. We walked on a layer of cool ash over the still glowing embers. We felt the heat rising to our faces, but the cold air rushed in below our knees.

Keyes took a keen interest in Secunderabad, the town of 180,000 people which had spontaneously, almost un-noticed and with no planning, grown up to support the garrison. It had become a noisome slum. Grainstores, wrote Bazalgette, brought rats:

Rats brought fleas. Fleas brought plague, for which there was no known cure. If plague could not be cured, perhaps rats could be controlled. This would involve re-building the town with rat-proof houses, and the opportunity would be taken to lay out wide streets and introduce drainage. Houses were built on concrete plinths, with wide overhang all round so that rats could not get in. The scheme was mainly self-financing, as sites on the main streets could be sold for high prices.

Sir Terence persuaded a wealthy banker to donate three lakhs (£22,000) to build a model village to replace the worst slum area. Control was given to the local Temperance Society and an Indian Christian engineer undertook, with volunteer specialists, to supervise the project. The banker agreed to double his donation if he were rewarded with a baronetcy with special remainder to his third and favourite son, but had to be content with a knighthood.

This work so impressed one of Hyderabad's revolutionaries that he devoted all his talents and energy to it.

For the whole of his nine years on the Frontier, Herbert Thompson had longed for a posting to the states, preferably in the southern half of India. When he heard he was to be Secretary to Keyes's successor, Duncan George McKenzie, he was overjoyed.

Apart from ending my nine years' service with Leah for the Rachel of my hopes, Hyderabad was a posting beyond my dreams. The Resident at Hyderabad was almost an ambassador, the state was in size not much smaller than France. In the context of an Embassy, the Secretary corresponded to Counsellor and Head of Chancery, with in addition direct administrative duties over what were known as the Administered Areas . . . So at one and the same time I was Sessions Judge and Inspector General of the Police (a contingent of 800 men), Prisons, Medical Services, Forests and Registration. Never before or since have I been such a Pooh-Bah. Theoretically I could arrest a culprit, try, sentence and receive him into my jail.

The Nizam was conspicuously loyal to the King: they belonged to the same trade union. The drama of the Abdication unrolled while I was in Hyderabad. When Edward VIII was closeted incommunicado in Fort Belvedere, the Nizam was so disturbed that he refused to go to bed for four days and insisted on his eldest daughter, who shared his bedroom, joining in his vigil. When at last the King resolved to abdicate and I telephoned the news, the Nizam's immediate reaction was, 'We have a King-Emperor. We can now go to bed.'

16

The States, the Politicals and Federation

It was characteristic of Hyderabad that it should send its own delegation to the Round Table Conference in London, rather than participating in a general states' delegation. Its leader was Sir Akbar Hydari, its members Trench and the Political Secretary, Nawab Mehdi Yar Jung; its secretary was Sir Akbar Hydari's son, Saleh, who was later to be the last Governor of Assam before Independence. It was proposed at first that they should all stay at the Hyde Park Hotel; but Saleh Hydari cased the joint and reported that the delegates' wives might be shocked by the Island Race's mating habits in Hyde Park, viewed through binoculars from the hotel windows. So, instead, they stayed at the Savoy, in tolerable comfort but to the displeasure of Trench's colleagues in the Political who were also attending the Conference but on the pay-roll of the parsimonious Government of India, and were billeted in more modest establishments down the Cromwell Road.

Before they set out the Nizam instructed them that they must throw Hyderabad's considerable weight behind Federation, which he saw as the only form a Dominion of India could take. They did so, and Hydari made a notable impact on the Conference.

Congress did not take part in the first Conference. Its leaders were in jail – self-sought, of course, as part of their Civil Disobedience Campaign. But the Viceroy, Lord Irwin, persuaded Gandhi and the other leaders to come out of jail and take part in the second Round Table Conference, in the winter of 1931-2. Gandhi was made Chairman of the Sub-Committee charged with finding a place in the new Constitution for the 'Scheduled Castes', that is to say, the sweepers and other Untouchables for whom he was always expressing a special concern. It was a disastrous selection: from first to last he made not a single constructive suggestion, and afterwards went on hunger-strike against a proposal that the Scheduled Castes should have special representation. But he was much lionised and May Trench met him on many social occasions.

No doubt he was a saint: everyone says so. It reflects discredit only on me, not on him, that I thought the aura he gave out was not of saintliness but of dreadful halitosis – the result, presumably, of all that health food, or perhaps London did not agree with him. He was busy being nice to Moslems and sat next to Amina Hydari at luncheon. She complained of being almost asphyxiated.

It was the second Round Table Conference which gave the princes second thoughts about Federation. They saw that Congress had no wish whatsoever to accommodate them. Congress did not want Federation in any case: it would give the Moslems a permanent, semi-separate role. What Congress wanted was a unitary state, governed by itself, with the Moslems in a permanent minority, second-class citizens unless they chose to throw in their lot with Congress. If the princes came into a Federation, they and the Moslems might form an unholy alliance which could challenge Congress supremacy. If there was no Federation, sooner or later the princes would fall like rotten plums from the tree.

While the first two Round Table Conferences were in session, the British Government had been Labour, led by Ramsay MacDonald. It was not the most successful ministry in our rough island story, but at least it had many of the right ideas about India, and genuinely wanted the sub-continent to achieve Dominion Status. The Third Round Table Conference took place under the aegis of the National Government, of which the voting strength was overwhelmingly Conservative, and most Conservatives viewed Dominion Status for India as an unfortunate necessity, to be postponed as long as possible. The die-hard wing of the party took its lead from Winston Churchill who was stubbornly hostile to any political concession. As a British cavalry subaltern he had served briefly in India forty years earlier, but had spent the long, hot afternoons perfecting his prose-style by reading Gibbon rather than increasing his knowledge of India by learning Urdu. He knew nothing of India and did not want to learn. He disliked and distrusted Indians. The errors of a great man are so much more damaging than those of a pigmy.

With the impetus from Westminster relaxed, the princes grew less keen every month on Federation. They could not agree among themselves on what they wanted. In March, 1932, Trench wrote:

Some want a bi-cameral legislature, others a uni-cameral one; some want the legislature to be small, others want a large one so as to get individual representation for as many states as possible. All seem to disagree regarding the system on which the states' representatives in a

Federal Assembly will be selected. In the meanwhile time passes and delays are dangerous.

Keyes was a keen Federalist, and much regretted the princes in general, and the Nizam in particular, backing away from it. He wrote to the Political Secretary, Sir Charles Watson, in January, 1933, that the Nizam had told him that he wished as a Faithful Ally to play a part in Federation, but the only obstacle was the way he had been treated over Berar. This posed a problem. When the provinces became self-governing under the new constitution, how could a territory of which the Nizam was sovereign be governed by a Congress Provincial Government? If Hyderabad joined the Federation, Berar should surely come in as part of Hyderabad. The Nizam undertook, if Berar were returned to him, to give the people there 'popular control and autonomy'. Keyes persuaded him that this would set an embarrassing precedent. How could he grant 'popular control' to some of his subjects and not to all? In the end, after Keyes's departure, the disputed territory continued its left-handed association with the Central Provinces, with the Nizam's flag flying beside the Union Jack; and his heir, the Sahibzada Azam Jah, was allowed to assume the title of 'Prince of Berar', which meant nothing but gave him much pleasure. 'To this,' Keyes informed Watson, 'I brought him.'

But now he and the other princes were weakening on Federation. For this Keyes blamed 'the muddy-minded babus of both colours' in the Political Department in Delhi, for whom he designed a special departmental tie, green with a yellow streak.

> They believed that, with the Chiefs* depending for their very existence on the Viceroy's special status, the Chiefs would accept their theories of Paramountcy and would lick the boots of their Political officers. They tried to prevent Federation coming up, and when it came up and held the field they tried to push it down with the argument that the Chiefs would have no safeguards for their sovereignty and autocracy . . . Now the Political Department is trying to frighten the Chiefs out of Federation by harping on the financial strings . . . They have succeeded so well that I don't think the Chiefs will come in unless the machinery is set up at once.

Keyes had the prejudices of the regimental soldier against the staff, and was unjust to them. It was they who advised the Viceroy, and the Viceroy, Lord Irwin, who wrote to the Secretary of State:

*A somewhat outmoded synonym for prince.

> I don't know where you get the idea that the Government of India is unsympathetic to the idea of an All-India Federation. This is really not the case, for while some of us, including myself, may have thought it very odd and very undesirable for the princes to tumble into a Federation three years ago, having committed themselves to it, we have always felt that it was impossible for them to keep out . . . I spend the greater part of my time canvassing the princes and exhorting them to take the plunge.

The passing of the Government of India Act in 1935 and the establishment of elected Provincial Governments, most of them Congress, on April 1st, 1937, brought the question of Federation to a head. There was provision in the Act for a Federation to be set up by Order in Council if at least half the princes, governing at least half of the states' subjects, agreed formally to accede to it. Lord Linlithgow succeeded Lord Willingdon as Viceroy in March, 1936. He was a Conservative, right of centre, but was convinced that a Federation of the provinces (four of which would be dominated by Moslems) and the states was the only way a united India could achieve Dominion Status within the Empire. He wanted to push the pace, but was restrained by the Secretary of State, Lord Zetland, who had to keep looking over his shoulder at Churchill's die-hards.

Linlithgow distrusted the Political Department. He seems to have had a personal prejudice against Sir B.J. Glancy, who was Political Secretary when he arrived. The obvious course would have been to make the Political Department responsible for selling Federation to the princes, through the Residents and Political Agents whom the princes knew and more or less trusted. Instead he formed a sort of special team of selected Politicals – Sir Arthur Lothian, Sir Francis Wylie and Sir Courtenay Latimer – to explain Federation to the princes, to hear and collate their objections and the safeguards they would require; but not to attempt to persuade them to join.

Conrad Corfield was convinced this was a mistake. The spectacle of a special team bypassing the Residents and Political Agents, whom they knew, aroused the princes' suspicions that they were being conned. However able the special team, it was, to use a military analogy, like breaking the chain of command by setting up a private army under an outside commander with an improvised staff.

It did not work. Of the eleven princes Wylie saw, not one was willing to federate. Their counter to the Viceroy's ploy was to employ their own constitutional lawyers to ferret out every snag in Federation and argue each point at great length. There were points which needed arguing. Under the Act, revenues from Customs and Excise would go to the Federal Government. Some states would lose considerably by this. How would they be compensated? Units in the Federation, whether provinces or states, would contribute on an equal basis to defence costs. But some states were already contributing, in cash or by ceded territories such as Berar. How much should they be credited for this? Given a general enthusiasm for Federation, such problems were soluble. But in the absence of enthusiasm, arguments about them gave unlimited scope for procrastination.

A problem which was not soluble was the attitude of Congress. Congress did not want Dominion Status within the Empire; it wanted complete independence. It did not want a Federation, with the possibility of an alliance between princes and Moslems. It set terms which it knew the princes could not accept – no state would be allowed to join that was not governed by an elected government; and states' representatives in the Federal Assembly must be elected, not appointed by the rulers.

Naturally the princes shied off. Congress was bound to be the dominant party in most of the provinces and at the centre. If Congress was so hostile, why embrace Federation only to be rebuffed? Better, surely, to hold fast to their treaties with the British Crown. Some rulers even saw accession to Federation as an act of disloyalty to the Crown.

Linlithgow hoped that, as a result of the work of his special team, by the end of November, 1938, the princes' opinions would be examined and collated, and any reasonable safeguards to their positions incorporated in draft Instruments which would be presented to them as a final offer. He would require a 'Yes' or 'No' answer within six months; and, provided enough said 'Yes', a Federation of India could be brought into being during the summer of 1939. He proffered a carrot in the shape of a generous slice of the Customs and Excise revenues, and an advantageous share of power at the centre – a third of the seats in the Lower House and two-fifths in the Upper House reserved for the states. There would still be loose ends, notably the amalgamation of innumerable petty states in Gujerat and Kathiawar, but once a Federation was in business these could be tied up. And then, he hoped, the parties to it (Congress, Moslems and princes), sharing responsibility, would rub along together and hostility would diminish.

In June, 1939, the more important princes held a special meeting in Bombay. Taking their lead from Bikanir and Bhopal, who nine years earlier had been all for Federation, they gave their answer: No.

Who was to blame? Linlithgow would probably have blamed the 'mediaevalism' of the Indian Political Service; also, perhaps, His Majesty's Government for applying the brake when a touch of the accelerator was needed. Keyes blamed the 'muddy-minded babus of both colours' in the Political Department in Delhi, as distinct from Residents and Political Agents in the field. Most Political officers blamed Linlithgow. Certainly Francis Wylie did, writing of Linlithgow's team, 'The whole circus was of course a farce. We had no direction, no line to advocate, the big idea being that you leave that to the princes, who were frightened out of their wits or clumsily clever with a whole litter of American lawyers . . . Where we let down the princes was in not giving them a lead.' Linlithgow, however, wanted the princes to be given a lead; it was Zetland who urged that the team's brief should be to discover what the princes thought about Federation, not to persuade them that it was to their advantage to join. Whether the princes would have followed a firm lead is questionable, but it does seem to have been the British Government, not anyone in Delhi, which failed in this respect.

Another Viceroy might have argued the case more strongly, but Linlithgow agreed with Zetland's caution. He was a man of great determination; he stood like a rock in the difficult circumstances of 1940-2. But his was not a dynamic, winning personality. The princes loved Irwin, they liked and revered Willingdon (while smiling at Her Excellency's idiosyncrasies). They respected Linlithgow, but another Viceroy might have persuaded the Cabinet to give more impetus to Federation, and to put it across the princes through the normal machinery of the Political Department, the Residents and Political Agents.

Conrad Corfield's contention that it could have been done seems to be supported by his and Herbert Thompson's experiences in the Rajputana States in 1938-9.

Thompson arrived in Rajputana to be acting Resident at Jaipur, keeping the seat warm for Corfield who was temporarily posted as Joint Secretary to the Political Department in Delhi.

> The task of explaining Federation to each state had been at last passed to the 'local' officers with instructions to get cracking. The task was made no easier by Pandit Jawaharlal Nehru who, in blood-curdling terms, had warned all rulers of the fate which awaited them when Congress took over the country. The more powerful states drew themselves up haughtily, but the smaller were as

> apprehensive as they were puzzled. When at last they faced the implications of a transfer of power, they realised that the protection of a paramount power might cease to be . . . Apart from it being our duty, we Political officers were eager to do what we could to sell the federal idea, though we knew perfectly well that if we succeeded the Political Service, and our jobs, would cease to be. Corfield and I used to compete in persuasion. I thought I had won the match by inducing the most charming of the backwoodsmen to federate. His last objection had been, that if the Federal Government controlled communications, would not Imperial Airways flying-boats violate his Maharani's purdah when she was enjoying the air on the Palace roof? I assured him that the pilot would not have the eyes to spy on the Maharani, and the Maharajah agreed to federate. But Corfield had been invited by his youngest ruler to draft his letter of acceptance. So he trumped my ace.

The princes had no wish to hear about details, or to have interpreted the small print which was so legalistic as to be beyond their comprehension. What each wanted to know was whether, by signing, he would be betraying the history and tradition of his state. Corfield believed that the individuality of each state could be preserved only by relinquishing some power to the Federation; but each ruler had to be persuaded in the light of his own circumstances. Only in the Rajputana States where a strong lead was given did the necessary 50 per cent of the rulers sign. It seems that the states, properly handled, were not beyond persuasion.

17

The States of Eastern India and Western India

There was a rag-bag of small states in eastern India in which relations with the Crown had been conducted through the Provincial Governments of Bengal, Bihar and Orissa, and the Central Provinces, with District Officers of those provinces performing the function of Political Agents. With the approach of provincial self-government, these arrangements had to be altered, for it was inappropriate that the Crown should be represented by an elected Minister of a Provincial Government, a Congressman at that. So in 1933 they were placed in direct relation with an Agent to the Governor-General for the Eastern States, a new creation, whose Residency in Calcutta had once been the mansion of Warren Hastings. All of these forty-two states were small, only six being entitled to gun-salutes. Most were very poor and backward, consisting mainly of hilly jungles teeming with tiger, bison, elephant and wild buffalo; inhabited by aboriginal hunting tribes such as the Gonds, still living by the bow-and-arrow, much addicted to witchcraft and human sacrifice, ruled by Rajahs and Maharajahs with somewhat dubious claims to Rajput status.

Reggie Bazalgette, Jack's brother, was the first Assistant Political Agent for the Orissa States, with headquarters at Sanbalpur. He found that the exiguous revenues of these states had mostly been appropriated by the Rajahs for their personal enjoyment; there were virtually no social services, and only the very worst of roads. He started negotiations with the rulers to improve matters and deprive Congress agitators of a target they could not miss. Congress propaganda was re-doubled. Early in January, 1939, Bazalgette heard of serious trouble in Ranpur State, with a mob threatening to burn down the palace. With two policemen, he set off on the eighty-mile drive, negotiating several trees felled to form road-blocks. Arriving in Ranpur, he found it quite impossible to drive through the crowd to the palace, so got out of his car with the two policemen and started to push his way through on foot. He encountered a bullock-cart draped with a sheet, from under which protruded several feet.

The driver of the cart shouted, 'Here are the bodies of the men the Sahib killed today!'

Bazalgette whipped the sheet off the cart, to expose several men very much alive.

'Kill! Kill!' roared the mob, and set upon him and the policemen with lathis,* battering the constables and beating Bazalgette to death.

Walter Magor was sent from Ajmere to replace him, although still under training. After a couple of months he was ordered:

> to proceed immediately to Rajgangpur in Gangpur State where I would meet a company of a Punjab regiment. There had been a 'No Rent' campaign, staged by the aboriginal Munda tribe, led by one Nirmal Munda who was to be arrested. We surrounded the village and I called on Nirmal Munda to come out. After some parleying with the headman, I noticed that some of the villagers were pulling bamboo rafters from the roofs and coming towards me. I then heard the noise of firing and was horrified to see men falling all round me. I immediately called out, 'Cease fire!' but about thirty people had been killed, and no order had been given to fire. The troops remembered that Bazalgette had been beaten to death a couple of months earlier. I arrested Nirmal Munda and took him to the jail in the state capital. I then brought the Diwan straight back to the village to hold a judicial enquiry into the incident, of which the proceedings were published at once, pre-empting a demand for an enquiry by Pandit Nehru.

Magor took leave to get married, and after a short honeymoon returned to Sanbalpur. The Political Agent, Major Searle, had a tame tiger-cub which slept for preference in Magor's bed.

> I took my wife to call on the Searles who had a long drawing-room with a parquet floor on which were laid Persian rugs. We were shown into the drawing-room but failed to notice that 'Widgie' was lying at the top of the stairs. As Daphne stepped on to the first rug, Widgie landed on her shoulders and they skated the length of the drawing-room to land at the Searles's feet. Quite a good introduction.

Nowhere were the problems of Federation more difficult than in the Western States Agency, north and north-west of Bombay. Supervised by a Resident and three Political Agents, these comprised 123 states varying in importance from Cutch, with a population of half a million and a seventeen-gun salute, to Santalpur, with a population of 413 (in

*A seven-foot, iron-bound bamboo stave.

1939) and no salute; and 163 'Talukas and Estates' governed directly by the Political Agents since their proprietors enjoyed no administrative or judicial powers.

Many of these states were fragmented, scattered over the map like pieces of a jigsaw puzzle waiting to be assembled. Political officers needed minds like computers to keep track of them. Their rulers were a medley of Rajputs, Kathis and the remote descendants of Pathan adventurers. The jurisdiction of the rulers of the small states was limited – some to non-capital offences, others to awarding sentences of two or three years' imprisonment, or fines of Rs 2,000 or Rs 5,000. Some were very poor, with an annual revenue of only a few thousand rupees; others rich with railway and customs revenues. One of the richest rulers was the Jam Saheb of Nawanagar, nephew of the famous 'Ranji' who had captained England and Sussex at cricket and was several times elected Chancellor of the Chamber of Princes.

The rulers and their states presented a picture of infinite variety and much interest to Politicals who were connoisseurs of the bizarre. Gujerat* was considered an excellent training ground for the young Political; the work was complicated, but most of the states were so small that it did not much matter if he made a few mistakes.

How had such an administrator's nightmare ever come into existence?

For most of the seventeenth and eighteenth centuries, Gujerat was under Mogul rule. It was then over-run by Mahrattas until, in the early nineteenth century, the Mahratta power was broken by the East India Company. By that time there were a few more or less established rulers governing more or less orderly tracts of country, but most of the land was occupied by free-lance captains and robber barons. The Company took over and ruled only a very small part of the country; over most of it the fluid, chaotic situation was frozen, encapsulated; the captains and barons recognised as Rajahs and Nawabs of the areas their disorderly bands were plundering, their position and rights guaranteed by the Company. In E.B. Wakefield's words, 'The stream of history was suddenly arrested, the current of change and development ceased to flow.'

How on earth could the pieces of the jigsaw puzzle be rearranged into a few units, economically and politically viable, fit to take their places in an all-India Federation?

*Gujerat was a geographical expression, applied to much of Bombay Presidency as well as to the Western Indian States and the Baroda and Gujerat States.

23 The boy Maharajah of Piploda refreshes himself after his installation as ruler. On his left is the Political Agent, J. Bradshaw.
24 The Maharajah gives an audience to his subjects

25 *Above left*, F.M. Bailey disguised as a Hungarian prisoner-of-war in Tashkent, 1918
26 *Above right*, Havildar Awal Nur and Daffadar Kalbi Mohamad on a secret mission with Bailey
27 *Below*, Bolshevik troops photographed by Bailey in Tashkent

Wakefield took over the Sabar Kantha Agency in 1937. He found rulers varying in quality. The Rajah of Tharad 'combined the appearance of a buffalo with the mentality of a mule' (a cruel libel on that sagacious animal) and grossly misgoverned his 54,000 unfortunate subjects. But the Thakur of Sudasna (32 square miles), who could trace his Rajput ancestry back 2,000 years, was an admirable ruler of his 7,000 subjects. 'In England he would have been a village squire and Chairman of the Bench of Magistrates. In Gujerat, in 1937, he was ruler of a state enjoying the protection of the Paramount Power.' But he was a giant compared to the Thakur of Vaktapur whose sway (also guaranteed by the Paramount Power) extended over a mere 4 square miles.

Some of Wakefield's predecessors had been less than diligent in supervising these potentates, and he found his office piled high with 'TOO DIFFICULT' files on quasi-legal, quasi-political disputes between little states, which had rumbled on about practically nothing for years. Some of these cropped up on tour: 'In Wao, Lalage was presented with a valuable diamond and emerald necklace which, of course, she refused to accept.' (The Rana of Wao had a long-standing territorial claim against the Thakur of Tharad.) A unique sight on tour, seen nowhere else in the world, were the herds of wild asses on the salt-flats beside the arm of the sea known as the Gulf of Kutch.

The Residency at Sadra was a fifteenth-century fortress on a bluff overlooking the river Sabarmati. During the monsoon the humid heat was utterly depressing, and the boredom even worse.

> From bank to distant bank the broad Sabarmati river became a turgid muddy torrent. Fields were flooded, roads were awash. For eight weeks Lalage and I did not leave Sultan Mahmud's fort except to take walks in the immediately surrounding countryside. We felt like prisoners taking their quota of permitted exercise . . .
>
> Studying the habits and behaviour of birds and animals was our only outdoor occupation. Brown monkeys with red bottoms abounded and were a scourge to the countryside. Being sacred they could not be killed, but the local Thakur spent a large sum of money every year in trapping them. When they had been trapped they were put into cages and sent away to be released twenty or thirty miles away . . .
>
> In the evenings, lacking anything better to do, we would sit indoors watching lizards stalking their prey. The four walls of our drawing-room were their hunting ground, and moths their favourite prey. The odds, we calculated, were about six to four against the moth.

Claude Bremner was also sentenced to twelve months in Sabar

Kantha. It was his 23-year-old wife's first experience of India, a tough introduction. But she found compensations. From the old fortress Residency she looked down the river.

> It was beautiful. The women washed their clothes, banging the garments on stones. I could hear their laughter and their singing. Occasionally a shepherd would lead his sheep and goats down to the river. There were prickly bushes around, from which would stalk peacocks, and there were black-faced monkeys, waiting to see what damage they could do. I was frightened by the sounds of the old fort, the tropical darkness and the cries of the wild animals, jackals and laughing hyenas.

On Christmas Day they played the Westminster bells on the gramophone. 'It was quite beautiful. It felt like the first Christmas.'

Compared to Sabar Kantha, the states in direct relation to the Agent to the Governor-General and those of Western Kathiawar were the height of sophistication and opulence – Piccadilly, the rue de la Paix and Fifth Avenue. Dhrangadhra (thirteen-gun), although it had an area of only 1,167 square miles and a population of 89,000, was as modern and well administered as any district in British India. In Nawanagar there was first-class cricket, golf on an admirably laid-out course, and tennis up to Wimbledon standard coached by three professionals, an Italian, a Swiss and a Yugo-Slav.

The Resident and the Political Agent, Western Kathiawar, lived in Rajkot. When Frank Pearson arrived as Under Secretary in the autumn of 1938, the Resident was E.C. Gibson, an *aficionado* of Kathiawar with a pleasantly cynical approach to the vagaries of government. It was an area redolent of politics: Jinnah was a Kathiawari, Gandhi a Gujerati. When Pearson was in Rajkot the Political Department tried to convince the rulers that Federation offered the best chance of their survival in an independent India. Congress on its part staged agitations in a number of states, pressing for more democratic forms of government and it was this agitation which eventually frightened the princes and led them to turn down Federation.

Congress was very busy in Rajkot State, where a ruthless and wily Diwan, Darbar Shri Viravalla, had debauched the young Thakur with brandy and dancing girls to such a degree that he himself had virtually taken over the state. He had the unusual distinction of seeing off Gandhi.

The circumstances of their encounter were that 'Sardar' Vallabhai Patel, a Gujerati, sought to trump the Resident's ace by negotiating with the Diwan for the setting up of a Reforms Committee to devise a democratic constitution for the state. It was to be composed of three state officials and seven non-officials, appointed by the Thakur on the recommendation of Congress – in fact, Congress nominees. The Diwan double-crossed Vallabhai Patel (not the easiest thing to do) and accepted only three of those named by him. Patel then accused the Diwan of breach of faith and Gandhi descended on the state, proclaiming that political prisoners in the state jail were being tortured. He was given every facility to inspect the jail, found no evidence of ill-treatment, and subsequently announced that he would fast until death unless all seven of the Congress nominees were appointed to the Reforms Committee.

The Diwan remained unmoved.

After a few days' fasting – his regimen did not exclude the consumption of goat's milk, orange-juice and water well laced with glucose – the Viceroy sent a letter asking him to take nourishment and come to Delhi to talk things over. Pearson delivered the letter.

> I presented myself at the bungalow where Gandhi was living. On the verandah his disciples sat cross-legged, spinning on the charka; among them an English Quaker, Miss Agatha Harrison.* I was told that I might enter but it was the Mahatma's day of silence and he could not speak to me. He sat cross-legged on a simple string bed, propped up by pillows; a simple white cotton garment was all he wore. His very shrewd eyes glistened through steel-rimmed glasses. We bowed to each other in silence and I presented my missive. There was an air of peace and dignity. After a few words to his supporters, I withdrew.

Gandhi accepted the Viceroy's invitation, and also his suggestion that the question of whether or not there had been a breach of faith – highly probable in the case of the Diwan – should be referred for an opinion to the Chief Justice, Sir Maurice Gwyer.

Gwyer gave an opinion favourable to Gandhi (one up to the Mahatma) who came bouncing back to Rajkot determined, as he said, to 'settle the Rajkot business once and for all'. He called on the Resident and was met at the Residency by Hugh Rance, newly arrived as Assistant to the Resident, who, like Pearson, was a 3rd Gurkha. 'He [Gandhi]

*She had swallowed Congress propaganda to such a degree that, while describing to Lord Linlithgow the sufferings of state subjects, she wept copiously.

leapt out of his car like a two-year-old and we shook hands warmly. He looked like a rather jovial old male witch.'

He seemed to have won hands down, but the Diwan was still unmoved. Gandhi, however, was too clever by half. Thinking to form a united front against Rajkot State, he promised places on the Reforms Committee to representatives of the Moslems and of the landowners. He then discovered that Congress Hindus would lose their built-in majority in the Committee, and went back on his promises.

The Diwan sat back and let events take their course.

The Mahatma was then accused of breach of faith. Everyone was cross with him, everyone felt he had let them down; and he had the embarrassing experience of being on the receiving end of a hostile demonstration such as he had so often arranged for others, with angry men waving black flags in his face. Emitting a dense cloud of philosophic verbiage to cover his retreat, he withdrew from Rajkot, never to return. All he had achieved was to strengthen the position of a thoroughly corrupt and despotic Diwan.

Nawanagar was always a problem state, largely because of the position and personality of 'Late His Highness', the famous cricketer 'Ranji', whose reputation in England, as the only Indian prince of whom most Britons had ever heard, far exceeded his virtues as a ruler. Test cricket captain, A.D.C. to the King, close friend of C.B. Fry and a host of other Establishment figures, he was, like Bikanir, virtually untouchable.

Rance's Resident, Gibson, took him out touring more than many Residents would have done, starting with a tour to Nawanagar, which was a very agreeable experience. The Jam Saheb then was 'Ranji's' nephew, Digvijaysinhji, almost as fine a game-player as his uncle. They bathed, played tennis and golf for a couple of days, and then crossed the Gulf of Kutch in the Jam Saheb's launch to the larger, but more backward, state of Cutch.

> We had two nights in Bhuj, the state capital, an ancient walled city and the Maharao, a nice old man of about 75, insisted on the gates being locked at ten o'clock each night and the keys being deposited in his palace. Cutch was about two hundred years behind the times.
>
> On the third day we went to the sea-side palace at Mandvi, a delightful spot. The Maharao's grandson, Prince Madansinhji, was about the same age, 27, as I, and we took to one another immediately. He took me out pig-sticking.
>
> Early in the morning we rode out, only Madansinhji and I having spears . . . When we arrived at the seaward side of the sugar-cane, the

locals started walking through it, beating tins and shouting and making a general hullabaloo. There was the sound of something crashing through the undergrowth and a large boar broke cover about forty yards from us.

Rance was an experienced pig-sticker – just as well, for a wild boar can easily disembowel horse and man: it has often happened.

Normally all available spears would have set off in pursuit, but as I was his guest, Madansinhji held back and I galloped off on my own. By the time I caught up with the boar, we were on the hard sand of the sea-shore. As I drew close enough to spear him, he turned to charge. The spear transfixed him, my horse slipped on the wet sand and we all came down together. However, I managed to hold on to the reins with my left hand and the shaft of the spear with my right, and as long as I could do this, I could prevent the boar getting at me and the horse. We danced around for what seemed ages but cannot have been more than a minute or so before the rest of the mounted party arrived and the boar was despatched. It was a hefty brute, 32 inches at the shoulder and weighing about 250 pounds . . .

After this playing golf in Cutch and Mandvi seemed rather tame.

A certain rich and famous Kathiawar ruler whose state included a sea-port once accosted Cyril Hancock.

'Why do you hate me, Hancock?' he asked.

It was a difficult question to answer. Hancock could hardly reply, 'Because Your Highness is such a bloody hypocrite – sounding off on the Chamber of Princes about loyalty to the Crown and a prince's duty to his subjects, while you grab three-quarters of your state's revenue for your private purposes and make a fortune smuggling pearls.'

18

Indian Politicals outside India

Some of the most interesting posts for the Indian Political Service were not in India at all. There was an officer based on Bushire who was Resident for the small Arab states on the southern shore, and Consul General for Persia, having under him various Consuls and Vice-Consuls, mainly officers of the Indian Political. The climate was vile; the opportunities for sport non-existent; the social life negligible; there was neither air-conditioning nor ice. But the Gulf had its *aficionados* who would not willingly serve anywhere else. Also its *non-aficionados*, who would. The work was different from anything in India, on the fringe of the 'Great Game', with Germany the opposition from 1907 to 1917. One Indian Political there in 1915 changed the course of history.

He was Captain W.G. Neale, First Assistant and in charge at Bushire while the Resident, Sir Percy Cox, was in Basra as Chief Political Officer to the Mesopotamian Expeditionary Force.

Bushire is a desert island of coral and old oyster-beds, just above sea-level, connected by a sandbank to the Persian mainland. Persia in the First World War was neutral, inclined towards Germany; and about two miles from Bushire lived the German Consul, Dr Helmuth Listemann, a dapper little fellow with a 'Kaiser moustache', inclined to stand on his dignity and to take offence. Half a mile from the Consulate was the house of a German businessman, Karl Eisenhut, who was up to no good.

In Bushire itself was a detachment of Bombay Grenadiers, to guard the British establishments there. On August 4th, 1914, social relations between the British and the Germans, hitherto quite cordial, ceased. This did not, however, prevent Leslie Hastings, a lively subaltern, from climbing up on to the roof of the German consulate one dark night and hoisting the Union Jack. Great was his chagrin in the morning on seeing the Union Jack still there . . . but the German flag flying over it. There was nothing he could do but return to the Consulate roof and haul down his country's slighted emblem, watched by Dr Listemann with a twinkle behind his spectacles. They had a few polite words and parted.

There was another German in south Persia, Wassmuss, an adventurer often compared to Lawrence of Arabia, who was stirring up the tribes to make trouble along the Indian frontier. In March, 1915, Neale received information that the three Germans were plotting to sabotage the submarine cable and to bring in tribesmen to attack the scattered houses of the British community. He obtained from Sir Percy Cox permission to arrest Listemann and Eisenhut – or, rather, to kidnap them, for he had no powers of arrest in Persian territory, and they had done nothing for which the Persian authorities would apprehend them.

For the operation on the night of March 9th-10th, 1915, two snatch-squads were formed, one under Neale, the other under the Vice-Consul, C.J. Edmonds of the Levant Consular Service. Both were accompanied by two officers and a squad of Bombay Grenadiers. Neale decided with all delicacy that he, as a married man, should take Eisenhut who had a young bride, while Edmonds tackled Listemann.

Listemann's first words on being awakened were, 'Oh, it's you again, Hastings, is it?' Edmonds entered Listemann's room to find him already out of bed and Hastings 'with a broad grin on his face like a kitten showing off its first mouse'.

Listemann drew himself up and said stiffly, 'Mr Edmonds, you are a member of the regular Consular Service and must know that what you are doing tonight is contrary to international law.'

Edmonds replied, 'I am sorry to inconvenience you. I am not here to discuss international law but to carry out my orders. I must ask you to come along quietly.'

He asked Listemann for his keys.

'Keys! Keys!' shouted the Kaiser's man in Bushire, pulling a handkerchief and a box of matches out of his dressing-gown pocket and flinging them on the floor, 'That is all you allow me to take and you ask me for keys!'

The sound of a galloping horse was heard, reminding Edmonds of the need for haste. If the Persian Governor were to hear of this outrage and send soldiers to rescue the victims, the situation would be fraught with embarrassment. First they had to walk half a mile to Eisenhut's house, where a carriage would be awaiting them.

'Will you walk a little faster, Dr Listemann?'

'No, I will not, Mr Edmonds.'

'Then I'm afraid you will have to be pushed. Here are your clothes, Dr Listemann. Perhaps you would like to put your trousers on.'

'No, I will not put my trousers on.'

'As you wish. But I must urge you to walk faster if we are to avoid unpleasantness.'

'Very well.' As they reached Eisenhut's house he added, 'And *now*, gentlemen, as I understand that there is a *lady* coming, perhaps I *had* better put my trousers on.'

The Eisenhuts came down. Listemann was not amused by Neale's cheerful, 'Sorry to disturb you, Dr Listemann, but war is war, you know.' He turned his back on Neale, for the Germans refused to recognise the diplomatic status of the Indian Political Service. Later, as he was taken aboard a Royal Indian Marine warship, he recovered his composure and asked Edmonds to look after his horses and his dogs.

After he had been taken off to internment, they searched his house and found, wrapped in woollen underpants, the German Diplomatic cypher-books. These were sent to London and made possible the de-cyphering of the Zimmermann* telegram which was instrumental in bringing the United States into the war.

Another Political officer stationed in Persia during the war was Lieutenant Colonel F.M. Bailey. He was an accomplished all-round naturalist: the beautiful Himalayan Blue Poppy was named after him, *Mecanopsis Baileyi*; and he was fluent in Russian and German. Summoned to Delhi in haste, he was ordered to proceed to Tashkent in Russian Turkestan, there to try to persuade the local Bolshevik Commissars to carry on the war against the Germans. Travelling quite openly, in uniform, he reached Tashkent after a journey of many weeks, via Gilgit, the Pamirs and Kashgar. He soon found he was on a fool's errand: the Bolsheviks had no intention of fighting anyone except the White Russians, whom the British were supporting, and the Emir of Bokhara who had taken to strangling their emissaries. Moreover Bailey's own position was delicate. Because it was British policy not to recognise the Bolsheviks as the legitimate Russian Government, he had no diplomatic credentials and certainly no diplomatic immunity. They regarded him, not without reason, as a spy.

Some Russian friends who were White in sympathy tipped him off that he was about to be arrested and shot, so he went into hiding. Russian Turkestan was full of soldiers of the Austro-Hungarian Army, released from prison-camps when the Bolsheviks made peace; and Bailey was able to obtain the uniform and papers of one of these. Under the eyes of the Cheka sleuths shadowing him, he disappeared into one house as Lieutenant Colonel Bailey, and emerged from another, further down the street, as an Austrian soldier. The first papers he got were not

*Zimmermann was the German Foreign Minister. He instructed the German Ambassador in Mexico to offer the Mexicans Texas, Arizona and New Mexico as the price for declaring war against the United States.

very satisfactory: he might easily meet someone who really did come from the town of which he purported to be a native. But he eventually acquired the papers of an Albanian. He thought it improbable that there could be many Albanians in the Austro-Hungarian Army, or any in Tashkent.

A few days after giving the Cheka the slip, he drove a hay-cart out of Tashkent into the countryside. For many months he lived in the utmost peril, sometimes in an isolated bee-farm in the mountains, sometimes in the city. He believed, wrongly, that British forces from North Persia were advancing on Tashkent, where they would be welcomed by the Kirghiz population and would have no difficulty in driving out the Bolsheviks. So he collected all the information that would be useful to them, wrote it out in invisible ink and sent it by secret courier to Meshed. He got in touch with the local Moslem and White Russian resistance and sent messages to Kashgar asking the Consul General Lieutenant Colonel Percy Etherton, a colleague in the Political, to give their agent Rs 200,000. The Bolsheviks would certainly have shot him had he fallen into their hands and it was a miracle that he didn't. In Tashkent one of his worries was that his bull-terrier, which he had left in the charge of his White Russian friends, would recognise him in the street and come up grinning and wagging its tail.

The political and military situation was complicated. South and south-west of Tashkent was the semi-independent, barbarous Emirate of Bokhara, part of the Tsarist Empire but now at war (more or less) with the Bolsheviks. Further west, in North Persia, were British and White Russian forces fighting the Bolsheviks on the Merv front. South of Bokhara was Afghanistan, which in the summer of 1919 was at war with India. Tashkent resounded with eye-witness accounts of the gallant Afghans advancing on Lahore, Delhi, Calcutta, while Indian Moslems rallied as one man to the cause of Islam and Revolution.

Bailey decided he must get out, with the information he had accumulated over fifteen months. His safest way would be through Bokhara to North Persia. He therefore joined the Bolshevik Secret Service, in which there were many ex-prisoners of war, and volunteered to go on a perilous mission to Bokhara where, so he had heard, the English spy, Bailey, might be lurking. Since five of their spies had been strangled in Bokhara, the Bolsheviks were delighted to find a comrade so zealous for the Revolution. Bailey and his White Russian friends took tickets on separate trains to the Bokhara border and crossed it into comparative safety. But only comparative: the Bokharans were the most fanatical of Moslems, and the Emir viewed with understandable suspicion a Faranghi wearing Austrian uniform and claiming to be a member both of the Bolshevik Secret Service and of the Indian Foreign and Political Department. However, Bailey was not actually strangled, but was allowed to stay in Bokhara under surveillance.

One day two men dressed as Bokharan merchants presented themselves to him and smartly saluted. They were Daffadar (cavalry sergeant) Kalbi Mohamad, a Hazara from eastern Afghanistan, and Havildar (infantry sergeant) Awal Nur, a Pathan, both of the Guides. They had been sent from the British forces in North Persia with a caravan of rifles for the Emir of Bokhara. They were very fine men, a credit to their corps. Eventually, making the right approaches to the right people, Bailey, the two Guides and his White Russian friends obtained the Emir's permission to leave for North Persia.

From Bokhara they rode for three weeks across the terrible Kara Kum desert, their only map torn from a Victorian travel-book. In Turcoman dress, with huge Turcoman sheepskin hats, they hoped to be taken for Turcoman brigands. Their lives depended on finding a particular well, with neither trees nor buildings to mark it, and led by a guide who admitted he had lost his way. They chanced upon the well, but it was 700 feet deep, and they had not half that length of rope. But their luck was in: a party of nomads arrived who lent them enough rope to draw water. After a skirmish with Bolshevik border guards, Bailey and the two Guides reached Meshed safely, together with the White Russians, Bailey's reports, his butterfly collection and the bull-terrier.

The German challenge in Persia was formidable. Wassmuss and his colleagues were tough, dedicated men who did great work for their country in keeping the tribes on the boil. The Allies countered them by setting up a thinly held cordon, 700 miles long, from Meshed to the Arabian Sea, manned in the north by the Russians and in the south by the British with tribal levies stiffened by Indian cavalry. It was fairly effective until the Revolution in 1917 when the northern end of it dissolved, and the way was open for agents to pass through to Afghanistan and the Indian Frontier. By rapid improvisation the defecting Russians were replaced by more levies and Indian troops, a job mainly for the Political. (All this time, it should be remembered, Persia was neutral.)

In 1918 B.J. Gould, who had been Assistant Private Secretary to the Viceroy, was posted as Consul to Seistan, the eastern province of Persia. From the railhead he travelled by lorry along a rough track lined with dead camels in varying stages of decomposition. 'Dead camels have a stale, sweet smell, and it was difficult to hold breath long enough to take gulps of clean hot air.' His Consulate at Duzdap (later renamed Zahidan) was a long bungalow with immensely thick mud walls and domed ceilings finished off with a sort of plaster made by pounding nodules found on the shore of the nearby Lake Hamun. There was a Consulate doctor, a British manager of the local branch of the Imperial Bank of Persia, and three British officers of the Seistan Levy Corps. After a few days there he rode 350 miles to meet his predecessor, Colonel Prideaux, from whom he was to take over, at the summer Consulate in Birjand. On the way he crossed Lake Hamun by a sort of punt made from hundreds of reeds bound together: Moses and the bullrushes. From Birjand he rode on to Meshed to make the acquaintance of the Consul General and General Malleson, commanding British troops in Persia. He then rode 700 miles back to Duzdap. He did not regret the fleshpots of Simla.

His main responsibility was looking after the levy corps. The Baluchis of Seistan knew everything there was to know about camels, deserts and raiding. They boasted that when a Baluchi was offered water by a soft oasis-dweller, he replied, 'Dog, I drank yesterday.' They were ideal material for a desert levy corps; and for every Baluchi enlisted, there was one less raider. When the Afghan War started in the summer of 1919, there were raids from both east and west. Gould was authorised to increase the levy corps from 1,400 to 2,400. Despite the great difficulty in finding Persian-speaking British officers, they coped splendidly until the end of 1920 when British troops were withdrawn from Persia and the Seistan Levy Corps was disbanded. Although a .303 Lee-Enfield rifle was worth two or three years' pay, in six years they lost only seven rifles.

It was not to be expected that Persian officials would approve of this military activity on their territory, but it was Gould's job to keep on good terms with them. He was particularly friendly with the Governor of Seistan, known by his title of Shaukat ul Mulk, the 'Glory of the Dominion', who ruled his people in the best traditions of oriental autocracy. One day Gould happened to mention that two levies had deserted. The Shaukat replied that he really did not know what Gould was talking about: it seemed to him inconceivable that a foreign consul could be employing armed Persian subjects on Persian soil. But, he added inconsequently, if he himself were enlisting men for watch-and-ward, he would never dream of enlisting them from that particular clan. Gould took the hint.

Gould went home on leave and returned to Duzdap with a wife who took to the life like a duck to water. She rode beautifully; learned to speak Persian with a better accent than his, since his was tainted with an Urdu intonation; produced two sons in the next two years; and was a great social asset with the local officials and tribesmen. 'The Little Lady' was particularly friendly with the Shaukat's wife, which of course helped Gould. One day the Shaukat asked for advice. Persia was to have a Parliament, with elected members. There was a problem about elections in Seistan – not about who should be elected, for that had been taken care of, but what sort of majorities would be considered suitable? Gould suggested a mix of runaway majorities and close-run affairs, which was duly arranged.

The Shaukat's hospitality was unbounded. For a typical party the guests – Persians, British, Belgian officials of the Persian Posts and Telegraphs, a White Russian general or two – would assemble for drinks (which the Persians, although Moslems, did not eschew) and conversation; then, in leisurely succession, luncheon, siesta, tea, tennis, bath, dinner, bridge. Sometimes after dinner a knife would be spun, top-wise, on the table. When it stopped spinning, the person at whom it pointed had to make an extempore speech, in any language, or mixture of languages, or – if words failed him – by gestures. Finally the guests would take their leave in the customary polite formula, 'I now proceed to remove the causes of inconvenience.'

With the disbanding of the levy corps, raiding increased. One unfortunate railway official was carried off into Afghanistan for ransom. To keep him quiet on his camel, his kidnappers stitched his right hand to his left ear. The Persian throne was usurped by a tough Colonel, Reza Shah Pahlevi. By the time Louis Pinhey arrived in Zahidan (formerly Duzdap) in 1931, *pax Persianica* had been restored by placing captured highway robbers in barrels of concrete, with just their heads sticking out, beside the road on which they operated. Disliking foreigners almost as much as highway robbers, Reza Shah had closed down the railway from Baluchistan, so that Pinhey and his newly wed wife had to travel for hundreds of miles in excruciating discomfort in a hired lorry over a no-road.

Arriving in Zahidan, they found that Persians, fearing the monarch's displeasure, would not associate with them, which inhibited their social life. However, a fair number of travellers passed through (as hastily as possible) including the Canadian archaeologist who discovered Pekin Man; and the ubiquitous, redoubtable 'Mrs Pock', the running boards and luggage-rack of her car piled high with rolled Persian rugs on which she had not the slightest intention of paying one penny in customs duty at the Indian border.

When Pinhey had a day's partridge shooting with some Baluchi Sardars, he was accused of stirring up tribal rebellion. When Reza Shah forbad the flying of a Union Jack in the consulate garden, which was legally Persian soil, Pinhey transferred the flagstaff to the consulate roof, legally British soil, where it was much more conspicuous. Dictators can be teased by those with diplomatic immunity.

The Political Department delighted in sending young married, or about-to-be-married, officers to the Gulf and Seistan. Jack Bazalgette and his wife, Jo, were decanted at Bushire in 1935 and accommodated in an octagonal cottage known as the hashti.* Its peculiar shape was the result of bygone departmental guile. The Persian Government having said that the British could have for the Under Secretary's house as much land as could be covered by a tent, the crafty Resident of the day had spread a large tent, with its flaps and walls, flat on the ground so that it covered an area similar to the ground-plan of a seaside bandstand. On that the hashti was built.

> Jo in her bath saw a line of fleas advancing on her, at the hop, across the white-tiled floor. 'What a dirty man', she said, 'the last Under Secretary must have been.' However at dinner our hostess greeted us, 'How are your fleas? Ours are ghastly.' We had arrived in the 'flea season' when the barley is cut and the fleas come storming into the houses.
>
> As Under Secretary I seemed to have neither work nor status. To give me something to do I was told to sort out the archives which dated back to 1750. The early correspondence was mainly commercial, written in beautiful copperplate handwriting, perhaps chiding the Agent Resident for slowness in selling the shipment of woollens sent him two years ago, and his reply that woollens would not move in that climate. We found an invoice for Scotch whisky at seven shillings a dozen. That moved.

Jo was made honorary Personal Assistant to the Resident. Her first job was to bottle a 6-gallon cask of overproof whisky. The fumes were such that she could barely stand after completing it.

> In the 1930s the most valuable product of the Gulf was the pearl. Arab divers brought up oysters from a great depth, and merchants

*Hasht: eight in Persian.

would carry fortunes in pearls wrapped in small ragged pieces of red cloth, roll them out on to a table-top or the palm of a hand, turn them over judiciously to admire their colour and beauty, grading and matching them.

The winter in the Gulf was glorious, all that the Mediterranean is said to be and not so cold. We did not fear the summer, for was there not unlimited sea to swim in? Little did we realise that the water-temperature could rise to 96° and one can sweat as much under water as out.

Besides, a man bathing in quite shallow water was attacked by a shark. An Indian clerk from the Consulate office dashed into the sea and belaboured the shark with his umbrella, driving it off with its victim's leg. It was an act of incredible bravery.

Long before Parliament made slavery illegal, British Agents in the gulf were trying to suppress the slave-trade. Any slave 'taking bast' by touching the flagpole outside the Residency would be granted his certificate of manumission. Bazalgette signed a certificate for an African who had swum ashore from a dhow and taken bast.

In the autumn of 1935 Bazalgette was posted as Consul in Kerman, 1,000 miles away by road. Kerman was the capital of a province, headquarters of an Army Command, and there would have been there a lively social life but for Reza Shah. So the Bazalgettes' society was restricted to Indian merchants, European carpet-dealers and the staff of a Mission Hospital. He would invite, say, the Governor to dinner, but the Governor was nearly always 'indisposed'.

Then there was a shift of policy. His Imperial Majesty decreed that, to bring Persia – or, rather, Iran – into the twentieth century, women must discard the all-enveloping chaddar and go about unveiled. Many did not like doing this, so it was decreed that only prostitutes might wear the chaddar, and any man might accost them. Moreover, to encourage the ladies in social intercourse, officials must hold parties for other officials *and their wives*, and to these parties foreigners must be invited. So the ladies of the town discovered a new source of income, hiring themselves out not for the traditional purpose, but as surrogate 'wives' of officials whose wives were too shy to go out. The Bazalgettes found it disconcerting meeting the same lady as Mrs Schoolmaster on one occasion, and Mrs Major on another.

Bazalgette was moved on to Khorramshah, a busy post. It was the main port of entry into Iran from the Gulf, and only ten miles away was the Anglo-Iranian Oil Company refinery at Abadan. There were a couple of thousand British Oil Company employees, and 5,000 Indian craftsmen, for all of whom the Vice-Consul at Khorramshah had a responsibility. He had a divided personality.

> Some of our work went to London via the British Legation at Teheran, some to New Delhi via the Political Resident, some to our Consul at Basra in Iraq. The crews of British ships came into consular jurisdiction and had to be signed on and off. With the number of British tankers arriving, loading and leaving every day, there was plenty of work for me . . .
>
> Much of my work came from the Indian community. To protect Indian workers from exploitation abroad, the Government of India forbad them to leave India until their work-contracts had been approved. A copy of the contract was then sent to the nearest British consul, to whom the Indian could appeal if he felt himself wronged.
>
> British employees of the Oil Company had no such protection. Many had been delighted at the generous terms offered them. But with the Hitler threat, the Company was expanding rapidly and could not live up to its promises, for example in housing. These youngsters found living in a tent with temperatures up to 120° unbearable, and the social amenities not all they were cracked up to be. Many wished to go home. They were reminded of their advances of pay, and the clause in their contract which enabled the Company to recover full passenger rates for repatriation by tanker. I was shocked at the ruthless decisions made by the Company.
>
> We started our family during the years we were in Khorramshah, and Jo went home in the summer of 1936 to have John. We were having customs problems when she returned, and I feared heavy duties on clothes and baby foods. We came off the mail steamer in our launch and the Customs Officer leaped aboard. 'Anything new to declare?' he asked. Jo held up John and said, 'Yes. This.' He laughed and left us in peace.

John Cotton, not yet married but engaged, arrived in Bushire in June, 1937.

> It was the hottest time of year in the Gulf, and it really was hot, much worse than Aden. Owing to the shallowness of the coastal waters, ships had to anchor four or five miles out and trans-ship their cargoes into dhows. On shore, harbour facilities were rudimentary; nevertheless Bushire was then the chief port of Iran. There was no air-conditioning. The water from the local wells was so brackish as to be

almost undrinkable for those not born to it. The Residency had its own plant for condensing sea-water. But to function properly a sea-water distillation plant has to have cold water to condense the steam, and there was no cold water.

As Under Secretary, Cotton was told to find himself something to do in the Town Office. He tried to study Persian, but did not get far because no Iranian national was allowed to teach him. Every now and then the Shah thought up another anti-British tease, such as imposing quarantine restrictions on the Resident and his staff when they returned from touring on the Arab shore of the Gulf: they had to live in tents on a barren little island until the danger of infection was judged to have passed.

In September he flew back to India to get married, returning with his bride in October. 'Although I had done my best to prepare Mary for the somewhat Spartan life in Bushire, she was rather taken aback by the reality.'

At Kuwait they were invited to watch the first oil being brought to the surface, but the bit at the end of the drill dropped off, so they were cheated of a historic moment.

In the New Year, Cotton graduated from the Town Office to the confidential office at the Residency. This was more interesting, giving him an insight into the complex political problems of the Gulf, with Iran on one side and, on the other, a whole collection of petty shaikhdoms and sultanates, then backward and indigent, now immensely rich and owning half the West End of London. He toured extensively with the Resident, generally in H.M.S. *Bideford* which was stationed in the Gulf to discourage gun-running and the slave-traffic.

We stopped and boarded two suspicious-looking dhows but the search yielded nothing. On our return we ran into such a fierce northerly gale that the *Bideford* only just made headway. It gave me pleasure that, while most of the officers and men were sea-sick, I wasn't.

Perhaps the greatest Arabist in the Political was Harold Dickson. His father served in the Levant consular service successively at Beirut, Damascus and Jerusalem, and he was suckled by a girl of the great Anizah Badawin group, which in Arab eyes made him a sort of honorary Anizah, a high status-symbol. He served as an Indian cavalry captain during the early months of the Mesopotamian campaign, but his fluent Arabic took him through a side-door into the Political as Assistant

Political Agent at Suq ash Shuyukh, an insalubrious spot on the Euphrates. After a happy year there he was transferred, most unwillingly. But when he called at the office of the Chief Political Officer, Sir Percy Cox, on his way to his new station, he was greeted on the verandah by most of the Shaikhs of Suq ash Shuyukh come to petition 'Cokkus' that he be not moved. Cox was not amused, but eventually accepted that this was not a put-up job and allowed Dickson and the Shaikhs to have their way.

He spent most of the next twelve years in Mesopotamia, living, working and travelling with the Badawin. In 1929 he was posted Political Agent, Kuwait. Nothing could have pleased him more. He identified completely with the local Badawin, 'more lovable than any other race on earth'. So did his wife. They became supreme experts on Badawin camels, horses, falconry, raiding, genealogies, feuds, migrations, customs. Dickson committed his knowledge to a massive volume which Freya Stark described as 'conscientious, detailed, authoritative and indispensable' to travellers in that region. His former chief, Sir Arnold Wilson, a rival author, said of it, 'You're a very good Political officer, but you can't write a damn.'

His first job in Kuwait was to sort out a rebellion by a very likeable vassal of Ibn Saud, operating from Kuwait territory. With some assistance from the R.A.F. (who machine-gunned him by mistake) he persuaded Shaikh Ahmed of Kuwait to deny the rebel sanctuary, and get the rebel to surrender and Ibn Saud to pardon him. So successful was his diplomacy that he became the lifelong friend of all three. Meanwhile his wife took into her care the wives and children of the rebel during the tortuous negotiations. Thereafter two problems kept him busy. The first was the need to frustrate the knavish tricks of British and Iraqi officials in Bagdad who thought they should inherit the Turks' sovereignty over Kuwait, especially with all this talk of oil there. The second problem was the oil itself.

As a romantic he must have hated the thought of a camel-culture changing into a Cadillac-culture; as a realist, he realised that it was inevitable; as Political Agent, he had to help Shaikh Ahmed make the best possible bargain for himself and his people.

Since 1923 the Anglo-Persian Oil Company had been negotiating with the Shaikh for concessions. In 1927 the Gulf Oil Company of Pennsylvania joined in the scramble, and the Shaikh was in the happy position of playing one off against the other. It was like bargaining in the souk for a gigantic prize. But the rivals combined into the Kuwait Oil Company and presented him with joint proposals which fell far short of his ideas. There then appeared, like a genie out of a bottle, the 100 per cent British company, Traders Ltd, which bettered the Kuwait Oil Company's offer. Shaikh Ahmed said he would accept the offer of Traders Ltd provided His Majesty's Government approved, and H.M.G.'s approval of the plum going to a wholly British company rather than to an Anglo-American consortium was highly likely.

But Dickson was determined that Shaikh Ahmed should not be conned. He smelt a rat, and reported to the Political Resident that Traders Ltd was merely a front for the Anglo-Persian, bent on double-crossing Gulf Oil, its partner in the Kuwait Oil Company, and securing a monopoly for itself. At the India Office Gilbert Laithwaite, the Permanent Secretary, scouted Dickson's conspiracy theory: 'Colonel Dickson may be right, but it is a most discreditable if not impossible story.' Doubtless Laithwaite was right. No oil company could possibly behave in this reprehensible way . . . could it? If there was a conspiracy, it recoiled on the conspirators. The Kuwait Oil Company promptly overbid Traders Ltd, accepted the Shaikh's terms and in the Agency house signed with him the concession agreement, witnessed by the Political Agent.

Two years later Dickson retired. By the good offices of Shaikh Ahmed, he was appointed Local Representative of the Kuwait Oil Company and lived on in the Agency, leased to him in perpetuity by the ruling family, until his death twenty-one years later. He became far more than an oil company employee – Shaikh Ahmed's closest friend and adviser, and Political Agent again during the war. Aged 90, his widow still lives in the Agency, one of the last landmarks of old Kuwait. As an Arabist she is as distinguished as her husband, with a string of publications and decorations to prove it.

The most extraordinary things always seemed to happen to Leslie Chauncey – shooting his Resident, disposing of the result of a Dowager Maharani's indiscretion; as a mere Under Secretary negotiating a treaty with an Arab Shaikh; and burying his Resident at sea. (Not the one he shot.)

> Colonel Sir Hugh Biscoe, the Political Resident, had been trying to get the Shaikh of Sharjah to lease a landing-ground for Imperial Airways and the R.A.F. Through three days of argument in intense hot weather, the Shaikh still demurred, and it was decided to return to H.M.S. *Bideford* and sail the next morning. That night the Resident died from a heart-attack. We sent messages to Teheran and Delhi,

and to the India Office to try to contact Lady Biscoe, who was in England, to ask whether a land or sea burial was required. Contact could not be made, but I was certain that his widow would prefer a sea-burial. So back to sea we went, and the burial took place.

I then had the idea that if I returned to Sharjah and told the Shaikh that he had killed the Resident with his arguing, he might out of remorse complete the agreement. That is how it turned out. Our signal reporting success crossed one from Delhi to the effect that no useful purpose would be served by our pursuing matters with the Shaikh.

The terms were one lakh (£7,500) a year rent; six rifles for guards; the mail steamer to call once a fortnight; no flag or Political officers; and the wind-direction-cone on the airfield to be in the Shaikh's colours.

Hugh Rance, posted with his young wife to Bushire, served under the Resident, Sir Trenchard Fowle, who set himself up as the Grand Old Man of the Gulf, presiding there for seventeen consecutive years. He was crusty and set in his ways. When one Political Agent, with due regard for economy, sent him a brief telegraphic report on some unimportant matter, Sir Trenchard fired back the magisterial rebuke, 'Do not use telegraphese when telegraphing to me.'

Sir Trenchard had a radio. It went wrong and there was great despondency, but Jane fiddled about with it and eventually gave it a despairing kick, which brought it instantly to life. She acquired great merit with Sir Trenchard by this achievement.

Towards the end of July we all moved up to the summer headquarters in Shiraz. Shiraz was about 6,000 feet above sea-level, in a fertile plain and grapes were widely cultivated. When we went out for our early morning ride the peasants would feed not only us but our horses with bunches of grapes.

Sir Trenchard's offer, in August 1939, to stay on indefinitely was, to his indignation, politely refused. He was succeeded by Major Geoffrey Prior, a stripling of 42. One of Rance's more delicate tasks was to draft a letter for Prior's own signature recommending that he be promoted to Lieutenant Colonel lest the Shaikhs and the R.A.F. officer commanding in Iraq feel slighted by having a mere major set over them.

In Afghanistan Britain maintained a diplomatic presence at Kabul where the Minister, Counsellor and Secretary were officers of the Indian Political Service but (because of the Service's Machiavellian reputation) provided with passports describing them as members of the Diplomatic Corps, which deceived no one but saved Afghan faces. In normal times it was a pleasant, undemanding post with a bracing climate, riding, skiing, trout-fishing and a lively cosmopolitan social life. Our interest was that Afghanistan remain neutral between Britain and Russia, with a slight leaning in the right direction. As this was more or less what the Afghans wanted, relations with the Amir's Government were generally easy. Only once a week was there a rush of work, coding and de-coding, to catch the weekly mail-boat from Bombay.

But B.J. Gould, appointed Counsellor in 1926, struck a more difficult time. It started with a fire in the Legation. The dry timber blazed furiously and there was little water to quench it. They saved as much of the Chancery records as was compatible with saving the horses. The Secretary, George Kirkbride, with a spirit only to be expected of a former officer of the Poona Horse, battered his way into the cellar and rescued the best of the wine. By breaking down a little side-door, they were able to escape into the street and were taken in by the Italian Minister.

And where, during these dramatic events, was His Britannic Majesty's Minister Plenipotentiary, Sir Francis Humphrys? Actually, he was in the Italian Legation, paying a social call on the Minister's beautiful wife, whom he rather fancied. A chuprassi was sent with a note apprising him of the emergency but, not liking to interrupt the burra sahib's dalliance, squatted with it outside the front door until the burra sahib emerged. By that time there was little left of the Minister's house, his office and the halls where he gloried and drank deep.

The new Legation was on a 25-acre site three miles outside Kabul. The Counsellor's most pressing task was to plan the new gardens; and, indeed, do most of the manual work himself, looking rather like a bespectacled coolie as he toiled away with mattock and shovel. Loraine Gould had a more demanding assignment, advising the court dress-maker, a French lady, on the appropriate garb for the Amir Amanullah, his Queen Souraya, court officials and ladies to wear on their forthcoming European tour. It was the sort of problem on which one would expect a French couturière to consult, if anyone, a compatriot, but the Little Lady took it in her stride. (She was, incidentally, not without official influence: Kirkbride was instructed to bring all important files to the Counsellor in bed, so that she could peruse them.)

The results of her fashion-guidance were disastrous. Afghans were appalled by films showing the Queen and her ladies unveiled; and members of the Majlis, the Afghan Parliament, were outraged at having to wear western morning clothes – striped trousers, frock-coats and cravats – for the opening session; at which, furthermore, they were harangued by the Amir for three days on their need to pull themselves together and emulate the unbelieving West. Amanullah, hailed only a few years earlier as the Sword of Islam, was denounced in the mosques as an infidel.

In November, 1926, most of the Kabul garrison marched away to deal with a rebellion near the Khyber Pass. Taking advantage of its absence, a small-time bandit named Bacha Saqao ('The Water-Seller's Brat') led his ragged army against the capital. They stopped first at the British Legation, where the Minister met them at the gate and advised them to move on, which they did. There was skirmishing between the rump of the Kabul garrison and Bacha Saqao's rabble, with the British Legation in no-man's-land. Afghan artillery joined in, not with conspicuous accuracy, and a few shells exploded in the Legation compound: the Gould's cook was loud in his complaints at finding a corpse in his kitchen. The diplomats kept out of the line of fire, encyphered long situation reports and de-cyphered demands from London and New Delhi for reports on the situation.

The Amir had two Junkers transport planes, and there were rumours that he contemplated flying off in them to Kandahar. Gould arranged with the German pilots that, when they were airborne, they would fire a green Very Light if the Amir were aboard, and a red one for the Queen. Gould stood at a Legation window to watch the take-off. First plane – red light – so the Queen had flitted. Second plane – at that moment a bullet hit the teak window-frame, showering Gould's face and scalp with sharp splinters. But for his glasses, he would have been blinded. On the same day the Superintendent of the Chancery got a bullet through his thigh.

A *coup d'état* in Kabul spells danger for foreigners. In 1841 and 1879 it had resulted in massacres. This time the telegraph line to India was cut; and the Afghan wireless failed just as Humphrys was asking New Delhi to evacuate the Legation women and children by air. But an R.A.F. plane flew over and dropped a wireless set which functioned well. At the same time Bacha Saqao withdrew from the capital and there was a lull in the fighting.

Advantage was taken of this lull. Snow had fallen. Through it, long before dawn on December 23rd, a party of women and children, led by Humphrys, stole out of the Legation and headed for the airfield. They kept silent, for bandits might be prowling around.

As it grew light a Wapiti, a troop-carrying Victoria and three

D.H.9A.s from Peshawur landed on the airfield, took them aboard and flew away.

It seemed a long time before we heard that our twenty-three women and children had reached Peshawur safely. In case any of our telegraphic reports had failed to reach Delhi, Loraine took with her, intimately concealed, many pages of thin paper copies.

On January 10th the Water Seller's Brat again advanced, and four days later Amanullah lost his nerve and abdicated. Bacha Saqao entered Kabul and proclaimed himself Amir.

As he would be unlikely to remain Amir for long, Humphrys and Shaikh Mahbub Ali, the Oriental Secretary, performed prodigies of diplomacy in getting all the foreign Legations and the new Amir to agree that the Afghans should be left to settle their differences without foreign interference; and that every foreigner who wished to leave would be flown out, and the Legations closed. The Government of India organised a fleet of troop-carriers to evacuate 300 British and Foreign nationals to Peshawur in February, while the Russians arranged to take out their people and the Turks to Tashkent.

The staff of the British Legation were the last to leave. It was snowing, and heavier snow was expected. Gould collected on the airfield several hundred men with shovels to clear a runway 700 yards long. They were getting on nicely when an Afghan officer arrived and asked what they were doing to his airfield. However, he was not out to obstruct; indeed, he brought 300 of his own men to help. They could not possibly clear a runway wide enough for a Victoria troop-carrier's wing-span, but they cleared one to take the wheels and trampled down the snow on each side. The French and Italians were flown out safely. Then it was the turn of the British, led by His Britannic Majesty's Minister with the flag which had flown over the Legation wrapped round his waist. They were seen off by a diminutive Pathan clerk who volunteered to stay behind as caretaker.

A few months later Bacha Saqao was defeated and put to death by Afghanistan's best general, Nadir Shah. He proclaimed himself Amir, and a very good one he became.

He was still Amir when Paddy Keen arrived as Under Secretary in Kabul in 1938, his first Political posting. He arrived longing to exercise his Pushtu in interviews with officials of the Afghan Ministry of Foreign Affairs. But Pushtu, although the official language of Afghanistan, was regarded as rather common by Top People, who spoke Persian (with an accent that Persians deplored) and perhaps a little French. Keen was able to ski every day from December 7th to March 17th. When the ground was not snow-covered or frost-bound, there were mounted paperchases for the more horsey members of the diplomatic community, and trout-fishing in season.

On short leaves he went camping and exploring all over the country: there seemed to be neither danger from bandits nor restrictions in the name of security. At Bamian, the junction of the old Silk Road from China to Constantinople and a side road from India, there were gigantic cliff-statues of Buddha, carved from the living rock, so massive as to resist even Timur Lang's iconoclasts. Beyond these were enchanting lakes, high up in the mountains, and further still cotton-mills at Phul-i-Kumri, largely staffed (for whatever motive) by Germans. Further north in Turcoman country, Keen met at a tea-house a group of Pathans from a colony which had been established there to stiffen the resistance to Russian penetration.

The most far-flung of Indian Politicals was the Consul General in Kashgar, capital of Sinkiang (Chinese Turkestan). Officially his job was to look after Indian traders in Kashgar and the string of oases along the southern edge of the Gobi Desert. In the nineteenth century there had been a fair amount of traffic between Sinkiang and India, but Chinese officials discouraged it, and trade goods moved more easily east to China or west to Russia than south over three terrific mountain ranges to India. So by 1920 this trade had dwindled to practically nothing, but the traders stayed on, hoping for better times. So the Consul General's official *raison d'être* remained, but his real job was to find out what the Russians were doing, and if possible stop them doing it.

Lieutenant Colonel Percy Etherton was a skilful player of the Great Game, fanatically anti-Bolshevik, convinced that they were bent on establishing their rule over Sinkiang and from that base sending agents and propaganda into India. In all of which he was absolutely right. He conducted a one-man campaign against them, protected only by his diplomatic status and with no military resources but a platoon of Gilgit Scouts to guard the Consulate. He was eight weeks' trek from Srinagar, over the Pamirs, the Hindu Kush and the Great Himalayan Range; the Russians were less than a week's ride, by an easy road, from the railhead at Andijan, and had large military forces at hand.

But in the Indian traders, who saw themselves ruined if ever the Russians prevailed, he had the rudiments of an intelligence network. In each oasis their doyen was a junior official, with low-grade consular status, known as the Aksakal. These were mainly Afghans, but loyal to their British employers, and kept ears and eyes open. Etherton sent out his agents to collect information about Russian forces on the frontier, their strength and efficiency and loyalty to the Bolshevik regime. He intercepted propaganda material being sent down to India. He kept a watch on Soviet agents in the country and badgered the Chinese authorities into expelling them, and stopping more coming in. The measure of his success is that most of the agents sent by the Russians into India were caught.

In the long run, though, the Russians could exert more pressure than the British. A Soviet Consul General was installed at Kashgar, with more money and a far larger staff than his British rival. Gradually every Chinese official, civilian and military, seemed to acquire in the background a Russian 'adviser'. Lorries began to appear on the dusty roads, all Russian. The province was torn by a chaotic, three-sided civil war, all sides apparently enjoying Soviet support. The British Consul General and his Indian trader protégés became lackeys of imperialism, a focus for discontent. Surprisingly the British Consulate was not closed down, and its mail – carried by horsemen to Tashkurgan in the Pamirs, where they met and exchanged bags with riders coming up from Gilgit – was not obstructed. But when Indians were imprisoned, flogged, and had all their property confiscated, there was precious little the British Consul General could do to help them. It was equally useless to protest to the Chinese who were not masters in their own house, and to the Russians who would say it was none of their business.

All this made Kashgar a frustrating post for Etherton's successors. Apart from intelligence-gathering, there was little to do – except to ride in the flat, dull environs of Kashgar, play polo with the Gilgit Scouts escort, read in the well-stocked library. To someone such as the ebullient Packman, Kashgar was pretty dull: the nearer one got to it, the less romantic Tartary seemed to be. But it was far from dull for Thompson-Glover whose wife, watching the civil war from the Consulate balcony, got a bullet through her shoulder. The difficulties of getting her to Srinagar were such that the Russians did the decent thing and took her by car to Andijan, thence across Asia and Europe by rail. It was five years before they made another friendly gesture. After Hitler invaded Russia, the Soviet Consul General invited his British colleague to join him in a duck-shoot.

B.J. Gould's career in the Political was extraordinarily varied. From Kabul he went to the Kurram, to Waziristan and to Baluchistan, where his wife died of typhoid and he himself was buried under the ruins of his house in the Quetta earthquake. From there he went to be Political Agent, Sikkim (fifteen-gun, the only Buddhist state in India). In that capacity he was chosen to represent the British and Indian Governments at the installation in Lhasa of the Fourteenth Dalai Lama, the first European ever to witness such a ceremony.

According to the Buddhist faith, death is followed by re-birth, either up or down the scale of creation according to one's merit. Thus a virtuous shepherd might be re-born as a monk, a robber as a snake. One's object in life should be to merit re-birth on higher and higher planes until at length one attains 'Nirvana' or the blissful state of nothingness. A person who, having earned Nirvana, consents to be re-born for the sake of his fellow-creatures is called a Bodhisattva. The Dalai Lama is a Bodhisattva in whom is incarnate the God of Mercy.

The Thirteenth Dalai Lama had governed Tibet since 1893, and died in 1933. There followed a long search for the new Dalai Lama, the child in whom he was reincarnated. There were various signs by which he could be identified, besides a physical and mental resemblance to his previous incarnation, and a preference for associates of the late Dalai Lama.

In the autumn of 1939 the child, four years old, was discovered and was brought to Lhasa. All the signs were there: this, without doubt, was he.

The British Mission at his installation consisted of Gould himself, Dr Staunton of the Indian Medical Service, and Rai Sahib Sonam, Gould's Sikkimese Personal Assistant. They arrived in Lhasa on February 9th, 1940, after a three-week ride from Sikkim. On arrival they presented silk scarves to the Regent, the Prime Minister, and the vacant throne of the Dalai Lama, and drank ceremonial tea. They then proceeded to the Norbhu Lingka, the 'Jewelled Garden' monastery, where the child was staying until his installation at the great Potala monastery.

On entering the frescoed Hall of Audience Gould saw:

> a solid, solemn but very wide-awake boy, red-cheeked and closely shaven, wrapped warm in the maroon-red robes of a monk, seated high on his simple throne, cross-legged in the attitude of a Buddha . . . I noticed the steadiness of his gaze, the beauty of his hands, and the devotion and love of the abbots who attended him. All seemed to be aware that they were in the presence of a Presence.

A column of people approached the throne, each one being given the appropriate blessing, with one hand, or two, or a touch on the forehead. Then Gould was motioned forward. 'I presented a white scarf. A scarf which had been blessed by the Dalai Lama was placed round my neck, and two small, cool, firm hands were laid steadily on my head.'

Twice tea and once rice was served, as a form of mutual hospitality which was also a sacrament. At the end of the audience Gould presented his gifts to the small boy – a gold clock with a nightingale which popped out and sang, a pedal motor-car and a tricycle.

The Dalai Lama was lifted down from his throne and walked out hand-in-hand with two abbots. In came his 8-year-old brother, eager to see how the presents worked. If he did not find out, he said, His Holiness would certainly beat him. Soon he was driving round the audience hall in the pedal-car.

This was a day before the installation, the essence of which was the Dalai Lama taking possession of the Potala, the seat of authority in Tibet. A tumultuous procession assembled at the Norbhu Lingka to escort him thither. There were ladies of the leading families in headdresses embroidered with seed-pearls, coral and turquoises, wearing eight-inch ear-ornaments of turquoises and gold, gem-studded charm-boxes, silk robes of every colour. There were troops of tumblers and dancers with masks and eagle-feather headdresses; sheepskin-clad shepherds; monks of every age from four to eighty, wearing maroon-coloured robes and turning prayer-wheels. There were the Dalai Lama's servants, grooms, cooks, attendants, carrying banners to ward off evil spirits; High Lamas, the State Oracle, the Chief Secretaries. Then, through clouds of incense, shuffled along the men carrying the Dalai Lama's gold palanquin with him invisible behind gold curtains. Next came the Regent, in gold robes, under a gold umbrella; the Dalai Lama's father, mother and brothers, and abbots from outer monasteries. Finally came a gigantic monk doorkeeper of the Potala who, with a stentorian voice, ordered back the crowds.

Long before dawn Cabinet Ministers, civil and ecclesiastical dignitaries and the British Mission had assembled in the great, square audience hall of the Potala for ceremonial tea-drinking. A burly lictor bellowed for silence. This was broken by a blare of trumpets, the main door was opened and there entered 'at a brisk pace a small figure in golden robes and pointed yellow hat with long flaps over the ears', his hands held by two abbots who helped him on to the throne. For the next five hours civil and church officials prostrated themselves, offered their scarves and were blessed, each according to his rank. Then there was a rush to tables piled high with sweetmeats, pastries, whole roast yaks, oxen and sheep. The Dalai Lama was lifted down from his throne and departed.

The next day was given over to rejoicings at what was, in Tibetan eyes, not the installation of a new ruler, but the return after a six-year absence of an old and much-loved friend. More formal gifts were presented – from the British Mission not toys for a child, but a brick of gold, ten sacks of silver, three rifles, six rolls of broadcloth, a gold watch and chain, field-glasses, an English saddle, a picnic-case, three stoves, a musical-box, a garden hammock, a pair of budgerigars. Other gifts included two horses from the Maharajah of Sikkim, bags of gold-dust, a six-foot elephant-tusk, a rhino-horn, holy books, golden silk clothes, slipper-shaped silver ingots.

Similar ceremonies were performed for eight days in succession. Gould was amazed that a 4-year-old boy should appear neither tired, bored nor fretful. The British Mission's gifts were a great success, especially the budgerigars, which the Dalai Lama would hardly let out of his sight. But when they seemed to pine in the Potala, at great self-sacrifice he put them in the care of the British Mission's wireless operator, a budgie expert. 'Not all children are so thoughtful. Not all are so greatly loving and greatly loved.'

19

In Foreign Parts, 1939–45

In September, 1939, the younger Politicals applied to join, or rejoin, the Army. Except for those still on probation, none were allowed to do so. They accepted their inglorious fate with varying degrees of resentment, not markedly consoled by pep-circulars from the Viceroy assuring them that they could best help the war-effort by carrying on business as usual. Even those on probation who were sent back to their regiments did not stay there for long. The Indian Political Service in wartime was subject to the conflicting pressures of Parkinson's Law and the cessation of recruitment from the Army; so it held fast to its own, or ensured that they went to semi-military, semi-Political jobs.

Thus Hugh Rance returned to the 2nd/1st Gurkhas, but was soon shunted off to the Nepalese Contingent. Walter Magor returned to the Poona Horse, but then went to the Staff College and the staff of the Adviser to the Indian state forces. Paddy Keen was pulled out of his battalion of Frontier Force Rifles to join the Intelligence Bureau at Quetta, which sent him to Persia* and the Western Desert before he was recalled to the Political. Johnny Raw returned to the 3rd/11th (Rattray's) Sikhs at Chaman, but not for long: he was winkled out of it to prepare a civil defence scheme for Quetta.

Persia was crawling with busy Germans, and until Hitler turned on his friend Stalin in June 1941, it seemed likely that Germany and Russia would make a joint attack on India. Even after that possibility was removed, to the British Government the greatest danger seemed to be a German drive through the Caucasus to the Persian and Iraq oilfields, without which Britain would have to surrender. So large British forces were retained in Persia to guard against this, and many Politicals stayed there too.

Among the troops in Persia was the Afridi Battalion, raised in 1941. The idea was a good one: to make use of the special skills of the Afridis in mountain warfare if the Germans should reach the Caucasus. There were plenty who pointed out the risk of having a whole battalion

*Persia was properly now Iran; but it continued to be called Persia lest, as Iran, it be confused with Iraq.

composed of a tribe which, although of great fighting quality, was devious, volatile and much given to internal feuds. But it was a calculated risk. The Afridi Battalion was very much a Politicals' unit: it was the brainchild of Sir George Cunningham, Governor of the North-West Frontier Province, its Pathan officers, N.C.O.s and nucleus of trained men all volunteers from the Frontier Corps, the Politicals' private army. Among its officers were Roger Bacon, Political Agent, Khyber, and Robin Hodson, his Assistant Political Agent.

Another corps which would have had a modest part to play if the Germans had broken through was the Mekran Levies, the special care of the Assistant Political Agent, Mekran, who in October, 1939, was T.L. Brownsdon. The corps consisted of 500 rank-and-file, half Baluchi, half Brahui, with 250 well-bred trotting camels. About half the corps was at headquarters, Panjgur, the remainder distributed in Beau Geste forts along the 250-mile border with Persia, their role being to discourage raiding in either direction. The camels were beautifully groomed, fed partly on lucerne grown under karez-irrigation at Panjgur, and had hardly any of the unpleasant sour smell usually associated with them. On patrol they could easily do thirty miles a day, at eight miles an hour.

Brownsdon visited all the outposts, generally stopping a night or two and often patrolling with the levies. He learned Baluchi, a rewarding language for the connoisseur, of Persian origin. He was very cut off from the world. Twice a month a camel orderly carried the outgoing mail to Pasni, a small port on the Gulf, and returned with the in-coming mail. The Europe-to-India telegraph line, erected in the nineteenth century, was long out of use, but its posts still straggled and leaned drunkenly across the desert, and someone had hung a wire along them so that messages in morse could, with long delays, be sent to Quetta. Towards the end of Brownsdon's time he was provided with a wireless set, with which he could communicate with Quetta twice a day: it transformed life in Panjgur. With the outbreak of war, R.A.F. planes came more frequently, bringing the luxuries of fresh bread and fish.

Two unusual incidents occurred in his time there.

> One of our levies, who suspected the Punjabi schoolmaster of having an affair with his wife, cut off the schoolmaster's ears, nose and penis. He then cut off his wife's ears and nose.
>
> I also discovered in an outlying fort two old screw-guns, designed to be taken to bits and carried by camels. They were muzzle-loaders, fired by pulling a lanyard. The men regularly went through the drill of

> loading etc., but no one could remember them ever having been fired, though there was some ammunition. This was too much for me, an ex-Gunner, so we had a test-firing . . . The gun-crew were rather apprehensive, but we doubled the length of the lanyard so that they could get behind a rock. The order to fire was given, the lanyard was pulled, and there followed a mighty boom as the gun recoiled about six feet and the shell went zooming off to explode a mile away. It was a great success, and we felt we could take on any U-boat which came prowling round Pasni.

Brownsdon, despite the isolation, the heat and the savage sandstorms, rather enjoyed his time in Mekran. So did Raw, posted there after preparing the civil defence scheme for Quetta.

> It was a howling desert, in which the only real greenery was along two widely-separated east-west water-courses. These supported very large numbers of date-palms of many different varieties. The Mekrani lived solely for his dates (except when sex intruded) and conversation with him was almost wholly restricted to this unexciting subject.

When the Germans reached Stalingrad, Raw took the levies into Persia for a long tour, showing the flag and putting it to the chiefs that if the Germans came through, the tribes should do their utmost to harass them. The route to India along the coast (which Alexander had followed) seemed a probable invasion route. The chiefs promised to do their bit, provided the British armed them.

> The 500-mile camel ride was a great success, and achieved a remarkable degree of friendship with the tribes. We all, including the camels, got back in good fettle. I myself, fit as I was, lost nearly a stone with the prolonged jogging.

For part of this excursion Raw was joined by Walter Magor whose specific job was to make 'tank-maps' (i.e. maps showing the practicability of the ground for tanks) of the approaches to India from the west. They were lent by a local Nawab a Brahui slave as mess cook, and guided over mountain tracks by an outlaw whose life-style required him to reside very close to the border. Magor, as a cavalryman, was less than enchanted with camel-riding, and found the animal-management fairly basic: 'If one went lame on the near fore, the remedy was a bang with a rock on the off hind, and he would then go sound.'

> Before we crossed the border, we sent a man ahead with a formal letter written in Persian to the Governor of Persian Baluchistan. Two

days later the man returned with a message from the Governor regretting that he did not understand classical Persian, and suggesting that we try French. We completed maps of the area showing such motorable tracks as existed, tankable country, and suitable areas for ambushes and guerrilla activity.

Michael Hadow was in the I.C.S. To get a little closer to the war, he transferred to the Political at the end of 1941. His first job was as Liaison Officer to the Chinese Mission, under Chiang Kai Chek and Madame Chiang, in New Delhi. Madame Chiang had a lot of charm and was tough as old boots. The Generalissimo was hopelessly unpunctual for which of course Hadow was held responsible. Then the British Ambassador to Russia arrived in New Delhi on his way to Moscow, and asked for Hadow as his Private Secretary. 'I jumped at the chance, and within three days was on my way.'

All the foreign diplomats had been banished by Stalin, 'for their safety', to Kuibishev. Hadow visited Moscow only to present his credentials, shaking hands with Stalin who reeked of cheap scent. In Kuibishev there was no work for him to do, and no contact with Russians if they could avoid it. Hadow made inventories of furniture, learned to encypher and de-cypher at speed; and watched a great deal of ballet.

I at least learned Russian and how to get on with Soviet officialdom. Of course we all realised that Stalin was a monster with imperial ambitions. His behaviour towards his allies was appalling. Yet he was a necessary evil if we were to win the war. We must therefore co-operate while standing up for ourselves and not letting the Russians get away with anything.

In the autumn of 1942 Hadow was posted to Meshed, in the Russian-occupied zone of Persia.

My Consul General was Claremont Skrine, also of the Indian Political. Skrine, as indeed the British public, was brainwashed by the 'Good old Uncle Joe' syndrome, and 'lean over backwards to please our gallant allies'. Hot from the Soviet Union I shocked Skrine and his wife by my views. I think they thought me an agent of Goebbels. They studiously courted the Russian Consul General, and could not understand the Russian reluctance to mix socially. I on the other hand spoke Russian and was accepted by them as a man who had seen Russia at war and had even shaken hands with Stalin. I therefore often got my own way with travel permits, the needs of our people on the transport route, the evacuation of the Poles from Siberia etc. If I didn't get my way, I played the Soviet Consul General off against the Officer Commanding the Russian troops. If all else failed I complained like hell until they yielded. I cultivated close social contacts with the Consulate and the military, and particularly with the N.K.V.D. which my Russian experience had taught me to recognise.

Meshed lay on the road we built and maintained from Quetta to Soviet Turkestan. Up this we ran a fleet of lorries carrying supplies to Russia. Being in the Russian zone, although allies we were constantly harassed; had to get passes for every journey we made (on our own road!); and were followed and watched everywhere we went.

Skrine was a passionate cine-photographer. The Russians saw him filming some shaggy horses being led to water by their slovenly Uzbek troopers. He was promptly arrested and taken to their H.Q. Two hours later he was allowed to phone our Consulate. I went straight round and saw their Brigade Major, a smug little bastard whom I knew fairly well. 'We have a man whom we caught filming military subjects. He claims to be the Consul General Skrine.'

I was taken to a cell in which sat Skrine, twittering with excitement.

I told the Russian that he knew perfectly well the man was Skrine, as he had been to official functions at the Consulate. I would, however, identify him formally. I said that I realised that to his mind filming third-line Asiatic troops amounted to espionage, but he must try to cultivate a sense of proportion, and to behave like a civilised human being. I would make a most serious complaint to my Government. He was certainly shaken, and I left with Skrine and his camera, but they had exposed the film.

The next drama was the arrival at Hadow's house, disguised as Armenian lorry-drivers, of five American airmen who had taken part in the Doolittle raid on Tokyo and then landed in Siberia and been interned. They had escaped from internment; but the Russians, if they got their hands on them again, would certainly lock them up, on the grounds that they had violated Soviet neutrality towards Japan. Hadow sought instructions from Teheran and was told to get them out to India.

By this time I knew the Russian check-points on the road, usually manned by illiterate Uzbeks, and their general inefficiency. I took the Americans in a jeep, unloaded them with a local guide out of sight of each check-point, and picked them up on the road later, at some agreed spot to which they had walked through the hills. After the last check-point I handed the vehicle over to them to drive to the British

28 R.H.D. Lowis (*left*) and T.A.F. Noble (*right*) with Tochi Scouts and Khassadar Subadar Darim Khan, I.O.M., Croix de Guerre, in Waziristan
29 E.N.S.A. party – the only European women ever allowed to Miranshah in 1943. Noble's orderly seems to be trying to sell them daggers.

30 Malik Mehr Dil, Mahsud, gives Pandit Nehru (*left*) a piece of his mind. The Political Agent, R.V.E. Hodson, tries to cool matters.

31 A Mahsud Jirga confronts Pandit Nehru

> zone. I then hitchhiked back to the main Russian check-point where I found my nasty little Brigade Major in charge. I told him that my jeep had broken down and I must get back to Meshed for a mechanic. He was effusively friendly and entertained me to tea and vodka, till a Persian bus came along. It was crowded to the roof, so he threw off two Persians to give me a seat.

Hadow also kept an eye on the Polish evacuation centre in Meshed, set up to bring out of Siberia the surviving Poles whom the Russians had imprisoned there in 1939. Able-bodied men and women were forwarded on to join the Polish Army in the Middle East, children and mothers to Bombay. This gave Hadow an unexpected bonus: 'Shortly before leaving Meshed, I married a Polish lady.'

Tom Rogers was posted as Vice-Consul in Bushire. Within a month of his arrival, British forces from Iraq entered Persia to compel the Persian Government to expel German agents, give depth to the defence of the oilfields and open up a supply route to Russia. It was a neat, almost bloodless, unscrupulous and necessary bit of bullying.

> Charles Stewart and I were the only senior staff in Bushire on the night the British troops crossed the border. The powerful Qashqai tribe north and east of Bushire were harbouring German agents, so we decided to take no chances, and burnt the cyphers.
>
> We felt better for it until Delhi, with the benefit of hindsight, informed us rather tartly that replacements would be slow in coming.

In peacetime the problem of the Vice-Consul in Bushire was to fill in his working hours. In wartime all sorts of jobs were laid on Rogers's devoted shoulders. He liaised with technical experts assembling trucks for Russia. He took over propaganda – or, rather, when it is on our side, 'information' – sending out optimistic news bulletins in Persian, setting up a reading room, and showing war-films in the hinterland from a van 'which also became a mobile surgery run by the Residency Medical Officer with me as barker and interpreter'.

The allied occupation of Persia had disrupted its internal economy and reduced its exports as there were no ships to carry them. Some areas stagnated, others prospered with war-demands for labour and contracts. Food, therefore, had to be imported for the population, at considerable cost in allied shipping and lives. Persian officials being what they were, the distribution could not be left to them, but had to be supervised by the Consular staff.

Rogers became involved in an enquiry into the death of the Russian

Vice-Consul who was in Bushire to help in setting up the supply-route to Russia but spent more time with the Swiss wife of a Persian official. Was it the suicide (to which Russians are notoriously prone) of a remorseful philanderer, or murder by his betrayed spouse? The local court plumped for suicide.

He set up a coast-watching service to look out for German and Japanese submarines; and liaised with the Middle East Anti-Locust Unit. 'Poisoned bait for the hoppers was their weapon, but occasionally a sack of untreated specimens was brought to my cook for turning into locust-curry.'

He was sent to re-open the Consulate at the port of Bandar Abbas, which had been closed since 1919. There his good relations with the local Persian authorities were impaired:

> when two wild (I believe Turkish) members of a small detachment of irregulars commanded by Tom Mitford got drunk one night. Beating on the door of the Governor's house, they demanded to see his attractive wife ... Tom understood, if unhappily, that the allied interest demanded his commando's immediate re-deployment.

But not before the Turks showed their mettle when a large fish, a tunny at least six feet long, leaped aboard Rogers's launch at night, crash-landing on him and the Turks as they slept on deck, and nearly capsized the vessel.

> We tackled the fish rugby-style at every point of its slippery anatomy. After a tough struggle which we were never sure of winning, the sea-invader was clubbed into submission.

(Well might Hadow observe that, in the Political, consular duties were peculiar. 'One meddled in local politics, ordered the Governor about, told the military what to do, etc. Yet the local Persians did not seem to resent it, whatever their politicians in Teheran may have felt, and relations were cordial.')

Rogers enjoyed the Gulf's wartime variety: the Royal Navy organising convoys and American experts displaying efficiency, sureness of touch, know-how in despatching cargoes to Russia; Peter Fleming asking genially if he was 'the local flogger of wogs'; Bertram Thomas of 'Arabia Felix' haranguing the bedouin about our war; a Red Russian pilot flying White Russian and British locust-hunters. In mitigation of Bandar Abbas's fiendish climate there was a tiny grove in the mountains with a pool filled by sulphur springs. It was seldom visited except by Rogers, locust-hunters and an occasional truckload of ladies of the town whose rule seemed to be 'Pool-day is off-day'.

Britons at war like forming private armies. Rogers at Bandar Abbas formed and commanded a private navy, of which the *raison d'être* was the presence in the Gulf of German and Japanese submarines. (One was sunk there by the R.A.F.) His operations originated with a report that Jask lighthouse had stopped working and that ill-wishers were signalling with red and green Very Lights to enemy submarines. So the Vice-Consul was rowed ashore with muffled oars. Carrying maps and air-photos in a waterproof package, he scrambled up the rocks and prowled round Jask village in the dark, looking at the lighthouse and watching out for suspicious persons. Alas, he found none. What he did find was two R.A.F. men reconnoitring for a landing-strip. Despite their denials, it seemed probable that they had fired off a Very Light or two in a moment of boredom-relieving exuberance. But obviously enemy agents could signal convoy movements, so vigilance and a sea-going vessel were needed.

When he found hired launches unreliable, the Royal Indian Navy provided him with a Cutch-built dhow with sails and an auxiliary engine. With this he patrolled the area – not, of course, to attack submarines, but to report their presence and seek news of them from local fishermen. A submarine would be unlikely to attack an innocent dhow, for it was seeking bigger quarry. Rogers and his crew of five Arabs and Persians lived on rice, dried shrimps, fish and Persian bread. They never saw a submarine, but checked siting reports. Once they stopped a dhow with two brothers, notorious pirates and slavers, aboard.

> There were guns, slaves and smuggled goods below deck. As if by some man-o'-war of an earlier age, the prize was escorted into Bandar Abbas where a grateful Governor undertook to bring the culprits to justice. I believe it had been a good many years since a British ship seized a vessel engaged in piracy and the slave-trade.

Rogers kept watch, by launch and dhow, on the coast, which extended for 550 miles to the border with British Baluchistan: for movement by sea was far easier than by the execrable roads which zigzagged from the coast far inland and back. All in all, Rogers had three busy and thoroughly enjoyable years in a part of Asia which others found a hell-hole: 'I was strangely attracted by that vast wilderness of hot salt sea and endless rocky shore.'

Paddy Keen was not. Sent to the Gulf after being extracted from the Intelligence Bureau, he found the heat, the humidity and the prickly-heat unbearable. He too used a dhow to supervise coast-watchers and seek submarines. But the frequency of mechanical failure whenever he wished to proceed in an easterly direction convinced him that his Persian crew had no thirst for glory.

Creagh-Coen, in his book *The Indian Political Service*, remarked that 'during World War II nine Political officers and two sloops of the Royal Indian Navy kept the Gulf quiet.'

The Arab specialists in the Indian Political were in the habit of being right, while the British Foreign Office was wrong. Before and during the First World War the Indian Politicals – Cox, Wilson, St John Philby, Dickson, Shakespear – all advised that the Arab to back was Abdul Aziz Ibn Saud, Emir of Nejd and leader of the aggressive, puritanical Wahabi sect, the Ironsides of Arabia. Shakespear, one of the greatest of travellers though he never wore Arab dress and his camels always carried a few cases of Hock and Moselle, was killed fighting for Ibn Saud against his tribal enemies, the Ruwalla. St John Philby ended his career in Ibn Saud's service, and Dickson in the service of Ibn Saud's kinsman, the Shaikh of Kuwait. But the Foreign Office followed instead the advice of the Lawrence lobby and put its money – a great deal of it – on Ibn Saud's rival, Hussein, Sharif of Mecca.

From this original error of backing a loser many misfortunes were to flow. Ibn Saud, the rising star in the Arabian firmament, for many years viewed Britain with suspicion, sometimes with hostility. To gratify the Sharif of Mecca, who was interested (as Ibn Saud was not) in Palestine, conflicting promises were made to the Jews and the Arabs, with consequences which are with us to this day. The Emir Faisal, eldest son of the Sharif, was promised the throne of Syria; a promise which could not be kept because the French, who had other ideas, flung him out. As a consolation prize, he was foisted on the Iraqis, who did not in the least want him. Thus Britain was at odds both with the most able, vigorous and formidable of the Bedouin, Ibn Saud, and with the radical Arab intelligentsia based in Bagdad. Worst of all, it was the Americans, not the British, who developed the Saudi Arabian oilfields, and the Arabian-American Oil Company became the most powerful force in the Arabian Peninsular. Mighty consequences of one error!

Tom Hickinbotham was a Political who got on so well with Arabs that when he was Political Agent in Bahrein he used to be invited to tea *à deux* with the Shaikh Hamad's senior wife, Ayesha. The Shaikh had four wives, each with her separate establishment, and when he spent the night with one of them, the lucky lady used to fly the Bahreini flag over her house. But to signify a visit of 'Mr Tom Bottom', as she called him, Ayesha used to fly the Union Jack, much to the amusement of her husband's subjects.

In 1942 Hickinbotham was Political Agent in Kuwait, just before the little Shaikhdom floated off on a tidal wave of oil. He was invited by Ibn Saud, now King of Saudi Arabia, and unquestionably the top Arab, to visit him at his capital, Riyadh. It was the wish of the King that he wear Arab dress and grow a beard, so as to attract as little attention as possible. 'To be without a beard would cast the gravest reflections on a person's moral character.'

They set off in a station-wagon and Dodge truck, accompanied by a one-legged guide of great renown, and by their insurance-policy, a noted follower of the Shaikh of Kuwait and prominent member of the Rashaida tribe. Marauding tribesmen would hesitate to bring down on their heads the wrath of the Shaikh and the Rashaida.

They drove across an eternity of desert. A heat haze shimmered in the distance and mirages magnified the smallest object until even close by it was almost unrecognisable. They halted for the night, and drove on at two-thirty in the morning so as to cross the Dhahna Sands while the dew still had a binding effect on the surface.

> These sands are not continuous but are a series of ridges. The first was the most troublesome because this half-mile of fine reddish coloured sand rises abruptly to a considerable height. Determination was essential, and going full out in third gear I took the steep slope as fast as the car would go and pressed on over the top with the accelerator hard down, bumping and skidding to the extreme discomfort of my passengers. If I had eased up we would undoubtedly have stuck: it was essential to maintain momentum if we were to avoid hours, if not days, of exhausting work digging ourselves out.

The station-wagon got through. The lorry stuck, but as its crew had plenty of food and water, they left it to be rescued later.

At the last oasis before Riyadh Hickinbotham arrayed himself for his arrival at the capital, in white with a thin brown cloak edged with gold thread, and a white headcloth held in place with a black twisted woollen rope. Fifteen miles short of Riyadh they were met by a large American car containing the Chief of Police and Rushdi Mulhas, Chief Assistant to the Foreign Minister.

> We drove through hundreds of black goats' hair tents of tribesmen who had assembled to receive their annual gifts of grain and money

> . . . Not less than nine thousand tribesmen were present each day and in addition there were fifteen or twenty thousand indigent folk who benefited daily from the King's bounty.

No sooner had Hickinbotham been left alone in the palatial guest-house when a servant arrived and placed an empty saucer on each of the side-tables.

> I enquired what they were for, and was told, for the convenience of visitors. I noticed with surprise the obvious outlines of a cigarette-case in the pocket of the servant's garment as he stooped over the table. I had not realised how time had softened the harsh puritanism of the Wahabis . . . There was in fact as much smoking in Riyadh as in Kuwait, but it was indulged in discreetly inside the house.

His siesta was interrupted by Rushdi Mulhas, informing him that Ibn Saud would receive him in half an hour.

> I dressed in fine white cotton clothes, added black socks and evening shoes, and completed the picture with my best gold-embroidered cloak and white muslin headcloth tastefully embroidered with white forget-me-nots.

He drove to the Marabah Palace and entered, alone, the very long reception room.

> On the left was a row of richly upholstered sofas and armchairs in which were seated Arab gentlemen, some wearing the gold 'agal' on their heads which proclaimed their relationship with the King. Away in the far right-hand corner, seated in solitary state with a telephone on a table to one side, was His Majesty King Abdul Aziz bin Abdur Rahman Ibn Saud. The dignity of that figure, swathed in a black cloak with a red and white headcloth, was far greater than I had expected. I was impressed by the aura of power which surrounded him alone in his great chair removed from his relations and counsellors. The other people in that great room just did not matter.
>
> I greeted him with the usual complimentary phrases, uttered by both of us, as we shook hands. In obedience to a wave of the royal hand, I sat down next to him and we talked of the weather and how hot it was, of the Shaikh of Kuwait and his health, the tribes, the water-melons of Jahra (a village near Kuwait) which were famous.
>
> Coffee was served . . . A few minutes later His Majesty's conversation flagged and, feeling that the time had come for me to retire, I asked permission to withdraw.

Next day Hickinbotham met the Crown Prince, the Amir Saud, and they discussed the relative merits of the Hyde Park Hotel and the Dorchester, the danger of electric fans giving one colds in the head; and the impossibility of pleasing everyone in the annual distribution of bounty and the hearing of petitions. (A problem not unfamiliar to Hickinbotham's colleagues in Waziristan.) He had another interview with Ibn Saud, this time alone. The King spoke on world affairs. This was at the blackest point in the war. The Germans were advancing on the Caucasus, the Japanese were at the gates of India, and Rommel was about to destroy the British armour and advance almost to Alexandria.

> I was struck by the bold line of his nose and jutting beard. I tried to keep my eyes on his, but now and again I let them fall and received a smart tap on the knee and was called to order by a peremptory 'Listen!' He touched on the Palestine question and said he had pointed out to the more extreme Arabs that direct action against the Jews would bring them into conflict with Britain to their eventual undoing. He declared that an Axis victory would mean the end of Arab freedom, and therefore he had warned the Arabs that whatever their feelings about Palestine they must do nothing to hinder Britain at this time, rather they must do all in their power to aid her. He turned to recent events in Iraq [where Rashid Ali's pro-Axis coup had been defeated] and deplored the fact that the Army had become involved in politics. It was, he said, the very worst thing that could happen to any army. He said that he had warned Rashid Ali but the warning had gone unheeded.
>
> He paused and gazed out of the window for a moment or two and then suddenly asked me if I knew how to deal with Arabs. On my murmuring a few words, he gave me his own views on this subject. They were, to use force and diplomacy. By the skilful use of these two elements, there was nothing that could not be achieved. Force was the real essential and to be preferred. Diplomacy was to be used only when adequate force was lacking.

After about three-quarters of an hour's discourse, he seemed tired, and Hickinbotham – who would willingly have listened for much longer to the words of a master – asked permission to withdraw, which was given with a charming smile. This from the man whom the Foreign Office had cold-shouldered in 1914-18.

Hickinbotham spent two days looking at impressive new irrigation schemes, the desert green with corn and lucerne and criss-crossed with canals. Then he drove back to Riyadh for a formal dinner with the King.

I had arrayed myself in my last set of clean white clothes and a black cloak. As I moved to my place on Ibn Saud's right hand at one end of the cloth spread on the carpets, I saw mountains of rice, no less than three sheep roasted whole, and dozens of supplementary dishes. The officials sat on the same side of the cloth as myself and the princes on the opposite side, at some distance from the King. Never did his relatives sit close to him. Negro servants stood behind us and one in particular busied himself in attending to my needs. He would have made an admirable children's nurse, but having left the nursery some years ago, I found his ministrations something of a nuisance. Ibn Saud had kicked off his sandals at the edge of the carpet and sat bare-footed. The rest of us wore patent leather evening shoes which I had been informed was now the etiquette of the court. Ibn Saud and I were the only two who ate with our hands and made no use of the knives and forks provided. All the rest of the company picked delicately at the food; not so the King, who ate heartily . . . We rose, washed the grease from our fingers in bowls held by the servants and returned to the roof where coffee was served. Immediately after which rose-water and incense made the rounds and the party broke up with Ibn Saud's rising and bidding us good-night . . .

Next morning I busied myself with my packing and then embarked on the formidable task of remunerating the servants, many for just being servants and for nothing else. Before I had dealt with them to their satisfaction, an emissary from Ibn Saud arrived to distribute largesse and garments to my party as is customary. I myself was presented with a gold watch and a small gold dagger and cloaks and headcloths.

After a farewell interview with Ibn Saud, Hickinbotham set off on the long drive back to Kuwait. It had been a memorable visit. A pity there had not been more such visits twenty-seven years earlier.

Edward Lydall was posted from Miranshah to be Secretary to the Legation in Kabul. The contrast between Afghanistan and Waziristan could not have been more marked. No one sniped at him on the Afghan roads, and if anyone had done so the authorities would simply have cut off the right hand of the headman of the nearest village. In Miranshah they lived like monks; but Kabul was full of attractive women of many nationalities.

The Legation itself, outside Kabul, was enclosed by a high wall, and in the middle stood the imposing residence of the Minister, Sir Kerr

Fraser Tytler, who was under the delusion that his staff respectfully referred to it as 'The Big House'; actually they called it 'The Bin'. Within the wall were houses for the Counsellor, the Military Attaché and the Legation Surgeon, but not for the Secretary, who had hitherto boarded with the latter.

> A tradition had, however, started to establish itself whereby the Secretary became, almost ex officio, the *cavaliere servente* of the Surgeon's wife. It was with a view to breaking this tradition that I was allotted two rooms in the Legation building itself.

Not at all like Miranshah.

The Minister had been there too long – Secretary to the first Minister to Afghanistan, Counsellor to the second. Perhaps in consequence there was a faint air of dottiness about the Legation. Almost on arrival Lydall overheard a revealing conversation between two of his colleagues.

> 'It's really rather provoking,' remarked one inmate. 'My wife keeps on threatening to throw herself out of the window. Admittedly with three feet of snow on the ground, she wouldn't hurt herself, but it gets on one's nerves in the long run.'
>
> 'You don't know how lucky you are,' returned the second inmate. '*My* wife keeps throwing the teapot at me, and that *does* hurt.'

Kabul contained the Embassies of Persia, Turkey and Russia; and the Legations of Great Britain, France, Germany, Italy, Egypt and Japan. (At the outbreak of war social relations with the Germans were severed.) This galaxy of diplomatic talent produced dinners of paralysing tedium.

> One frequently had to choose a conversational partner from between the lady on one's right who spoke only Kurdish and the lady on one's left who spoke nothing but Japanese. On such occasions we would line up before the Legation Surgeon who would dole us out each a tablet of Benzedrine. We would then prance joyfully into dinner, quite prepared to converse with a deaf-and-dumb Hottentot. Timing, however, was an important factor. If he distributed the Benzedrine too soon, everything would suddenly go blank half-way through the pudding.

Lydall organised social entertainments, ran the Legation library and de-cyphered an occasional telegram. On national days he had to send to other Embassies and Legations visiting cards marked 'P.F.' (*Pour féliciter*)', to which his irritated opposite numbers would have to reply with cards marked 'P.R.' (*Pour remercier*). 'In this way, it was felt, international amity was encouraged.'

His warmest relations were with the Italians. Every so often he would have to write to them on the lines of:

> '*La Légation de Sa Majesté Britannique présente ses compliments à la Légation Royale d'Italie et a l'honneur de lui avertir que . . .*' Whereupon Quaroni and Anzilotti would get together, rubbing their hands and chuckling, and draft a reply to the effect that they entirely agreed with what I had written except for my use of *avertir* with the dative.

Lydall was also responsible for war-propaganda. His duties consisted of first putting into the wastepaper basket vast masses of material from the Ministry of Information, and then producing a daily news bulletin beginning with a picture and ending with a joke. These were sent out to all Embassies and Legations (except the German). During the phoney war this was not a particularly onerous duty, but after Dunkirk it became very tiresome to think up new excuses for every defeat, and new ways of making the point that the English always won the last battle. He continued to swap propaganda with the Italians, but the Legation messenger who visited the Italian Legation preserved the convenances by never actually setting foot on enemy territory. Not so the Italian Minister's [Russian] wife, who delighted in coming up to Lydall at parties and saying, '*Now* I am going to embarrass you.'

T.L. Brownsdon was at the Legation in the humbler role of Attaché, concerned mainly with cypher work, a terrible chore.

> The volume of work was enormous. Some of the less secret codes could be handled single-handed; but the most secret needed a team of three. Only gazetted officers were allowed to handle them, and it was quite a job getting a team together. The code-books were kept in a large safe in my office, which contained also a loaded revolver, a bottle of petrol and a box of matches.

The Minister's cousin was appointed assistant Attaché to lighten the load. She became very quick and expert at the work, but at first found it puzzling.

> 'Edward, here is a cypher telegram which comes out like this: "Unfounded students sigh on Siamese lagoons." Can that be right, do you think?'
>
> 'I suggest, Esmé, that you are using the wrong code-book.'

'So I am. But *what* a pity! It conjures up a so much more romantic picture than most of the telegrams we receive.'

Early in 1941 there suddenly arrived a party of diplomats from Bagdad to set up an Iraqi Legation. What could they be up to? The only Iraqi in Kabul, apart from the diplomats, was their chauffeur. Eventually it transpired that their object was to persuade the Afghans to declare the Jihad, the Holy War, against Britain, to coincide with Rashid Ali's coup in Iraq. But the Afghans were not yet quite certain who was going to win, and would not be persuaded.

Sir Kerr Fraser Tytler was a diplomat of the old school, who believed that the Afghans could best be induced to remain neutral by an occasional word murmured into the ear of an influential figure of the Afghan Establishment. All other wartime diplomatic activity, he considered, was full of sound and fury, signifying nothing. In 1941 he was succeeded by Sir Francis Wylie, one of the stars of the Indian Political Service, who favoured more positive action.

'Do you think, Edward,' he would say to his Secretary, 'that you could *possibly* find out whether the Germans have any money in the Afghan National Bank?' Simple. I asked the (Afghan) manager of the bank to lunch and he gave me a complete list of all the Germans who had accounts at his bank, together with details of the balance to the credit of each.

Wylie asked me what was going on in the German Legation. As luck would have it, I had met a German communist youth who attended all the meetings in the Legation and was delighted to tell me about them.

Such information could be quite important, as there were at least 200 Germans in Afghanistan – diplomats, businessmen, managers and artisans in the cotton-mills – most of whom were doing what they could for their country, notably by smuggling arms and money to the Faqir of Ipi, so that the British would be obliged to retain considerable forces in Waziristan. Afghan foreign policy was based on strict neutrality between Britain and Russia, playing one off against the other, and on not annoying the Germans who looked like winning the war. So long as Anglo-Russian relations were frigid, it was not difficult for the Afghans, faced with a British demand that these Germans be expelled, to hedge and procrastinate.

When Hitler invaded Russia, the entire staff of the British Legation was invited to luncheon at the Russian Embassy. After innumerable toasts in vodka and champagne, Lydall and his colleagues 'wove our way back to our offices and wrote indecypherable notes on our files.' At first the Afghans welcomed this new development: like many others, they expected the Russians soon to be annihilated. Then it suddenly dawned on them that they were faced with an entirely new situation, Britain and Russia (more or less) in accord. They were confronted with a joint démarche, demanding the expulsion of all Germans and Italians.

What should they do? Germany might still win. Again they procrastinated, an operation in which they were adept. But as a consequence of information given by Wylie to a sceptical Minister of War, an arms-smuggling convoy was ambushed, two Germans killed and ten mule-loads of rifles and ammunition captured.

> As a result of this, the Afghan Government did expel every German with the exception of the Minister and a skeleton staff. Through a neutral we received an urgent request that they be sent out via India, for if they were sent out via Russia, they would never get through alive. They left in a lorry convoy to Peshawur, thence in a sealed train to Karachi and a neutral ship to Europe.

Lydall had to issue them with visas for India, a curious action in the middle of a war.

The Japanese were determinedly social but had very weak heads. Lydall attended a garden party at their Legation.

> Soon they were all lying insensible in the grass while we sang excerpts from *The Mikado* over them, to the scandalised disapproval of the Germans looking over the wall of their next-door Legation. This was about the last we saw of the Japanese, for in December, 1941, there occurred Pearl Harbor.

Lydall was transferred to Calcutta to ease relations between Chinese purchasing missions, Calcutta businessmen and the Indian and Bengal Governments, which had hitherto been marred by a total lack of linguistic or any other understanding. Knowing not a word of any Chinese language, he was comforted by the thought that his replacement at Kabul spoke fluent Mandarin and Cantonese, but not a word of Persian or Pushtu.

In Calcutta Lydall cultivated friendly relations with our oriental allies in Chinese restaurants, provided them with lists of officials and others who might or might not be of use to them, and made up the diplomatic bags which were flown weekly to the British Consulate General at Kunming and Embassy at Chungking.

A rather broad definition of the word 'document' was applied to the contents of their bags. There would be boxes of cigars for the Australian Minister, laundry left behind by diplomats in transit, cosmetics for the staff of the Indian Agent General which they sold to the Chungking shops until I objected, a rubber dinghy in which the Free French were to go spying on a lake near Kunming, and the plaster cast of a wooden leg with which someone wished to curry favour with a one-legged Chinese admiral. Interest was added to the work by requests which I received from the various cloak-and-dagger men in Calcutta for mysterious packages to be sent by the bag. It was interesting to discover how many organisations were working away unbeknownst to one another.

After Fort Sandeman, K.P.S. Menon had served for three years as Diwan in Bharatpur, where he 'managed to keep on the right side of the Prince, the people and the Government of India, three elements whose interests did not always coincide'. He was then summoned to Delhi and, to his great surprise, offered the post of Agent General for India in China. The Foreign Secretary, Sir Olaf Caroe, warned him that Chungking was a beastly place, lacking most of the amenities, frequently bombed, with a vile climate; but the post was considered important. After consulting his wife, Menon said he would be glad to go provided she and their daughter could accompany him.

They flew there over 'the Hump', wild and stupendous mountains and jungles. Chungking had been bombed quite badly for two years, and few permanent buildings were still standing. It seemed to consist of little but bamboo and mud shacks.

The streets were insanitary and the smells overpowering, because of the careful accumulation of human faeces for manure. Zafrullah Khan, my predecessor, had advised me to undergo an operation to remove my sense of smell before leaving India. There were few recreations, and in the evening reading was difficult because the electric current was weak. One day a week electricity was cut off altogether.

The prices in Chungking were fantastic. When I arrived they were 140 times above the pre-war level. Within a year the prices had risen to 310 times.

Menon did not share the euphoric view of the Chinese widely held among politically minded Indians. 'Hindi, Chini, bhai, bhai' ('Indians and Chinese are brothers') was a Congress slogan. Menon did not feel at all brotherly towards the Chinese.

> In India we used to speak glibly of the spiritual affinity between India and China, but when I went to China I discovered that India had more in common with Europe.
>
> One of my earliest despatches to the Government of India was called *The Song of Soongs*. This amazing family, like the equally amazing Kungs, dominated China. T.V. Soong, Minister for Foreign Affairs, invited me to lunch soon after I had presented my credentials. But what manners! Soong kept his guests waiting for half an hour, and when he appeared had no word of apology to offer. When the lunch was over, we were hustled out.
>
> Accompanied by Anujee and Kunju, I went to tea with Soong's famous sister, Madam Chiang Kai Chek. The 'Madamissimo' turned on her charm as one turns on an artificial fountain, which rises higher and higher until one is wet with the spray.
>
> I met another of the Soong sisters, Madam Kung, a very worldly person with an altogether false sense of values. When I met Kung he had been Finance Minister for a decade. Though a descendant of Confucius, he looked like a pork butcher and had all the airs of a parvenu. In poverty-stricken China, he reeked of wealth, with his cars, carpets, lawns, central heating, swimming-baths, pictures and rows of footmen – a financial octopus.
>
> I remember a party thrown by Kung on New Year's Eve . . . It was the most vulgar party I have ever attended – vulgar in its excessive ostentation, artificial hilarity and the cavalier treatment of guests. General Wingate, Madame Sun Yat-Sen and myself sat at the same table. We were a strangely silent trio amidst the din caused by the cats, dogs, horses, pigs, for each table bore the mark of an animal and the guests at each table had to mew, bark, neigh or grunt. Throughout the party Wingate did not utter a word.

Menon noted acidly the near-canonisation of the Madamissimo in the United States, symbolised by her idealised portrait in the stained glass of a New York church, the Rector of which described her in a sermon as 'the First Lady of Christendom'.

The Chinese Government was not a bit interested in fighting the Japanese imperialism: 'The Kuomintang seemed more intent on pinning the communist "bandits" down in their dens', and the best Chinese divisions were employed in a blockade of the communist-held areas.

Menon had a useful window on young China in his daughter, Kunju, who studied at Chengtu University. The food was so poor that she had to keep up her strength by guzzling pea-nuts: 'I am the record pea-nut eater of the campus, but I would give anything for a slice of toast and a cup of Indian tea.' But the Chinese students could not have been kinder. Already, Kunju told him, the students were anti-Kung, seeing that rapacious family exactly as they were. It was no surprise to Menon when they turned against Chiang and the Madamissimo. 'I hope,' wrote Kunju, 'that this letter is not censored, but one of my friends actually said in a very low tone that he preferred Mao Tse-tung to Chiang Kai Chek.'

Menon was recalled to India for consultations, and on his return to Chungking made the adventurous journey overland via Srinagar, Gilgit and Kashgar. To cross the three great glaciers of the Karakoram he was lent the Mir of Hunza's favourite riding-yak. Menon did not at first take kindly to it, nor the yak to Menon, giving him a most malevolent look through red-tinted eyes. Bad-mannered, puffing like a porpoise, dripping saliva, it put Menon in mind of his enemy the Brigadier in Fort Sandeman. Yet once in the saddle, he felt as 'safe as Shiva on the sacred bull'. The yak moved over the glacier-ice with singular unconcern, placing its feet with the deliberation of a chess-player advancing his queen. 'One false move, and I would have been in one of those deep romantic glacier-pools.'

They crossed out of India in a snow-storm and rode over the plateau of the Pamirs, the 'Roof of the World'. All this time he had been a lone Hindu among Moslems who had a reputation for fanaticism. They had treated him with the utmost respect: 'that I was a Hindu did not matter. I was an Indian and the representative of the Government of India.'

Forty-six days after leaving Srinagar, he was met outside Kashgar by the British Consul General in a station-wagon brought there across Russia. Thereafter his journey lay eastward, by lorry, across the northern fringe of the Taklamakan and Gobi Deserts, an infinity of desolation save where there were small oases. In these oases were colonies of Indian traders, and Menon's main object on this journey was to give them what help he could, which was very little. Buffeted by civil wars, and finally smothered by Russian occupation (though Sinkiang was still nominally Chinese), commerce withered and died, and these unfortunate people could neither buy, sell nor depart.

He met Russians wherever he went, and found their hospitality – vodka extra strong for export – almost overwhelming. They did not quite succeed in drinking him under the table: 'not quite, but almost'.

Fourteen days out of Kashgar, he arrived at Urumchi, capital of

Sinkiang, where he stayed three weeks because snow blizzards made it impossible for a plane to land. The cold was such as he had never imagined; every night the temperature was fifty degrees below freezing. While Chinese officials in Urumchi politely discussed the Japanese war and Indian affairs, all they were really interested in was a local Moslem revolt. He was glad to leave this 'sinister town' and fly to Lanchow, on the Yellow river. They walked half-way across this on ice, and completed the crossing on goatskin rafts, dextrously steered between floating icebergs.

They saw in Lanchow Genghis Khan's tomb, guarded by Chinese soldiers and Mongol lamas; they saw the silver coffin containing his bones, the bow and arrow and spear he had wielded, and a gruesome banner bearing a large hank of human hairs, one from the head of each of his victims, 'and there were as many hairs on the banner as stars in the sky'.

One hundred and twenty-five days after leaving New Delhi, he flew from Lanchow to Chungking.

20

The Frontier, 1938-45

Hazara District, although part of the North-West Frontier Province, was in its character and outlook only half-frontier. It lay on the left or east bank of the Indus. Most of the people spoke Punjabi; only in the northern tahsil (Mansehra) was Pushtu generally spoken. The Deputy Commissioner was Political Agent in respect of the Pathan tribes of the Black Mountain and the small state of Amb, both on the left bank of the Indus. In so far as anyone had relations with the completely independent little republics of Kohistan, between the Pathan state of Swat and the Gilgit Agency, it was he.

Gerald Curtis was appointed Deputy Commissioner, Hazara, in April, 1938, and thought himself lucky.

> The D.C., Hazara, had a pleasant house on the fringe of Abbottabad which, at over 4,000 feet, was never excessively hot. He also had a summer residence under the deodars at Nathia Gali. Thus he was never separated for long from his wife and family. It was part of his duty to tour in the mountains on either side of the Kagan valley as far as the Gilgit border. No D.C., Hazara, need expect to be rung up in the middle of the night and be told that one of his villages was being raided, the noise of shots being heard as a background to the agitated voice of the reporter.

His main problem in 1938 was that the province had an elected Congress Government headed by Dr Khan Sahib. Not that Dr Khan Sahib was a bad Chief Minister: there were many worse, and he was on the best of terms with the Governor, Sir George Cunningham, who exercised a moderating influence over him. But he was bent on promoting a more egalitarian society. The British had relied on the landowning class, Pathan country gentlemen known generically as 'the Khans', very similar in taste and outlook to the country gentlemen who had in effect governed England before the Reform Act of 1832. To Dr Khan Sahib and his brother, although they belonged to that class, such élitism was all wrong. Whereas the British had made the Khans honorary magistrates, bestowed titles and jagirs on them, looked to them to preside over Jirgas under the Frontier Crimes Regulations, the

Congress Government missed no opportunity of cutting them down to size, preferring even urban Hindus. Dr Khan Sahib (who had married the daughter of a Yorkshire farmer) was genuinely concerned to side with have-nots against the haves of Pathan society, and to harry corrupt officials and oppressive landowners. He could not quite be brought to realise that Deputy Commissioners such as Curtis, although they made use of the Khans, were just as concerned as he to help the poor. In his Ministry were two Hindu Ministers, both wealthy businessmen; and one exceptionally able left-wing Moslem, the Revenue Minister, Qazi Ataullah, whose father had been a village mullah, a class of person not quite socially acceptable to the Khans, one of whom remarked contemptuously to Curtis, 'His father used to wash our dead.' But as Revenue Minister he had great power, which he deliberately used not merely to wrest control from the British, but to weaken the fabric of society. (The Government of Pakistan lost no time in putting him behind bars.) His first ploy was to try to abolish the Lambardari system, the keystone in the structure of rural society.

> A Lambardar was a hereditary headman. His first duty was to collect the land revenue and deposit it in the Tahsil Treasury. This system, surprising to European minds, worked well. Government responsibility was to protect the Treasury and convey remittances safely to the District Treasury. No low-paid officials were exposed to the temptations and risk of collecting large sums of money.
>
> The Lambardar's second duty was to report serious crime to the police and to take part in police investigation. His local knowledge might prove invaluable even though bias might have to be discounted.
>
> When he visited District Headquarters he was entitled to an interview with the D.C. at which he was kursi nisheen, entitled to the courtesy of a chair. He was thus able to bring his own and his villagers' sentiments to the notice of the head of the district.
>
> It always seemed to me that for 2½ per cent of the land revenue (which was the Lambardar's fee) the Government had made a good bargain. But the Minister did not want to hear this sort of advice.

The Lambardari system, reeking of privilege, was distasteful to the Progressive mind. But the Ministry was not able to abolish it before they themselves were out of office. They did, however, end the practice by which the D.C. was ex-officio Chairman of the District Board, so corruption flourished.

Law and order being no great problem in Hazara, the principal duty of the D.C. was to superintend the revenue system, securing punctual payment and maintaining accurate land registers.

> The great advantage of checking these on the spot, surrounded by an interested crowd, was that no one could get away with a blatant lie without contradiction. Every villager present knew what the truth was, though he might not care to reveal it to his own or his friend's disadvantage. The revenue system was designed to secure to all men, rich and poor, their rights in land. The title by which one was addressed, Gharib Parwar, Cherisher of the Poor, was not an empty honorific.

It was constitutionally correct, but politically unfortunate, that India was at war because Britain declared war, without a single Indian being consulted. It is possible, but hardly likely, that if Congress leaders had been tactfully consulted they might have supported the war-effort. As it was, Congress at first stood aside, and later instigated open rebellion timed to coincide with a Japanese invasion which Gandhi undertook to oppose by love and soul-force. This did not in the least affect recruitment for the armed forces – Congress-wallahs were not potential recruits – but it may have inhibited potential officers from coming forward. In the North-West Frontier Province, as in other provinces, Congress Governments resigned, and Governors became responsible for the administration. This made things easier for the D.C.s: there were no more of Qazi Ataullah's attempts to abolish privilege, élitism and integrity.

Fraser Noble was a young I.C.S. man just down from university. In accordance with a new arrangement, he and three others were posted direct to the North-West Frontier Province where they worked as Politicals although still on the I.C.S. cadre. His first mentor was Gerald Curtis, whom he greatly admired.

> The importance of being decisive was brought home to me. We would arrive breathless and sweating from the strenuous scramble up steep and stony paths and sit among a crowd of very noisy cultivators. The D.C. would put his questions and listen carefully to the outbursts they provoked. Suddenly he would shout, 'Silence!' Instantly the throng was quiet, and Gerald would pronounce his verdict. Invariably this was accepted without question, often with acclaim. What had been needed was a decision after a hearing of all sides.

Thus disputes which had festered for years were settled.

Noble usually did the first part of a tour by public transport, a charcoal-driven lorry, and then on foot, horseback or bicycle according to the terrain. A day's stage would be anything from twelve to twenty miles, plus detours to examine the scene of a dispute or some agricultural experiment. He might stop the night in a Forest Rest House, or in a tent.

There were by now few young men left in the villages: large numbers, all volunteers, had joined the Army.

> Talking to the villagers about the war was an important part of the work of a touring officer. Wireless sets were rare and rumours were rife. Enemy propaganda spread through various channels, though it was received on the Frontier with more scepticism than All-India Radio or the B.B.C. news . . . At that period the war news was pretty gloomy. Even the most remote villagers knew it, and wondered what had happened to the British who had ruled them for generations . . . The people did not welcome the prospect of a British defeat. They regarded the Germans as cruel, and Japanese as rubbishy Hindus of a sort . . . They had no difficulty in understanding the threat from the Caucasus or Persia; but Soviet communism was the enemy of Islam, and they found it hard to understand why the British, who only a few months ago had been faced by an alliance between Germany and Russia, should now wish them to regard the Russians as friends.

The growing shortage of food-grains was beginning to cause concern, and the Punjab Government had banned its export from the province, to the great inconvenience of the people in Hazara who were accustomed to import Punjab wheat. A flourishing wheat-smuggling system developed, with which Noble was not altogether out of sympathy; he negotiated with his opposite number in the Punjab an unofficial understanding on these matters.

Noble, who had a degree in economics, was credited with an expertise which he thought slightly bogus, and was made responsible for food-stuffs and price controls.

> The important thing was to get private trade working again by ensuring that adequate supplies were at the D.C.'s disposal to meet an emergency, and to make these available below the formal market price (and well below the black market price). The scheme worked. Within a few days hoarded stocks emerged, bringing prices tumbling down, and our emergency depot ceased to be under pressure.

By October, 1943, Noble was ready for a change. He was posted to Miranshah as Assistant Political Agent, North Waziristan.

It was a German objective to keep the Frontier a-boil so that the British would have to retain there a large number of troops. Throughout the war there were never less than five regular brigades in Waziristan. What prevented the Frontier going up in flames, as it had in 1919, was the presence of Sir George Cunningham, Governor of the North-West Frontier Province and Agent to the Governor-General for the tribal areas from 1937 to 1944. General Wavell, the Commander-in-Chief, said that Cunningham was worth a division of regular troops on the border. No one knew the Frontier and its people so well. He was infinitely capable and always calm. His physical presence – he had played rugby eight times for Scotland – was persuasive, and its impact softened but not weakened by a warm, slow smile. When in 1942 Congress launched its 'non-violent' rebellion (which could hardly have been more violent) and the Viceroy, Lord Linlithgow, urged him to arrest all Congress leaders, Cunningham (said his Secretary, Johnnie Dring) 'put him off with a soothing reply'. He knew he could control the Frontier without locking up men of the calibre and potential usefulness of Dr Khan Sahib. He had his contacts everywhere, including a sort of private intelligence service of pro-British Mullahs, so that he was never taken by surprise.

The Kurram Agency, home of the ever-loyal Turi, remained staunch. Despite the war it was decided to go ahead with a long overdue Land Settlement there. The Settlement Officer – somewhat junior for such a responsible post – was Captain B.K. Kapur, a cadet of a Hindu family which for over 100 years had played an important part in the administration and military affairs of the Punjab. Although a Hindu, he was exhilarated at serving among Pathans, 'simple and friendly, tough and strong, who kept rifles as others did walking-sticks'. He liked, too, the whole atmosphere of the Frontier, the comradeship between senior and junior Politicals, between British and Indian. Forty years on he recalls:

> Khassadars, Maliks and Kurram Militia showed no difference in their treatment or respect to me as a Hindu from their treatment or respect to Moslem or British officers. I toured extensively, camping in scores of villages, and received nothing but friendship and hospitality. Those among them who are alive today would remember me and receive me with the same warmth as they did in the past. Settlement Officers are remembered for generations.

So well did he do the Kurram settlement that he was sent to do the first settlement on a cash basis of Quetta.

In Waziristan it was business as usual, only more so. Jirga after Jirga of Mahsuds and Wazirs swore that any Russian or German who dared cross the border would get a bloody nose. (Two intrepid Germans were caught by the Kabul Khel Wazirs carrying money to the Faqir. The Kabul Khel cut off their heads and kept the money.) The tribes contributed quite generously to war funds. They enlisted in any unit which would take them, though not many units did. Stimulated by lucrative contracts, they constructed anti-tank defences across all possible invasion routes. And they continued to snipe convoys, blow up bridges, kidnap Hindus and occasionally give battle against regular troops and Scouts. From the Axis Legations in Kabul they received rifles and light machine-guns, howitzer shells for the Faqir's simple but quite effective cannon, and, above all, money. This money enabled the Faqir, for the first time in Frontier history, to pay and feed a full-time guerrilla force known as the 'Gorwekht Militia', from the Gorwekht mountains straddling the Afghan frontier on which he was based. No longer were hostiles obliged to commandeer food from resentful villagers and go back home when they could commandeer no more. The Gorwekht Militia was the hard core for larger lashkars of part-time hostiles. As trained regulars left for the main war, the troops who remained consisted of half-trained men. So the South Waziristan and Tochi Scouts had to carry a heavier burden, and in the case of the latter to expand rather too fast for efficiency and training. 'It is,' wrote one Commandant of the Tochi Scouts, 'not the best musketry training to hand a man a rifle and tell him to go and shoot a Wazir.'

In North Waziristan the general pattern was of continuous minor operations, with now and then something more major. In South Waziristan the Mahsuds generally sat on the fence. They disliked Wazirs, and their chief spiritual mentor, the Mullah Fazal Din, was a professional rival of the Faqir of Ipi, competing for 'voluntary' contributions from the faithful as for an Anglican vicar's Sustentation Fund. So every rupee collected from Mahsuds for the Faqir meant one less for Fazal Din. But although the Mahsuds as a tribe were not hostile, they included gang-leaders, any of whom could raise a lashkar of several hundred men, making quite a formidable army if several joined together for an operation. When Mahsuds did fight, they were well-led and their actions well-planned, effective and bloody.

The most truculent Mahsud clan was the Shabi Khel, who inhabited the desolate, almost inaccessible mountains south of Sararogha. They wanted no dealings whatsoever with the Government, 'neither your honey nor your sting'. Early in the war a gang of Shabi Khel hit the jackpot – holding up a car, killing the driver and kidnapping the passenger, a Hindu officer of the Indian Medical Service, Major Dugal. They hustled him off to a cave in the Shabi Khel country and sent, through intermediaries, demands for a substantial ransom. The Political Agent, South Waziristan, was Lieutenant Colonel Abdur Rahim Khan, a large landowner in Peshawur District. His Assistant Political Agent, Sararogha, was G.H. Emerson. They were under great pressure from Mrs Dugal, who not unnaturally besought the Political Agent daily to ransom her husband before he was killed or matrimonially damaged. Meanwhile the kidnappers amused themselves by sharpening knives in the unhappy doctor's presence and discussing which part of his anatomy should be cut off first to expedite payment. In fact he suffered only from apprehension and fleas, but that was bad enough. Emerson asked the head Shabi Khel Malik, Pir Rakhman, a fine figure of a man with long ringlets and Old Testament prophet's robes, whether he thought the Major would be freed. 'Well, you know,' replied Pir Rakhman frankly, 'he is a golden egg.'

The Shabi Khel country was bombed, after the customary warning leaflets had been dropped. Many bombs failed to explode which was a bonus for the Shabi Khel, who put them under bridges and culverts, lit fires alongside them and withdrew to watch satisfactory explosions. Eventually the Government agreed that a ransom of Rs 30,000 should be paid, but deducted it from the Shabi Khel Maliks' allowances. Major Dugal was then released. Emerson was told:

> I was to recover two British-made rifles* from each of the twelve known kidnappers of Major Dugal. How I was to do this, when none of the men were in our hands, was not very clear. However, I sent for some of them on safe conduct and started bargaining. One outlaw sat cross-legged in my room and told me the whole story. They had not intended either to kill the driver or to kidnap Major Dugal. But when they found him in the car they decided he would be worth keeping.
>
> 'You know, Sahib,' he said, 'we would have accepted Rs 3,000 paid at once for him.'
>
> 'That is very interesting,' I replied, 'because, between ourselves, we advised the Government to offer this very sum.'

*A proper Lee Enfield Service rifle made in a Royal Ordinance factory and probably captured or stolen from the Army; of far higher value than a rifle of similar appearance made in a tribal rifle factory.

> 'I know,' he replied. 'The more fuss that was made, the higher rose our price. We kept him in a cave and took great care of him. The Maliks came and told us we were making the name of the tribe stink to high heaven. What is that to us? (we said). When have you Maliks ever given us a share of your generous allowances? You can start now. If you want the Major, you can pay for him . . . They paid well, Sahib.'

One day at Sararogha a tribesman came in clutching two medals, the I.O.M. and the I.D.S.M., which he had won in France.

> We then discussed the war now being waged, during one of its darkest moments. He had not the slightest doubt that we would win. 'The Germans are not supermen,' he said, 'we beat them before and we will beat them again.' I was greatly heartened.

Yet this man, wearing his medals, had probably fought against us in 1919. The Mahsuds did not regard themselves as allies of the Germans or Russians nor as shaking off the gyves of colonialism which hardly affected their way of life. They laid their ambushes, sniped at convoys, blew up bridges partly for Islamic zeal, partly to maintain the 90 per cent independence which they already enjoyed, but mainly for gain. And Lieutenant-Colonel Abdur Rahim Khan met guile and bad faith with equal guile and bad faith.

The only disagreement Emerson ever had with him was over the arrest of an outlaw while he was a patient in a Scouts hospital.

> I felt that someone who had come for medical treatment was trusting us to care for him. Abdur Rahim took the view that he was fully entitled to meet cunning with cunning. I was very unhappy about the proposal, and Abdur Rahim said he wanted the arrest made but would not ask me to have any part in it. My Pathan Assistant said I was being much too scrupulous: the tribesmen themselves would admire his cunning rather than deplore his duplicity . . . I must admit that the attitude of the tribesmen bore this out. It must in fairness be added that we had not made any promise of safe-conduct and that the outlaw had tried to come incognito.

It was the constant endeavour of the Faqir of Ipi to embroil the Mahsuds in his war, and of the Politicals to keep them on the fence. One day the Faqir announced that he would visit his friends the Mahsuds. Emerson was spending a few days in Brigade Headquarters in Razmak, and the news provoked a Gunner Major into launching a tirade against the Political's softness in their handling of hostiles. Emerson asked:

> what he [the Gunner Major] would do about the proposed visit of the Faqir. He replied that, having found out what house the Faqir was staying in, he would blow it down by fire from his medium battery in Razmak. I asked him if he would guarantee dropping a shell on the exact spot where the Faqir was. He admitted that it might be necessary to fire a few ranging shots. I asked him how much of the village would be left after a few ranging shots.

Emerson went on to point out that this would provoke exactly what the Government in wartime was most anxious to avoid – full-scale Holy War by the Mahsuds in alliance with the Wazirs. But something had to be done about the visit.

> I sent for the Maliks and asked if we were now at war. They made light of the matter. Of course they could not refuse shelter to so famous a visitor. They would have to go through the motions. But they did not want him stirring up hostility in their villages, and they would give him the minimum hospitality for the shortest time that protocol required. He would be moved from one village to another and with any luck would be gone within a fortnight.

In the event the Faqir's visit achieved nothing but some contributions to his Sustentation Fund.

This was all the small change of Waziristan operations. At any time the Mahsuds could, if they wished, assemble for battle against Government forces. But they would do so in their own time and for their own cause, not to oblige the Faqir. They did so choose in December, 1940, just after Johnny Dring arrived to take over South Waziristan from Abdur Rahim Khan.

> I found on my arrival that plans had been made for the Razmak column to march out against the leading Mahsud hostile, Mohamad Hayat. The plan had been leaked. When I tried to get to Razmak, our lorries were held up in Shabi Khel territory. There was a lot of firing and shouting between the hostiles and my escort of leading Maliks. It was impossible to get through so we retreated to the Scouts post at Sararogha. I simply *had* to accompany the column, so the R.A.F. picked me up and landed me at Razmak at dusk after the gates had been closed. The lone walk to the perimeter was rather hair-raising.

Early next morning the brigade column, four miles long, with three battalions and ample artillery, set out from Razmak to chastise the insolent Mohamad Hayat. In nine cases out of ten he would have withdrawn before overwhelming force, melting away into the mountains where he could not be brought to battle. This time, however, he decided to fight. As Mahsuds were generally well-informed on such matters, he may have learned that one of the three battalions, of a Punjab Regiment, was not very well trained. Dring, who had been in the Guides and knew how such things should be done, watched proceedings with a critical eye.

> Piquets were sent to the hilltops to protect the road as usual, but some of the fundamental principles went awry. When the advance guard reached the campsite at Tauda China, the battalion on piquet duty started to run for the camp in complete disorder. Sixty-six men were killed, including the Colonel. The men said he had given up the struggle and shouted 'Every man for himself'. It was the worst Frontier incident for many years. The whole column was bogged down in bivouacs in the snow for four weeks. Another brigade had to be brought up from India just at a time when the object was to reduce frontier garrisons.

For the next couple of years the Mahsuds were good as gold (about 3 carat), somewhat to the disappointment of Pat Duncan who took over from Emerson. He was an Ulsterman who, when at Oxford, had been best man at the wedding of a future Prime Minister, Harold Wilson. His wife, a natural linguist with a First in Modern Languages, spoke perfect Mahsud Pushtu. He was a more militant character than Emerson, inclined to egg on the Scouts rather than discourage their military ardour. Of this they did not entirely approve: it was not what they expected of a Political. However, in April, 1943, several Mahsud gangs, responsible for most of the murders, kidnappings and general mayhem of the past ten years, joined in a large lashkar to ambush a convoy from Wana. They were brought to battle, and the Scouts were in difficulties when Duncan came trundling along the road in his van, eager for the fray and bringing two 3-inch mortars intended only for post-defence and with no carrying-gear. Nevertheless, at this point they were invaluable: by superhuman efforts they were manhandled to the point from which they could support the platoons in difficulties; and with their help, the Scouts were extricated and the Mahsuds discomforted.

They had their revenge seven months later, just after Gerald Curtis had taken over from Dring. The Commanding Officer of a Gurkha battalion in Razmak decided to run a training exercise on the slopes of Shuidar mountain. It was a very rash thing to do: no one in his right senses in Waziristan took out a single battalion without supporting arms. The Political Tahsildar, a Pathan, warned him but he paid no attention. Up Shuidar the Gurkhas went. This annoyed the Mahsuds of the Abdullai clan, and the drums beat to arms. Sniping started: the training exercise suddenly became real, and a Gurkha was killed near the top of the mountain. Because of the Mahsud habit of mutilating dead and wounded, the Colonel was determined to bring down the body. There were more casualties, more delays; the shooting increased and attracted more tribesmen. (Barren hills sprouted men whenever a show like that developed.) Another Gurkha battalion was sent out from Razmak to reinforce the first. In the twilight the exultant Abdullai chased both battalions right back to Razmak and the gates had to be closed while many men were still outside. In the final tally, taken next day, it was established that there were over fifty Gurkhas killed, many knifed in the darkness, and some fifty rifles plus Tommy-guns and light machine-guns lost.

Taking his meals in the brigade mess, Curtis was well aware how the soldiers felt about this shocking episode (especially officers of Gurkha regiments at the rout of their 'little men'), about the casualties and the loss of weapons, the ultimate disgrace by Frontier standards. They were inclined to blame everyone but themselves, especially the Politicals: unfortunately Duncan, acting Political Agent before Curtis's arrival, had authorised the operation on Shuidar. Nothing in Curtis's previous experience gave him any guidance on what to do now, but he had at hand a wise Pathan Assistant Political Officer. The Abdullai were ordered to return all the weapons they had captured, plus a lot more as a fine, and to evacuate two hamlets, the fortified towers of which would be destroyed by artillery.

They evacuated the hamlets, but did not return any weapons. Curtis, who had held a commission in a Territorial battery, watched subsequent proceedings with interest.

> Each hamlet was enclosed in mud-coloured walls with turrets at the corners, and furnished with a lofty, slim and rather elegant watch-tower. Two batteries were involved, one of 4.5 inch howitzers and one of 25-pounders. The 4.5s began, and after a couple of registering rounds, started knocking down the walls . . . The 25-pounders took on the towers. They scored repeated hits, but the shells passed through, leaving the towers standing. The mud, goats' hair and timber structures were extraordinarily tough. Eventually a hit from a 4.5 destroyed one tower. The other was left standing but in a

precarious condition. That afternoon the Abdullai brought in some of the lost weapons.

They were ordered to bring in the remainder – or else. They did not, so the R.A.F. took a hand. After due warning, a third fortified hamlet was bombed. A lucky hit exploded a dump of explosives or ammunition: there was a flash and an immense cloud of dust, after which neither walls nor tower remained. The rest of the lost weapons, 100 rifles as surety for future good behaviour, and the fine were brought in that afternoon.

Curtis started with a huge prestige-point; four sons, all by the same wife. 'Four sons, four rifles!' exclaimed the tribesmen in admiration and envy, as he got down to mastering their very difficult dialect of Pushtu.

> A large part of the day was spent listening and talking to Mahsuds . . . I used to see each Malik separately in my office. All were disarmed before entering, but my Mahsud orderlies on duty outside my office carried weapons. They sat on the steps and occupied their leisure by knitting thread spun by their women from the wool of the fat-tailed sheep. It was rough and stiff, and although the finished pullover was warm, it felt like a coat of mail . . . Any Mahsud could argue plausibly and in persistence could outclass the importunate widow. To give anything to a Mahsud was merely to create claims for more.

One of the Political Agent's problems was that by tribal custom all rewards and promotions should be awarded on a clan basis, according to an established pecking-order, irrespective of merit. But every tribesman was an aggressive egoist, determined on the one hand that his services should be suitably rewarded, and on the other that a reward to anyone else was a breach of custom. There was a Shabi Khel Malik, Gul Khan, who had been a Subadar in the Kurram Militia which, alone among the Frontier Corps, recruited a platoon of Mahsuds, a triumph of hope over experience. His platoon, annoyed by a promotion being given according to merit, not to the clan whose turn it was, had deserted with their rifles. Subadar Gul Khan had then been informed that his services were no longer required, and he could depart without his pension. This he thought unfair, since he had advised the Commandant against that promotion. He badgered Curtis to intercede to get him his pension, which Curtis undertook to do though he did not like Gul Khan: 'with an eye like that, if he were a horse, no one would buy him'.

Long before any reply could be expected from the Political Agent,

Kurram, Gul Khan stopped Curtis's car in the road, waving a written petition.

> I got out of the car and he told me his story yet again. I watched him carefully and took his petition and got back into the car without turning my back. I felt I had been lucky to escape without a knife in my guts. However, Providence intervened. Gul Khan's aged father married a young wife and begat a son. This was too much for Gul Khan: he had been robbed of his pension, and now his father's long life and unnatural virility were going to deprive him of much of his birthright. He killed his father, his young stepmother, and his half-brother. But even in Waziristan there were limits. The Shabi Khel Jirga banished him, and he departed to Afghanistan.

Like other Political Agents, South Waziristan, Curtis believed that something must be done to improve Mahsud agriculture and make them less dependent on raiding. He calculated that for a population of about 88,000 the tribe had less than 3,000 acres of irrigated land. There was much more un-irrigated land, but the crops it produced were meagre, relying on a capricious rainfall. To see for himself sites for land improvement schemes, karezes, small dams and simple irrigation works, he went on many long tours on foot, with only a tribal escort, wearing Pathan clothes:

> including a pagri, the end of which I used to draw over my red face if I did not want to be too conspicuous.
>
> At night I was allotted a room which opened out into a small courtyard overshadowed by a tall watchtower . . . all surrounded by a wall, loopholed and furnished with a wooden gallery on which riflemen could stand. I never felt uneasy about my safety. But when I heard the evening call to prayer and realised that I was the only man paying no heed to it, I had a feeling of isolation.

Curtis obtained money for wire netting to strengthen the walls of the Mahsuds' terraced fields and the earth banks they built to hold up seasonal flood water, and for simple irrigation schemes. But shortage of water was the lesser part of the problem: the greater was shortage of soil, which could not quickly be remedied.

With all its shortages and economic dislocations, the war brought the Mahsuds some economic benefits. The Army would not recruit Mahsuds in any capacity which involved them being given rifles: the temptation to desert would be too great. But two Mahsud labour battalions were raised, and a Motor Transport Company (Mahsuds are good natural mechanics) for service in Burma, where they did very well. There was also the Mahsud Convoy. Following the Shahur Tangi ambush in 1937, supplies for Wana were sent in weekly convoys of lorries owned, driven and escorted only by tribesmen. It could be argued that the ambush was thereby rewarded; but the system worked, and the tribes made far too much money out of it ever to attack the convoy.

Wartime rationing brought more headaches for the Political Agent. Cloth, kerosene, timber, sugar were all rationed, and distributed by contract. These contracts were highly lucrative, and their tribal allocation fiercely disputed. During a temporary shortage of wheat, Curtis arranged for gram (split peas) to be imported.

> It was not a popular grain. Mahsud Jirgas spared me no detail of what a diet of gram did to their digestive processes. Then even gram ceased to be available. My appeals to the Food Controller fell on deaf ears. I recorded my anxiety in my official diary, and received a sharp reprimand from the Governor. However, thereafter the wheat I needed arrived monthly. Had I allowed the situation to deteriorate, there might have been another major Mahsud war.

The Ahmedzai Wazirs of the Wana area could be almost as troublesome as Mahsuds. That they were not, in Curtis's time, was due largely to his Assistant Political Agents in Wana. The first was John Dent, a direct entry to the North-West Frontier Province, a Scot and a more equable character than Duncan, but remarkably quick off the mark. He was dining with a Wazir Malik when he heard that two Army rifles had been stolen, and instantly took out a force of Scouts to surround the houses and take hostages of the offending clan. The rifles were returned. Under his patronage the Wana Hunt – 8½ couple, hunting generally a drag but sometimes getting a line on a jackal – was seldom sniped at to the detriment of sport. He was succeeded by Captain Mohamad Yusuf Khan, M.C., who had served four years with the South Waziristan Scouts before being invalided out with pleurisy. His spare-time interests were hunting, show-jumping and classical music. Wherever he was posted, Scouts and Khassadars were treated to Beethoven, Handel and Mozart played loudly on a very expensive gramophone. No one knew better than he the 'form' in Waziristan, the intricacies of tribal politics.

In North Waziristan the situation was rather different. The Faqir of Ipi's war grumbled on year after year, *piano* for months at a time, then blazing up *fortissimo* for a few weeks, but seldom on a scale sufficient to involve the Razmak and Bannu brigades. It was the Tochi Scouts' war, and junior Politicals were much involved in it.

The Faqir had several home-made cannon, firing 3.7 howitzer shells, which could penetrate the walls of a Scouts post and explode unpleasantly inside. With one of these pieces, his Gorwekht Militia started to shell the Ghariom Scouts post, killing several of the garrison. After use it was trundled back into a cave, safe from artillery and bombing from the air. His reputation would rise if he were allowed to get away with it: the gun must be captured or destroyed; or at least the cave must be blown up so that the gun could not fire with impunity. A force of several Scouts platoons made a night approach march, deployed at dawn and advanced on the cave. With them went the Assistant Political Agent Bryan Becker, to sort out any political complications that might ensue. As they got near the cave, they came under fire. A Scouts officer, John Auret, recalls:

> As I doubled smartly for cover, I noted Bryan sort of waddling. I thought he was putting on an act and was about to tell him not to play the fool when he swayed and called out, 'They've got the Assistant Political Agent.'

Becker took a bullet through the thigh.

> Not wanting to be a nuisance, I got myself carried back by my orderly and two or three of the bodyguard who happened to be around. The bullet, having gone through my thigh, creased the forehead of my Political Assistant, a big, fair Turi, Ghulam Yayyah (of blessed memory). He died of it a few days later.

A useful double for the Faqir.

Becker was replaced at Miranshah by Fraser Noble, from Hazara. His boss was Jack ('Lotus') Lowis. Johnny Raw found it:

> a delight to see him [Lowis] dealing with a recalcitrant tough who, in the face of his impeccable salty Pushtu and humour, was soon eating out of his hand. His handling of a Jirga, with the back-row boys screaming at him, was equally effective. He would produce some appalling proverb which had the rest of the Jirga in stitches and shouting at the hecklers to sit down and shut up.

Noble was fascinated by Waziristan.

> It was harsh, arid, rocky, weird, lonely, forbidding, threatening, rugged, misshapen, strange, alien; yet at times it had a spectacular

beauty and breath-taking colour. One feared the ferocity of the people and abhorred their cruelty, yet admired their sturdy manliness, democratic pride and love of freedom; and warmed to their hospitality and ready wit and humour. Calculating their bluff and working out counter-measures, seeking information and sifting the wheat from the chaff, was an intellectual exercise which tested one's patience and equanimity.

In Miranshah there was a squash court, and a professional imported for the cold weather from Peshawur, a member of the family which after the war produced many world squash champions. 'He had the special talent of forcing one to raise one's game.' On Sunday afternoons there was vigorous basketball with the Scouts: 'its version of the rules much more physical than I had bargained for'.*

It was far too dangerous in North Waziristan to go round on foot accompanied only by tribal escorts. Noble travelled:

> in a Ford Vanette which carried seven or eight of my bodyguard, or in the 3-ton lorry which carried up to 30, many on the roof, and therefore awake, otherwise they might fall off: if they were awake, they might be alert. The bodyguard was chosen to include one or two representatives from each of the more important clans in the Agency, and most of them were the sons or nephews of respected Maliks. There was a reassuring *esprit de corps* among them, and they would often sing cheerful Pushtu love-songs as we sped along. Their Subadar was a villainous-looking Kabul Khel whose close-set eyes and wispy beard and the dirty black turban carelessly wrapped round his chin and slopping over his face made a first impression that was anything but reassuring. But he was nearly twice their age and certainly twice as experienced and three times as cunning, and I came to feel safer whenever Gul Behram was around. On one of the occasions when shots were fired at me the driver reacted very fast, screaming orders to the escort as he accelerated towards cover. The shots passed behind the lorry, the sniper misjudging its speed. He was on the far side of the Tochi river; the bodyguard shouted curses and imprecations as they dashed through the water in his direction.

Shortly after Noble left, two Politicals, Campbell and Bromhead, were wounded by snipers who were better judges of a lorry's speed.

*Basketball, with fierce tackling and no holds barred, was a favourite Scouts' game because it could be played behind walls, under cover from casual sniping.

Any important Scouts operation was accompanied by a Political, to identify prisoners, question friendlies, warn the tribesmen to sin no more. Noble accompanied a barampta* to search a village for hostiles who had been holding up mail lorries, killing and kidnapping Hindus travelling on them.

> Some of the men we wanted had ingenious hiding places, one in a tiny cell cunningly constructed in a nondescript heap of bricks. We had to threaten to use grenades before he came out with his hands empty. A man cornered in this way often decided to run amok, with dagger or pistol, and could kill several of his hunters before they could stop him . . . There was a miserable woman lying in a cot in a dark corner, under a sheet. She was said to be ill with fever. Jack decided to accept the story, but as we were withdrawing, I said, 'It's not a woman, you know – look at the hair on her hand.'

Noble's main responsibility was the charge of about 1,100 Khassadars – inspecting them; ensuring that they were on the job, piqueting the road on Road Open Days; paying them; questioning them for information and listening to their complaints. They often invited him to delicious feasts of pilao, liver and kidney kababs, local oranges, grapes and walnuts.

Although Noble was very fit, the night gashts were an ordeal, and for the credit of his service he must keep pace with the Scouts. One night gasht involved:

> incredible scrambling in the dark over rocks, and several times waist-deep through an icy stream . . . In nine hours, we halted only twice for twenty minutes . . . When I traced our movements on a map, I was astonished at the distance we had covered. In the last hour we did five miles.
>
> [On another], as we climbed the moon shone to ease our way, and the going became very rough and precipitous. Suddenly the moon went behind a great bank of cloud and we were in pitch darkness. I had no sense of balance or direction. Having scrambled over a rock, I was aware that the man ahead of me was much higher, and realised that he was climbing a vertical cliff. I could find no foot-hold, but my outstretched hand brushed against the root of some shrub of shrivelled tree. I cannot recall ever being so frightened. Some instinct

*An operation to surround a village at night and search it at dawn, looking for wanted men, stolen property, or victims of kidnappers.

made me haul on the root, and it held. I pulled myself up and on to a narrow ledge. I was aware that there were other men crouched there, waiting, and thankfully I waited with them. Some time before dawn there was enough light to start moving again.

They did not find the gang they were looking for, but were sniped at as they withdrew, and did not feel safe until the Scouts' own field-gun in Spinwam post began firing over their heads.

Sir George Cunningham often visited the Agency, on one occasion to see on his death-bed an old Tori Khel Malik called Shahzar Khan, who years ago, when Cunningham had been Political Agent, North Waziristan, had been a notable hostile. The dying man presented the Governor with a handsome robe of honour, black with gold embroidery, which had been given him by the Amir of Afghanistan for his prowess against the British in 1919. He then put in a word for an outlaw from British India, a multiple-murderer, whom he was harbouring. The Governor promised to look into the case and see if he could be pardoned. They then adjourned to a repast capped by splendid oranges from Shahzar's own garden. When Sir George enquired of Shahzar's sons of the outlaw, they pointed quietly to the man passing round the oranges.

Lowis went down with malaria, so Noble had to act as Political Agent. This coincided with one of the Faqir's attempts to bring the Mahsuds into his war. He established himself in the Shaktu valley, which was the boundary between the Tori Khel Wazirs and the Mahsuds. His presence excited the young men of both tribes, so he could not be allowed to stay there. He had to be moved on by a judicious combination of political pressure and air-action – without, by over-reaction, doing his work for him. A nice calculation. It was difficult to pinpoint his exact position.

[Noble] . . . had a session with the Intelligence Bureau in Peshawur on air-photos and cross-examined scores of would-be informers. I twice took Gul Behram and a bunch of friendly Maliks on reconnaissance flights. They had never flown before, and prudently turned towards Mecca to say their prayers before venturing into the plane. But once they were airborne, they showed no signs of nerves, rushing from one side of the plane to the other in response to such cries as 'There's Gul Zamir's kot!' After the second flight we were reasonably confident that we knew, to within two or three hundred yards, where Ipi's new headquarters were, and Sir George agreed that we might drop the warning notices that it was a 'proscribed area' liable to be bombed and machine-gunned at any time.

Of course there was no hope of bagging the Faqir. But by the time his hosts had been living for a few weeks in flea-ridden caves, grazing their livestock only at night and watching their towers being knocked down (very costly to rebuild) the Faqir was in disrepute, and was invited to return to the Gorwekht mountains, where he could do much less harm. His former hosts used unexploded bombs not only for blowing up bridges but, as one demonstrated to Sir George Cunningham, for blasting rock to make an irrigation channel.

Every good thing comes to an end, though; and eventually Noble had to leave the job he loved and go to one he hated, bound to a desk in Peshawur.

In 1943-4 there was a serious shortage of food-grains on the Frontier, aggravated by the incompetence and corruption of the Provincial Government.

A year earlier, when Congress instigated a rebellion in the United and Central Provinces, a number of Congress Members of Legislative Council in the North-West Frontier Province had been interned. Others defected to the Moslem League. Congress thus lost its parliamentary majority, and a Moslem League Provincial Government was formed, neither notably efficient nor oppressively honest, under Sardar Aurungzeb Khan whom Herbert Thompson had known as a leading member of the Peshawur Bar. The Congress Opposition ran rings round it.

Sir George Cunningham set up a small team of Politicals to deal with a dangerous situation: Dring as Secretary to the Food and Civil Supplies Department; Arthur Wooller, fresh (or, rather, somewhat jaded) from the Gulf, as his Deputy; together with Noble as Controller of Rationing.

Noble was appalled by the cumulative effects of petty dishonesty on the supply system. Even in Tribal Territory Jirgas denounced 'controls', a word which, as it entered the Pushtu vocabulary, acquired pejorative implications.

> There was a genuine food shortage, and after months of ministerial intervention in the work of district officers, public confidence in the system of distribution had been shaken. The normal channels of supply had dried up, in anticipation of higher prices and the bonanza of the black market. The Moslem League represented the big landowners; Congress, professing the interests of the labourer, the landless, the underdog, found it easy to mount demonstrations against the Ministry. At a critical period of the war, the Frontier was

faced with violent political dissension and the breakdown of the procurement and distribution of food supplies.

Poor harvests and a shortfall in imports from the Punjab, whence grain had been sent to relieve the Bengal famine, had caused people to hoard. The Governor made a personal appeal to large landowners to deliver grain, but was disappointed at the result. The Ministry ordered a registration of stocks, but the opposition of the landowners was obstinate and compliance was patchy. The Moslem League Government, acting in this way solely to protect the poor (the rich could shop in the black market) was denounced by Dr Khan Sahib and former Ministers for harassing the landowners.

However, in September, 1944, the Government of India allocated larger supplies from the Punjab to the North-West Frontier Province. Local procurement then dramatically improved as those who had been hoarding grain, disappointed in their hopes of rocketing prices, hastily unloaded their stocks on a falling market.

With supplies improved, an equitable system of distribution was needed. That was Noble's job, to be done:

> without either losing the confidence of the Ministry or undermining its precarious stability. Ministers would want constantly to intervene, to be associated with any success the officials achieved and to disclaim responsibility for mistakes. The grain dealers, nearly all Hindus and supporters of Congress, boycotted the Government's efforts and were frostily uncooperative.

The grain dealers' boycott made it necessary for Noble to acquire facilities for receiving and storing the grain. He appealed to the Army, and was instantly allotted some empty barracks and military railway sidings where large consignments could be unloaded quickly. He had to set up an official, monopolistic retailing system. Fortunately one Hindu trader, a stout and cheerful young contractor, co-operated. Without his expert knowledge of the trade and his contacts with dealers in the Punjab, Noble's task would have been impossible. 'No doubt he benefited financially: he earned it.' Ration depots were established where service would be clean, dependable and quick: in Peshawur City alone there were over 100 such depots. Another Frontier Political, Alastair Low, as Finance Secretary, sorted out the problems of funding such an unprecedented enterprise in the face of unending objections from the Finance Department.

Peshawur is a turbulent, cosmopolitan city, full of foot-loose independent characters, and its women-folk make themselves heard behind the purdah, [complaining shrilly] that enquiries of the rationing department's staff were an intrusion into the privacy of the Islamic family . . . But a week after the scheme started the Governor made an unheralded tour of the city's ration depots and found conditions vastly different from July when the people had been sulky and hungry, the trade disorganised and supplies scarce.

Herbert Thompson was also in Peshawur at that time, not overjoyed at being appointed Revenue and Divisional Commissioner, 'one of the most exhausting jobs that ever fell to me'. His predecessor, a devout member of the Oxford Group, believed in leaving all decisions to God, and the Almighty had been somewhat dilatory in revenue matters. Thompson found:

chaos, including a room full of files which my wife discovered on taking possession of our official house while I was assuming charge of an office proudly displayed as empty of all pending work. For six weeks I worked daily from 6 a.m. until 2 a.m. next morning.

The Chief Minister, Thompson's old friend Sardar Aurungzeb Khan, was:

inexperienced and not particularly effectual, but I was fond of him. He used to blow in at odd moments to discuss any sort of subject. One evening he raised the subject of a licence to fell timber in a reserved forest. Earnestly I explained that this was fundamentally wrong in the fight against soil erosion. After trying to argue me round to his own view, he confessed, 'As a matter of fact, my Cabinet does not like it, but they said that if you agreed, they would too.' Then he added with a grin, 'I *did* so want to help one of my supporters.'

In Kohat District there was a new dimension to the problems of rationing. The Deputy Commissioner, Kohat, was responsible for political relations with the Orakzai tribe – tough, well-armed, much recruited into the Army and Frontier Corps, but living in Tribal Territory and not administered at all by the British. They were as a rule fairly amenable, but with their neighbours had joined the general tribal rebellion in 1919. They occupied a key-position between the Afridis, who in any large-scale conflict would probably be hostile, and the Wazir-Mahsud group who were already more or less hostile. To keep the Orakzai quiet Cunningham sent to Kohat as Deputy Commissioner one of the old and bold, Shaikh Mahbub Ali, commonly known as 'the

Shaikh', who thirteen years earlier had been Oriental Secretary to the British Legation in Kabul.

A landowner from Peshawur, 18-stone of political craft and guile, the Shaikh kept the Orakzai quiet. But he ran the district exactly as though it had been part of the Kingdom of Afghanistan. By 1944 it was clearly time for the Shaikh, now well beyond reach of want, to move on. 'Lotus' Lowis as D.C., Kohat, and Johnny Raw as Assistant Commissioner, Hangu, had to cleanse the Augean stables. To Raw it was an eye-opener.

> *How* Kohat had been administered! Apart from such little matters as curious results in magisterial cases, general corruption and nepotism, it became clear that all commodities such as sugar, cloth, kerosene etc. which were strictly rationed and had been on ration cards since early in the war had disappeared in their entirety into the black market. No ration-cards had ever been issued in any part of the District. Lotus and I set about remedying the situation and before long everybody had a ration-card. No one had seen ration-cards before and their purpose had to be explained.

Edward Lydall as D.C., Nowshera had a different sort of problem. Most of the inhabitants of the North-West Frontier Province supported the war-effort and enlisted in very large numbers; but there was a noisy Congress/Redshirt minority who opposed it by such bold measures as shouting anti-war slogans. Their leader in Nowshera was a tongawallah (cab-driver) named Ghulam Mohamad, with the rank of General in the Redshirts, a very nice little man. But he was offended by Lydall (described in his speeches as a bloodsucking tyrant) writing and circulating a poem lampooning him. He came to Lydall's bungalow to make a formal protest, and an agreement was drawn up: if he would stop making anti-war speeches, Lydall would stop writing poems about him.

Some time later he again called on Lydall with another complaint. Since he had stopped agitating against the war, everyone was saying that he must be in the D.C.'s pay.

'Well,' said Lydall, 'so you are.'

'That,' said the General, drawing himself up with dignity, 'is not the point.'

In order to restore his reputation, he had to be sent to prison.

'All right,' said Lydall. 'But one good turn deserves another. If I send you to prison, you must promise to start a pro-war movement when you come out.'

'Certainly, Sahib. How much jail would that earn me?'

'I thought about a week.'

'No, no! I must insist on at least six months.'

They compromised on two months. Ghulam Mohamad was sentenced for conspiring to commit sabotage, and departed to prison with a broad wink at the Honourable Magistrate.

When Dr Khan Sahib held an anti-war meeting in Nowshera, Lydall sent a Police Sub-Inspector to hand him a basket of lemons with the D.C.'s compliments, and with winks and nudges to give the public the impression that the doctor too was in his pay. (He was not.) However, the doctor was made of sterner stuff than the tongawallah and was not easily put out; so Lydall urged the local mullahs, supporters of the Moslem League, to go and heckle him. This they did: the result was a mini-riot, and Lydall made a formal complaint about Dr Khan Sahib's conduct, following this up with a satirical ballad about the Doctor. The refrain went with a swing:

I'm Khan Sahib, the Red-shirt hero,
I'm Khan Sahib who fears duress,
I'm Khan Sahib the anti-British,
I'm Khan Sahib, I.M.S.
I'm Khan Sahib the Moslem tiger,
I'm Khan Sahib, the Hindu mouse,
I'm Khan Sahib of the Congress
And Khan Sahib of Government House.

The doctor was furious, for his sense of humour did not extend to jokes about himself. Lydall was somewhat embarrassed subsequently to find himself next to Mrs Khan Sahib at a luncheon in Peshawur. (The doctor did not believe in letting his anti-British sentiments inhibit his social life.) But he need not have worried.

'Oh, Mr Lydall,' she said, 'I *did* so enjoy your poem about my husband. Our daughter Miriam has learned it by heart.'

21

In the States, 1939–45

The 'phoney war' hardly touched India and made very little difference to Politicals in the states except in so far as they longed to return to the Army. There was a greater plenitude of paperwork, and slightly fewer officers to keep it circulating, but otherwise not much change. However, when the war moved closer, they found themselves in charge of civil defence, rationing, propaganda, riot control, even the command of military and police units.

While petrol rationing made touring more difficult, other wartime factors made it more purposeful. When food was rationed, Residents could tactfully indicate the impropriety of 9-course banquets. When 12-bore cartridges, golf-balls and fodder for polo-ponies were in short supply, it was difficult for the most evasive ruler to divert an intrusive Political Agent. How could the two days of his visit be filled? Only by taking him round such schools, dispensaries, agricultural schemes and recruits in training as could be produced.

For instance, Maharajah Yadavindra Singh of Patiala, as good a games-player as his father and a far better ruler and man, put a lot of effort and money into agricultural development based not on grandiose works by tractor, bulldozer and borehole-driller, but on what would now be called 'intermediate technology', within reach of the ordinary farmer with the help of a village artisan and a team of well-diggers. He invited the Resident, Herbert Thompson, to choose any village in the state to inspect. Thompson, studying the map, selected the most remote and inaccessible. 'I knew you would!' laughed His Highness. 'It is the only one I haven't got round to.' It was the sort of thing that could hardly have happened before the war, certainly not in Patiala ruled by Bhupindra Singh. The Resident would have been taken to shoot duck, watch cricket and polo, eat gargantuan meals – anything but inspect 'village uplift'.

Dudley Biscoe's first wartime posting was as Under Secretary to the Resident for Mysore, stationed in the salubrious climate of Bangalore. He was housed in what had been a billiard saloon; it was like camping in a desert.

Mysore (twenty-one-gun, population 6·5 million) had had a chequered history. In the eighteenth century it had been the realm of the Moslem usurpers, Hyder Ali and Tipu Sultan; the East India Company restored it to its former Hindu rulers, and when in 1831 the populace rebelled against them, turned them out and took over the state itself. Fifty years later the state was revived and handed back to the Hindu ruling family. So in effect it had been in existence only since 1881, and the administrative system of British India continued. It was progressive, though not (as Lord Willingdon observed) without an element of eyewash. There was a Representative Assembly with powers rather less than those of the House of Commons in Tudor times. It was part-elected, part-nominated; it had the right to be consulted in matters of taxation and in asking awkward questions about the administration (but not too awkward). There was a Legislative Council with an unofficial but not an elected majority: in English historical terms, most of its members were 'placemen', nominees of the ruler. So although much was made of its 'bicameral legislature', it was not, from the Maharajah's point of view, oppressively democratic. But in other ways Mysore was very advanced, with quite good roads, active and efficient agriculture and veterinary departments, light and heavy industries, coffee-plantations, hydro-electric power and the most productive gold-fields in India. In 1939 it had a Moslem Diwan of great ability, Sir Mirza Ismail.

The Maharajah was not a Rajput, though he would have liked to be considered one. At great expense he acquired a genuine Rajput bride, but throughout the lengthy wedding ceremonies she complained at being married to a man of low caste. Deeply hurt, when the ceremonies were concluded and without consummating the marriage, he presented her with her own palace and never set eyes on her again.

Biscoe, from Baluchistan, found Mysore very strange.

> There was considerable industry and railway workshops in Bangalore. My only judicial work was in the children's court. I found that I could give naughty boys the cane, and after one or two canings which no English public school boy would have regarded as in the least severe, the children's court came to be regarded as a lion's den, and crime fell right off.
>
> I was astonished at how much paper it takes to fight a war. It just poured in, and we had to pour it out again. The work was greatly helped by the very high level of administration in the state: we simply did not recruit clerks who were not B.A.s. English was spoken by all educated people.
>
> The Secretary was Humphrey Trevelyan, a brilliant man. Once a

long despatch from the Viceroy arrived. Humphrey marked it to the office, 'Please analyse.' A day later it came back analysed with a suggested reply. Humphrey sent it back marked 'Please draft accordingly.' He corrected one or two words, sent off the reply and finally marked the file 'H.R.* may care to see this.' I tell this partly to show how good the office was and partly how confident and competent Humphrey was.

The Darbar supported the 'phoney war-effort' gladly and efficiently. A few Congress agitators were restrained, a few enemy aliens were interned, generally on the advice of the French parish priest in Bangalore. It was all very quiet, except for the rustling of files and petty correspondence.

Mysore was in the front line compared to the three Madras States, Travancore (nineteen-gun), Cochin (seventeen-gun) and Pudukotai (eleven-gun) to which 'Heb' Todd, after working in London during the blitz, was posted as Resident.

> We had a lovely old Dutch house on an island in Cochin harbour, dating from the days of Dutch rule – large rooms and wide verandahs . . . We had a second Residency at Trivandrum, the capital of Travancore . . . We drove up through attractive tea-gardens to Munnar, some 5,000 feet above sea-level, where we lived in a state bungalow on a pretty jungle-clad hillside. There was a club, a small race-course and a golf-course with proper grass greens. The usual round of social life prevailed.
>
> Luxurious, easy-going days . . . There was a hill-lake where we stayed in an old house-boat with a flat roof. We used to tour round the lake in this and had some very good views of wild elephants and bison disporting themselves in the water . . . To us who had come from battle-scarred London it seemed fantastically unreal.

It was almost as great a change for Norval Mitchell to move from Waziristan to Bastar State, as Administrator (because the Maharajah was a minor) of the wildest jungle tract in India, inhabited by aboriginals who were generally (but to the expert, inaccurately) known as Gonds. Previous Administrators had been I.C.S. officers from the Central Province. With one exception, these had taken the view that Bastar should be preserved in aspic, without schools, hospitals, police-stations, forestry development; the happy naked hunters discouraged from practising human sacrifice, but otherwise left as God had made them.

*H.R. The accepted office abbreviation for Honourable Resident.

Mitchell, touring on horseback, in bullock-carts and by elephant, found that Bastar was no Garden of Eden. Shifting cultivation – burn the jungle, grow crops for three years in the ashes, then move and burn some more – was destroying the environment, and decimating the wild animals on which Gonds relied for the protein in their diet. They suffered hideously from diseases due to malnutrition, especially yaws. The few schools and dispensaries which had been started did no good because the Hindu staff treated Gonds as sub-humans.

With the help of a resident anthropologist, Verrier Elwin, who had a Gond wife, Mitchell set up a few forest dispensaries and a few primary schools, where the emphasis was on teaching practical skills rather than book-learning; he compiled a simple primer of the Gond language and insisted that all Hindus employed in the state make some attempt to learn it. He shot some tigers which were killing cattle by the score. He noted, but did nothing to draw anyone's attention to, the huge iron deposits which thirty years later were to bring to Bastar all the blessings of Indian industrial society.

When the Japanese war started, he was transferred to be Political Agent, Orissa States, just where the Japanese were expected to strike first in their invasion of India. There was nothing to stop them. They had command of the Bay of Bengal, and there was only one Indian division to defend 900 miles of coastline. The Eastern States Agency, regarded previously as a backwater, suddenly became important. Through it passed the railways to Calcutta and Assam; one of its states, Tripura, was just behind the front in Burma; the Orissa States were the equivalent of Kent and Sussex in 1940. This large, inchoate Agency, with a multitude of small backward states and poor communications, needed a human dynamo to make it an asset, not a liability, to the war-effort. It got one in Cyril Hancock.

Mitchell and his Assistant Political Agent, Dudley Biscoe, did what they could to prepare for a Japanese landing, but it was not much.

> With the Diwans of the states we organised refugee routes, emergency food arrangements, a census of bicycles so that when the alarm was given, the police might remove the chains. There was a mixture of farce and good sense in this: a vision of a frustrated foe being unable to pedal away to the west, and a much clearer vision of local transport being denied. The state engineers prepared all bridges for demolition. Police made ready to sink all river boats.

For first news of a landing, reliance was placed on the chaukidars (watchmen) in the coastal villages. One of them, after refreshing himself too liberally with palm-toddy, did report little yellow men swarming ashore. The Deputy Commissioner of Balsinore spent all night burning the currency notes in his Treasury and dumping the coins in a well lest they fall into enemy hands.

The Rajah of Dhenkanal was to be arrested at the first news of a Japanese landing. Biscoe found him an unlovable character, steeped in drugs and drink, a known supporter of Congress. But Hancock, with hindsight, was inclined to think the Rajah misjudged. 'The fact that he was a Member of the Magic Circle who mystified cultivators by producing rupees out of their ears made me very uneasy.'

Some ass in Delhi issued an order that, in the event of invasion, all Politicals should stay put and collaborate with the enemy to keep essential services running: this despite evidence from Malaya and Burma that the enemy had no intention of collaborating with any British officials, only of beheading them or locking them up. Hancock treated this order with the contempt it deserved. He would, he informed Delhi, take to the jungle with as many armed police and aboriginal bowmen as he could muster and harass the enemy until he was scuppered. Mitchell (recently in South Waziristan) and Biscoe (recently in Fort Sandeman) went one better. There were in the area many Pathan traders and moneylenders, no strangers to guerrilla war and very willing to form guerrilla bands provided the Government gave them rifles and hand-grenades. With this proposal Mitchell and Biscoe went to the Resident.

> His receipt of my message was enthusiastic. His only criticism was that I had not proposed a scale of blood-money graduated to the rank and importance of our victims . . . Biscoe was sent in his official car, Union Jack fluttering, to the Fort in Calcutta to indent for our weaponry and arrange for its delivery.

The Japanese were held in Burma, their raids on Colombo were defeated and their aircraft-carriers withdrew from the Bay of Bengal. The danger of Japanese invasion receded; but a new peril loomed.

When Britain declared war on Japan, Nehru's first reaction was to be proud at last of being British. He, Vallabhai Patel and other Congress leaders would have co-operated against an enemy far more of a threat to India than Germany was. But Gandhi called them to heel. In obstruction and disruption and generally negative measures he had no match: it was only when constructive policies were required that his shortcomings became apparent. He scorned the British Government's offer of Dominion Status immediately after the war, 'a post-dated cheque on a failing bank', and demanded that Britain immediately 'Quit India'. He envisaged an easy Japanese victory, followed by Japan handing over India to the Indians – or, rather, to Congress. If the Japanese seemed disposed to stay, they could be removed by love and soul-force. Since the British did not seem willing to oblige him, he (with the other Congress leaders in dutiful chorus) launched a campaign of open opposition to the war-effort. It would, of course, be 'non-violent'. (In the Mahatma's view, blowing up 'small' railway bridges was not violent.) Like a long-awaited bush-fire, the rebellion blazed through the United, Central, Bihar and Orissa Provinces, and the Eastern States.

> Railways were one of the main targets. Stations were destroyed, signal-boxes put out of action, rails torn up. For three weeks rail communication between Delhi and Calcutta was cut off. There were some shocking murders of railway staff. Two Canadian Air Force officers in an immobilised train were induced to give up their revolvers, and then hauled out of the train and beaten to death.

An R.A.F. plane, patrolling the line, was compelled to ditch in a river: as the crew swam ashore, villagers pushed them under with poles. Biscoe saw the sequel.

> I found myself in a small state where a mob was programmed to meet next morning and march on the palace. I was able to wire Calcutta where Colonel Hancock alerted the R.A.F. A mob did indeed assemble in a large mango grove. While no attack was reported the air-gunners did, as was customary, test their guns after they were air-borne. By some sort of coincidence a number of men in the mob were wounded and the mob broke up. This was just as well, as we could have mustered only a total of nine rifles among us if the need had arisen.

After railways, police-stations and district treasuries were attacked. The police were amazingly true to their salt: Mitchell heard of no case of them surrendering, although if they were overwhelmed, as was often the case, they were burnt to death.

The first of the Orissa States to be hit by the rebellion was Talcher (non-salute). A mob tried to burn down the palace. The Rajah, a stout-hearted young man, ordered his twenty policemen to charge the insurgents and arrest the lot. This they did, but the jail superintendent refused to admit 200 prisoners to a jail built for forty.

Hancock arrived for consultations.

> What he said was in the highest degree encouraging: this affair was an

acute national emergency, and no officer of his need look over his shoulder at remote authorities when coming to grips with insurgents. He stood by this throughout.

Hancock returned to Calcutta, and Mitchell and Biscoe embarked on a four-week campaign, Biscoe first in Nilghiri State, Mitchell in Talcher. Mitchell had as his striking force a platoon of Crown Representative's Police (see pp.307-8), Punjabi Mussulmans armed with old rifles bored out to make ·410 muskets firing buckshot, fairly effective up to about thirty yards. The Subadar was an old soldier, the constables young and untried. There were also some thirty Talcher citizens, enlisted as Special Constables and armed with lathis. They recovered much of the looted railway property in Talcher, and then set off across the flooded country for a village where a headman had been murdered. They came to a narrow defile with a river on one side and a precipitous wooded hill on the other.

> This seemed an obvious place for an ambush. I therefore sent twenty of the Special Constables on an encircling movement to the right . . . Having given them half an hour's start, the rest of us moved into the defile . . . When we were half-way through, there came a crashing noise from above us. I thought we had disturbed a herd of bison and I stood uncertainly, waiting to see which way they went. Among the Specials was a Pathan trader, with whom I used to converse in Pushtu, feeling a friendliness for a man from the Frontier . . . As I stood, he pushed me roughly against the vertical bank on the inner side of the road. He stood over me, arms extended over my shoulders and hands against the bank, and told me to stoop. The flanking party then moved in and caught six men. My forces were too few to escort prisoners. Some form of summary punishment was indicated, and for this purpose I had brought the Talcher state magistrate and a doctor. The doctor examined them to see if they were physically fit to stand a beating. His approach with a stethoscope was one of the most formidable weapons in the suppression of the rebellion . . . None of the culprits, who had been rolling rocks down on us, received more than four strokes, and they were then released. The effect was immediate.

Biscoe noted that the instrument of correction was a bamboo cane, which Ooriyas (inhabitants of Orissa) believed would cause impotence. They were sensitive on this point. Young Ooriya women were healthy and strapping wenches; Ooriya men were weedy, feeble creatures, often unable to satisfy their wives. It was a male privilege to eat husked rice; women had to put up with the husks which, removed by parboiling in the form of a jelly, contain all the vitamins.

Word of their draconic measures preceded Mitchell and Biscoe, so that the latter stages of their march became a triumphal progress, 'with village musicians and dancers coming out to conduct us in through welcoming arches'.

For Mitchell the days that followed were very unhappy.

> After twelve years of working for Indians I believed that it was all worth while. Every district officer remembered the years of friendliness and trust. It seemed that this had all gone. The name of the prophet of non-violence was being blasphemed. I doubt if the prophet minded. We showed the flag by marching through the state. I recognised a Congress leader walking in the opposite direction. The hatred in his face was shocking.

Meanwhile the apostle of non-violence, with Pandit Nehru and others, languished in the Aga Khan's palace in Poona.

Mitchell acquired a second platoon, Sikhs. In one village where he was levying, Frontier-wise, a collective fine, he saw a constable breaking open a woman's money-box. He moved the men away and sent for the Subadars commanding them. To do nothing to stop the police looting would be craven; to act precipitately might provoke a mutiny, for these men were not proper soldiers, nor had they ever been subject to military discipline. He told the Subadars that every man must deposit his loot behind a clump of bushes. When this had been done:

> I went down to see the results. On the ground lay an astonishing miscellany of private possessions and jewellery. My inclination to weep was strong. The men had, however, been shamed into this surrender and I could now proceed to salvage their honour. I called the headman and elders and showed them what had been done on my orders; and I explained that all these articles might be claimed from the state treasury as soon as the fine was paid.

At the next village they got a hostile reception – drums thudding, conches blaring against them as they marched along a forest track. At the outskirts of the village they were met by a very brave little man, the sub-inspector of the village police post, normally manned by six constables but four were away on routine duties when the mob came roaring against him. If, as seemed extremely likely, he and his two men were to be hacked into pieces or burnt alive, he had resolved to die in proper order: his buttons polished, his uniform clean and starched.

> He marched up smartly to me and saluted. Behind him was the pandemonium of shouts, conches and drums. I was able to make him hear me when I spoke, but he was unable to speak. Determination to do his duty had governed his conduct, but he could not control his jaws or his voice.

Mitchell and his two platoons had arrived in the nick of time. Before attacking the insurgents Mitchell suggested that they shout their war-cries. The suggestion was well-received, and as they advanced they roared, 'Allah-o-Akbar!' and 'Sat Sri Akal!' He posted one platoon to guard his flank and rear, and advanced with the other.

> Our advance guard, four men, was moving down a narrow lane when the enemy charged. I told them to fire one round each. A man in the mob was hit in the shoulder and the rest withdrew. It became clear that a heavier attack was coming. I drew up my party in an open space and faced the mob which thronged the narrow lanes. Arrows, shot on a high trajectory over the houses, fell among us, one at my feet. Then they charged us. An aboriginal, fighting drunk, came at me with an axe. My pistol* was in my hand, my finger on the trigger, when the Subadar crashed his lathi down on the man's head. The Subadar had raised his lathi again for the death-blow when I came to my senses and jabbed my walking-stick into the ground beyond the man's face. The lathi, deflected, slid down it and hit the ground.

Mitchell had to retain the initiative, but had no wish to kill any of the misguided aboriginals. Realising that the policemen, wearing boots, would move much slower than the barefooted insurgents, he told them to fix bayonets, shout their war-cries and charge. This they did, and the mob fled.

He felt very bitter, not at those who had tried to kill him, but at the comfortable, embusqué Congress-wallahs who had stirred them up, seducing the simple aboriginals from their jungles and priming them with drink. It was the aboriginals, skilled bow-and-arrow hunters, who were the danger.

A group of villages in Gangpur State were refusing to pay land revenue. They were inhabited by aboriginals converted to Christianity – and to much else – by a German Lutheran missionary who had

*It was a ·22 automatic, a lady's handbag weapon, lent to him by the Rajah of Talcher.

decamped to the Fatherland just before the outbreak of war. It was they who had murdered the Political Agent, Reggie Bazalgette, in 1939 and maimed for life a policeman; it was they who had attacked Walter Magor a few months later. Their challenge could not be ignored.

Mitchell issued them with formal notice that arrears of land revenue must be paid, otherwise it would be collected by force. He obtained six extra platoons of Crown Representative's Police, and recruited 200 Special Constables. It was not too many to deal with rebels whose numbers ran into six figures. He also arranged for plenty of bullock-carts to be available. When the deadline for payment had passed, he moved on the largest village at night, planning to surround it as though in a Waziristan barampta.

> The Subadars were very intelligent, and the exercise went as though all had done it often before. At my end of the line we enjoyed a bonus. When the moonless darkness had absorbed us all, I walked forward very quietly to a small clump of mango trees, and saw in the starlight a number of men asleep under the trees . . . A few minutes later we found we had taken prisoner, in complete silence, six of the leaders of the rebellion. By the time we moved into the village it was daylight and our bullock-carts started to roll in. We seized every scrap of movable rice we could find, huge balls of rice, of a diameter of about four foot, confined in thick ropes. The Tahsildar stuck on each ball a label with the name of the owner on it and told them they could have their rice back the instant they paid their land revenue in full. The subversion collapsed.

It collapsed not only in the Orissa States but elsewhere: the rebellion was over, and smiling faces instead of looks of hatred met Mitchell and Biscoe whenever they walked abroad.

Thereafter Mitchell found his job as Political Agent, Orissa States, very agreeable. The rulers were decent men, but of varying capabilities as rulers. Good and bad, all were respected, indeed loved, by their subjects. Nilghiri State, scene of some of the worst troubles, had to be brought under the Political Agent's management, through a good Diwan. Mitchell hated to deprive the Rajah of his powers; he was an extremely nice man, with cultivated tastes and a special interest in Indian ballet. As a constitutional monarch he would have done very well, but as an autocrat he was hopeless.

> The interview in which I communicated to him the Government's decision was distasteful to me. It was made less so by his quiet and

dignified, even friendly, acceptance of the orders. He also welcomed the new Diwan whom I appointed.

Bonai State had an elderly, pleasant and hopelessly incompetent Rajah, but an energetic Diwan whose main interest was in primary education and children's nutrition. Every child at school, by order of the Diwan, had to consume every day with great benefit to his health a saucerful of cold, raw, germinated gram. The Diwan also organised the first agricultural show in Bonai, at which the *pièce de résistance* was the burial alive of a very holy man, and at the conclusion of the show the miracle of his survival.

A small man, stripped down to his loincloth, embellished with ashes and various pigments, and looking rather glum, was led forward. In a trice he was sitting in the hole. A board was placed over the hole, over the board was heaped the excavated earth to the depth of a foot, and all was made tidy by bashing with spades.

As the speeches droned on Mitchell became more and more worried about the holy man slowly suffocating. The Resident, Cyril Hancock, was made of sterner stuff: 'his facial expression was a combination of academic interest and a wish for someone to offer him attractive odds'. After a lengthy tour round the exhibits, Mitchell hastened back to the grave. There was no one there but the holy man's disciples, chewing pan and awaiting orders. These they very quickly received. The holy man was exhumed, alive but in a coma, looking like a boxer recovering from a knock-out.

The jungle-dwellers of Talcher State turned from insurrection to the more wholesome pursuit of the round-up of wild elephants in order to catch young ones for training. Slowly, over several days, a herd was driven into an immensely strong stockade. In among them then went a few large, tame elephants which separated the youngsters from adult animals and prodded, shoved and jostled them into submission, until they were led docilely away to begin a life of, one hopes, contented slavery.

Tripura, the most eastern of the states in Hancock's charge, bordered on Assam, and was vulnerable from the directions of Arakan and Kohima. Military and R.A.F. units proliferated. Tripura's own small but efficient state forces (the people were related to Gurkhas) were absorbed into the Fourteenth Army. The Maharajah, although zealous for the war, complained that the brutal and licentious soldiery, of whom not one in a thousand had ever heard of him, did not respect his susceptibilities or the dignity of his state. The Army, on the other hand, complained that state officials were obstructive. It was fortunate that Hancock had an M.C. and a good military record in Mesopotamia, where General Slim, Fourteenth Army Commander, had also fought. Hancock and his Secretary, Redpath, tackled Slim on the subject, and that great man, with all his preoccupations, said, 'Leave this to me.' It was just what Hancock needed. An Assistant Political Agent was posted to Tripura specifically to liaise with the Fourteenth Army, and there were no more complaints on either side.

The most north-easterly of the Indian states was Manipur (eleven-gun). To Edward Lydall, posted there from the Frontier early in 1943, it seemed like the Land of the Lotus Eaters; for although there were noises off, they were quite a long way off. That, indeed, was its attraction for the Political Agent, a genial and affluent bachelor named Gimson, who had selected it as a sort of Eventide Home for the twilight years of an undistinguished career. He was no respecter of persons: when Lord Linlithgow asked for a whisky-and-soda, Gimson, who had plenty of whisky but saw no need to waste it on Viceroys, replied firmly, 'I'll give you a rum-and-water.' On the other hand, as Lydall remarked, 'persons were no respecters of him. "Obviously 1911 vintage," commented Wylie with a sniff. "As cheerfully inefficient as ever," noted Lord Wavell.'

Lydall's job was the even less demanding one of President of the Manipur State Darbar (P.M.S.D.) The Maharajah, a rotund and moon-faced young man, had been, before his accession, exiled by the Darbar for attempted murder, having with malice aforethought cut down the tree in which resided his father's soul.

> He was simple and friendly, and as he was for religious reasons officially a teetotaller, he liked coming to my bungalow to drink tumblers full of gin, indistinguishable in the eyes of his subjects from glasses of water.

The state consisted of some 800 square miles of paddy-fields tilled by fairly diligent Assamese, and 8,000 square miles of jungle-covered mountains in the depths of which lurked more or less mongoloid Naga and Kuki tribes whose keenest wish was to remain out of sight and out of mind. The Maharajah's sway covered the plain, but owing to a past rebellion, the P.M.S.D. administered the hill-tribes. The state capital, where Gimson and Lydall both lived, was in an overgrown village named Imphal.

The Darbar consisted of six Manipuris, none of conspicuous attainments, with Lydall as President. Its writ ran only in the Imphal plain. Its decisions had to go to the Maharajah for formal approval.

If he failed to approve, I had the right of appeal to the Governor of Assam. This only happened once, when His Highness refused to ratify the Darbar's proposal to reduce the number of state holidays (about one day in three, plus Sundays) on the grounds that they were necessary to honour the 'sylvan deities' of Manipur. Gimson was able, however, to persuade him that in these stirring times so many holidays were inappropriate.

Lydall's portfolios included Revenue, Fisheries, Budget, Police, Medical and Public Works – a broad contribution.

The state income was about ten times what it had been before the war. With the Army established in the Imphal plain, money flowed in, and among other places it fetched up in the pockets of the dancing-girls. Night after night they performed at regimental parties, there being much competition among the troops to attract a dancer's attention by holding a ten-rupee note on one's head until she grabbed it. I calculated that the girls had each collected several lakhs of rupees, and assessed them to pay Income Tax. They were outraged, and some of them even went to jail for a day or two in protest before paying up.

(But Lydall remained on cordial terms with their doyen, 'the Divine Mambi'.)

His main duty was the administration of the hill-tribes, which involved much touring on foot, his baggage carried by porters. Disputes were often settled by a form of ordeal by water.

First the parties swore an oath inviting the spirits of the water to do terrible things to them if they were lying. They then immersed themselves in a river or pond, and the first to appear above the surface lost the case. It was an excellent system, and there was no appeal.

In Manipur the punishment for murder was by public hanging, and this, like much else, had to be organised by the P.M.S.D. Lydall fortunately had to arrange it only once, and it was a painful occasion because he had become very friendly with the murderer who, in prison awaiting execution, refused to eat unless he was provided with a plate. But the jail superintendent insisted that if the murderer were provided with a plate, he would cut his throat with it, unless, perhaps, the Sahib . . . So every day Lydall sat and chatted with the condemned man who ate, as he wished, off a plate. When the day of execution came, Lydall arranged that he be befuddled with opium when the drop fell.

He had, of course, many dealings with the Army.

> Colonel Holbrook, for instance, the cheerful head of 4th Corps Intelligence, sought my help in the matter of a member of the Maharajah's family, with whom the Japanese were thought to be negotiating. 'But,' I protested, 'he's half-witted.' However, I offered to let Holbrook decide for himself, and invited them both to a garden party to celebrate the fall of Mussolini. Holbrook exchanged a few words with the princely dim-wit. No danger from that quarter, he decided.

Lydall also saw a lot of the R.A.F., 'who would come to my bungalow primarily to drink but also to tell me what they thought of the Army'. These feelings showed themselves at siting-boards, convened to select sites for air-fields in the Imphal plain. Lydall's presence was much in demand, as he was not infrequently the only person present who was on speaking terms with all the others.

For some months these and other preparations for recapturing Burma proceeded. Then, suddenly, in March, 1944, the Japanese struck first. Kohima, in the hills ninety miles north of Imphal, was cut off, and Imphal almost so.

> Based on Arakan experience, 'boxes' with defended perimeters were established, such as 'The Keep' which included Corps Headquarters and the main airstrip, and 'The Citadel' which included Gimson's Residency, my bungalow and Area Headquarters. The Maharajah's palace was not included, so I invited him to join me. His Highness thanked me but explained that he could not move without the state Deity, a large block of wood called Gobindji, and Gobindji could not move westwards. So His Highness and Gobindji spent 'the Flap' unprotected, with the Japanese only four miles away. Each day I sent him a briskly encouraging account of the fighting.

With most of the state either enemy-occupied or being fought over, there was little administration for Lydall to do. Every morning he would attend 'Morning Prayers' at Area Headquarters, and on the way back he would pass a group of hill-tribesmen in his garden busily engaged in brewing rice-beer, known as 'zu', for distribution to the troops in the front line. With the road from Assam cut, Imphal was being supplied by air, and there was no room in the planes for a drink-ration.

Largely to maintain morale, the Darbar met regularly.

I particularly remember one meeting during an air-raid, when we retired each to his own trench in the compound, members taking it in turns to bob up above the surface to make a speech or record a vote.

Such was the renown of Lydall's zu that many military officers dropped in to liaise with the civil authority; including 'Paul', a colourful Field Security Officer:

'*My dear*!' said he, 'I don't know whether I'm coming or going.'

'What has caused this slight uncertainty?' I enquired.

'Well, my dear, a most *unnerving* thing occurred yesterday afternoon. I was ringing up Pat, the Assam Rifles Quartermaster, about some *squalid* matter of military routine – we'd arrested one of his Gurkha officers as a Japanese or something of the sort – when I happened to ask him what the latest news was.'

'Over the telephone? What about Security?'

'My dear, I *know*. Most naughty and reprehensible. But worse was to follow. "The Japanese," said Pat, "have just captured Wangjing."* *Quite* untrue, my dear, as you know. But *I* didn't. So I made a noise like a whole series of exclamation marks. "What's the matter?" Pat asked. "My *dear*," I almost *screamed*, "I'm in *Wangjing* myself!" Really most unsettling.'

'Have some zu?' I suggested.

'My dear, a tot *couldn't* be more welcome.'

He departed on his motor-cycle, and there arrived an orderly of the Assam Rifles with a note from Pat. He delivered it with a tremendous clashing of heels and a sweeping gesture of salute. 'The Sub-Area Commander,' began the note, 'in considerable perturbation, sings:

The cannon that boom in Wangjing, tra la,
Have broken the British front-line . . .'

I seized my pen and wrote a second verse:

The cannon that boom in Wangjing, tra la,
Have placed us in jeopardy great;
So I've got to take under my wing, tra la,
A most unattractive young king, tra la,
And Gobindji the God of the state.
And that's what I mean when I say or I sing:
'Oh bother the cannon that boom in Wangjing!'
Tra la la la la la.

*A village some twenty miles south-south-east of Imphal.

In due course Kohima and Imphal were relieved, the tide of war receded into Burma, and Imphal's day of glory was over. So, with the arrival of the first lorries of whisky and beer, was Lydall's renown as a dispenser of good cheer.

However his part in the struggle for democracy was not quite over. A special irregular unit, 'Lydall's Lightfoot', was formed from hill-tribesmen, to scour the jungles for Japanese stragglers. Generous rewards were offered for any brought back alive. None was – only a number of shrivelled yellow ears, in matchboxes.

The operations of Chinese–American forces in the extreme north of Burma resulted in one of the most bizarre tasks ever given to a Political officer. The authorities were horrified to discover that Chinese officers carried maps which showed the border between India and China (including Tibet, over which the Chinese claimed suzerainty) well south of the MacMahon Line negotiated between the three parties in 1913, delineated in Delhi on a more or less blank map and ratified by the Indian and Tibetan Governments but not by that of China. The disputed area, which not even the most intrepid explorers had penetrated, had no value whatsoever, economic, political or strategic; but it was intolerable that the Chinese should thus annex it by default.

So in November, 1944, Major A.E.G. Davy was instructed to show the flag there and establish friendly relations with, and between, two tribes of mongoloid headhunters and slave-raiders, armed with bows and poisoned arrows – the Daflas and the Apa Tanis. He was further enjoined to announce 'that within an area where he judged our influence to be effective, all raiding for slaves and cattle must cease, and all claims . . . must be submitted to him'.

It was a project of the wildest fantasy. Merely to move through the country was a major undertaking, since the hills were steeper, the jungle thicker and the rainfall heavier than anywhere in Burma; and over much of it there was a heavy snowfall. The Daflas and the Apa Tanis, who had never before seen a white man or an Indian and were perhaps never to see one again, were by no means willing to provide porters for Davy and his escort of Assam Rifles, and generally decamped into the jungle on the approach of an authority of which they had hitherto been totally unaware. Davy was accompanied by two enemy aliens, an Austrian anthropologist and his wife who had been working in a neighbouring area since 1939. They were charming, and most helpful; and soon after the end of the war in Europe were arrested as spies.

Davy's four-month journey was an unpublished and quite pointless epic. In the spirit of 1845 rather than 1945, he submitted proposals for the construction of motor-roads and air-fields, staff quarters, an Assam Rifles depot, and for the enrolment of a porters corps. The Imperial Government, he argued cogently, should develop and administer the area as a buffer against China which would probably soon turn communist. Everything he planned and everything he wrote made good sense. But May, 1945, was hardly the time to plan and write it, and no one paid any attention to his advice.

In May, 1941, John Cotton was moved from Mount Abu to be Under Secretary to the Resident at Hyderabad when all the political drama of the 1920s and 1930s had subsided. There was no pressure on the Nizam except to support the war-effort, sending his state forces to fight, contributing huge sums for Spitfires and anything else that was needed; which he was very willing to do.

As Under Secretary, Cotton performed the usual magisterial and administrative chores in Secunderabad and the Residency Area, and in the afternoons did his share of the political work.

But early in 1942 there was suddenly apparent the prospect of a Japanese landing on any practicable beach between Bengal and Ceylon. The only division available to counter-attack was based on Secunderabad, and the Hyderabad Lancers were deployed to watch 900 miles of coast.

Secunderabad was an obvious target for Japanese bombers, and within easy reach of their carriers. Cotton, as District Magistrate, was appointed A.R.P. controller of the Leased Areas.

> We enrolled ex-soldiers and retired officials whom we trained to do the various jobs which experience in the U.K. had shown were needed. We created the necessary services – Air Raid Wardens, Fire Services, First Aid detachments, Heavy Damage Repair Units etc. The Police were expanded. The Nizam's State Railways helped with materials and technical advice.

He was also in charge of petrol and oil rationing; and by what seemed a happy inspiration, conspired with the local manager of Shell to make petrol go further by diluting it with 12 per cent ethyl alcohol, a by-product of the sugar-cane industry. The result was to bring all motor transport to a halt: 12 per cent was too much. Eventually, by trial and error, they found that 8 per cent was about right.

When the Congress 'Quit India' rebellion blazed up, there was rioting in Secunderabad where Hindus were in a large majority. The Superintendent of Police asked Cotton to come at once.

> The students were on the rampage. They had attacked the teaching staff, and now they had taken to the streets and were inciting people to join them. There were acts of violence all over the city – point-duty policemen attacked, shops looted, pedestrians molested and motorists stoned. On the first day a number of students were arrested, and released after schoolboy chastisement. They gave no more trouble, but the criminal element in the bazaars were harder to deal with. Rioting went on for several days and the Secunderabad police were becoming exhausted as incidents multiplied in different areas. We requisitioned for them the motor transport of the Civil Defence Services. Finally I obtained reinforcements from the Hyderabad City Police, under their Inspector General. These Moslem policemen stood no nonsense from Hindu mobs. When about 10,000 defied them in the main street and from the roof-tops, hurling down brick-bats, the I.G. ordered the police to fire tear-gas containers into the rear of the mob, and then drove those in front back on the smoke. When a similar situation developed in a side-street, I was with a small force of police armed with lathis only. Behind me, however, we had half a dozen armed police. After lathi charges had failed to disperse the mob, I read the Riot Act. The Superintendent then brought up the armed police and ordered them to load. Seeing that we meant business, the mob began to back away, thus averting a very ticklish situation.

They never had to ask for military help, and soon the trouble subsided.

Jack Bazalgette, on returning from the Gulf, was lucky in his posting as Under Secretary (and soon Secretary too, the posts being combined) to the Resident for Kolhapur and the Deccan States. Kolhapur, his headquarters, was a nineteen-gun Mahratta state with a population of 1 million, the ruler of which, Rajaram Maharaj, enjoyed great prestige as the direct descendant of the Mahratta national hero, Shivaji. There were seventeen smaller states in the Agency.

Kolhapur, 2,000 feet above sea-level, had an equable climate.

> When we arrived, it was a blaze of colour. Every road seemed to be an avenue of trees in full bloom; the umbrella-shaped 'Gold Mohur' with blossoms varying from golden yellow to flame, the blue Jacarandas and the amaltas with cascades of yellow. Houses were covered with Bougainvillaea in different colours, and with Trumpets of Jericho.

As Under Secretary, Bazalgette had the usual hotchpotch of chores – Administrator and Magistrate for the 2-square-mile Residency Area, Treasury Officer for the region's reserve of currency notes, rupees, postage and revenue stamps. Every morning he was also a soldier again.

The Kolhapur Infantry, 600 strong, was a nice set of middle-aged Mahratta gentlemen; their drill and turn-out were impeccable; they performed perfectly their duties on ceremonial parades and state occasions; they made themselves useful about the palace gardens. Their military potential was rather less than that of the Yeomen of the Guard. The descendant of Shivaji longed for them to go to the war, but they were simply not able for it. So the state raised a Motor Transport Company, which did well in the Middle East. But His Highness was determined to contribute fighting troops, and so badgered the authorities that Bazalgette was told to get on with raising a new, active service battalion, the Rajaram Rifles. There were no officers to spare for this: Bazalgette must do the best he could, bricks without straw.

There was, however, plenty of enthusiasm. Recruits poured in, and the Diwan detailed as officers a number of university students, militarily ignorant but desperately keen. Bazalgette felt it was:

> essential to teach these youngsters at once that an officer's job is not to stand about and look handsome in a smart uniform, but to be ready to tackle anything the troops had to do. For this I had to give a lead myself, so my routine started before dawn, cycling two miles to their camp to be on P.T. or drill parade, to take a cross-country run, followed by musketry or simple tactical exercises till mid-day, when I cycled home to lunch, and an afternoon's work in the regimental or Residency office, sometimes until 8 or 9 at night.

A considerable problem was feeding the Rajaram Rifles, with wartime prices steadily rising and no rations from the Indian Government. Bazalgette had an idea, though. One of the state's expenses was for fuel to burn garbage and nightsoil. Why burn it? Compost it, and grow vegetables for the Rifles. At first there was opposition from the state authorities. The whole idea was simply disgusting! But Bazalgette pressed on regardless, and was soon turning out, on an experimental scale, clean, dry, powder compost, quite without smell. The results, in the regimental vegetable gardens, were phenomenal:

> sugar-cane as thick as your wrist where before it had been only finger-thick . . . Once we had our sweepers trained, the Diwan had

them train the Kolhapur City sweepers, and within a year the Municipality was making Rs 100,000 from the sale of the garbage of a city of 100,000 inhabitants.

As for the Rajaram Rifles, the Inspector General of Indian state forces was so impressed that he provided regular Indian Army officers to take over from Bazalgette and complete their training for active service. Bazalgette was not allowed to accompany them overseas, but is proud that they are now a regular battalion of the Indian Army.

As the Japanese drew closer, many rich Bombay businessmen evacuated themselves to (and, indeed, in) Kolhapur, where they felt safer than within gun-range of the sea. They were known derisively as the 'Jitter jees'. One, at the Club, was bemoaning a severe attack of diarrhoea, giving (as some Indians will) lurid details.

'It's all your fault,' said a lively Kolhapuri lady, 'you will listen to the Japanese radio, and look at the effect on you! If you'd listen to the B.B.C. you'd be as constipated as the rest of us.'

Rationing, propaganda and civil defence all fell to the Secretary/Under Secretary's lot. Among his odd jobs, though unconnected with the war, was taking an inventory of the state jewellery.

> 'I know,' said my friend the Finance Minister, 'that you are very busy, but this will not take more than two or three days, and it is rather important for us.'
>
> It took seventy-five sessions of three to four hours each, and upset my routine for months. Rao Bahadur Indulkar and I, with a trusted jeweller and a confidential clerk, sat in the Palace strong room. There were no safes or strong-boxes or even proper jewel-cases; but biscuit-tins, sweet-jars and any odd container filled with unwrapped pearls, diamonds, emeralds and rubies. Each item had to be listed, weighed, described and approximately valued.

Among the smaller states of the Deccan Agency, the most interesting was Aundh (population 78,000; area 501 square miles, much fragmented). It was unusual in that its Rajah was a Brahmin, descended from a clerk in Shivaji's service.

> The Rajah was a gentleman of the old school, a saintly man devoted to the welfare of his people. An artist himself, he had one of the finest collections of Indian schools of painting. He was a student of physical culture and modernised an ancient Hindu routine of prayer and exercise. Every child in the state had to do fifteen minutes every day

> before lessons started. I have never seen such splendidly healthy and happy children as in Aundh schools.
>
> When his eldest surviving son, Appa, returned from Oxford, the Rajah entrusted to him the task of framing a constitution. Appa Sahib's proposals were based on the ancient Indian system of elected village Panchayats or Committees of Five. The elected village head would go to the District Council, which would send an elected representative to the state council.
>
> There was an immediate outcry from neighbouring rulers of 'Communism' and the Resident told me to investigate.

Bazalgette immediately took to Appa Sahib, and found that his ideas, so far from being Marxist, represented grass-roots democracy, entirely suited to Indian conditions. Moreover, the Panchayats decided all simple law suits, civil and criminal. 'It is not easy to get away with barefaced lies in front of neighbours who know what has been going on. Pleaders and "professional witnesses" were at least discouraged.'

The Special Branch found Appa Sahib highly suspect, a rank Commie. He actually wore a Brasenose blazer and dhoti: what further proof was needed? He was admittedly a Nationalist, and might well have been interested at the start of the 'Quit India' rebellion if Bazalgette had not stood up for him. Proof of his quality was that he went through the electoral mill, from Panchayat to state Council, and inevitably became his father's Prime Minister. But he remained a Nationalist, and a sort of freelance supporter of Congress; and after Independence went on to a successful career in the Indian Foreign Service.

Rajaram Maharaj was passionately keen on anything to do with horses – racing, breeding, buying, selling and especially driving them in a four-in-hand over the rolling downlands of Kolhapur, in pursuit of blackbuck to be hunted with tame cheetahs.

> The vehicle was a four-wheeled brake, drawn by four horses. The driver and one passenger sat on a high box with a pilot close behind them, gripping a post and watching out for rocks, ravines or other dangers. Two cheetahs, hooded, lay beside their keepers on the flat deck of the brake, and the passengers sat along the sides, holding on for dear life as the brake crashed in full gallop across country, bucketting about like a speedboat in a rough sea. Once when Jo's parents were with us, her father found a nice, thick rope to hold on to, until it was revealed as a cheetah's tail.
>
> Several attempts may be made to cut off a buck from the herd before it is close enough to loose a cheetah. Then the brake stops, the

cheetah is unhooded and released. He jumps down and quickly assesses the quarry, beginning a fast stalk. Then he is off at over 40 m.p.h. He can keep this up for about a quarter of a mile, but that is about his limit: if he has not killed he gives up. He does not spring at a buck's back, but slaps his hindquarters, tripping him up, and like a flash is on to his throat. He does not draw blood, but has a stranglehold. The keeper comes up with a knife and slits the buck's throat, giving the cheetah a ladleful of blood as a reward. He is then hooded again, perhaps his coat is put on, and he goes home.

It is tremendously exciting. The thrill of speed across country, the skill of the driver, the *élan* of the cheetah, are not to be forgotten. But it is hardly an efficient way to reduce the depredations of blackbuck on the villagers' crops.

Among the amenities of Kolhapur were sausages produced on a large scale by the inmates of a Polish refugee camp. They were much enjoyed by the Europeans, and the Poles did a thriving trade. After a time some villagers complained to the Resident that there was a dearth of donkeys, the Poles having bought them all. Soon there were no more sausages.

The Resident, Herbert Thompson, and by extension his Secretary/Under Secretary, Bazalgette, were deeply involved in the problems of the Kolhapur succession, which were tortuous, dramatic and possibly homicidal.

Shahu Maharaj, ruler in the early years of the century, had one daughter, Akka Saheba, born in 1894, and two younger sons. Akka Saheba was the termagant, the rider, the pig-sticker, who married Tukojirao, Maharajah of Dewas Senior, and left him as soon as she had presented him with a son (see pp. 148–50). She returned to Kolhapur where she made herself a perfect nuisance. One day when her father was away on a conference, she said to her two younger brothers: 'Come on, boys, let's go pig-sticking.' The elder had a fall and was killed. The younger, Rajaram, succeeded to the gadi in 1922 and was still ruling when Bazalgette arrived. He had no children by his first wife, so married a second, and had none by her either. His efforts in that direction were not assisted by his sister's jeers at his impotence. Possibly she was already hoping that, if he had no heir, her son would inherit the gadi.

In great secrecy, Rajaram Maharaj's second wife was impregnated by artificial insemination, he being the donor. When the nine months were up there was tremendous excitement, guns and fireworks, parades and processions. Alas, the child was a daughter. His Highness was undaunted. 'Our family,' he said, 'always has daughters first.'

Before there could be a repeat performance Rajaram Maharaj developed a huge carbuncle, from the complications of which he died. Who was to succeed him? Succession in Kolhapur had to remain in the male line, even by adoption, and be confined to blood-descendants of Shivaji. There were three major factions. The traditionalists insisted that the nearest descendant in the male line, and of Shivaji's blood, must be found and adopted. The Akka Saheba, elder sister of the late Rajaram Maharaj, now Dowager Maharani of Dewas Senior, intrigued in favour of her son, Vikram Singh, Maharajah of Dewas Senior and a major in the Mahratta Light Infantry. (Despite a good war record, he had one drawback as an officer: the tendency of his Mahrattas to cluster round him in battle, to protect the descendant of Shivaji against enemy bullets.) Finally the Dowager Maharani and Regent of Kolhapur, Rajaram's widow, hoped that her daughter might succeed to the gadi, after a suitable childhood marriage.

The rival claims of both Dowagers were based on successions through the *female* line and neither favoured the traditionalists' proposal that a boy be found, and adopted, who was descended from Shivaji. (Dowager Maharanis often made a great deal of trouble in such matters. When the Resident in Rajputana complained of two Dowagers there, old Maharajah Pratap Singh replied unanswerably, 'Well, who abolished suttee?')*

The traditionalists had their way, and a six-week-old boy, son of a Daffadar in the state cavalry, descended from Shivaji, was very reluctantly adopted by the Dowager Maharani. Intrigue seethed about him like a witches' brew, and unprecedented precautions were taken against poison – British nurses and a carefully screened staff. The little boy thrived until he was five, when the nurses departed and the staff was changed. He began to waste away and soon died.

The traditionalists were overwhelmed by the general desire to have as Maharajah a strong man who would see Kolhapur through the difficult years ahead. Vikram Singh was reluctantly adopted by the Dowager-Regent, left Dewas and came to Kolhapur. So the Akka Saheba won, but much good it did her: her son ruled for only a short time before Nehru abolished all the states.

From April, 1944, until early in 1946 Norval Mitchell was Diwan in Kolhapur, fully realising that it was the twilight of the state. The Regent (the Dowager Maharani) was well-disposed to him, but took no active part in government.

*The ceremonial immolation of a widow on her husband's funeral pyre.

Mitchell took particular interest in the Public Health portfolio. His pet project was called the 'Village Sub-Dispensary Scheme'. There were scores of Government dispensaries, and those in charge were devoted men, although not particularly well qualified. But the supply of drugs was inadequate, and the 'doctors' (to give them that courtesy title) needed more help.

> It was a simple task to increase the supply of medicines. Villagers who wanted a sub-dispensary must provide a room, a table, a chair, and a cupboard with lock and key; also someone suitable to act as Sub-dispenser, often the local schoolmaster. The latter would attend a three weeks' course at Kolhapur, and then go home with an honorarium of Rs 5 a month, the key of the cupboard and a stock of twenty things . . . He would have been taught that medicine number 6 was for the treatment of malaria, for dysentery number 8 . . . Every patient had to pay one anna for each day's treatment: if nothing was charged, no one would have any faith in what was prescribed.
>
> The success of the scheme was immediate, and the demand too great for the Department to meet it quickly. As Finance Minister, however, I saw to it that money was available . . . When I left Kolhapur there were more than two hundred and twenty of these sub-dispensaries in operation.

He was also able to establish a leper colony in the late Maharajah's estate with 300 acres of agricultural land around it.

> One hundred lepers with their families, also often infected, could be accommodated, and soon there was a waiting list for admission. They could be cured in the sense that leprosy could be arrested by a drug called Promin, though there could be no restoration of damage already done. They always seemed very happy. I hope that funds were available for the colony's continuance in later years.

Funds probably were available. Whatever might happen to Kolhapur State, in his work as Minister for Public Health and Medical Services, Mitchell was not building on sand.

Bazalgette's next job was an extraordinary one, even by Indian Political standards: Assistant Commandant of the Crown Representative's Police at Neemuch.

Neemuch was an old, run-down cantonment in Central India, its empty barracks and bungalows dank and crumbling under the attacks of white ants; a depressing place.

The Crown Representative's Police was a para-military force of battalion strength, officered partly by Army and partly by police officers, raised in 1938 to cope with situations in the states which were beyond the state police but did not call for the intervention of the Army, and where police from neighbouring provinces, mostly governed by Congress, might not be readily available. The idea was good, the execution ruined by Treasury parsimony and the refusal to take account of wartime inflation. The men were disgracefully underpaid – Rs 18 a month; they were underfed – out of this miserable pay they were expected to feed themselves and their families; they felt neglected and disgruntled, for they were all men of martial races who saw their brothers in the Army being better paid, better fed, enjoying rapid promotion as the Army expanded, and actually fighting; while they rotted in penurious and ignominious idleness in Neemuch. Their Medical Officer reported to Bazalgette that they were suffering from malnutrition and vitamin deficiency; the Adjutant had to reduce the prescribed Physical Training because the men were not up to it; and there was not a single officer who would not give his soul to be somewhere, anywhere, else.

At least the malnutrition could be tackled. Bazalgette discovered that watered-down milk was being sold to the men by a contractor at four annas a pint: far better milk could be bought in villages for one-and-a-half annas a pint, so men were sent out on bicycles with large containers to buy it. Grain, too, could be bought much cheaper in the villages than from the contractor; and sugar direct from the Controller of Sugar. They had a little money in various regimental funds which, with the men's approval, could be spent on developing a vegetable garden. Their greatest asset was 600 bored, under-employed yeomen farmers, longing to get to work.

Among them was a water-diviner, who told them where to sink wells, named after the Afridi and Mahratta platoons which dug them. The Sikhs built a bund and diverted a small stream into a storage lake. The Punjabi Moslems started a citrus orchard. Large quantities of compost were made, to the annoyance of a Municipal Counsellor who had a lucrative contract to remove all the battalion's filth. Quite soon excellent vegetables were being grown, and the men began to look like soldiers. Bazalgette found it 'a joy to see the glow coming back to their skins and to watch them fill out on good food, clean rich milk and healthy work'.

Nor were they wholly denied the excitement of more or less active service. Two platoons did well under Mitchell and Biscoe in the Orissa States. A company also served in Khairpur, a state in Sind, in a dirty, brutal little campaign against the Hurs (see pp. 314-15).

As the Japanese were driven down through Burma, attention began to shift from eastern to western India, from war to post-war politics. Independence, Dominion Status, Partition, Federation were all in the air.

Gujerat-Kathiawar was politically a key-area: homeland of Gandhi, Vallabhai Patel, Jinnah; bubbling with Congress agitation; containing one of the largest, richest and most progressive states, Baroda, and scores of the smallest, poorest and most backward; ruled by some of the most dim-witted, and some of the most intelligent princes, including one, the Gaekwar of Baroda, who was in strong sympathy with Congress, provided he could retain after Independence his wealth and privileges. If Federation could be sold here, it could be sold anywhere.

Even during the war some progress had been made in that direction. In 1942 John Shattock, Secretary to the Resident, Western India States, conducted a vigorous campaign to persuade some of the smaller states to accept 'attachment' to larger ones. The larger, 'attaching' states, such as Baroda and Nawanagar, would take the little ones, geographically and dynastically close, under their wing, so that they could share Big Brother's law courts and police services. It was more face-saving to the 'attached' states than the more logical course of scrapping them altogether. But they did not like it. The Talukdar of Bhadwa (population 1,401) challenged in court his state's attachment to Gondal, the Maharajah of which, a Doctor of Medicine, had done so well on the Bombay Stock Exchange that his subjects paid no direct taxes. The Talukdar won his case, and the Mother of Parliaments had to take time off in the middle of the war to pass an Act legalising the attachment process.

But the war had still to be won, and in Kathiawar there was an embarrassing obstacle to victory. This was none other than His Highness the Jam Saheb of Nawanagar, Chancellor of the Chamber of Princes, nephew of the great Ranji, a favourite of many Conservative politicians and of the British public who probably confused him with his illustrious but devious uncle. In 1940 Worth, the Secretary, was told by the Jam Saheb's step-brother, Revenue Minister of the state, that his loyalty to the British Crown made it impossible for him to remain in his step-brother's service: he was on his way to Delhi, where he hoped for some job connected with the war. He gave no further details, but shortly afterwards:

> The Bombay Salt Commissioner told us that cargoes of contraband goods were being shipped from Porbandar [closely connected with

> Nawanagar] and Bedi [in Nawanagar] to Basra, eventually reaching Germany. It was hard to believe that the Jam Saheb could be a party to this trade, but a word was said and the trade stopped.

Probably more effective in stopping this racket was the British occupation of Iraq in 1941. But if the Jam Saheb could not better himself by trading with the enemy, the introduction of rationing provided him with other strings to his bow (see p. 311).

In November, 1944, there was a tremendous upheaval caused by the amalgamation of Baroda and Gujerat with the Western India Agencies. Cyril Hancock was the first Resident, and John Cotton the first Secretary, of the enlarged Agency. Cotton found Hancock 'a real live wire, comparatively young, but highly experienced. To me he was a kind and considerate chief, but he was a glutton for work and a hard taskmaster.'

This was just as well, for his predecessor had been that member of the Oxford Group who in Peshawur had left all decisions to God and a roomful of pending files for Herbert Thompson. God had been equally dilatory in Baroda.

The Resident toured constantly, pushing and bullying the princes to put their states in order in preparation for whatever might come. Cotton sometimes accompanied him, frequently by rail as the more important rulers had their own railways with their own saloons, which were put at the Resident's disposal. Even on tour, for Cotton the flood of files did not abate.

> Every day the office messengers would arrive from Rajkot bringing large black boxes stuffed with files and reports which had to be studied and minuted to the Resident for orders. In the evening the boxes would be returned with drafts for typing and instructions for the Political Agents. The next morning a new set of boxes would arrive. While the Resident was being entertained by the rulers and taken to inspect public works or the occasional shikar trip, I would remain behind in the guest room of the palace devilling away at the files.

That was the division of work: the Resident dealing with the rulers and influencing them in the right direction, the Secretary landed with the bumf.

Robin Hodson arrived as Under Secretary, straight from the Afridi Battalion. He found it all rather perplexing, especially the Food Controller's work. The state of Jawhar, for instance, produced surplus rice, but much of it was of poor quality. In normal times this would have been left to market forces, but now the ex-Adjutant of the Afridi Battalion had to conduct long negotiations with the experts in Bombay on the quality, price and quantity of Jawhar rice bought by Bombay Province. 'The ruler of Jawhar was obstructive and his Diwan a crook.' Well, well!

He was not the only crook. The production of ordinary white cotton cloth, worn by nearly every Indian all the year round, was restricted so that factories could turn out stout cloth for uniforms. It had to be rationed. The Jam Saheb appropriated to himself the entire quota of his state and made millions by smuggling it to Arabia where it fetched an enormous price. A heavy-handed ruler, he simply ignored his subjects' complaints. These, however, came to the ears of the Resident and the customs authorities in Bombay. It was a very serious matter which, if proven, could and should result in his being deposed. But the Jam Saheb! The sainted Ranji's nephew! The Chancellor of the Chamber of Princes! The consequences in Britain and India, the discredit it would throw on the whole princely order, would be horrific. Cotton, instructed to make a delicate investigation, found it was probably a true bill; but by then the war was over, and it was a bad time to disgrace one of the most articulate and influential princes. So the matter was dropped. But the Jam Saheb was mortified that in the Victory Honours List His Majesty did not bestow on him any mark of royal approbation, not even promotion to Lieutenant-General, on which his heart was set. Although His Highness knew well what Cotton was up to, and Cotton knew that he knew, the matter was never mentioned between them.

Edward Lydall followed Cotton as Secretary.

> The Resident, who was somewhat of a martinet, constantly toured the larger states preaching the gospel of modernity and efficiency, lest they be vulnerable to Congress subversion. Their responses varied. The Maharajah of Cutch, a benevolent autocrat, listened attentively to Hancock's admonitions and then made his sole contribution to modernity and efficiency: could not the Cutch Darbar be known in future as the Government of Kutch? This, after much correspondence with Delhi, we managed to secure for him.
>
> The Maharajah of Morvi had built himself a new Palace with an indoor swimming-pool, a wife on every floor and pornographic frescos on the walls. He had recently been warned off the Bombay turf for doping his horses, and his dearest wish was that Hancock should secure his rehabilitation.

The Nawab of Junagadh (whose Gir Forest contained the only wild lions in India) was very vulnerable, a Moslem ruling over Hindus. But he was far too shy to discuss these weighty matters with the Honourable Resident, and really interested only in his scores of gundogs, whose nuptials were arranged after all the genealogical researches, and consummated with much of the ceremony of a state wedding.

Not even Hancock could charge the Gaekwar of Baroda with being inefficient or obscurantist. Yet he was in disrepute with the Political Department for his matrimonial arrangements were untidy, a sure recipe for palace intrigue and dynastic troubles. Having decreed monogamy for his subjects, he took a second wife without formally discarding the first. The new wife was already married to a Hindu, and the most expeditious way of cutting this embarrassing knot was for her to embrace Islam and be automatically divorced. She then returned to the Hindu faith and was wedded to His Highness. He was most desirous that she should be recognised as his second Maharani, and be called 'Your Highness'; but at this the Viceroy jibbed, possibly under instructions from the brother-in-law of the Duchess of Windsor; so officially she was known as 'The Lady Sita Devi'. There was a golf tournament, at which Lydall won the Men's Open, and was presented with a cup by the Lady Sita Devi 'to whom I had to make a bow combining gratitude and non-recognition'.

Lydall still carries in his mind:

> such pictures as that of a cricket-match in which the Thakur Sahib of Dhrol took part – all thirty-six stone of him; and that of a musical evening when His Highness of Porbandar soulfully played the violin while I sang some Brahms and Lady Hancock accompanied us on the piano.

Hodson contributes an agreeable picture of Sir Cyril Hancock at a moment of crisis in Baroda. The Resident and Secretary were both away on tour when Baroda was afflicted with twenty-nine hours of torrential rain. The river overflowed its banks and water ran feet deep through the city and Residency Area; and from the menagerie came the roaring, trumpeting and bellowing of apprehensive animals. In the Residency:

> sofas, chairs, papers and all the contents of office, drawing-room and dining-room were carried upstairs by all male hands. The safe was too heavy to move. I told the servants to take their families into the Residency and camp on the landing and staircases where they blackened the walls with their cooking-fires.

The Treasury was locked and the key was with the Treasury Officer who lived in the city, so the currency notes, coins, stamps and opium had to be left to their fate. The bush-telegraph warned Hodson that the Resident was on his way back, but how could he arrive, other than by parachuting in? While Hodson was pondering on this problem, and wading from the office to the Residency, he was astounded to see the considerable backside of the largest state elephant rounding the corner of the drive and surging through water up to its girth. On top, in a howdah, like a reincarnation of Clive or Warren Hastings, sat the Resident. On the arrival of this dynamic *deus ex machina*, the waters began to subside.

The aboriginal Dangs inhabited some jungle-covered mountains in the extreme north of Bombay Presidency. They were animists in religion, worshippers of animals and trees, and divided into fourteen minute states each of which was governed by a Rajah or Naik, nearly all illiterate. When Hancock and Cotton went to visit them, they were received with great jubilation.

> Witchcraft was a tenet of the religion of these tribes, and one night we witnessed an extraordinary manifestation of it. Surrounded by elders in a jungle clearing, illuminated by the flames of a large bonfire, we were treated to a feat of levitation the like of which I never witnessed before or since. A youth in a trance-like condition was laid on a string bed a few yards from where we sat. The firelight was strong and we could detect no trickery. A witch-doctor, for want of a better term, stood over the boy intoning prayers and charms against a background of drumming and chanting by the bystanders who were gathered in the darkness some distance from the bed. After these rites had continued for perhaps fifteen minutes, the bed with the boy on it started to rise slowly to a height of about four feet, and there it hung suspended in mid-air. The witch-doctor, to convince us that there was no deception, passed the blade of a sword several times above, beneath and along the sides of the bed. We retired to our tents completely mystified by what we had seen.

All the Dangs wanted of the twentieth century was that they be left alone after Independence, as they had been before. What a hope!

No princes supported the war-effort more zealously than those of Rajputana, in money and in personal services, in India and on various fronts. The Maharao of Bundi won an M.C. in Burma, commanding a tank troop of Probyn's Horse. He was one of many thousands of first-class volunteers from Rajputana who fought Germans, Italians and Japanese. That was what Rajputs were for.

The same was true of the Punjab States – total dedication to the war-effort, and the provision of hundreds of thousands of fighting men. In addition, the Punjab was the granary of India, sending millions of tons of hard grain to less well-endowed areas.

But the state of Khairpur, included in the Punjab States Agency although it is geographically part of Sind, was rent by the bizarre little Hur campaign. The Hurs originated in the Sind Deserts. They were partly a semi-nomadic tribe addicted to dacoity (armed robbery), partly a semi-heretical Moslem sect, and wholly a nuisance to everyone in contact with them. They owed allegiance to a charismatic, black-bearded giant known as the Pir Pagaro. Like the Grand Master of the Assassins in mediaeval Syria, he commanded the devotion of disciples who would butcher with axes anyone he specified. The Pir Pagaro himself confessed to the policeman who finally arrested him that he had no belief in God; but many of his followers believed he was God. Once, when he was in a mosque and the mullah, turning towards Mecca, presented his back to the Pir, a furious Hur, brandishing his axe, seized the mullah by the throat, pointed to the Pir and shouted, 'Don't you understand that God is there?' No one dared protest.

From the proceeds of robberies, extortions, kidnappings, rail hold-ups, the Hurs had ample funds, with which they employed skilled armourers and bomb-makers. They were well armed and very elusive in their deserts, which they and no one else knew. The Pir declared himself an ally of Japan.

He evaded pursuit by dodging about between the Sind Desert and the neighbouring deserts of Rajputana, and a hide-out just inside Khairpur State. Conrad Corfield had just taken over as Resident, Punjab States, when he received a telegram to say that Hurs had ambushed a police party and hacked to death the Khairpur Chief of Police.

> On arrival at Khairpur next morning I found it a city of the dead. Every door was barred and every window shuttered. The morale of the state police was at its lowest ebb . . . A detachment of the Crown Representative's Police was soon on the spot to restore morale in Khairpur, but the Sind Government now had to face wider disturbances. The Governor had little support from his Ministers. They not only depended on the votes which the Pir could control but were terrified of the personal vengeance he might wreak. Lord Linlithgow then decided that the Pir must be removed from the scene.

The subsequent campaign took two years, and sucked in troops and police to the equivalent of a division, including parachutists, the Mounted Infantry of the Zhob Militia, a company of the Crown Representative's Police and, from time to time, Jack Bazalgette. In the end the Pir Pagaro was hanged for numerous murders, and no more was heard of the sinister Hurs.

The survival of the states, through some form of Federation, was a cause to which Corfield was passionately devoted. In Rajputana, just before the war, he had put great pressure on the princes to accept Federation, and with some success. Now, as Resident of the Punjab States, he returned to the charge.

Some of the rulers were beginning to realise that the war must soon end, and their troubles would then begin. To withstand Congress attacks they must provide services and development to compare with those in the provinces. But where was the money to come from? Corfield went into it thoroughly with rulers and Diwans. Most princes had considerable reserves derived from their family estates, marriage settlements and diversions from surplus state revenues in the past. But how much of these was properly the ruler's, and how much belonged to the state? In tedious negotiations with each ruler a division was made; and state funds were allocated for roads, education, agriculture and other development, or put aside for the future.

Corfield was less successful in persuading them to impose checks on their own autocratic powers. Long and hard he argued that they would have a better chance of survival if they did so.

> The general response was that the Paramount Power had made the treaties and must keep their promise of protection whatever the future position might be. I could hardly say then that the Paramount Power might be leaving. The decision had not been made, and the war which required their support was still being waged.

More enjoyable was touring on horseback and on foot in the twenty-two small Punjab Hill States – glorious, forested mountains, a bracing climate and simple, lovable people. Plans had been made to build a huge dam where the Sutlej river was squeezed into a narrow gorge in Bilaspur State. Its purpose had nothing to do with the people of Bilaspur: it was to provide hydro-electric power and irrigation in the plains.

> What concerned the Rajah most was the extent of the area which would be flooded and how many villages would be submerged. He

invited me to accompany him on a tour of those villages. I expected to be faced with irate villagers who had been warned that their homes, their temples and their ancestral fields were to disappear for a project which did not interest them and would bring them no advantage. I was amazed to find that they listened quietly to the Rajah's explanation of the value of the project to others with a resigned fatalism at the prospect for themselves. The Rajah was 'their father and their mother', and if he said it was necessary for them to move, he must be right, though they hated the idea. If he promised that they would be given alternative land and compensation, they trusted him to see that the promise was kept. No district officer would have been given the same reception.

22
The End of It All

With the end of the war, the Viceroy, Lord Wavell, had to tackle the problems of bringing India forward into Independence which had been left pending in 1939. He had repeatedly urged Churchill, who was not interested in India and had other matters to worry about, that some thought be given to this even before the war was over; but he and Churchill disliked and distrusted one another, and no attention was paid to his advice. When the Labour Government came into power in July, 1947, they took the greatest interest in India, but only in getting rid of it as quickly as possible.

The basic difficulty was the refusal of 100 million Moslems to be dominated by 350 million Hindus and Sikhs. There could be no compromise, no real shifts in opinion, since a Moslem could not become a Hindu or a Hindu (except in very rare circumstances) a Moslem. Since 1909 the Moslems had tried to ensure their political survival by separate electorates which would enable them to make up in solidarity what they lacked in numbers. This, of course, angered Hindus as tending to divide the nation. (Moslems denied that there was such a thing as an Indian nation.) In 1940 the Moslem League, representing the vast majority of Moslems, decided that their political survival could be ensured only in their own Moslem state of Pakistan, amputated from India. So how could they be fitted into an India which they had formally renounced? It was made more difficult by the personality of their leader, Mohamad Ali Jinnah, a Bombay lawyer. Westernised; prickly; quick to take offence; without an atom of humour or, it seemed, humanity; speaking no language but English and far from orthodox in his religion, he was a most improbable leader for a party of which the ethos was Islamic. But he was utterly uncompromising, he would not concede an inch: if Congress wanted freedom for India, they must concede freedom for Pakistan. The fact that he was dying of T.B. did not make him any easier to deal with.

The third piece in an insoluble Rubik's Cube puzzle was the states themselves.

When in 1939 Federation had been shelved 'for the duration', the position had been that Congress was immovably against it, fearing that they might be faced by an alliance of princes and Moslems which would endanger their control. The princes had turned it down because of the hostility to them of Congress, which would be the largest party in any central Government; and because they feared to lose the considerable measure of independence which the Paramount Power allowed them. The Moslem League was not much interested: although not yet committed to the concept of Pakistan, they were moving in that direction, and the states were an Indian, not a Pakistan problem. Conrad Corfield's appointment as Political Adviser to the Crown Representative in June, 1945, was a signal that Federation was again a live issue.

The Political Adviser was the head of the service. (This was a new creation. In pre-war days the Political Secretary had been head of the service, the Foreign Secretary his 'number two'.) The departmental hierarchy can best be shown diagrammatically.

Political Adviser

- Political Secretary
  - 2 Joint Secretaries
  - 2 Deputy Secretaries
  - Under Secretary
- Secretary for External Affairs
  - 3 Joint Secretaries
  - 7 Deputy Secretaries
  - Under Secretary

These were the denizens of the corridors of power. Naturally they attracted from officers in the field the resentment and ridicule that any headquarters staff does, but any officer with ambition hoped at one time or another to serve in Delhi. The qualities required were good judgment, which could not be developed without experience in the field; the ability, succinctly and precisely but omitting no major factor, to put a case for a senior officer's decision, and to incorporate that decision in a letter which could not be misunderstood – all according to a procedure laid down by Lord Curzon. He knew his stuff.

Corfield, when he arrived in Delhi as Political Adviser, had just been on leave in England. He was met by the Political Secretary, Cecil Griffin, who told him that relations between the Political and the princes could hardly be worse. The Standing Committee of the Chamber of Princes had wished to include on the Chamber's agenda for the next meeting a formal demand for an assurance that their relations with the Crown would not be altered without their consent, and a complaint of a recent tendency to alter them. The Political Secretary, responsible to the Viceroy for producing the agenda, had advised him that these matters should not be aired in public. So the Standing Committee had resigned.

It was time to mend fences, and soon after Corfield's arrival the Nawab of Bhopal, Chancellor of the Chamber, was given the assurance they wanted, that Paramountcy would not be transferred from the Crown to the future Government of India without the princes' consent; while the princes gave an undertaking that their consent to changes in the constitution would not be unreasonably withheld. The complaint that the Political Department had over the years whittled down the princes' powers was an old one, and not without substance. Corfield agreed that, provided the interests of the country as a whole and the people were not jeopardised, the rulers were entitled to expect Britain to keep strictly to the treaties; but time was too short to examine and re-examine every alleged infringement of the treaties over the last fifty years. Bhopal agreed to leave it like that, and the Standing Committee withdrew its resignations.

At the January session of the Chamber of Princes, the Viceroy again assured them that Paramountcy would not be transferred without their consent. He again urged rulers of smaller states to merge into more viable units, and rulers of larger states to govern more efficiently and set up representative institutions. Corfield caught the eye of a Punjab prince who smiled because he had heard all this before. Would they now do anything about it? Would they have time?

In March, 1946, a British Cabinet Mission headed by Sir Stafford Cripps arrived to expedite progress towards Independence. It was agreed that the Viceroy should set up a new Cabinet composed of Congress and Moslem League members; and that a Constituent Assembly be formed, on the basis of one member for about a million people, to frame a loose federal constitution for a united India. The Cabinet Mission drew up a memorandum as a guide for formulating a policy towards the States. This memorandum seemed to be an extremely important document, although it was later to be ignored by the British Government, the Indian Cabinet and the next Viceroy. Its salient points were: that Paramountcy could and would not be transferred to an Indian Government; that it was for the states to decide the terms on which they would accede to a federal India; that all rights surrendered by the states to the Paramount Power would be restored to them; and that, while negotiations on the terms of accession proceeded, there would be a standstill agreement on financial and economic affairs, including rail and other communications.

Corfield, as Political Adviser, had the right of attending any Cabinet meeting at which anything affecting the states was to be discussed. He did not feel this was enough; but when he suggested that there be a more formal recognition of the princes' right to be consulted, there was a stony silence from the Congress members of the Cabinet, broken at length by the suggestion that Corfield be replaced by an Indian. Later he told Lord Wavell that he thought this an excellent idea, provided an Indian could be found who was acceptable to Congress, the Moslem League and the princes. Wavell smiled and made no comment.

On June 10th the Standing Committee of the Chamber of Princes decided to set up a states' Negotiating Committee to negotiate on behalf of all states with a parallel committee of the Constituent Assembly the terms on which the princes would come in. The Nawab of Bhopal very quickly set up this committee of fourteen princes and Diwans; but the Constituent Assembly, seeing no great urgency in making things easier for the princes, took six months to set up its own committee. Negotiations were to start in February, 1947.

It was perhaps unfortunate that the Chancellor at this critical time was the Nawab of Bhopal. He was a very able man, and a good ruler, but his own position, as the Moslem ruler of a mainly Hindu population entirely surrounded by Hindu India, was insecure; and, although other princes greatly respected him, a Moslem would not carry as much weight with the Rajput and Mahratta princes as a fellow-Hindu.

However, so far, so good.

Meanwhile, at the furthest end of the political spectrum, Robin Hodson had in June, 1946, been rescued from controlling prices and rations in Baroda to be Assistant Political Agent in South Waziristan, the job he had always wanted. His fellow Assistant Political Agent was Captain Mohamad Yusuf Khan; his Political Agent was Major J.O.S. ('Jos') Donald, an officer deeply imbued with the traditions and ethos of the Frontier, of which his father had been Chief Commissioner. The Resident, Waziristan, was Packman.

Rationing of food-grains, sugar, cloth, kerosene etc. had inserted many new bones of contention into an area which did not lack them anyway. The system was to allocate a contract for selling (say) rationed sugar to one Malik: he would sell it to a syndicate of other Maliks in his own or a related clan; and they, for an agreed percentage as their remuneration, would sell the sugar and divide the profits among their clansmen. The greatest care had to be taken to allocate the contracts fairly – or, rather, in accordance with the Mahsud/Wazir ideas on fairness, based on the traditional clan pecking-order. Otherwise there could be serious trouble.

Pir Rakhman, the huge, bear-like Shabi Khel Malik, was bitterly affronted at not being allocated the cloth contract for the year. There is little doubt that he was responsible for a tragic series of events.

On June 21st a gang blocked the road with rocks and, when the Political Agent's car came along, shot out his tyres, hauled him out and frog-marched him off to a cave in the Shabi Khel country without his bodyguard lifting a finger to protect him. The news first reached Mohamad Yusuf, together with a note from Donald asking for food, whisky, blankets and P.G. Wodehouse novels, which were sent.

Packman then sent Maliks to the Shabi Khel demanding Donald's immediate release. They in return demanded 1 lakh (£7,500) ransom, and immunity from punishment. At a Mahsud Jirga Packman flatly refused to pay a penny or to make any promises of immunity. But these, as everyone knew, were the beginnings of a bargain. The Government would follow the procedure it had followed in other cases. The ransom would be paid, the victim released, and the Government would then recover the money, plus a fine, from the Maliks' allowances of the offending clan or, spreading its net wider, of the whole tribe. The wider the net was spread, the greater the satisfaction of the culprits. So the Maliks 'persuaded' Packman to pay up now, and recover later. The money was taken in sacks by the Maliks, who handed it over to the Shabi Khel. Donald was released, and went on a few weeks' leave.

The Mahsuds afterwards claimed that Packman *had* promised immunity. Hodson, who was present at the Jirga, was certain that he did no such thing: it would have been out of precedent and out of character. It was the invariable practice to make a clan guilty of such a fell deed smart for it – not in person, but in pocket. After due warning by leaflets, the offenders' fortified towers would be bombed. There would be no casualties, but a great deal of trouble and expense repairing them. It was also said by the Mahsuds that Donald, while in the cave, had promised immunity. This, too, seems unlikely. He and his kidnappers would know that such a promise, extorted under duress, would weigh nothing against the determination of higher authority to punish the outrage.

The question now was, who should be bombed? The rest of the tribe insisted that the Government's wrath should be visited only on the Shabi Khel. The Shabi Khel would not come in under safe conduct to discuss the matter but sent messages that the trouble was due to the misallocation of the cloth contract, for which they were not to blame. Other people had profited from this, so other people could now pay up.

The decision went against the Shabi Khel, and Hodson dropped leaflets on them warning that they would be bombed unless they returned the ransom-money, plus a fine of 100 good rifles. There being no response, they were bombed intermittently from August 10th to September 10th, and six of their villages were damaged. But they still did not bring in the money or the rifles; and short of a military operation, which was out of the question, there was no way of forcing them to. So, according to tribal and frontier custom, the tribe as a whole had to be punished for the sins of a few of its members. Donald, back from leave, by his handling of a very difficult Jirga, got the Maliks of the whole tribe to agree that the ransom money could be deducted from their allowances, and that they would collect the 100 rifles. It seemed that the whole affair was satisfactorily settled.

On September 24th, Hodson went down to Tank on routine business and breakfasted with the Political Agent, who seemed moody and depressed. While preparing for his return, he heard a pistol shot from the bathroom, went in and found Jos Donald mortally wounded. Beside him was a note, 'I have failed in my duty. I have lived a lie.'

Afterwards it was rumoured that he had committed suicide as a protest against the Government shaming him by bombing the Shabi Khel after he had promised them immunity. Hodson is certain that this was not so. Jos Donald shot himself through a misguided sense of shame – at having made a nonsense of the cloth ration, and at having been humiliated while his bodyguard stood idly by. He felt he had let the side down. His was one more name added to the list of Politicals killed by the Mahsuds.

In the North-West Frontier Province the Moslem League Government, unpopular because of rationing and its partiality to the 'haves' of Pathan society, was defeated in a vote of confidence in the Assembly. The consequent General Election was won by Congress, and in January, 1946, Dr Khan Sahib was back as Chief Minister. Almost the first thing he did was to transfer responsibility for rationing from district officers to Congress hacks. It seemed a crafty move, but it recoiled against him: Congress now suffered the odium for imposing 'controls'. Moreover, the people who had voted Congress in, largely to tease the British, now saw to their amazement that the British really were on their way out, and that they had saddled themselves for the next three years, if not for ever, with government by Hindus. Pakistan was now the issue. B.K. Kapur, one of the few Hindu Politicals who knew the Frontier well and got on capitally with Pathans, believes that, so much did they dislike the idea of Punjabis in control, they would have chosen union with India but for the thumping of Islamic drums. But in the circumstances of 1946–7, with communal riots and massacres down-country, Islamic fervour was bound to be high. Hodson saw in Waziristan charred fragments of the Holy Koran being displayed as evidence of Moslems being persecuted in Calcutta.

The centre for this upsurge of fanaticism was Peshawur. Cunningham had retired: his successor was Sir Olaf Caroe, as great an expert on Pathans (he published a book of Pushtu poetry translated into English), but perhaps not as imperturbable a man for the day when heaven was falling. The D.C., Peshawur, was imperturbable enough – Dring. It was reputedly the toughest job on the Frontier, with one division, Charsadda, a Redshirt stronghold; and Peshawur City a hotbed of Congress, Afghan and Tribal intrigue. But Dring had his relaxation. Norval Mitchell, newly arrived as Financial Secretary, went to call on him. The orderly at his house said, 'The Sahib has gone to the dogs.' For a moment Mitchell, whose Pushtu was rusty, thought this rather cheeky. Then the penny dropped: the D.C. was also Master of the Peshawur Vale Hunt, and had gone to the kennels to see the hounds fed.

Dr Khan Sahib would not believe what to everyone else was plain as a pikestaff: that Congress had won its last election on the Frontier. He insisted that if the charismatic Jawaharlal Nehru were to visit the Frontier in person, the situation might still be retrieved, the Pathans would be content to stay in India, and Pakistan would be aborted. Nehru was by now Foreign Minister of the new Interim Government of India, in which Congress and Moslem Leaguers quarrelled incessantly and could agree on nothing. Nothing loth, he announced a visit to the Frontier in October. One of the Joint Secretaries of the Department of External Affairs was detailed to accompany him: 'Jogi' Crichton had been Political Agent, North Waziristan, and knew pretty well what was in store. 'We're for the Death Ride,' he told Mitchell.

Nehru's party flew to Peshawur. On the airfield, behind a cordon of troops and police, was an enormous crowd waving black flags, shouting Moslem League slogans and well-flavoured abuse. Dring outwitted them by posting a large force of police by the main exit, and taking Nehru out by a back-gate to Dr Khan Sahib's house. The mob followed. Mrs Mitchell, cycling along the Mall with her baby in the cycle-basket, came face to face with them and the leaders quickly cleared a way for her.

At Dr Khan Sahib's house the mob broke through the police cordon and into the garden to make clear their disapprobation of the Pandit. Next day Nehru's party flew on to Miranshah where the Political Agent,

'Benjie' Bromhead, had managed to persuade a Wazir Jirga to meet them in his garden. Dr Khan Sahib's brother, Abdul Ghaffar Khan, opened the ball with a speech informing the Wazirs that they were poor, ignorant 'jungli' folk, and the Congress was determined to give them hospitals, and schools where they would be taught religion, and to civilise them. The Wazir spokesman, recalls Gerald Curtis:

> then replied more in grief than in anger that Abdul Ghaffar Khan had got it all wrong. They were a free people. They intended to remain free. They wanted no schools, and no hospitals, nor did they need instruction in the teaching of Islam from a man whose son had married a Parsee and whose brother was married to a Christian. This remark infuriated Dr Khan Sahib who called them paid toadies of the British. Whereupon they leaped to their feet and raged round the Pandit and his party. There was pandemonium. At the centre were the Pandit, Abdul Ghaffar Khan and Dr Khan Sahib, all of whom had lost their tempers, arguing with each other, and outside the ring were the Wazirs howling foul abuse.

Not without difficulty, the party extricated themselves and made their way to the airfield, whence they flew to Razmak, where Hodson, acting Political Agent, had assembled a Mahsud Jirga to meet them. As they walked to it, Nehru said to him and Packman, 'You're a poor set of men to be frightened by such spineless wretches.'

The Mahsuds found it almost impossible to believe that the British were being driven out by a bunch of babus, but they gathered in the Residency garden to hear what the head babu had to say. Hodson watched with some apprehension.

> It was customary to address a Jirga from a chair, the Jirga squatting on the ground in front. To my astonishment Nehru rose to his feet and advanced with his arms in the air as though addressing a party rally in Allahabad. When his voice rose to a crescendo, he informed them that he had come to free them from the slavery of the British. At this the entire Jirga rose in anger and Captain Mir Badshah's father, an old white-bearded Malik named Sher Dil who had certainly been out against us in 1919, advanced on Nehru with raised walking-stick shouting, 'You have the effrontery to call us slaves of the British! We've never been anyone's slaves, and we're certainly not going to be yours. If you ever show your face here again, we'll circumcise you. And furthermore, Hindu, our private parts are of extraordinary size,

as you will find out to your cost before long.' With that parting shot, still quivering with rage, he stumped out.

These words, being in Pushtu, were lost on Nehru, but not on Dr Khan Sahib and his brother. An elderly Malik with a henna-dyed beard, who had been in the Army and spoke Urdu, had come with a prepared speech and intended to deliver it. He got up and handed a copy to Nehru. Then he squatted down, adjusted his spectacles and began to read from another copy.

One. We don't know why you people have come.
Two. We have always been free and intend to remain free.
[And so on down to]
Five. We and the British have a working arrangement which we both understand. If we deal with any kortunai* it will be with Mohamad Ali Jinnah.

This made Nehru frantic with rage. He said he was more powerful than the British and had kicked them out, swinging his foot. The Mahsuds greeted this with laughter and the meeting broke up in disorder.

At Wana the Ahmedzai Wazirs refused to meet Nehru, but some of the bazaar Hindus, 'suited-booted', i.e. wearing European clothes, came out with garlands to greet him. 'The Wazirs with one accord ran upon them, scattered the garlands, removed the nether garments of the suited-booted and the dhotis of the rest and chased them back to camp.'

Nehru next tried the Khyber, and was stopped by an angry, stone-throwing mob. The Political Agent, Major Mohamad Kurshaid, at the peril of his life plunged into the mob and got them to desist, but Nehru's party had to return to Peshawur without speaking to a single Afridi. A single Afridi, however, spoke to them, an old man standing beside the road and jabbing with an umbrella.

'What does he say?' asked Nehru.

Packman translated. 'He says he'd like to stick this umbrella up your arse and open it.' But the story is apocryphal: it may be just another Packie story.

The next day Curtis, who was D.C., Mardan, was told to see Nehru through his district to the Malakand. They got there safely, and spent the night with the Political Agent. Listening to the radio, they heard Mehr Chand Khanna, the Finance Minister, accusing Politicals of

*A Mahsud word of contempt for Indians, cf. 'wog'.

encouraging the tribesmen to insult Nehru and deliberately endangering his life. Curtis 'looked at Nehru during this tirade and he did not seem altogether comfortable'.

Later in the evening he asked Nehru to come out on to the verandah, if he was not too tired, for a few private words. He told Nehru that there was no longer any trust between British officers and Congress. It must not be expected that they would stay on and run the Frontier for Congress after Independence.

> He [Nehru] asked how many of the cadre felt as I did, and I assured him that one and all did. That shook him a bit. Though he did not say so in so many words, he left me to conclude that there were no men to replace us. I said I could give him a list of Pathans straight away, out of my head, to replace us. Finally I said it was unthinkable that we should plan to insult a man of his eminence or imperil a life, the loss of which must embitter Anglo-Indian relations. He thanked me for my frankness and we parted friends.

Next morning Curtis was unavoidably detained and, through a misunderstanding, the return-convoy started without him. He drove very fast and caught them up near the bottom of the pass.

> The Pandit's car was stopped. Out of it got Dr Khan Sahib, his clothes stained with blood. I jumped down and ran to the car. Three windows were broken. The Pandit was cut on the chin. Abdul Ghaffar Khan had a cut on the nose. Dr Khan Sahib was waving a Mauser pistol. I pointed out that it was a mistake to start without me. I would deal faithfully with any opposition provided they travelled in a Frontier Constabulary lorry. I begged them to do so. They declined. There was nothing I could do but put myself in front of the Pandit's car and a Frontier Constabulary lorry behind it, the press in their cars next and a Frontier Constabulary lorry at the tail. We were still in the Agency and not in my district. A few miles down a party of men threw dung into the Pandit's car, covering the faces of all with it. When we were clear I stopped the convoy. A couple of cars containing Moslem Leaguers were passing by. As they would obviously prepare opposition down the road, I tried to stop them but had to jump for it. Out jumped Dr Khan Sahib shouting, 'Shoot the buggers! Shoot the buggers!' All the famous politicians now got out squealing with rage and saying I must fire on any crowd I saw by the roadside. Dr Khan Sahib said he was Minister in charge of Law and Order and ordered me to do so, and the Pandit said if we fired, all the crowds would run

away. What a party! I said I could not agree to fighting my way through a settled district. I fetched my lathi police and heard from them that considerable opposition might be expected on the road. So I determined that I would not move a yard until the Pandit, the doctor and Abdul Ghaffar Khan were safely ensconsed in a Frontier Constabulary lorry. They resolutely declined. I then, astonished at my own eloquence, made a speech to Nehru telling him what a fine chap he was and what international importance was attached to his person. It did the trick. They got into the lorry. Meanwhile an old bird with a long red beard arrived from nowhere and said he was the uncle of a Tahsildar I had in Waziristan. He suggested going across country by by-roads. I agreed. The convoy turned and we reached Peshawur with no further opposition.

Dr Khan Sahib embraced me on arrival and acknowledged that on the whole it had been better not to shoot. Mrs Khan Sahib emerged and asked me to lunch. I sat down with Nehru's secretary, a little black Christian from Travancore. He attacked our Frontier policy. He explained how Congress was going to win over the tribes by loving kindness. I said, 'I will give you a text from the Bible, yours and mine. "Let not he that putteth on his armour boast himself as he that putteth it off!" ' It closed the conversation.

Nehru had been led up the garden-path by Dr Khan Sahib. He had behaved foolishly, sometimes hysterically, but with considerable courage. By the time he left Peshawur he must have realised how worthless were Dr Khan Sahib's assurances that the Frontier was solid for Congress. Politicals, who did not love the Pandit, would have been less than human if they had not viewed his misadventures with equanimity, even with politely concealed levity. He on his side would have been less than human if these events had not fortified his hatred and distrust of the Indian Political Service. At a judicial enquiry no evidence was found to support allegations that Politicals had instigated the demonstrations against Nehru but Nehru continued to hate them.

Meanwhile Politicals carried on as though the show would run for fifty years. What else could they do? Cower down waiting for the end? Thompson, as Resident for the Punjab States, rejoiced in the good government of Patiala – all the better in that the Diwan had served with him in the Royal Flying Corps, surely the only Sikh fighter pilot on the Western Front in 1916–18. He straightened out, yet again, the perennially tangled finances of Khairpur. He worsted Pandit Nehru in a skirmish over Faridkote.

Nehru had a particular prejudice against Faridkote, perhaps because, being well governed by its young and popular Rajah, it did not tally with his ideas about the states. The railway ran through the capital of the state, within a stone's throw of the state Secretariat; and the line, with the railway station, was not state territory but part of British India. Nehru therefore ingeniously proposed to hold a public meeting in the station premises at which he would denounce the Rajah and all his works. The Rajah, wrote Thompson:

> protested to me. An excitable man, he threatened to shoot Nehru if he came. I knew this was merely an explosion of temper, but Sikhs are martial and passionate folk, and it was not impossible that some loyal subject of the Rajah might emulate the murderers of Thomas à Becket. Through the Political Adviser, Conrad Corfield, I urged that the Viceroy lay a restraining hand on his Deputy Prime Minister, as Nehru then was. After a gentle but unfavourable reply, I ventured to return to the charge. Corfield rang me up. We argued. Finally he said, 'I see you disagree with His Excellency.' 'With great respect, I do,' I replied. 'Very well, I am to tell you – ' pause, and I wondered what was coming, 'I am to tell you that Lord Wavell has complete confidence in your handling of the Rajah and leaves you to do whatever you wish.' But Nehru did not hold his meeting in Faridkote station. What a Viceroy to serve!

As often as he decently could, Thompson went up into the cool to see how Jack Bazalgette was getting on as Political Agent, Punjab Hill States. Bazalgette's was a wonderful job for the last four years, given him, no doubt, because he had been afflicted with jaundice and a gastric ulcer, and needed a job in a good climate. It was heaven to live:

> in a large and comfortable house, with a very rewarding garden, 7,000 feet up in the Himalayas, with a magnificent scenery of range after forest-clad range, and the backcloth of the everlasting snows; to have absorbing, interesting work, with authority which seemed unlimited, to do what I believed was right. 'Hill States' is somewhat of an understatement. These were truly mountains, between the Punjab and Tibet. Our lowest land was over 2,000 feet above sea-level, our highest in Bashahr State rose to well over 23,000 feet. These high mountains and deep valleys sheltered 31 states, each ruled by its Rajah or Thakur.

There were only some 30 miles of motorable road, along Kim's Hindustan-Tibet Road, opened to extract timber essential for the war-effort, such as walnut-wood for rifle-butts.

Touring was on minute hill-ponies, teetering along the narrowest of paths often across the face of precipices; or, more safely, on foot. Right to the end Bazalgette was urging his kinglets to share Diwans, or Chief Justices, or police training facilities; and to produce proper annual budgets, setting aside for their Privy Purses a set percentage of the state's revenue and not overspending this. And right to the end they obstructed any erosion of their sovereignty.

One who suffered greatly from a cash-flow problem in his private life made an ingenious attempt to remedy it by arranging for his state Treasury to be burgled and sharing the swag with the burglar. When this came to light, the Political Agent could only 'advise' him to go and live in Dehra Dun, on a pension, while his state was taken under administration until his son grew up. He thanked Bazalgette a year later for having relieved him of responsibilities which he found increasingly burdensome.

> The Divine Right of Kings had a very real meaning to the subjects of even a bad ruler, and I was impressed by the devotion of the people even in such cases. One of my most conscientious rulers chided me for deposing a horrible fellow who had gone beyond the limit of misrule. 'You must remember the Gods have made him Rajah, so who are you to undo their work? If he is a bad man, the Gods will punish him. Are you the tool of the Gods?'

Bazalgette may not have been the tool of the Gods, but he was petitioned by a Goddess, an experience unusual even in the Indian Political Service.

> She was sitting in her palanquin, under a very fancy umbrella, dressed in beautiful long robes and surrounded by priests dressed in saffron robes, standard-bearers, peacock feathers, fans. She greeted me respectfully through her High Priest. She could hardly do otherwise, for she was but a foot high, made of solid silver. She complained that the Rajah had stolen her water, diverting a water-channel which should have run into her fields. Would I please intervene, since the Rajah was under the influence of the state Goddess, a lady with whom she was not on good terms. I made notes and promised a personal investigation.

In most states the state Goddess was accommodated on the top floor of a squat tower which was the Rajah's palace. In this one building was concentrated all the authority, temporal and spiritual, of the state. On the first floor were the police-station and jail; on the second, the Treasury and law courts; on the third, the Rajah himself. And the ground floor was crammed every night with cattle, sheep and goats, an effective form of central heating but conducive to the spread of tuberculosis. In one state the Goddess forbade the drinking of milk. All must be given to her. The priests made it into butter and ghi, which they sold on her behalf. 'I am sure that some early priest had realised the connection between cow's milk and tuberculosis.'

Bazalgette's heart was set on getting the little Rajahs to combine and form a Hill States Confederation. He nearly succeeded, but Congress scotched that idea, bullying and bribing each in turn, persuading them that their best chance of survival was immediate surrender.

The last Resident in Udaipur was George Kirkbride. He was usually accompanied on tour by his wife, Nancy, and his 20-year-old daughter, Mary, for whom this was a wonderful experience after the monotony of wartime rural England, living with grandparents and training as a nurse.

> A tour started very early in the morning, while it was still cool. First the Green Bus set off, carrying servants, Dad's camp clerk with files and typewriter, a couple of chuprassis (office messengers) gloriously attired in red serge gowns, gold cummerbunds and snow-white turbans. Then Mum and I, wearing bush hats (never topis) and sensible khaki trousers and shirts, would take our seats in the open Chev. Not until Dad came down the front steps did the driver whip the khaki cover off the Union Jack on the bonnet, with a glance at us that said, '*You're* not entitled to this!'
>
> The roads were awful, with red dust settling on us from above or billowing up through the floor. Any driver coming towards us, seeing the Union Jack, would stop so that we did not get his dust, and we would slow down so that he did not get ours. The little wooded hills and valleys were lovely, and even the stony deserts had a stark beauty.
>
> About mid-day we would arrive at the place chosen for lunch, a shady mango-grove perhaps, or beside a pretty jheel. There would be carpets laid out for us to sit on, a white table-cloth and food nearly ready.
>
> Then on through the hot, drowsy afternoon, to arrive at our destination about tea-time. It might be a dak bungalow, where the servants would have the floors swept, the beds made and tea ready.

After tea we rambled with the dogs through the jungle, or beside a jheel, carrying binoculars for bird-watching, and a gun to shoot something for the pot.

If we were spending the night with a ruler or one of the Thakurs (feudal nobles) our host would meet us three or four miles outside the town with a motorcade of hangers-on. There would be a flurry of greetings and we would drive on, Dad in the front car with our host, Mum and I eating dust behind. We always had to change for dinner, Dad into a dinner-jacket, Mum and I into long dresses. The food was seldom good, unless we had remembered to ask for Indian food, when it was delicious. The men generally talked politics or shooting, not much catch for me.

After dinner Mum and I had to pay our obligatory visit to the ladies in their zenana, rather an ordeal as they were generally very shy and spoke only the most rustic Hindi which we could not understand. Occasionally there would be one who had come out of purdah in Delhi or Bombay (never in Udaipur) and spoke Urdu, or even English. The topic of conversation would then be children, and the misfortune of my not being married. They were always beautifully dressed in glittering saris and jewels. I greatly admired their small-boned grace and pale skins, but some looked as though they could do with a brisk walk.

Kirkbride had considerable difficulty in discovering what, if anything, was being done in the way of development in Mewar, the most conservative and feudal of Rajput States. 'The annual administration report for which one waits with hope sadly deferred would show that something was being done somewhere. As it is, one has to find out by devious methods.' However, by 'hard pounding' he persuaded the improvident Darbar to accumulate three months' reserve of grain for Udaipur City.

There was potential wealth in minerals, and embryo industrial development.

At Zawar the lead and zinc mine is now in the hands of a private company. I was able to visit the mine with the Government of India's geological expert, and it does appear that as a long-term proposition it is one of the state's more valuable assets. In the flat lands of the north-east an enterprising Marwari has accepted my geologist's tip and found fairly good emeralds. The emeralds were found in mica which far exceeds lead and zinc in its commercial possibilities. Central Mewar is a-glitter with mica, transported to the factory by

> bullock-cart, and the profits are immense. But where there is mica, there is sweated labour.

Sweated, that is, in terms of wages, but the working conditions were not bad, as good light was essential. Mary watched the women workers:

> sitting on cool and pleasant verandahs, paring pieces of mica in the first stage before it went to more experienced workers to be separated. It looks like a piece of thick, muddy-coloured talc, some of the pieces about six by eight inches. They are separated by a fine, knifelike tool into infinitely thin strips. Very trying for the eyes, which is why it must be done in light, open verandahs.

There was a mill for spinning and weaving locally grown cotton. It had only recently come under control of a (state) Factory Act, which allowed children of twelve to work nine hours a day for six days a week.

> For this they get twenty-two rupees a month. Their fathers can get as much as sixty and their mothers thirty. So a family can do quite well provided the small matter of education is abandoned. A sense of historical perspective may however be retained by reading the Report on the Employment of Children in England in the year 1842. In comparison, the present conditions of child-labour in Mewar are enviable. Nevertheless this is Mewar's danger-spot, the place where industrial reform, however unwilling, is finding its starting-place.
>
> As for the medical services, it is best not to dwell on them, for it does one no good. The T.B. Hospital is the Belsen of Udaipur. It is a dreadful place. Although only five miles from the capital, it is short of milk, devoid of transport, and supervised by a medico on whom Quincey's opium-eater would have nothing. I protested, not for the first time, and chose the Development Minister as my target. As, however, he has never seen it, the conversation was one-sided.
>
> About the roads I will say as little as possible, for I have already said enough. On my present tour I was accompanied by an officer of the Colonial Service who had spent many years in West Africa. At the end of our first day of 120 miles he said, 'Well, I am thankful we do not have to travel like this in Africa. If this is your usual experience no one could call you pampered.'

In this state, still largely feudal in its structure, local government was mainly in the hands of the First Class Nobles holding their lands directly from the Maharana, such as the Thakur of Badnor. Kirkbride noted less than half a dozen prisoners in the Badnor lock-up, and a police force of only thirty-five – arguments that there was no law and order problem. Conditions in the hospital were grim, but the doctor, who had served in both world wars, was obviously well-liked; and in the school were forty clean little boys and girls, all polished up for the occasion, 'but it was easy to make them laugh and I do not think their fat stomachs were due to spleen'.

> We saw the Thakur among his people, and those who spend their time abolishing these relics of a feudal age would have had to think again could they have seen the friendly relations between master and man or have understood the amiable and quiet-voiced discussions about water and all that that implies.

The most ancient place in Mewar was Nagda. There was a very old Jain temple, with a huge, gleaming, black god, Santinath. It was, Mary noted:

> made of smooth black marble and gives a great feeling of repose. Long, smooth, black limbs beautifully modelled, and an open, slightly smiling face. I thought the very red lips disarming. On Santinath's either sides are white images apparently of women: the left one peeps coyly from the corners of her eyes, while the other surveys the world with widely smiling mouth and laughing eyes.

Their favourite tour was to Dungarpur whose Maharawal was their friend. The state was well-governed by him and his Diwan, who was his brother, Virbadra, an Oxford graduate. There was, of course, a panther shoot.

> [Mary] was in a machan with Virbadra who fortunately did not expect one to take a very intelligent interest in the shoot. When the sun went off the machan we had an hour of bird-watching. We saw Common Ioras so big and brilliant that we had to think twice before deciding that they were Ioras at all, and lots of lovely Grey Tits, White Bellied Minivets, White Bellied Drongos, and a Horned Eagle I had not seen before. I could have stayed there for hours.
>
> The palace is built round a central courtyard in the midst of which is the Palace of One Room. The courtyard is mainly of white marble but all the carvings of the Gods and some really human animals and flowers are done on slabs of grey stone, and there is some pink stone worked in somewhere. Up steep narrow old stairs was the nuptial chamber where the girls of the Dungarpur house spend their wedding night. This room is fun. One little alcove was decorated entirely with

114 willow-pattern plates let into the wall. The rest of the room was coloured glass mosaic and lacquer work, mostly of lotus design. There were two enormous silver chairs and a silver bed hung from the ceiling like a cot. The best things were some exquisite old Rajput pictures. H.H. showed us an emerald lingam the size of a small bird's egg, in an exquisite gold tassie set with rubies and white sapphires.

At dinner Dungarpur could talk of nothing but politics, which was understandable enough in those days. Intelligent and articulate, he was dedicated to the concept of a bloc of states, reaching to the sea, strong enough to negotiate with Congress and secure good terms for joining India. Although his was only a medium-sized state, fifteen-gun, he took a lead in this. Kirkbride felt:

> that H.H. is getting into very deep political waters and that he and his two admirable brothers feel a chill wind such as they have never known. H.H. said, 'Well, we have had our differences with the Political Department, but at least we felt secure.'

Less serious was the Maharajah of Partabgarh, 'an inveterate boozer and rather an ass, but really amusing and likeable. His English is perfect and he is a born mimic.' He formed the Partabgarh Luncheon Club, with a tie almost identical with that of the M.C.C. George Kirkbride (who could also be a clown) had always wanted to belong to the M.C.C. but never quite made it: however, he did join the Partabgarh Luncheon Club, and wore its tie on all cricket occasions. It gave him the greatest satisfaction.

In February, 1947, the states' Negotiating Committee was due to begin talks with the parallel committee of the Constituent Assembly on the terms on which the states could join an Indian Union. But before the talks even started, the states' committee suffered a body-blow. Baroda ratted. On the pretext that his Diwan had been left out of the committee, he announced that he would join the Constituent Assembly and negotiate entry terms on his own.

He was at first the only rat. The other rulers stood by the Negotiating Committee, which extorted from Nehru the valuable concessions that he accepted in full the Cabinet Mission's memorandum with all of its implications, that he had no wish to interfere with the monarchical form of government, and that the states' delegates to the Constituent Assembly need not be elected: they could be nominated. He was to go back on these assurances, but for the moment he seemed to have made significant concessions. Having done so, he and Vallabhai Patel resorted to the time-honoured imperial practice of 'Divide and Rule'.

Rajput princes had never been conspicuously ready to unite against a common foe. Confronted by Mogul or Mahratta enemies, Rajputs had invariably turned to rend one another; and Mahrattas had no more cohesion. To Bhopal, Dungarpur and a few others, it was crystal-clear that only by sticking together and negotiating together could they extort from Congress terms on which they could join the Union without losing all their independence. But it was child's play for Nehru and Patel to persuade some princes, jealous of others, that they would do better to climb on the bandwagon now, rather than take a lead from a Moslem Nawab. Those most easily persuaded were princes who employed Diwans from British India, generally Madrassis, often on the advice of the Political Department. These Diwans might be able administrators, but they owed their masters only the loyalty of a hireling. They probably had some sympathy with Congress, and they certainly had an eye to their career-prospects in an India governed by Congress. Baroda had a Madrassi Diwan, as had Bikanir,* the next to defect. Bikanir's was Sardar K.M. Panikkar, a communist fellow-traveller whose ability, power of persuasion, drafting skill and Machiavellianism were to be major factors in the princes' failure to show a united front. By the end of April eight rulers – Baroda, Bikanir, Jaipur, Jodhpur, Udaipur, Rewa, Cochin and Patiala – had individually joined the Constituent Assembly. They were not thereby formally committed to joining the Union; merely to taking part in the formulation of terms on which they might join. But they destroyed the states' Negotiating Committee. Jaipur, Jodhpur and Udaipur also had Madrassi Diwans.

Corfield was as disappointed as Bhopal. They had hoped that if the princes as a bloc joined the Constituent Assembly, so might the Moslems who were holding aloof, because together they could match Congress. But with the demise of the states' Negotiating Committee, it seemed that the last chance was lost of preserving the unity of India.

On February 20th, 1947, Corfield went in for his weekly talk with the Viceroy. Wavell passed him a letter across the table, 'What do you think of that?' The Viceroy had been sacked, in the curtest and most inconsiderate manner, the public announcement being made on the day of his daughter's wedding.

He was sacked not because he thought the British could hold on to India: he knew, and had frequently submitted to Churchill's Govern-

*Not the famous Maharajah Ganga Singh: his son, Maharajah Sadul Singh.

ment, that this was impossible; but because he (like Gandhi) would not promote the partition of India. If Indians could not stick together, they must separate; but this should be their responsibility, by their own act, not by the act of His Majesty's Government. Wavell's plan was to hand over power province by province, with adjacent states; retaining power at the centre while details, including the position of the states, were being settled. But the Labour Government would not wait or retain responsibility indefinitely until Moslems, states, Scheduled Classes could be slotted into their places in a predominantly Hindu country. They were dead-set on quitting India at once, no matter what happened afterwards. Of course if India, divided or undivided, were to choose to remain in the Commonwealth that would be very gratifying, and face-saving; but, be that as it may, they wanted out.

They chose well their successor to that man of honour, Lord Wavell. Earl Mountbatten of Burma was a war-hero – or at least a dynamic and competent war-organiser, with a persuasive personality, great vanity, great wealth, mildly socialist ideas and a much more socialist-minded wife. It was a bonus that he was cousin to the King, and had known on the polo-ground many of the Indian princes or their fathers. This at first made them well-disposed to him; until he had actually done so, many simply could not believe that 'Dickie' would let them down. He was in full agreement with the Cabinet's decision to quit India as soon as it could decently be done – or sooner. He had a Teutonic inability to see the trees for the wood, or distinguish the path of honour from the main chance. Unity of India? Forget it! Treaties with the princes? Scraps of paper!

He was politically naive and optimistic. He hoped that, although the sub-continent might be partitioned between India and Pakistan, a tenuous unity could be maintained in his own person, as joint-Governor-General of two Dominions. There was never a chance of this. Auchinleck might be acceptable as joint-Commander-in-Chief, but he was the hero of all Indian soldiers, Hindu, Moslem and Sikh. Indians hardly knew Mountbatten.

As war-supremo he was impressed by the big battalions, represented by Congress. He and his wife took to Nehru, with whom he had already made friendly contact, and swallowed everything he told them. Nehru on his part found in them something which had been lacking in his life, uninhibited friendship. But in the ambience of this friendship there was no place for Jinnah, the princes or, of course, Conrad Corfield. As an Admiral, Mountbatten would never have tolerated any interruption or by-passing of the chain-of-command. But as Viceroy and Crown

Representative he brushed off the advice of his Political Adviser on the grounds that Nehru had informed him otherwise.

However, taking over from Wavell on March 22nd, he attended three weeks later a Residents' Conference called by his predecessor. He stressed the need for speed, and left them to their deliberations.

The need for speed was obvious. Most officers, military and civil, were tired and stale after seven years of war and political altercation. As soon as they realised that the British really were on their way out, Indians in every kind of authority (including nearly half the officers of the I.C.S.), patriotically wanting independence for their country, had also to think of their future careers, and the folly of antagonising their future masters. The confidence, the efficiency and the impartiality of the services were draining away: the handover had to take place while they were still in control of events. So the Residents' Conference worked out a time-table to withdraw Political Agents by the autumn, and Residents by the end of 1947; and to close down the Political Department by March 1948.

Meanwhile Mountbatten accepted the inevitability of Partition and prepared his plan to hand over to the two Dominions in June, 1948; which did not conflict with the Residents' Conference time-table. Mountbatten gave the states a low priority when he sent his chief adviser, Lord Ismay, home in May to put his plan to the Cabinet. Corfield, therefore, arranged to accompany Ismay, lest the states' case be lost by default, to make quite sure that in the Mountbatten plan it would be unequivocally stated that the points made in the Cabinet Mission's memorandum of May, 1946, remained the policy of His Majesty's Government (see p. 319). If Paramountcy were not transferred, if all rights surrendered by the states to the Paramount Power were restored to them, and if there were to be a Standstill Agreement, the states would be able to negotiate reasonable terms.

This was quickly agreed by the Secretary of State; as, with minor administrative amendments, was the Residents' Conference time-table. Well satisfied, Corfield returned to Delhi.

There, however, Ismay informed him that since Pandit Nehru would not accept June, 1948, as target-date for the handover, the Viceroy was flying home to obtain the Cabinet's sanction to bring it forward to August 15th, 1947. The new date was announced on June 3rd. Always the showman, Mountbatten issued to all Government offices special calendars showing the number of days left. This was supposed to concentrate people's minds – as though they needed to be concentrated.

Obviously thirty-eight days were not enough to settle terms for all states, amalgamate those too small to be viable, move British and Indian troops out of cantonments in, for example, Hyderabad. Nor were some of the rulers markedly helpful. Obsessed with the legal aspects of the lapse of Paramountcy and intrigued by the thought of being able to do as they pleased after August 14th, they could not be made to see that there were economic and geographic compulsions upon them far more potent than the limitations of Paramountcy. No Indian Government could permit innumerable little Alsatias inside India. Their only chance was to form blocs able to negotiate from strength and to withstand economic and military pressure. One bloc comprising the states of Rajputana, the western part of Central India, Gujerat and Kathiawar would have had respectable economic and military resources and, above all, access to the sea, besides being astride the railways from Bombay to the north-east. But this Nehru was determined to prevent, and already some of the key rulers and Diwans had been got at. By the end of July, forty-three individual states had joined the Constituent Assembly. The Maharajahs of Bikanir and Patiala, with all the proselytising zeal of recent converts, urged their fellow-princes to do likewise as 'Dickie' would never let them down.

Pandit Nehru's hostility, and his readiness to renege on previous undertakings, is made clear (though his exact words were disputed) in a letter from Mountbatten to Corfield dated April 22nd:

> [Pandit Nehru] said he wished to make it clear that he had been misquoted in the newspapers, since the tenor of his remarks was not that he threatened rulers that they would be regarded as hostile if they failed to send representatives forthwith to the Constituent Assembly, but that the failure of rulers to take part in the Constituent Assembly would be behaving in a hostile manner. He added that failure to consult the will of their people in any way would also be behaving in a hostile manner.

The obligation to consult the will of his people did not, of course, apply to the Maharajah of Kashmir, whose people were mainly Moslem but ruled by Dogras and Kashmiri Pandits of whom Pandit Nehru was one.

Among the administrative details to be seen to before the end was the disposal of files in the Residencies and Political Department offices. Most would of course be handed over to whomever took charge – but not all. To be consigned to the India Office were those of great historical interest, marked T.H. (Top Historical) while they were being sorted out; to be destroyed were those which might compromise any living person or enable them to be blackmailed, marked T.S. (Top Secret).

There was in at least one Residency a third, unofficial, category, T.F. (Top Feelthy), to be passed round officers (not, perhaps, the Honourable Resident himself) and then destroyed. Among these was an ancient file regarding a long-dead ruler. Loaded with honours and long past orthodox princely pleasures, his favourite diversion was an occasional orgy with his intimates, brandy and champagne flowing like water, at the climax of which all would get down on hands and knees, nether garments removed, with a candle inserted into each. *But only His Highness's candle was lit.* The game – an uproarious and very harmless one provided you did not get burnt – was to light your candle from His Highness's. In the margin of the file, in faded copperplate handwriting, someone had enquired, 'Is this the offence known in the Indian Penal Code as arson?'

Nehru, on whom Herbert Thompson could always rely not to check his references, accused Corfield of having all the files destroyed, but the altercation led to the convening on June 13th of a special meeting to discuss the states. Corfield recalled:

> I had prepared a brief for Lord Mountbatten detailing the points for discussion. He had hardly completed his opening remarks before Nehru started on a tirade against the Political Department, saying I was trying to Balkanise India and should be indicted before the Federal Court for malfeasance. I saw Jinnah looking at Lord Mountbatten as though waiting for him to intervene and protect his Political Adviser. But nothing was said;* until Jinnah could stand it no longer and pushing back his chair remarked that, if proceedings were to consist of bombastic speeches and unjustified accusations, the sooner they were brought to a conclusion the better. Nehru calmed down and Lord Mountbatten proceeded with the points to be discussed.
>
> Nehru tried to argue that the Cabinet Mission memorandum did not mean what it said about the states' complete freedom to negotiate

*It seems that Corfield's memory was at fault. Minutes of the meeting record that the Viceroy did intervene to say that his Political Adviser was doing no more than carry out the policy of the Secretary of State, Lord Listowel. It was, in fact, Mountbatten who was deliberately diverging from the Secretary of State's policy in regard to the princes. Listowel protested, but did not press his protest in the face of Mountbatten's argument that he was the man on the spot; and that only by following his policy could India be quitted with the requisite speed. For details of these events from Mountbatten's point of view, see Philip Ziegler, *Mountbatten*, pp. 405–9.

new arrangements as independent units. Jinnah took the opposite view.

Legally Jinnah was right. In practice, for states which failed to combine into blocs strong enough to resist pressure, that legal freedom was illusory, and could be preserved only by an effective Standstill Agreement honoured by the new Government.

The meeting then proceeded to consider how the two new Governments could conduct relations with the states when the Political Department and its agencies had lapsed. For this purpose, it was agreed to establish a states' Department in two sections, one of which on Partition would go to India, the other to Pakistan.

The states' negotiating position was compromised by some rulers fantasising about exercising their undoubted constitutional right, after the lapse of Paramountcy, to remain separate from India as independent Commonwealth countries. The idea was absurd: no Indian Government could have permitted the Balkanisation of India, and no British Government could have provoked the Indian Government and opened the door to the most catastrophic conflicts by admitting such states to the Commonwealth. Not even Hyderabad could maintain its independence for long. Equally fantastic was the idea that a Hindu ruler of a Hindu people (Jodhpur) could join the Moslem theocratic Dominion of Pakistan. Unfortunately a few junior and middle-rank Politicals, emotionally involved in the survival of the states and hoping perhaps for exciting jobs in them, encouraged these fantasies. It is possible that Mountbatten and Nehru believed that Corfield was one of these. The canard is repeated, in at least one supposedly authoritative account of these events,* that Conrad Corfield intrigued to take some states out of India.

Nothing could be further from the truth. Corfield's attitude to these wild projects is clearly shown by one off-the-cuff remark and one retrospective passage in his book *The Princely India I Knew*. To a gullible member of the Viceroy's staff who asked if it was true that Herbert Thompson had accepted the post of Prime Minister in an independent Hyderabad, Corfield replied scornfully, 'Thompson would never be such a fool.' In his book he writes:

> I have never been able to appreciate why Nehru was so afraid of India disintegrating if the rulers had *technical* independence when Paramountcy lapsed. No state could have preserved actual independence

*Michael Edwardes, *The Last Years of British India*, pp. 186 ff.

> for very long. The country had been welded by the exercise of Paramountcy into too firm a structure . . . Nehru was inheriting most of the Indian Army and Civil Services; all the Central Government's offices and the bulk of the industrial complex developed for the war-effort . . . The people of the states would never put up for long with any interruption of railway, postal, telegraphic and currency amenities . . . I could only conclude that Nehru's anxiety was not as real as he stated and that his true aim was to weaken the bargaining power of the rulers by securing new political arrangements before Paramountcy lapsed, so that the states could be more easily absorbed after independence.

And what the Pandit told him, the Viceroy believed.

Corfield was dedicated to a very different concept, that of viable states or unions of small states joining a Federation of India. To this he had given his time and enthusiasm as Joint Secretary to the Political Department in the mid-1930s, as Resident in Jaipur in the late 1930s, as Agent to the Governor-General, Punjab states from 1941 to 1945, and lastly as Political Adviser. Nehru, through an intermediary (and Mountbatten in Nehru's absence), offered Corfield grudging apologies for the monstrous attack made on him; but they continued to distrust him; and he, them.

Mountbatten still hoped to be, after Independence and Partition, joint Governor-General of India and Pakistan. Any prospect of this coming about was ended by an event which, though trivial in Europe, was far from trivial in India. At Delhi airport, in the presence of a large crowd including reporters and newsreel photographers, Nehru kissed Lady Mountbatten. The incident sent a shockwave from end to end of India. Indians do not kiss even their wives in public, and respectable Indian women did not embrace, in public, or in private, men other than their husbands. There was much speculation, not all of it seemly, on the significance of that kiss. Herbert Thompson, who was present, was sure that it was not merely social, nor did it have any sexual implication. It was the kiss of Judas. By it Nehru betrayed his friend, Mountbatten, deliberately labelling him and his wife 'Congress property'. Jinnah was appalled. If ever there had been any chance of Mountbatten being acceptable as Governor-General of Pakistan, that ended it.

The reaction of the smaller rulers to these great events varied from the Appa Sahib of Aundh who had already made of his father's small state almost a Congress enclave, to a Rajah with a small state and a large drink problem who greeted a touring Political Agent with the words,

'They tell me you're quitting India. When you go, old man, take me with you.' And promptly fell flat on his face.

Meanwhile, on the Frontier, some unfinished business had been wound up.

In April, 1947, Norval Mitchell, newly appointed Chief Secretary, had prepared an appreciation of the political situation, in which he stressed that there must be a referendum on whether the North-West Frontier Province would go to India or to Pakistan. He predicted an overwhelming majority for Pakistan. The Viceroy decided to see for himself, in a visit to Peshawur. A huge and dangerous throng of perhaps 100,000 Pathans assembled to demonstrate to him that they would not, in any circumstances, be taken into India by a Congress Government which no longer represented them.

On his arrival at Government House the Viceroy was asked by the Governor, Sir Olaf Caroe, if he would confront this vast crowd in order to calm them down. Mountbatten agreed to do so, provided Dr Khan Sahib also agreed. Mitchell relates:

> Dr Khan Sahib was called, and spoke to the Viceroy privately. The Viceroy shortly afterwards informed the Governor that Dr Khan Sahib's response was that the Viceroy should indeed go to be seen by the people if he must; but he should know that the Governor had organised the demonstration. This evidence of Dr Khan Sahib's attitude is shocking.

Lord and Lady Mountbatten then went out and, with great courage, faced the crowd. They might very easily have been shot or lynched. So might Sir Olaf Caroe who (although this is not generally mentioned in accounts of Mountbatten's intrepidity) stood beside them. Mountbatten had impressive physical presence, of which he took full advantage. He had also, Mitchell noticed, rolled up the sleeves of his bush-shirt rather higher than usual, thereby revealing, as his hand came up to the peak of his cap, 'the hypertrophied biceps of a first-class polo player'. He could not have uttered a single word that the crowd would even have heard, let alone understood. But the Mountbatten magic worked: the vast inchoate mass cheered him rapturously, 'Mountbatten Zindabad!'

He did not, however, delude himself that they wanted union with India. At a meeting that evening in Government House it was decided that there should be a referendum. As Mitchell had predicted, a huge majority chose Pakistan. Two days before Independence Sir George Cunningham came out of retirement and arrived in Peshawur to be the first Governor of the North-West Frontier Province in the Dominion of Pakistan.

On June 25th, 1947, there was a great gathering of Rajput princes at Udaipur to form their states into the Rajasthan Union. Mary Kirkbride saw:

> Dungarpur in blue and white striped muslin turban which looks so attractive that I felt I must wrest it from him and cut it up to make a frock. Virbadra was even more beautiful in bright yellow turban, matched by a broad sash, a fine sword and jewelled buttons. Odd to think that he was at Oxford! Partabgarh, quite dotty as usual, in a pale lemon turban, rich brown corduroys (in this weather!) and white buttoned-up coat. When Dungarpur asked him what he was going to do about the Rajasthan Union, he said, 'Whatever you do', and that was that. The conference went off well, for ten princes signed the agreement and there are more signatures to come. I think its success was quite a surprise to everyone. In the evening Dad and I went down to the station to meet Ratlam and Kishengarh, and old Partabgarh turned up again. He said he had signed 'some damned paper, I don't know what it was about'.

The princes of Rajasthan dispersed, well satisfied with what they had achieved. Given an effective Standstill Agreement, cohesion among themselves and a modicum of support, or even neutrality, from 'Dickie', they should be able to obtain reasonable terms for their accession to India. They had further reassurance from a speech by the Secretary of State for India, Lord Listowel, in the House of Commons debate on the Indian Independence Bill:

> The states will be masters of their own fate. They will be entirely free to choose whether to associate with one or other of the Dominion Governments or stand alone, and His Majesty's Government will not use the slightest pressure to influence their momentous and voluntary decision.

Their satisfaction was premature. On June 27th, two days after the meeting in Udaipur at which was inaugurated the Rajasthan Union, the states' Department was set up, its Indian section under Sardar Vallabhai Patel. His Secretary was V.P. Menon, a Madrassi, able, devious and an implacable enemy of the princes. He virtually replaced Corfield as the Viceroy's Political Adviser. Menon proposed:

> that the active co-operation of Lord Mountbatten should be secured. Apart from his position, his gifts and his grace, his relationship with the Royal Family was bound to influence the rulers . . . Nehru readily entrusted Lord Mountbatten with the task of negotiating with the rulers on the question of accession.

It was also V.P. Menon who devised the gambit that brought about the princes' ruin. In breach of the Cabinet Mission's memorandum, and of assurances recently given by the Secretary of State in the House of Commons, rulers who had joined the Constituent Assembly were handed an ultimatum: the Standstill Agreement would apply only if they acceded to India before August 15th. But they need accede only for defence, foreign affairs and communications, and they were positively assured by Vallabhai Patel, in a formal communication from the states' Department:

> We ask no more from them than their accession on these three subjects . . . The Congress are no enemies of the Princely Order . . . Nor would it be my policy to conduct the relations of the new Department with the states in any manner which savours of the domination of one over the other.

But the ultimatum effectively abolished the Standstill Agreement. As V.P. Menon pointed out:

> If rulers acceded on defence, the Government of India obtained right of entry into any state where internal stability was threatened . . . Defence covered not only external aggression but internal security.

Furthermore, nothing would be easier than to ensure that there would be a threat to internal security. Nehru said frankly, 'I will encourage rebellion in all states which go against us.' The mere hint that this might happen would bring a recalcitrant ruler to heel. C.C. Desai, I.C.S., Joint Secretary to the states' Department, proudly quotes himself as telling the ruler of a small state, 'Either you sign what we have got now, or you don't sign at all, and you take the consequences of your action. Our Crown Reserve Police (sic) would walk into your state.' It was a general interference-licence as undefined and potent as that which the Paramount Power had occasionally used, with the minimum of force and the object of supporting, by a necessary purge, the princely order. In future its use, or the mere threat of its use, would not be occasional, would not be limited to the minimum of force and not be intended to support the princely order.

It would in most cases be even easier to apply irresistible pressure on a ruler by the control of communications. Lord Mountbatten made this brutally plain to the Maharaj-Rana of Dholpur, on July 29th.

> You asked me what I thought India would do to Dholpur if you did not accede. To the best of my knowledge and belief they will do nothing; that is precisely the trouble – nothing whatever will be done, and your state will remain in complete isolation in the centre of an indifferent India.

This could have been resisted only by a bloc of states with bargaining power and a seaport sticking together over the next few weeks while they bargained; but the Rajput princes' track record for unity was not impressive.

Already some of the Kathiawar and Gujerat States, headed by the Jam Saheb, had decided to form their own mini-union rather than go in with the Rajasthan Union. At their request Walter Magor, Political Agent, Gujerat States, chaired many meetings of rulers and Diwans which thrashed out quite a viable arrangement for joint services and administration within India. He was then casually informed that the Jam Saheb and some others proposed to take the Kathiawar States into Pakistan. Constitutionally they had a perfect right to do this; but with their highly politicised Hindu population, it was a concept from the wilder shores of impracticality. Magor heard the outcome.

> In July they were invited to a Garden Party at the Viceroy's House, where each in turn (as they told me shame-facedly on their return) was bidden to talk to the Viceroy supported by Sardar Vallabhai Patel; and was told that there could be no question of their joining Pakistan, they would be incorporated in India. Most of them agreed, feeling that they could not go against the wishes of the King's cousin. A few who were intransigent were taken to see Lady Mountbatten who told them peremptorily that they must do as they were told.

It seems extraordinary that a man as astute as the Jam Saheb's (Madrassi) Diwan could have lent himself to this crazy idea. Perhaps he did so tongue-in-cheek, an agent provocateur. However that might be, it administered the *coup de grâce* to the Rajasthan Union, which had counted on Jamnagar, the Jam Saheb's capital, for its seaport.

Among the Rajputana States Bikanir had already defected. Jodhpur and Jaipur (Madrassi Diwans), the largest in revenue and population, were the next to go; followed by Mewar (Udaipur), the most prestigious, with its Madrassi Diwan. Outside Rajputana, Patiala and Travancore had already surrendered.

The Nawab of Bhopal wrote an impassioned appeal to the Crown Representative.

> I beseech you, my dear Dickie, to try and appreciate my point of view and that of my fellow-rulers who have adopted the same attitude . . . Any state or group of states acceding to the Dominion of India under the present Mountbatten Plan would be relegated to the position of a permanent powerless minority at the mercy of the Congress Party whose avowed intention it is to wipe out the Princely Order from the political map of India.

But even Bhopal (Madrassi Diwan) threw in his hand before August 15th.

Was it a pipe-dream, that a cohesive group of states could hold their own as an integral part of a Dominion of India? The Maharawal of Dungarpur insists that it was not. The princes were convinced that Congress, like every other nationalist revolutionary movement, must split into left and right as soon as the nationalist revolution was achieved – the left headed by Nehru, the right, ironically, by their old antagonist Vallabhai Patel, whom many princes admired and even rather liked. On the right they would have found allies.

> Princes were not fools. Had they been left alone by Lord Mountbatten they would have enlisted the support of the landed aristocracy of the United Provinces and Bihar, not to speak of Rajputana, Central India, Kathiawar and Gujerat. The Moslems would have gladly supported them, as well as the Parsees and the Sikhs. Seventy per cent of the capitalists of British India would have done likewise, including Birla and Tata, both of whom were more akin to Patel than to Nehru. The Depressed Classes would have lent support to Patel, and the complexion of the country would have been changed. Princes would have gathered tremendous bargaining power and their position would have been unassailable. Their support would have been sought by most of the stable elements in India. Popularity was not the monopoly of Nehru alone. I have known princes who have held their own [in democratic elections] having lost their states not for a year or two but for twenty years.* A bloc of states in the Indian Union comprising 30 million people with an area of 300,000 square miles

*The Maharawal of Dungarpur was himself one of these.

(bigger than the present Pakistan) was a feasible proposition, and no dream. But it was not to be.

It was an end brought about by one man and his wife. By making them sign the Instrument of Accession the Viceroy perpetrated the rape of the states. Had the princes been left alone, Congress could never have got them to sign away their powers and heritage within a fortnight. *No, never.* Being a member of the Royal Family, many princes took Lord Mountbatten as a friend. Nothing could be further from the truth. No one wanted protection from the Crown if the Crown could not give it; but the princes expected justice and fair play, not lies and half-truths to beguile them into a snare.

As the princes were not coming quickly enough to heel, it was decided to hold a conference at which the Viceroy as 'honest broker' would persuade them all to sign Instruments of Accession to India (except, of course, those geographically in Pakistan). Corfield called the conference for July 25th; and then, feeling that he could not in conscience take part in it, departed on retirement.

The 'honest broker' deployed all his resources of charm, cajolery, bullying, jocularity and royal cousinhood. When the Diwan of Kutch, whose Maharajah was ill, said he could not sign the Instrument without His Highness's authority, Mountbatten mimed the action of a crystal-gazer and said, 'I can see His Highness wishes you to sign.' There were further exercises in arm-twisting on July 26th and August 1st, the A.D.C.s improvising 'Ayes' and 'Noes' lobbies; with much jollity Bikanir and Patiala pretended to go with the Noes. By the end of it, all but two large and three small rulers had signed on the dotted line – for defence, foreign affairs and communications only: they had Lord Mountbatten's guarantee that there would be no further encroachments on their sovereignty.

The two large non-signatories were Kashmir (Hindu ruler, Moslem population), which had not yet decided whether to join India or Pakistan, having a perfect constitutional right to join either; and Hyderabad (Moslem ruler, Hindu population). The Nizam decided that he would go it alone, joining neither India nor Pakistan, trusting in the wealth and strength of Hyderabad to maintain its independence, and confident of the support of His Majesty's Government for Britain's Faithful Ally. He had the constitutional right to do this, but his policy was wildly unrealistic. Without a sea-port, entirely surrounded by India, he could not possibly remain independent; the British Government had no intention of supporting the Faithful Ally; and his own people were overwhelmingly Hindu, Indian, Congress in sympathy. He sent a personal appeal, by hand of a special courier, to the King. But the courier was stopped at Delhi airport, presumably on orders from on high, and allowed to go no further. Nor was the Nizam any more fortunate in his approaches to Pakistan. Jinnah went to Hyderabad to discuss these. Most punctilious of men, he inadvertently presented himself to the Nizam with the top button of his long tunic undone. His Exalted Highness, not himself the most dressy of men, was outraged by this mark of disrespect from a mere Bombay lawyer and refused to shake hands. So Jinnah took himself off in a huff.

At midnight on August 14th it was all over. There are many descriptions of the poignant ceremonies, all over India and Pakistan, of hauling down the Union Jack for the last time. I shall not add to these. But in the states it was slightly different.

In Indore, for instance, there was a grand ball at the Maharajah's palace to celebrate Independence – not, *bien entendu*, India's independence from Britain, but rather Indore's independence, however short-lived, from India. Most of us were not exactly in festive mood, but brandy and champagne produced a sort of spurious gaiety. At about two in the morning the Maharajah's Military Secretary came up to me and said, 'Charles, are you man enough to shoot a tiger this morning?'

I was sufficiently tanked-up to offer to strangle a tiger.

'Well,' said the Military Secretary, 'There's been a cow killed about twenty miles out. His Highness knows you are disappointed at leaving India next week without getting a tiger, and he says you can have a go at this one if you like. One of the Palace jeeps will take you out.'

I drove back to my bungalow in the jeep, collected my rifle and (without remembering to change out of my dinner-jacket) drove out to the edge of the jungle, where a shikari was waiting. There followed a 3-mile walk along a muddy jungle path, during which the drink died on me and I felt less and less inclined for the chase.

The shikari laid a hand on my arm and whispered, 'The kill is in that clearing. We'll sit behind this bush.'

We did so, and as it grew light I made out a large tiger standing over the carcase of a cow. I fired, and it galloped off but I knew I could not have missed. By now I felt awful – splitting headache, queasy stomach, and a wounded tiger to follow with rather a light rifle, through thick monsoon jungle and grass six foot high.

We waited twenty minutes to allow time for the wound to stiffen, and then walked cautiously up to the kill. There was blood, and the marks where the tiger had torn up the ground as he turned to dash away. We found him dead in a nullah 100 yards off.

I am not proud of the episode. I would not now dream of shooting a tiger. But I tell the tale as this was surely an unusual way of passing a historic morning.

That day, there arrived at the Residency in Udaipur a small package addressed to George Kirkbride. There was a covering letter from the Maharawal of Dungarpur.

> My dear George,
>
> As there is no longer any official relationship between us, I hope you will give me great pleasure by accepting these small presents for yourself, Nancy and Mary, from your friend, Lakshman Singh of Dungarpur.

They had style, the princes of Rajputana.

At midnight on August 14th, 1947, the Indian Political Service came to an end. The older officers retired, with pensions and compensation which was reasonable, if not exactly generous. Hindu and Moslem Politicals had no difficulty in being re-employed in the services of India and Pakistan: they had qualities and experience which were much in demand. K.P.S. Menon had a most distinguished career in the Indian Foreign Service as Indian Ambassador to the U.S.S.R. and other countries. B.K. Kapur, a Hindu almost unique in his knowledge of and feeling for the Frontier, represented his country first in Lahore, then in Peshawur. Mohamad Yusuf Khan became President of Pakistan National Airline, and eventually retired to England so as to be within reach of Glyndebourne. Iskandar Mirza went one better: he became President of Pakistan.

Most of the British Political officers who wanted to do so found places in the British services – the Foreign Service, Colonial Service and various quasi-governmental organisations. In their new careers many did extremely well. Trevelyan became British Ambassador in Moscow, and ended up in the House of Lords. Cotton, Hadow and Fry all became Ambassadors. Noble became Vice-Chancellor of Aberdeen University. Others took contract jobs as Politicals in Pakistan, under Sir George Cunningham. One of these, Pat Duncan, was the last of many British officers to be assassinated by Mahsuds, ironically while doing a job which benefited no one but that tribe. He was engaged in selecting Mahsud families for re-settlement in a rich canal colony vacated by Sikhs, when he was shot dead at a range of a few feet. It was a blood-feud killing: the murderer's father had been shot by the Scouts in the Shahur Tangi action ten years earlier. The murderer was immediately shot by Duncan's Mahsud orderly.

In the holocausts which followed Partition, the princes, the state authorities and the state forces all showed up extremely well, except in Patiala where they showed up badly, butchering every Moslem they could catch. Hundreds of thousands of Moslems, fleeing from British India into the Rajput States, were succoured, protected, accommodated, fed and finally sent on their way to Pakistan, for which Pakistan has always been very grateful to the Rajput rulers.

As for the rulers themselves, all the promises and half-promises, the assurances and reassurances given to them by the British Government, the Cabinet Mission and the last Viceroy turned out to be – scraps of paper. The Congress Government was implacable. Within a few months of Independence rulers were arbitrarily stripped of their ruling powers; then of their titles; finally of the incomes which had been guaranteed them when they were deprived of everything else.

It was His Majesty's Government and the last Viceroy who delivered them, bound and helpless, into the hands of their declared enemies. The moral justification for this shabby treatment rests on two propositions: that the princes could not have been saved; that they should not have been saved.

It was clearly impossible for Britain to continue to hold India indefinitely in order to honour guarantees to the princes. It would have required large military reinforcements and a readiness to batten down all opposition, which was out of the question. The British people were not interested in holding India. Nor, probably, was it possible for Lord Mountbatten or anyone else to persuade Nehru to allow the princes to proceed with the formation of powerful blocs which were obviously intended to challenge Congress hegemony. But was it necessary for Lord Mountbatten to use all his power and prestige, and his relationship to the King, to push the princes into signing Instruments of Accession which they knew would be the death-warrants of their states? In the words of Chaudhuri Mohamad Ali,* 'Perhaps the Princes were doomed to extinction, but that they should have been coaxed and driven to the slaughter-house by the shepherd they trusted most adds poignancy to the scene.'

For Mountbatten's conduct towards the princes there are two possible explanations. Either he sacrificed them because future relations

***The Emergence of Pakistan*, p.232.

between Britain and India might be damaged by any denial of Pandit Nehru's wishes; or he believed that he was getting them the best deal available while he was still in a position to influence events. One would like to think that the last Viceroy of India was guilty of naiveté rather than cynical *Real Politik.* He believed everything Nehru told him; he wanted to believe everything Nehru told him. He may have taken at face value the promise of Congress to ask from the princes 'no more than their accession on these three subjects'. He told the King that he had done well by the princes, and seems to have been shocked when the Congress Government broke all its promises to them.

If he had not cozened and bullied them into signing Instruments of Accession before August 15th, the end-result for them might or might not have been the same: it could hardly have been worse. But at least Britain's hands would have been clean: there would have been no breach of faith.

Should the princes have been saved? Obviously not all of them. There were hundreds of tiny states which were not viable and would have been a constant source of trouble and friction. Clearly Hyderabad, with its Moslem Nizam and Hindu population, could not have survived. (Though this does not excuse Nehru's hypocrisy in applying different rules to Hyderabad and Kashmir: in the former the will of the people must prevail, in the latter the will of the ruler.) But there were many large and medium-sized states admirably governed, economically viable, with rulers and people devoted to each other. They did not, to be sure, enjoy the blessings of one man one vote; but when one looks round Asia and Africa today, can one honestly say that this is the hallmark of salvation, without which a country is damned? Might not India's history have been happier if there had been conservative elements to balance the left-wing, pro-Soviet bias of India's last hereditary rulers, the Nehru dynasty? Among the princes there was ability, integrity, dedication and patriotism which might have contributed much to India if they had not been bulldozed on to the scrap-heap.

Abbreviations

A.D.C.	Aide-de-camp
C.B.	Companion of the Bath
C.I.E.	Companion of the Order of the Indian Empire
C.M.G.	Companion of St Michael and St George
C.R.E.	Commanding Royal Engineers
C.S.I.	Companion of the Order of the Star of India
D.C.	Deputy Commissioner, in charge of a District
D.S.O.	Distinguished Service Order
F.R.G.S.	Fellow Royal Geographical Society
F.R.S.	Fellow Royal Society
F.R.S.L.	Fellow Royal Society of Literature
G.B.E.	Grand Cross of the British Empire
G.C.B.	Grand Cross of the Bath
G.C.I.E.	Grand Commander of the Indian Empire
G.C.M.G.	Grand Cross of St Michael and St George
G.C.S.I.	Grand Commander of the Star of India
G.C.V.O.	Grand Cross of the Royal Victorian Order
H.E.	His Excellency
H.E.H.	His Exalted Highness
H.H.	His Highness
H.R.	Honourable Resident
I.C.S.	Indian Civil Service
I.D.S.M.	Indian Distinguished Service Medal
I.M.S.	Indian Medical Service
I.O.M.	Indian Order of Merit
I.S.O.	Imperial Service Order
K.C.I.E.	Knight Commander of the Indian Empire
K.C.M.G.	Knight Commander of St Michael and St George
K.C.S.I.	Knight Commander of the Star of India
K.C.V.O.	Knight Commander of the Royal Victorian Order
K.G.	Knight of the Order of the Garter
K.T.	Knight of the Order of the Thistle
M.C.	Military Cross
O.M.	Order of Merit

Glossary

Barampta	an operation to surround a Frontier village at night and search it at dawn, looking for wanted men, stolen property, or victims of kidnappers
Begar	compulsory, unpaid labour on public works
Chaukidar	night watchman
Chota hazri	early-morning tea
Chuprassi	footman, office attendant
Daffadar	cavalry sergeant
Darbar	a ruler's council; the government of a state
Dhobi	washerman
Diwan	chief minister of a Hindu or Sikh state
Faranghi	'Frank'; a term, dating from the Crusades, applied by Moslems to Europeans
Firman	an edict by the Nizam of Hyderabad
Gadi	the throne of an Indian prince; literally, 'cushion'
Gasht	a patrol of the Frontier Corps
Gharib Parwar	'Protector of the Poor'; an honorific
Hamsayas	'Persons sharing the same shade', i.e. fugitives from British justice or from another tribe
Hartal	a one-day general strike and closure of business premises
Havildar	infantry sergeant
Itr	attar of roses, ceremonially sprinkled on important people
Izzat	honour; the respect in which one is held
Jhalsa	annual ceremonial tribute-paying in Gilgit
Jihad	Holy War
Jirga	a tribal assembly on the North-West Frontier
Jungli	wild, uncouth
Karez	a system, native to Persia and Baluchistan, of providing permanent running water in an arid country
Kharita	a formal commission from the Viceroy, acknowledging a prince as ruler of a state
Khassadar	an irregular tribal levy on the North-West Frontier

Kortunai	an offensive term, applied to Indians by Mahsuds; c.f. 'wog'
Kuhl	water-channel
Kui	a long, cylindrical bag of white or beige tweed, rolled up until it forms a beret-like hat
Lambardar	a local revenue collector, with other duties
Lashkar	a tribal army on the North-West Frontier
Lathi	a seven-foot, iron-bound bamboo stave
Machan	a platform built in a tree or stone tower
Malik	a tribal headman on the North-West Frontier
Nazar	a symbolic tribute paid to Indian rulers on special occasions two or three times a year by officials and nobles
Pan	betel-nut and spices wrapped in a vine leaf, presented ceremonially to important people
Panchayat	an elected village council
Patwari	a local revenue clerk
Powindah	nomads
Pukhtunwali	the Pathan code of conduct
Purdah	literally, 'curtain'; a woman in purdah does not appear unveiled in public
Ram	God; a Hindu deity
Ryots	peasants, cultivators
Sanyasi	a holy man
Sardar	chiefs of Baluchistan tribes; nobles in states
Sarkar	government
Shabash	'Well done!'
Sheriat	Moslem law
Shikar	any field sport, especially shooting
Shikari	a stalker or hunter
Sowar	trooper
Suttee	the custom of a Hindu widow immolating herself on her husband's pyre
Tahsildar	a revenue assistant and collector
Tongawallah	cab-driver
Vakil	a 'pleader'; a cross between a solicitor and a barrister
Vedas	Hindu holy books
Wazir	chief minister of a Moslem state; also a Pathan tribe
Zenana	the women's part of a house or palace; the harem
Zindabad	'Long live' (e.g. 'Pakistan Zindabad!')

Appendix 1

Biographical notes on Political officers mentioned in the text and on some other contributors

Showing: date of birth; date of entry into Indian Political Service; military rank, in the case of entrants from the Army; last appointment only in the service; subsequent career; decorations. An asterisk denotes a contributor to this book of otherwise unpublished material, held mainly in the India Office Library and Records.

Abdur Rahim Khan b. 9 Nov. 1898. April 1926. Major. Political Agent, Loralai 1944–7.

Bacon, R.N. b. 25 Dec. 1900. Nov. 1929. Lt-Col. Political Agent, Gilgit 1945–7. C.B.E.

Bailey, F.M. b. 3 Feb. 1882. Dec. 1905. Lt-Col. H.M. Minister, Nepal 1935–8. C.I.E.

Barnes, H.A. b. 27 Aug. 1900. May 1927. Major. Political Agent, Zhob 1939–40. Murdered at Fort Sandeman, Oct. 1940. C.I.E.

**Mrs M.O. Barnes*

Barton, W.P. b. 1871. I.C.S. 1899. Resident, Hyderabad 1925–30. K.C.I.E., C.S.I.

Battye, R.K.M. b. 30 Aug. 1905. June 1932. Major. Secretary to Resident, Rajputana 1946–7. Subsequently Colonial Administrative Service, Tanganyika.

**Bazalgette, J.E.A.* b. 24 Jan. 1907. Jan. 1933. Major. Political Agent, Punjab States April 1946. Subsequently worked for Dr Barnardo's Homes 1951–62 and with refugees in Turkey 1963–72.

Bazalgette, R.L. b. 8 July 1900. April 1927. Major. Political Agent, Orissa States 1938–9. Murdered 1939 in Ranpur State.

Beatty, R.N. b. 16 Nov. 1910. Tochi Scouts. Captain. Acting Assistant Political Agent, North Waziristan 1936–7. Murdered near Boya.

**Becker, H.B.* b. 12 Aug. 1913. Captain. Seconded to Political Service from South Waziristan Scouts as Assistant Political Agent, North

Waziristan 1943–5. Tobacco farming, Southern Rhodesia 1946–50.

Betham, G.L. b. 8 April 1889. March 1924. Lt-Col. H.M. Minister, Nepal 1938–44. K.B.E., C.I.E., M.C.

**Biscoe, D.H.* b. 12 July 1909. Dec. 1934. Major. Secretary to Resident, Punjab Hill States 1946. Subsequently appointments with Electrolux until retirement in 1974. M.B.E.

Bowen, J.C.E. b. 8 Oct. 1909. Nov. 1934. Major. Consul, Bushire 1945.

Bremner, C.E.U. b. 30 Aug. 1891. July 1919. Lt-Col. Consul, Portuguese possessions in India 1940–3. M.C.

**Mrs Anne Bremner*

Bromhead, Sir Benjamin D.G., Bt, b. 7 May 1900. South Waziristan Scouts 1929–32. Tochi Scouts 1937–8. Lt-Col. Political Agent, North Waziristan 1944–5. O.B.E.

**Brownsdon, T.E.* b. 26 June 1910. Jan. 1936. Major. Secretary to Resident, Mysore 1947. Subsequently Colonial Administrative Service, Kenya 1949–50. Worked with Independent Television Authority 1956–61. O.B.E.

Caroe, O.K. b. 15 Nov. 1892. I.C.S. 1923. Secretary External Affairs Department, Government of India 1939–45. Governor, North-West Frontier Province 1946–7. K.C.S.I., K.C.I.E., F.R.S.L.

Cater, A.N.L. b. 15 June 1880. I.C.S. April 1907. Agent to the Governor-General and Chief Commissioner, Baluchistan 1931–8. K.C.I.E.

Chauncey, F.C.L. b. 22 Dec. 1904. 1930. Major. Political Agent, Chattisgarh States 1945–7. Subsequently H.M. Diplomatic Service 1949–58. Personal Adviser to the Sultan of Muscat and Oman 1961–70. C.B.E.

Cobb, E.H. b. 15 Sept. 1899. Nov. 1924. Major. Home Secretary to Government of North-West Frontier Province July 1946. O.B.E.

Corfield, C.L. b. 15 Aug. 1893. I.C.S. 1925. Political Adviser to the Viceroy as Crown Representative 1945–7. K.C.I.E., C.S.I., M.C.

**Cotton, J.R.* b. 22 Jan. 1909. 1 Nov. 1934. Major. Deputy Secretary Political Department 1946–7. Subsequently H.M. Diplomatic Service. Ambassador to Zaire and Burundi 1965–9. K.C.M.G., O.B.E.

Cox, P.Z. b. 20 Nov. 1864. 1890. Major-General. British Minister, Persia 1918–20. High Commissioner, Mesopotamia 1920–3. G.C.M.G., G.C.I.E., K.C.S.I.

Creagh-Coen, T.B. b. 31 March 1903. I.C.S. Oct. 1935. Deputy Secretary Political Department 1946–7. Subsequently service with the Government of Pakistan 1947–53. Chairman Public Service Commission, Eastern Nigeria 1956-8. K.B.E., C.I.E.

Crichton, G.C.L. b. 30 July 1900. May 1926. Lt-Col. Counsellor British Legation, Kabul 1943–6. Officiating Secretary External Affairs Department April-Aug. 1947. Financial Adviser, Kuwait 1951–6. C.S.I., C.I.E.

Cunningham, G. b. 23 March 1888. I.C.S. 26 Nov. 1911. Governor, North-West Frontier Province 1937–46 and 1947–8. Rector, St Andrews University 1948–9. G.C.I.E., K.C.S.I., O.B.E.

**Curtis, G.C.S.* b. 4 Sept. 1904. I.C.S. May 1933. Deputy Commissioner, Mardan 1943–6. Subsequently farming in Essex. Chairman Essex National Farmers' Union. County Councillor and County Alderman. O.B.E.

**Davy, A.E.G.* b. 10 Dec. 1908. Oct. 1935. Major. Secretary to Resident, Central India 1945.

Dent, E.J.M. b. 6 June 1918. I.C.S. Nov. 1940. Assistant Commissioner, North-West Frontier Province. Remained a member of I.C.S. while serving in the North-West Frontier Province. O.B.E.

Dew, A.B. b. 27 Sept. 1867. 1897. Lt-Col. Agent to the Governor-General and Chief Commissioner, Baluchistan 1919–22. K.C.I.E., C.S.I.

Dickson, H.R.P. b. 4 Feb. 1881. Aug. 1915. Lt-Col. Political Agent, Kuwait 1929–36. Subsequently chief local representative Kuwait Oil Company. Author *Kuwait and Her Neighbours*. C.I.E.

Donald, J.O.S. b. 10 Oct. 1905. 1932. Major. Political Agent, South Waziristan 1946.

**Dring, A.J.* b. 4 Nov. 1902. 1927. Lt-Col. Chief Secretary, North-West Frontier Province 1947. Prime Minister, Bahawalpur State 1948–52. K.B.E., C.I.E., J.P.

Duncan, P.T. b. 16 March 1916. I.C.S. 1940. Assistant Commissioner, North-West Frontier Province. Subsequently Political Agent, South Waziristan, in Pakistan Government service. Murdered 1947.

**Emerson, G.H.* b. 3 Dec. 1907. I.C.S. Nov. 1935. Political Agent, Zhob 1945. Subsequently National Council of Social Service 1947–72.

Etherton, P.T. b. 4 Sept. 1879. Colonel. H.B.M. Consul-General and Political Resident, Chinese Turkestan 1918–24.

Fitze, K.S. b. 6 Jan. 1887. I.C.S. April 1915. Secretary to H.E. The Crown Representative 1940–4. K.C.I.E.

Fitzpatrick, J.A.O. b. 21 Nov. 1879. I.C.S. 1909. Agent to Governor-General, Punjab States 1927–35. K.C.I.E., C.B.E.

Fraser-Tytler, W.K. b. 26 Dec. 1886. 1919. Lt-Col. H.M. Minister, Kabul 1935–41. K.B.E., C.M.G., M.C.

Fry, L.A.C. b. 17 April 1908. 20 Nov. 1933. Major. Deputy Secretary

External Affairs Department. Subsequently H.M. Diplomatic Service. Ambassador to Brazil. K.C.M.G., O.B.E.

Gaisford, P. b. 28 Nov. 1891. June 1919. Lt-Col. Resident, Mysore 1944–6. Kt, C.I.E.

Gibson, E.C. b. 6 July 1886. I.C.S. June 1915. Resident, States of Western India 1937–42. K.C.I.E.

Gimson, C. b. 24 Dec. 1886. I.C.S. Feb. 1919. Political Agent, Manipur 1933. C.I.E.

Glancy, B.J. b. 31 Dec. 1882. I.C.S. May 1914. Governor, Punjab States 1941–6. G.C.I.E., K.C.S.I.

Glancy, R.I.R. b. 19 Sept. 1874. I.C.S. 1901. Agent to the Governor-General, Central India 1924–9. Member States Enquiry Committee 1932. K.C.S.I., K.C.I.E.

Glover, J.W. Thomson b. 30 July 1887. 10 April 1914. Lt-Col. Resident, Kashmir 1937–40. C.B.E.

Gould, B.J. b. 29 Dec. 1883. I.C.S. 1909. Political Officer, Sikkim, and for Bhutan and Tibet 1935–45. Kt, C.M.G., C.I.E.

Griffin, L.C.L. b. 5 Jan. 1900. I.C.S. Nov. 1927. Secretary to Crown Representative 1944–7. Kt, C.S.I., C.I.E.

Griffith, R.E.H. b. 4 March 1882. Nov. 1908. Lt-Col. Governor, North-West Frontier Province 1932–7. K.C.S.I., C.I.E.

**Hadow, R.M.* b. 17 Aug. 1915. I.C.S. May 1944. Under Secretary External Affairs Department 1946–7. Subsequently H.M. Diplomatic Service. Ambassador to Israel 1965–9. Ambassador to the Argentine 1969–72.

Hall, H.P. b. 9 Sept. 1913. Nov. 1937. Major. Director Food and Civil Supplies, Baluchistan 1945–6. Subsequently service in Colonial Office, Commonwealth Relations Office and Ministry of Defence 1948–73. Director of Studies, Royal Institute of Public Administration since 1974.

**Mrs Margery Hall*

**Hancock, C.P.* b. 18 Sept. 1896. 1920. Lt-Col. Resident, Western India States and Baroda 1943–7. K.C.I.E., O.B.E., M.C.

**Harrington-Hawes, D.G.* b. 22 May 1907. March 1934. Major. Deputy Secretary Political Department 1945–7. Subsequently Director-General International Hospital Federation 1962–75.

Heale, R.J.W. b. 24 Sept. 1876. 1903. Lt-Col. Agent to Governor-General, Central India 1929–31. C.I.E., O.B.E.

**Hickinbotham, T.* b. 27 April 1903. 1932. Major. Political Agent, Kalat 1945–7. Subsequently Governor of Aden 1951–6. K.C.M.G., K.C.V.O., C.I.E., O.B.E.

**Hodson, R.V.E.* b. 20 July 1914. Oct. 1939. Major. Political Agent, North Waziristan 1947. Subsequently with Ministry of Defence 1951–79. M.B.E.

Holland, R.E. b. 29 June 1873. I.C.S. June 1904. Agent to the Governor-General, Rajputana 1920–5. K.C.I.E., C.S.I., C.V.O.

Howell, E.B. b. 12 Feb. 1877. I.C.S. May 1904. Foreign Secretary, Government of India 1930–2. K.C.I.E., C.S.I.

Humphrys, F.H. b. 24 April 1879. April 1905. Lt-Col. British Ambassador to Iraq 1932–5. Subsequently Chairman Iraq Petroleum Company 1941–50. G.C.M.G., G.C.V.O., K.B.E., C.I.E.

Iskander Mirza b. 13 Nov. 1899. 1926. Major-General. Joint Secretary to Government of India Ministry of Defence 1946. President of Pakistan 1956–8. C.I.E., O.B.E.

**Kapur, B.K.* b. 12 Jan. 1910. April 1936. Captain. Deputy Secretary External Affairs Department, Government of India, April 1946. Subsequent career with Government of India Ministry of External Affairs. M.B.E.

**Keen, P.J.* b. 30 June 1911. Oct. 1936. Major. Under Secretary Political Department 1945–7. Subsequent career in H.M. Diplomatic Service. C.M.G., M.B.E.

Keyes, T.H. b. 28 May 1877. Jan. 1903. Brigadier-General. Resident, Hyderabad 1930–3. K.C.I.E., C.S.I., C.M.G.

Kirkbride, G. b. 16 April 1894. 22 March 1922. Lt-Col. Political Agent, Mewar 1943–7.

Latimer, C.R. b. 13 July 1911. I.C.S. Jan. 1939. Secretary to Governor, North-West Frontier Province, and District Commissioner, Bannu 1945–7. Subsequently H.M. Overseas Service. Office of High Commissioner for Basutuland, Bechuanaland Protectorate and Swaziland 1948–64. Minister British Embassy, Pretoria 1965–6. Kt, C.B.E.

Lawrence, H.R. b. 20 July 1878. April 1904. Lt-Col. President Council of State, Jaipur 1927–30. C.I.E.

Lothian, A.C. b. 27 June 1887. I.C.S. Nov. 1915. Resident, Hyderabad 1942–6. Author *Kingdoms of Yesterday*. Editor *Murray's Handbook for India, Pakistan, Burma and Ceylon*. K.C.I.E., C.S.I.

Low, A.P. b. 30 Jan. 1908. I.C.S. Nov. 1935. Financial Secretary to Government of North-West Frontier Province 1944. O.B.E.

Lowis, R.H.D. b. 5 Feb. 1905. Indian Police. Feb. 1936. Deputy Commissioner, Kohat Jan. 1946. O.B.E.

**Lydall, E.F.* b. 4 Aug. 1907. I.C.S. Nov. 1935. Secretary to Resident, Baroda and for states of Western India and Gujerat 1946–7.

Subsequently with Legal Division of Shell International Petroleum.

Mackenzie, D.G. b. 1 July 1883. I.C.S. June 1912. Political Agent, Hyderabad 1933–8. K.C.I.E.

Macnabb, R.J. b. 7 Feb. 1883. Jan. 1906. Lt-Col. Agent to Governor-General, Central India 1933.

**Magor, E.W.M.* b. 1 June 1911. Oct. 1937. Major. Secretary to Resident, Kolhapur and the Deccan States 1945–7. Subsequently Colonial Administrative Service, Kenya 1947–61. Home Civil Service 1961–71. C.M.G., O.B.E.

Mahbub Ali Khan, Khan Bahadur Shaikh b. March 1894. March 1915. Political Agent, Dir, Swat and Chitral Jan. 1946. O.B.E.

Menon, K.P.S. b. 18 Oct. 1898. I.C.S. Feb. 1925. Agent-General for India in China Sept. 1945. Subsequently in Indian Foreign Service. Ambassador to U.S.S.R. 1952–61. C.I.E.

**Mitchell, A.N.* b. 18 Dec. 1906. I.C.S. Feb. 1936. Financial Secretary, North-West Frontier Province Aug. 1946. O.B.E.

Mohamad Yusuf Khan South Waziristan Scouts, 1937–43. Captain. Assistant Political Agent, South Waziristan 1945. M.C.

Neale, W.G. b. 2 Oct. 1880. July 1906. Lt-Col. Deputy Secretary Foreign and Political Department 1928–30. C.I.E.

**Noble, T.A.F.* b. 29 April 1918. I.C.S. of which he remained a member while serving in the North-West Frontier Province 1941–7. Joint Deputy Commissioner, Peshawar. Subsequently Higher Education in Britain. Vice-Chancellor, Leicester University 1962–76. Vice-Chancellor, University of Aberdeen 1976–81. Kt, M.B.E.

Noel, E.W.C. b. 14 April 1886. Dec. 1912. Lt-Col. Deputy Commissioner, Mardan. C.I.E., D.S.O.

Ogilvie, G.D. b. 18 Feb. 1882. Dec. 1905. Lt-Col. Agent to the Governor-General, Rajputana 1932–7. K.C.I.E., C.S.I.

Packman, K.C. b. 14 May 1899. 1924. Lt-Col. Resident, Waziristan 1944–7. C.I.E.

Parsons, A.E.B. b. 5 Aug. 1884. May 1919. Major-General. Resident and Agent to the Governor-General, Baluchistan 1936–9. K.C.I.E., C.B.E., D.S.O.

Patterson, S.B.A. b. 18 March 1872. Nov. 1898. Lt-Col. Agent to Governor-General, Rajputana 1925–7. Political A.D.C. to Secretary of State for India 1928–33. K.C.V.O., C.S.I., C.I.E.

Pears, S.E. b. 1875. I.C.S. 1901. Chief Commissioner, North-West Frontier Province 1930–1. K.C.S.I., C.I.E.

**Pearson, Sir Francis Fenwick, Bt,* b. 13 June 1911. 1936. Chief Minister, Manipur State 1945–7. Subsequently M.P. for Clitheroe 1959–70.

Parliamentary Secretary to Prime Minister 1963–4. M.B.E., J.P.

Philby, H. St J.B. b. 3 April 1885. I.C.S. On Special Duty, Persian Gulf Nov. 1915. Chief British Representative Transjordania 1921–4. Subsequently travels and exploration in Arabian peninsular. Friend and Adviser of Ibn Saud. C.I.E.

**Pinhey, L.A.G.* b. 28 Oct. 1901. April 1929. Lt-Col. Political Resident, East Rajputana States, and Secretary to Resident, Rajputana 1946–7. O.B.E.

Prideaux, F.B. b. 26 Nov. 1871. 1895. Lt-Col. Political Resident, Persian Gulf 1924–7. C.S.I., C.I.E.

Prior, C.G. b. 9 Dec. 1896. 24 Aug. 1923. Lt-Col. Political Resident, Persian Gulf 1936–46. Governor, Baluchistan 1946. K.C.I.E., F.R.G.S.

Pritchard, H.R.N. b. 11 April 1879. Feb. 1905. Lt-Col. Agent to Governor-General, Madras States 1930–3. C.I.E., O.B.E.

**Rance, H.D.H.* b. 19 May 1912. Major. Nov. 1936. Assistant Political Agent, Bahrain 1946–7. Subsequently Colonial Administrative Service, Northern Rhodesia 1948–50. Diocesan Secretary, Diocese of Chichester 1961–76.

**Raw, W.G.* b. 6 Oct. 1910. Nov. 1936. Major. Home Secretary, Government of North-West Frontier Province 1945.

**Redpath, A.W.* b. 4 Sept. 1909. Nov. 1934. Major. Counsellor British Legation, Kabul 1947–8. Subsequently Pakistan Government Service and H.M. Diplomatic Service until 1975. C.B.E.

Reilly, B.R. b. 25 March 1882. April 1908. Lt-Col. Governor and Commander-in-Chief, Aden 1937–40. Colonial Office 1940–61. K.C.M.G., C.I.E., O.B.E.

Reynolds, L.W. b. 26 Feb. 1874. I.C.S. 1905. Agent to the Governor-General, Rajputana 1927–32. K.C.I.E., C.S.I., M.C.

**Lady Reynolds*

**Rogers, T.E.* b. 28 Dec. 1912. I.C.S. Aug. 1941. Assistant Political Agent, Quetta-Pishin 1946–7. Subsequently H.M. Diplomatic Service 1948–73. Ambassador to Colombia 1971–3. C.M.G., M.B.E.

Sandeman, R.G. Colonel. On special duty for Kalat affairs 1875–7. Agent to Governor General, Baluchistan 1887. K.C.S.I.

Searle, C.S. b. 29 Nov. 1895. June 1923. Major. Resident, Revenue and Judicial Commissioner, Baluchistan Feb. 1946. M.C.

Shakespear, W.H.I. b. 29 Oct. 1878. Jan. 1904. Captain. Political Agent, Kuwait 1909. On official mission to Ibn Saud 1914. Killed in tribal clash between forces of Ibn Saud and Ibn Rashid 1915.

Sharbat Khan, Mir b. 1880. 2 Sept. 1921. Political Agent and Deputy

Commissioner, Sibi 1932–5. C.I.E.

**Shattock, J.S.H.* b. 21 Nov. 1907. I.C.S. Oct. 1939. Chief Minister, Chamba State 1946–7. Subsequently H.M. Diplomatic Service 1947–67. C.M.G., O.B.E.

Skrine, C.P. b. 28 Feb. 1888. I.C.S. Oct. 1915. Counsellor British Embassy, Teheran 1946–8. Subsequently Chairman Permanent Committee on Geographical Names 1960–4. Kt, O.B.E.

**Thompson, J.H.* b. 9 March 1898. I.C.S. July 1926. Resident, Punjab States 1945–7. Kt, C.I.E. Subsequently rowing correspondent *Sunday Times* 1954–68. B.B.C. Appointments Department 1956–9.

**Todd, H.J.* b. 15 Oct. 1893. Indian Police. Oct. 1921. Resident, Eastern States 1944–7. Subsequently Chief Representative Iraq Petroleum Company, Bagdad 1952–9. Kt, C.I.E.

**Mrs. E. Tollinton.* Wife of H.P. Tollinton, Settlement Officer, Hazara 1941–7.

**Trench, C.P. Chenevix* b. 29 June 1914. Feb. 1946. Major. Under Secretary, Central India 1946–7. Subsequently Colonial Administrative Service, Kenya. M.C.

**Mrs C.P. Chenevix Trench.* Formerly Mary Kirkbride.

Trench, R.H. Chenevix b. 1876. 1901. Lt-Col. Member of the Nizam's Executive Council, Hyderabad 1927–35. Kt, C.I.E., O.B.E.

Trevelyan, H. b. 27 Nov. 1905. I.C.S. Nov. 1932. Joint Secretary External Affairs Department, Government of India 1946. Subsequently H.M. Diplomatic Service 1947–67. Ambassador to the U.S.S.R. 1962–5. High Commissioner, South Arabia 1967. Baron, K.G., G.C.M.G., C.I.E., O.B.E.

Wakefield, Sir Edward B., Bt, b. 24 July 1903. I.C.S. Dec. 1930. Joint Secretary Political Department 1946. Subsequently M.P. for West Derbyshire 1950–62. C.I.E.

Watson, C.C. I.C.S. April 1902. Political Agent, East Rajputana States 1917. Political A.D.C. to Secretary of State for India 1921. C.I.E.

Weir, J.L.R. b. 29 Jan. 1883. Feb. 1908. Lt-Col. Resident, Gujerat States and Baroda April 1937–8. C.I.E.

Wilberforce-Bell, H. b. 17 Nov. 1885. Jan. 1910. Lt-Col. Resident, Punjab States 1934–9. K.C.I.E.

Wilkinson, W.H.J. b. 31 May 1874. March 1903. British Envoy, Nepal 1924–32. C.S.I., C.I.E.

Wilson, A.T. b. 18 July 1884. 1909. Lt-Col. Civil Commissioner, Bagdad 1918–20. With Anglo-Persian Oil Company 1921–32. M.P. for Hitchin 1933–9. Pilot officer R.A.F.V.R. 1939–40. Killed in action. K.C.I.E., C.S.I., C.M.G., D.S.O.

Wingate, Sir Ronald E.L., Bt, b. 30 Sept. 1889. I.C.S. Oct. 1917. Revenue Commissioner and Agent to the Governor-General, Baluchistan 1935–7. C.B., C.M.G., C.I.E., O.B.E.

Wooller, A. b. 23 May 1912. I.C.S. Dec. 1939. Deputy Commissioner, Bannu March 1946. Subsequently H.M. Diplomatic Service 1947–72. High Commissioner, Mauritius 1968–70. C.B.E.

**Worth, M.* b. Dec. 1905. I.C.S. April 1933. Development Officer, Baluchistan, Political Agent and Deputy Commissioner, Quetta-Pishin 1945. Subsequently in Australian Government Service with Departments of Works and Housing and External Affairs.

Wylie, F.V. b. 9 Aug. 1891. I.C.S. May 1919. Governor, United Provinces 1945–7. G.C.I.E., K.C.S.I.

Appendix 2

Viceroys of India 1899–1947

Baron Curzon of Kedleston. P.C., G.C.S.I., G.C.I.E. 1899–1905.

The Earl of Minto. P.C., G.C.S.I., G.C.M.G., G.C.I.E. 1905–10.

Baron Hardinge of Penshurst. P.C., G.C.B., G.C.S.I., G.C.M.G., G.C.I.E., G.C.V.O., I.S.O. 1910–16.

Lord Chelmsford. P.C., G.C.S.I., G.C.M.G., G.C.I.E., G.B.E. 1916–21.

The Earl of Reading. P.C., G.C.B., G.C.S.I., G.C.I.E., K.C.V.O. 1921–5.

Baron Irwin. P.C., G.C.S.I., G.C.I.E. 1926–31.

Earl Willingdon. P.C., G.C.S.I., G.C.M.G., G.C.I.E., G.B.E., 1931–6.

The Marquess of Linlithgow. P.C., K.T., G.C.S.I., G.C.I.E., O.B.E., 1936–43.

Field Marshal Viscount Wavell of Cyrenaica and Winchester. P.C., G.C.B., G.C.S.I., G.C.I.E., C.M.G., M.C. 1943–7.

Viscount Mountbatten of Burma. K.G., P.C., G.C.B., O.M., G.C.S.I., G.C.I.E., G.C.V.O., D.S.O., F.R.S. March-August 1947.

Bibliography

Charles Allen and Sharada Dwivedi, *Lives of the Indian Princes* (Century Hutchinson, London, 1984)
F.M. Bailey, *Mission to Tashkent* (Jonathan Cape, London, 1946)
Sir William Barton, *The Princes of India* (Nisbet & Co., London, 1934.
Jack Bazalgette, *The Captains and the Kings Depart* (Amate Press, Oxford, 1984)
Sir Olaf Caroe, *The Pathans* (Macmillan, London, 1965)
Sir Conrad Corfield, *The Princely India I Knew* (George Thomas for the Indo-British Historical Society, Madras, 1975)
Sir Terence Creagh-Coen, *The Indian Political Service* (Chatto & Windus, London, 1971)
Sir Kenneth Fitze, *Twilight of the Maharajahs* (John Murray, London, 1956)
Sir Leslie Fry, *As Luck Would Have It* (Phillimore & Co., London, 1978)
B.J. Gould, *The Jewel in the Lotus* (Chatto & Windus, London 1957)
J. Glendevon, *The Viceroy at Bay* (Collins, London, 1971)
Peter Hopkirk, *Setting the East Ablaze* (John Murray, London, 1984)
Sir Evelyn Howell, *Mizh: a Monograph on the Government of India's Relations with the Mahsud Tribe* (Govt of India Press, Delhi, 1931)
John Lord, *The Maharajahs* (Hutchinson, London, 1972)
Sir Arthur Lothian, *Kingdoms of Yesterday* (John Murray, London, 1951)
Edward Lydall, *Enough of Action* (Jonathan Cape, London, 1949)
K.P.S. Menon, *Many Worlds* (Oxford University Press, 1965)
V.P. Menon, *The Story of the Integration of the Indian States* (Longmans, London, 1956)
Captain L.A.G. Pinhey, *Report on the Quetta Earthquake, 1935* (Govt of India Press, Delhi, 1937)
E.B. Wakefield, *Past Imperative* (Chatto & Windus, London 1966)
Philip Ziegler, *Mountbatten* (William Collins, London, 1985)

Special Sources

The States of Rajputana (i)

For Udaipur (Mewar)
India Office Records LPS/10/978, 979
R/2 Boxes 147, 148, 149
Private papers of C.G. Chenevix Trench

The States of Rajputana (ii)

For Bharatpur
India Office Records L/P & S/10/1090
Viceroy's correspondence with Secretary of State Mss Eur C/152/2
Mss Eur E/240/1
Mss Eur E/240/5

For Alwar
India Office Records L/P & S/13/1377
Mss Eur F/144/29
Viceroy's correspondence with Secretary of State Mss Eur C/152/2
Mss Eur E/240/6

The States of Central India

For Dewas Senior
India Office Records L/P & S/13/1123

For Indore
India Office Records. Viceroy's correspondence with Secretary of State Mss Eur E/238/8

The States of Gwalior, Baroda and Gujerat

For Baroda
India Office Records L/P & S/10/264, 296

Jammu and Kashmir

C.E. Bechhofer Roberts, *The Mr A Case* (Jarrolds, Norwich, c. 1950)
India Office Records, Viceroy's Correspondence with Secretary of State Eur Mss 238/8
R/2 TN 1075/211
R/1/1/917
R/1/1/1137
L/P & S/13/1261
Article by D.G. Harrington-Hawes, 'The Wanderers', in *Blackwood's Magazine*, June, 1948

The Faithful Ally

India Office Records Mss Eur F/144/63
L/P & S/11/272 P 4543 1926
Mss Eur F/131/31 (a) and (b)
Trench family correspondence

The States, the Politicals and Federation

India Office Records Mss Eur F/231/31 (a)

Indian Politicals outside India

Notes on the life of Lt-Col. H.R.P. Dickson provided by his son, Captain H.Y.W.S. Dickson

The End of It All

Letters of the Maharawal of Dungarpur to the author
India Office Records Mss Eur D/1006
Article by Sir Arthur Lothian, 'A Neglected Aspect of Modern History', in the *Quarterly Review*, October, 1962, pp. 392–402

Index

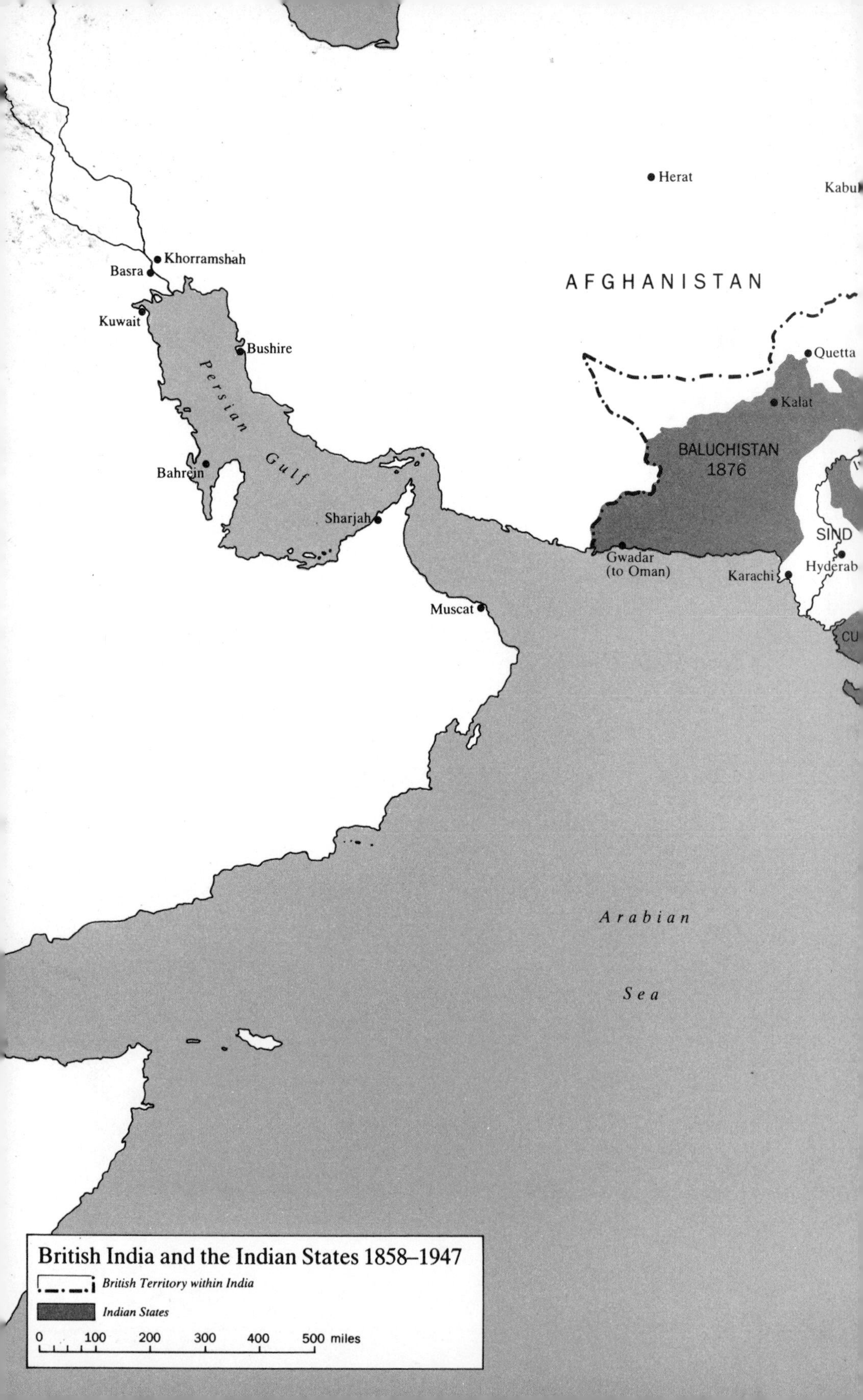
Herat
Kabul
Khorramshah
Basra
AFGHANISTAN
Kuwait
Bushire
Quetta
Persian
Kalat
BALUCHISTAN
1876
Bahrein
Gulf
Sharjah
SIND
Gwadar
(to Oman)
Hyderab
Karachi
Muscat
CU
Arabian
Sea
British India and the Indian States 1858–1947
British Territory within India
Indian States
0
100
200
300
400
500 miles